GENETIC STUDIES OF GENIUS

EDITED BY

LEWIS M. TERMAN

VOLUME III

THE PROMISE OF YOUTH
FOLLOW-UP STUDIES OF A THOUSAND GIFTED CHILDREN

GENETIC STUDIES OF GENIUS

Edited by LEWIS M. TERMAN

VOLUME I. MENTAL AND PHYSICAL TRAITS OF
A THOUSAND GIFTED CHILDREN

By LEWIS M. TERMAN and OTHERS

VOLUME II. THE EARLY MENTAL TRAITS OF
THREE HUNDRED GENIUSES

By CATHARINE M. COX

VOLUME III. THE PROMISE OF YOUTH: FOLLOW-UP STUDIES
OF A THOUSAND GIFTED CHILDREN

By BARBARA S. BURKS, DORTHA W. JENSEN,
LEWIS M. TERMAN, and OTHERS

ACKNOWLEDGMENT

The investigations reported in these volumes were made possible by an appropriation from the Commonwealth Fund, supplemented by an appropriation from the Thomas Welton Stanford Fund and by a gift from Mr. Max Rosenberg.

GENETIC STUDIES OF GENIUS

VOLUME III

THE PROMISE OF YOUTH

FOLLOW-UP STUDIES OF A THOUSAND GIFTED CHILDREN

BARBARA STODDARD BURKS
DORTHA WILLIAMS JENSEN
LEWIS M. TERMAN

Assisted by

ALICE M. LEAHY
HELEN MARSHALL
MELITA H. ODEN

STANFORD UNIVERSITY PRESS
STANFORD UNIVERSITY, CALIFORNIA

1930

PRINTED AND BOUND IN THE UNITED STATES OF AMERICA
BY STANFORD UNIVERSITY PRESS

PREFACE

This volume, the third in *Genetic Studies of Genius,* was definitely planned for before the first number in the series had been written. In view of the poverty of exact knowledge relating to the developmental histories of gifted children, it would have been unfortunate in the extreme if the subjects so extensively studied in connection with the preparation of Volume I could not have been followed further. The earlier investigation, costing more than $40,000 and the time of several workers for three years, made available for the first time measurements of a sufficiently large group of intellectually superior children to establish reliably the direction and extent of their deviation from unselected children in a large variety of physical, mental, and personality traits. The resulting mass of information, substituting, as it did, verifiable facts for unsupported opinion on so many questions, justified in itself all that it cost. It is obvious, however, that the value of the original data will be immeasurably enhanced if the career of each subject can be followed to its end. Whether or not this will be possible, only the future can tell. At the very least it is to be hoped that follow-up studies of these subjects may be continued for another twenty years, by which time the majority of them will be approaching the middle period of life.

It is also to be hoped that the present series of volumes can be extended by additional researches of the kind described by Dr. Catharine Morris Cox (now Mrs. Catharine Cox Miles) in Volume II—researches dealing with the childhood traits of outstanding geniuses of history. Both the "forward" and the "backward" types of investigation are necessary if genuine progress in the psychology of genius is to be made. Even the casual examination of a few score biographies should convince one that a tempting field here awaits the psychologist. It is the exceptional biographer who shows any real appreciation of the importance of the childhood period or who is able to interpret correctly the facts which he considers important enough to present. One contribution from this series should be an influence upon the writing of biography, particularly those phases of biography that have to do with childhood and youth.

v

If the study here offered is in some respects less interesting than that of Volume I, in other respects it may be
found of greater interest. The data it presents are less novel,
but they are perhaps even more significant, or potentially so.
The reader may at times feel that the amount of detailed
information presented is unnecessarily great; but it was
deemed better to err in this direction than to risk omitting
material which might acquire significance with the passing
of years.

Volume III represents the results of genuine collaboration. The general plan of the investigation was formulated
by me, but in many decisions relating to detailed procedures
all the members of the staff participated. In her capacity as
chief assistant throughout the investigation Dr. Burks made
invaluable contributions to the success of the undertaking.
The field work was done by Miss Leahy, Miss Marshall, and
Mrs. Oden, with some assistance from Dr. Burks, who, in
addition, handled the greater part of the office work. The
data presented in Part I were assembled under my direction
by Dr. Burks, assisted by a clerical force. Dr. Burks prepared the tentative draft of chapters ii to xiii, of Part I, and
is responsible for most of the statistical treatment of the data
in chapter iii on retests of intelligence. The data for the case
studies were assembled and written up in first draft by Dr.
Burks, Miss Leahy, Miss Marshall, and Mrs. Oden. Dr. Jensen's contribution is the interesting study of literary juvenilia in Part III. I am responsible for chapters i and xxvii
and for the final draft of the entire volume.

We wish to express our profound gratitude to the many
persons who have co-operated so helpfully to make the
study a success. Invaluable assistance was given by the
school officials and teachers in nearly all the cities of California and by many in other states. Special acknowledgment is due to the entire school personnel of Alameda,
Berkeley, Fresno, Long Beach, Los Angeles, Oakland, Palo
Alto, Pasadena, San Francisco, San Jose, and Santa Ana,
and to various individuals connected, respectively, with the
California Institute of Technology, Occidental College, Po-
mona College, San Jose State Teachers College, Stanford
University, the University of California at Berkeley, the University of California at Los Angeles, and the University of
Southern California. The co-operation rendered was by no
means limited to such formal matters as granting the field

assistants permission to enter the schools, examine school records, and use school buildings in the testing of subjects. School officers and teachers invariably took an active interest in the work and gave, all told, hundreds of hours of their time in supplying information about the subjects. Not once, in the course of the entire investigation, was any possible courtesy or assistance withheld either by the schools or by other social agencies.

Our indebtedness to the subjects themselves and to their parents and other relatives is greatest of all. The total number of hours contributed to the study by single subjects and the families of subjects ranged for the most part from three or four to ten or upward. The average was probably not far from six or eight. That so few refused this degree of co-operation, when in the majority of cases there could be no expectation of personal benefit, was one of the happiest circumstances connected with the investigation.

Acknowledgment is made elsewhere of the indispensable assistance given by those who read and rated the literary juvenilia as described in Part III. Each generously devoted between twenty and forty hours to this task.

Dr. Truman Lee Kelley gave valuable assistance in the investigation reported in Part III.

We are indebted to Marshall J. Kimball for preparing all the graphs, to Mr. and Mrs. Somerville Thomson for a careful proofreading of the entire volume, and to Mrs. Thomson for various kinds of assistance in preparing the manuscript for the press.

LEWIS M. TERMAN

STANFORD UNIVERSITY
June, 1930

CONTENTS

CONTENTS

PART I. METHODS AND RESULTS

PART IV. SUMMARY

PART IV. SUMMARY

APPENDIX

INDEX

LIST OF FIGURES

PART I. METHODS AND RESULTS

THE PROMISE OF YOUTH

CHAPTER I

PURPOSE, METHODS, AND PERSONNEL

The purpose of *Genetic Studies of Genius* is to throw light on the factors which make for superior achievement, particularly achievement in the realm of intellect. The importance of this field of investigation hardly admits of argument. How to identify the individual of extraordinary gifts and how to make the most of his potentialities are questions which philosophers, scientists, and educators have pondered from the days of Plato to the present moment. That the scientific study of genius should have had to wait until the middle of the last century was inevitable, considering the tardy development of biology, genetics, psychology, and the social sciences. With the growth of these basic disciplines the problems of genius become for the first time open to scientific approach. Already workers in great numbers have been attracted to the field which the pioneer researches of Galton and Cattell have opened up so effectively. Thanks to the rapid development in the underlying sciences, the outlook for progress in the study of genius was never so promising as it is today. The biology of genius, its psychological identification, the factors—innate and environmental —which mold it, and the social forces which limit its influence or make possible its utilization can now be investigated far more fruitfully than was possible even a couple of decades ago, and by methods which did not then exist.

Of the two approaches to the problem, one by the study of matured geniuses, the other by following the development of gifted children, it is the latter that is especially favored by recent scientific advances. However, as Dr. Catharine Cox has demonstrated in the second volume of this series, some of the newer methods are applicable also in the study of historical characters. Both procedures are in fact necessary, because each by itself fails to cover the entire ground. Studies of eminent individuals such as were carried on by

3

Galton, Cattell, and Cox give us information which can be secured in no other way. Similarly, studies of living gifted subjects whose development is followed from childhood to mature years make their unique contribution. Perhaps the majority of readers will be inclined to agree that the latter approach, if cultivated for a sufficiently long period, will probably bring the more significant results. It is the genetic method, and for this reason it is more likely to throw light upon causal factors and shaping influences than is the method which works backward from completed career to early life.

The genetic method, however, has one disadvantage. Inasmuch as one's ultimate achievement cannot be accurately predicted, we are not able to limit our study to just those children of a given population who are destined to achieve eminence. We must begin with a very large group of subjects who seem promising in early life, in order to stand a chance of catching many adult geniuses in our net. But even if few or none are caught, the labor will not have been lost. It is as important to know why some individuals who showed early promise achieve so little as it is to know why others of no greater apparent promise achieve so much. We would emphasize this fact in justification of the title that has been given to the present series: *Genetic Studies of Genius*. The title is not meant to imply that the thousand or more subjects who have entered into the investigations described are all potential geniuses in the more common meaning of that term. A few of the group may ultimately achieve that degree of distinction, but not more than a few. The achievement of the others may be expected to cover the entire range from near-genius to utter failure. The title of this series of volumes is none the less justified.

Volume I, it will be recalled, was devoted chiefly to the mental and physical traits of gifted children as these were evidenced in the results of tests, measurements, and observational reports at a given stage in their development. The investigations there described may accordingly be thought of as belonging to the cross-section type. They had for their purpose to give as concrete and quantitatively definite a picture as possible of the measurable traits of children having intelligence quotients above 140. How this picture might change with the passing of years was left for the most part to future determination. We say "for the most part," for the reason that in the course of the original study data were incidentally obtained which, indirectly at least, suggested certain tentative conclusions relative to the course which development tends to follow in such children. The data referred to are of two kinds: (1) the life histories obtained from the reports of parents, teachers, and school records; and (2) age resemblances and differences that came to light in the comparison of children tested and measured at the different ages from three to eighteen years. These data, in our opinion, pointed strongly to the conclusion that there is a marked degree of permanency in the main features of a true cross-section picture of a child with respect to his intellectual, social, moral, and personality traits.

However, to expect the picture to remain in all respects unchanged through the entire period of growth and development would be entirely unreasonable. Gifted children, like all other children, are subject to innumerable vicissitudes of environmental influence. Not even the most extreme of hereditarians would accord only zero or negligible value to the sum total of such influences. It is possible, moreover, that many of the traits which are to be accredited largely to original endowment are of the delayed type which become manifest only after a given stage of development has been attained. If this should be true, alterations in the picture would sometimes occur regardless of the effects of environment. It is clear, therefore, that cross-section studies must be supplemented by studies of the longitudinal type if we are ever to learn the true facts regarding the development of an individual child.

Since the longitudinal study, strictly speaking, is one that continues without cessation, it is obviously too costly to be applied to a large group of subjects. In fact, no satisfactorily thorough study seems ever to have been made of the development of even a single individual for the full period from birth to maturity. Under ordinary circumstances the best we can do is to make a series of cross-section studies of a subject at different stages of his developmental history. By comparison of these successive cross-section pictures we are able to secure what for practical purposes may be considered a longitudinal view of the growth changes. This is the method which has been planned from the beginning of the Stanford research with gifted children.

Almost eight years have elapsed between the date when

the majority of our gifted subjects were located and studied (1921–22) and the writing of this volume. During that period it has not been possible to follow constantly the development of each child. The available funds were sufficient merely to allow for the employment of a half-time assistant whose duties were of necessity limited to the handling of correspondence and to occasional interviews with parents and children. An effort was made to keep in touch with the subjects by sending to parents and teachers report blanks calling for certain physical, educational, and social data.[1] These report blanks were mailed in 1923–24, 1924–25, and 1925–26. Each year about 90 per cent of the Home Blanks were filled out and returned, but only about 75 per cent of the School Blanks. Although the information secured in this way was of considerable value, it was so limited in scope and in various respects so incomplete that it offered an insecure basis for conclusions or generalizations on anything other than school progress. The most important service performed by the annual reports was to keep us in touch with parents until such time as a more searching follow-up investigation could be made.

In 1927 a grant of $10,800 from the Commonwealth Fund, of New York City, made it possible to launch the researches which here are to be reported. The completion of the task was made possible by assistance from the Thomas Welton Stanford Fund and by a gift from Mr. Max Rosenberg, of San Francisco. Plans for the investigation were formulated during the spring and summer of 1927, and in September of the same year the field assistants began their work of testing children and interviewing parents and teachers. The field work required the full time of three assistants for a year, and the tabulation and interpretation of data and the preparation of the report required somewhat more than another year.

The length of the interval between the main search for subjects in 1921–22 and the follow-up investigation of 1927–28 was in several important respects favorable. In the first place, it was great enough to make the comparisons between earlier and later findings significant and interesting. An interval of half the length, for example, would have brought

---

[1] See Volume I, pp. 597 ff., for reproduction of the blanks used and for summary of data furnished by the first set of blanks sent out (1923–24).

out the trends of development much less clearly. On the
other hand, a much longer interval than six years would
have rendered all of the earlier tests unsuitable for repetition and would have made impossible many of the quantitative comparisons which we considered extremely desirable. Contacts would have been more difficult to establish
and many more subjects would have been lost. Finally, and
by no means least in importance, the interval selected was
a most fortunate one on account of the research staff it was
possible to secure. Everything considered, it would seem
that the investigation could hardly have been better timed,
particularly if a second follow-up can be made after another
interval of ten or fifteen years.

The new study was planned toward the accomplishment
of two purposes: (1) to serve as a check upon the correctness of the conclusions presented in Volume I; (2) by obtaining various kinds of data not obtained in the earlier
investigation to help to complete the picture of the typical
gifted youth.

In regard to the first of these purposes, it has not seemed
necessary to check elaborately the raw factual data summarized in Volume I. Of the substantial correctness of those
data there can be little doubt. There is every reason to believe that any group of subjects selected in the same way
and studied by the same or similar methods will show essentially the same tendencies to deviation from children of the
generality that we have found. Specifically, we should fully
expect to find any such gifted group superior to unselected
children of equal age in the following respects: they would
have a much larger proportion of near relatives who had
achieved notably more than ordinary men and women
achieve; they would be slightly superior to average children
in health and physique; their mean educational achievement, however measured, would be vastly superior to that
of unselected children; the amount of unevenness in their
abilities would differ very little from that which obtains for
children in general; they would be found superior to unselected children in trustworthiness, emotional stability, zeal,
social adaptability, leadership, common sense, and almost
every other desirable trait of personality or character,
though in some of these their superiority would be much
less marked than in the intellectual processes.

In regard to conclusions based upon or growing out of

factual findings of the kind just mentioned, the situation is different. Here there is endless need for additional evidence. We do not yet know to what extent the superior achievement of relatives is indicative that the gifted subject comes of biologically superior stock. We do not know how much the IQ and school achievement fluctuates during the period of mental development. We do not know whether such unevenness of ability as is found tends to increase or to decrease with age. We do not know whether age brings improvement or deterioration with respect to personality traits. We know all too little about the resemblances and differences between our gifted group and those individuals who in mature life achieve eminence of a degree that ranks them popularly in the class of geniuses. We know still less about the type of education that is best for gifted children.

It will be a long time before we shall be able to give a final answer to all of these questions. On some of them we believe that a little light will be shed by continued study of the same gifted group, and it is this conviction which is responsible for the investigation here reported.

Realizing fully that few of the problems relating to gifted children could be solved with finality by our investigation, and not knowing whether or not later follow-up studies of the same group of subjects could be made, we gave considerable thought to the selection of procedures and methods. At best only a small fraction of the data which one would like to have could be collected. After much thought the following schedule was adopted:

Intelligence tests. The Stanford-Binet Test for subjects below the ninth grade, and one form of the Terman Group Test of Mental Ability for all others. Scores on the Thorndike Intelligence Examination to be summarized for all of the subjects who had taken this test as applicants for admission to Stanford University. Scores on the Stanford Scientific Aptitude Test were already available for another group.

Achievement tests. The Stanford Achievement Test for subjects in grades four to eight. The Hotz Algebra Tests for subjects in grades nine, ten, and eleven. The Stanford Literary Comprehension Test in grades nine, ten, and eleven, and for all subjects under twenty years who were not attending school. The Iowa High - School Content Examination for high-school seniors and college freshmen. Scholastic marks of subjects in high school and college to be secured. Ratings of sample poetic and prose productions of certain members of the group on the Jensen Scale for Rating Literary Juvenilia.

Tests of non-intellectual traits. The Woodworth-Cady test of emotional stability for all subjects in grades four to eight, also for more advanced subjects who resided in or near San Francisco. The Wyman Interest Test for those who took it in 1922. The Stanford Masculinity-Femininity Test for Los Angeles subjects in grades nine to twelve, or over twenty and not attending school. The George Washington Social Intelligence Test for high-school seniors and college freshmen, and for subjects under twenty who were not in school. The Watson Test of Social Attitudes (fair-mindedness) for high-school seniors and college freshmen. The Strong Test of Occupational Interest for boys of the Regular group over fifteen years of age, and for boys of all groups who were registered at Stanford.

The age range of the subjects was so great that no test, whether of intelligence, achievement, or personality, was suitable to all. Moreover, because of limitations of time and funds it was not possible in the case of most of the tests to give them to all of the subjects for whom they were applicable. However, in each case the number tested is large enough to give a fairly reliable sampling. To find out how a group of a thousand gifted subjects compares with a norm group, it is not necessary to test all of the thousand. By testing a random sampling of one hundred to two hundred of the thousand we learn almost exactly as much as if we had tested all.

The testing schedule was planned only for the subjects who had originally qualified for the gifted group on the basis of scores on an individual test (the Stanford-Binet). The schedule of follow-up blanks for other types of information was as follows:

1. Home Information Blank, four pages, for parents of all children up to and including age nineteen and for older children if in Main Experimental group.[1]

2. Interest Blank, two pages, for all children up to and including age nineteen and for older children if in Main Experimental group.

3. Information Blank, two pages, for all children of age

[1] For an explanation of the composition of various subgroups included in the gifted group, see chapter ii.

twenty or beyond, unless members of Main Experimental
group. This blank combined most of sections 1 and 2 above.

4. Trait Rating Blank, two pages, twelve traits, for use
by parents of Main Experimental group, Outside Binet
group, and Special Ability cases up to and including age
nineteen; also for teachers of children in these three groups
if they were still in high school or had graduated recently.

5. School Information Blank, two pages, for teachers of
children in all groups who were still in high school or had
graduated recently.

6. Supplementary Blank, one page, for subjects who
were married.

7. Report on Home Visit, for field visits at homes of Main
Experimental group, Outside Binet group, and Special Ability cases within field workers' range.

8. Report on Conference with Teacher, for field visits at
schools of subjects in the three groups. This report was not
a rigid part of follow-up routine.

9. Report on Conference with Child, for field visits with
children of the three groups. This report was not a rigid
part of follow-up routine.

The essential parts of the above-listed blanks are reproduced in the appendix.

The numbers for whom various kinds of information
were secured are given in connection with the presentation
of data relating to separate items contained in the blanks.
Apart from the report blanks listed above there were forms
for weekly reports to the Director by the field assistants,
form letters to parents and teachers, and forms on which
certain data were reported to parents when a report was
requested.

Much information that would have been desirable could
not be secured with the funds available. For clinical purposes it is unfortunate that each of the tests given could not
have been given to every subject for whom it was applicable.
There are many valuable kinds of achievement tests, special
ability tests, and personality tests that could not for reason
of expense be given to any of the subjects. It is especially to
be regretted that the medical examinations and physical
measurements of the earlier investigation could not be repeated. However, viewing the matter retrospectively we
feel that with minor exceptions the choices which were made
in connection with the testing and report schedules were not

unwise, and that if the investigation were to be repeated with the same limitations of time and funds there are few changes we should wish to make.

The investigation was especially fortunate in the personnel of its staff. Miss Helen Marshall, at present instructor in psychology at Stanford University, had been one of the field assistants in the original study and had helped to assemble much of the material of Volume I for publication. As her work in the follow-up study was done in the same city where she had worked originally (San Francisco), she was able to make contacts more readily and to obtain a greater amount of information regarding her subjects than would have been possible for any other person. In the Bay region she was ably assisted by Mrs. Melita Oden, a graduate in psychology at Stanford who had had considerable experience in clinical psychology and social work.

For Los Angeles and cities near it we had hoped that Dr. Florence Goodenough, who had covered that territory in the original study, might be secured. As Dr. Goodenough was unable to leave her work at the University of Minnesota, we secured instead one of her students—Miss Alice Leahy. The choice could not have been more fortunate, for Miss Leahy was superbly equipped in every attribute that contributes to the making of the ideal field assistant. One of the co-authors, Dr. Burks, also devoted almost half a year to the collection of field data. It is no exaggeration to say that whatever value this study possesses is to be credited first and foremost to the rare competence and devotion with which the field labors were carried through.

Dr. Jensen's study of literary juvenilia, although not in the strict sense an integral part of the primary investigation, has furnished such interesting data with respect to the literary ability of a small group of our subjects that we are fortunate in being able to include it as Part III of this report. Dr. Jensen's scale makes it possible to compare the best literary productions of gifted children with the juvenile productions of eminent authors. Her application of the scale appears to warrant the conclusion that a few of our subjects have shown about as much evidence of literary genius as was shown at corresponding ages by leading English authors of the last three hundred years. This suggests, as do many other parts of our investigation, that there is incomparably greater wealth of potential genius in the general population than the statistical incidence of eminent persons would suggest. Society has no greater problem than to discover and make the most of these little-known resources.

The main purpose of our study has been to find at least a partial answer to the question how gifted children turn out. It may be assumed that this is the question which above all others average readers will desire to have answered. It is also safe to assume that a good many readers, because of inevitable preconceptions, will be on the alert for evidence pointing to deterioration of ability. It is highly desirable that no such evidence should be overlooked, but we feel it necessary to forewarn the reader against a prolific source of error in rating the ability or achievement of subjects attending high school or college. We refer to the selective factors that give a higher and higher average level of ability in successive school grades above the seventh or eighth. The child who ranks as the best in two hundred of the school's twelve-year-olds can not be expected to rank as the best in two hundred of the eighteen-year-olds who are still in school. A more nearly comparable rank would be the best in thirty or forty. It is so easy to overlook this ever-rising standard of comparison with the older subjects, and so fatal to just conclusions to do so, that one must be constantly on guard against committing the mistake.

Another source of error tending in the same direction is encountered when comparisons are made between gifted and other subjects of the same school grade without taking account of the difference in age which is usually present. For example, when we compare high-school seniors of our gifted group with the generality of high-school seniors, we are not only comparing the former with the best ten or twenty per cent of young people in general, but with the best ten or twenty per cent who are some two years older. We estimate that our subjects who in ability or achievement rate at sixteen years of age anywhere within the best decile of high-school seniors, or at eighteen within the best quartile of college sophomores, have achieved a status which is fully in harmony with an earlier IQ rating of 140 or 150. Moreover, it is no certain indication of deterioration in intelligence if the achievement of a given subject falls far below the levels we have indicated, since it is notorious that an indefinite number of factors other than intelligence contribute to an individual's scholarship standing.

CHAPTER II

FOLLOW-UP PROCEDURES

General Aims of the Field Work

It was the goal of our investigation to obtain, for a group large enough to provide statistically reliable results, data that would be sufficiently authentic, comprehensive, and specific to give something of a clinical picture of each individual subject. Ideally, our study should combine the painstaking methods of case study with the condition of wholesale numbers demanded by statistical biometry. The degree of success with which the first aim was accomplished can be judged from the illustrative case studies given in chapters xiv to xxii. Our files contain data for between three hundred and four hundred of the children in our group as complete as for the children described in these case summaries; they contain illuminating though less complete data for a far greater number. That the criterion of large numbers was met will be seen in the tabular summaries at the end of this chapter, wherein are reported the results of our efforts to secure co-operation from all the cases with whom the investigation was concerned in 1921–22.

The four field assistants, after spending three weeks at Stanford in preparation for the year's work, went into the field with the following major objectives:

1. To administer the follow-up tests of intelligence, school achievement, and personality, and to distribute information blanks to teachers, parents, and the children themselves.

2. To trace down every clue from the home and school environment, and from the child himself, that would contribute to an understanding of his development.

3. To complete our records of sibships by testing all sibs of appropriate age not previously tested by us.

4. To re-establish cordial relations with the families of our cases, building through friendly contact and through such helpful advice as could be proffered, toward many years of continued co-operation.

13

Classification of Gifted Groups

Desirable though it would have been to secure for every one of the 1,470 boys and girls on record in our files the complete schedule of information from several tests, home and school visits, and interviews with the subjects themselves, to do this was physically and financially out of the question. It was clear from the first that some of our cases would have to be followed through correspondence. Although the large majority of our group have remained in California, a considerable number have moved to distant places, and their homes now span half the globe. Furthermore the funds at our disposal, while ample for a rather reasonably thorough follow-up of a large, representative group of our gifted children, were not sufficient to permit as intensive study as one could wish of all the cases who remained within accessible range.

At the time Volume I of this series went to press in 1924, our total group consisted of the sub-groups given in the table shown on the opposite page.

In addition to the 1,444 cases in Table 1, there were 211 cases in our files who failed by a small margin to qualify but have been followed up.

The following statements are necessary to make clear to the reader the composition of the various groups listed in Table 1.

1. The 643 "Regulars" of the Main Experimental group are the children located by the original field assistants during the 1921-22 search for gifted children. With few exceptions they were located in the public schools through a system of nominations by classroom teachers as described in Volume I, chapter ii.

2. The 35 siblings of our Regulars either qualified for the group on tests made a year after the original survey, or were later transferred to the Main Experimental group from other classifications. The number 35, however, is no indication of the total number of sibships included in the gifted group, for nearly 150 of the 643 Regulars have one or more siblings also among the Regulars. Two or more gifted Regular subjects were furnished by each of about 65 families.

3. The Outside Binet cases include the pre-high-school subjects who qualified for the gifted group on the basis of a Stanford-Binet test but were not located by Stanford assist-

ants during the 1921–22 search. In addition to 128 cases that had been located between 1911 and 1921, the group contains 228 cases tested by volunteer assistants in various cities.

TABLE 1

CLASSIFICATION OF THE GIFTED GROUPS

I. *Main Experimental group*
    1. "Regulars" used in tabulations................643*
    2. Siblings of above (including two twins below
       standard) 35
    3. Parents refused co-operation................. 6†
                                    ——   684

II. *Outside Binet cases*
    1. Parents co-operating 250
    2. Parents not co-operating 106
                                      ——   356

III. *Outside Group Test cases*
    1. Parents co-operating 299
    2. Parents not co-operating.................... 78
    3. Deceased 1
                                      ——   378

IV. *Special Ability cases*
    1. Parents co-operating 21
    2. Parents not co-operating.................... 5
                                      ——   26

      Grand total 1,444

* Two of the 643 had died by 1924.
† In addition to the parents of these six cases, the parents of six cases counted in the 643 above gave inadequate co-operation.

4. The Outside Group Test cases include 309 high-school pupils located through a co-operative survey of 95 California high schools; they include also 69 cases located in pre-high-school grades. The entire number, 378 in all, qualified for the gifted group on the basis of group mental tests—the Terman Group Test in all but eight cases.

5. The Special Ability group is composed of 26 cases showing unusual talent in some special field, but failing to qualify for any of the other gifted groups. It does not include cases of undoubted special ability that were able to qualify on the basis of IQ.

It may be added that in all classifications except the Main Experimental group the children listed as having "parents not co-operating" are not in most cases children whose par-

ents have refused to co-operate. The term is justified by the
fact that a number of volunteer assistants who sent in test
blanks for children listed in the "Outside" groups never
approached the homes of the children to secure the supplementary questionnaire material. Also, test blanks for gifted
children were sometimes sent to us by people having no
connection with Stanford, and residing in remote sections of
the state or even in distant states. Under such circumstances
we did not always attempt to establish contact with the
parents for it was imperative that we devote most of the
funds and facilities at our disposal to intensive study of the
Regular group located and tested under standard conditions.
Thus our files serve as a repository for test records of a
number of children who are not being followed by us. Some
of these records, though not supplemented by information
concerning educational progress and home background,
may have considerable future interest in the light of these
children's later achievement.

CASES FOLLOWED PERSONALLY AND CASES FOLLOWED BY CORRESPONDENCE

By far the most complete data were obtained originally
for the 643 Regular cases of the Main Experimental group,
these being the subjects who were selected under the most
nearly uniform conditions. For these reasons the bulk of
Volume I was devoted to statistical treatment of data from
the group of Regulars alone. At the beginning of the 1927–28
follow-up it was therefore decided that results of greatest
comparative value would be obtained if the field assistants
concentrated their time upon making contacts with, and
testing the members of, this single group. The statistical reports of the present volume are based entirely upon individuals of the Regular group except in chapter xiii where
the follow-up results for the High School and Special Ability
groups are briefly summarized, and occasionally in discus-
sions where the inclusion of other than Regular cases is definitely specified.

In addition to the 643 Regulars of the 1921–22 study are
the 35 siblings of these children who qualified at a later date,
or were later transferred to the Main Experimental group
from other groups. For obvious reasons it would not do to
follow up our Regulars by tests and personal interviews,
leaving for office correspondence their brothers and sisters

who also belong to our group. Then, too, the Outside Binet group, in addition to a number of cases contributed by volunteer testers in various cities, contains 121 cases that had been studied rather thoroughly by Stanford prior to the large-scale investigation of 1921–22, and perhaps a hundred other cases with whom we have been in fully as close touch as we have been with most of the Regulars. Also we have been in close touch with most of our small group of 26 Special Ability cases, and we felt that it would be of particular interest to find out what had become of children whose special talents were not supported by intelligence of the highest order.

Because of all the foregoing considerations, we decided to include in the group to be followed up personally by the field assistants all of the children who had been originally tested by the Stanford-Binet scale and who were, at last report, accessible to the three central regions where the field assistants had their headquarters, i.e., Los Angeles and adjacent cities; the San Francisco Bay district; and Fresno and the Peninsula district in which Stanford University is located. Of such children there were about 900.

In the cases of over 350 children who originally qualified for the Stanford study on the basis of group intelligence tests, as well as those of the 200 children among our Regulars, our Outside Binet group, and our Special Ability group, who live too far away to be approached personally, contacts with homes, schools, and colleges were made by correspondence. Needless to say we attempted, through such correspondence, to re-establish a cordial rapport with each case. Realizing that to hold the interest and co-operation of these cases over a period of years without person-to-person contact of any kind required special effort on our part, we gave a great deal of attention and time to the correspondence side of the follow-up. Each set of information blanks received by mail from any of these cases was acknowledged by a personal letter ranging from half a page to two pages in length. Many of the parents and children, upon filling in and returning the blanks, asked advice regarding educational and vocational plans, or problems of a more intimate nature, such as home discipline. Many of the children acted upon our offer to summarize the data in our files concerning their ability for college entrance committees, for committees upon college scholarship awards, or for prospective employers.

In the cases followed up by the field assistants, as well as in those followed up only by correspondence, report blanks were returned to us by mail. Since these cases had had recent personal contacts with the field assistants at the time the blanks were left for them to fill out, the receipt of their blanks was acknowledged merely by printed office forms, except when the blanks contained inquiries, requests for advice, or information of exceptional importance. Under such circumstances, fully as much attention was devoted to acknowledgment and reply as in the cases of children followed up through correspondence alone.

The organization and execution of the follow-up correspondence consumed approximately half of an assistant's time for the greater part of a year, as well as considerable of the Director's time.

WORK SCHEDULE OF FIELD ASSISTANTS

It has been mentioned that before starting their work in the field, the assistants spent three weeks at Stanford in preparation. One week was devoted to checking up their Binet procedure to insure uniform administration of tests. The greater part of the time was spent in looking up and recording information from the case folders that would be of assistance in the follow-up of individual subjects. On a special blank printed for the use of the assistants, record was made by a clerk of the name, address, IQ, birth date, and parent or guardian of each member of the gifted group. These blanks were sorted according to locality. The assistants then proceeded to extract from the files such information as concerned deaths, separations, and remarriages of parents, name of the assistant originally making contact with the case, parents' occupations, the names, birth dates and test scores (if known) of siblings, degree of parental cooperation, attitude of the family toward the child's education, and facts or developments in the child's life about which special inquiry should be made. The blanks were thus prepared to serve as work sheets during the entire investigation. Duplicate copies of the work sheets were mailed to five of the field assistants who had served on the study in 1921–22 with the request that each make notations regarding any matters that might be helpful to the present assistants in their work with particular children. Dr. Florence Goodenough, Dr. Dorothy Yates, Miss Beatrice Lantz, Miss Florence Fuller, and Mrs. Elizabeth Kellam De Forest generously contributed many hours to this task. Though it was possible in the large majority of cases to extract all necessary information from the Stanford files, there were a good many instances in which suggestions made by the original field assistants proved of material aid in making contacts.

Once the assistants were in the field, their program involved the following procedures:

1. Look up and verify the present addresses of subjects.

2. Telephone or write for appointments to call. Make home calls and cover as completely as a half hour or hour permits the topics listed on Report on Home Visit Blank (reproduced in Appendix). Leave Home Information Blank, Trait Rating Blank, and Child's Interest Blank to be filled out and mailed to Stanford.

3. Make school calls, interviewing teachers of the children upon the topics listed on Report on School Visit Blank (reproduced in Appendix).

4. If possible, interview the child at home, or at school, or later at the time of the follow-up tests.

5. Make arrangements with the schools to give follow-up tests, and then proceed with the test schedule (outlined above, on pp. 8–9).

6. Select children who for special reasons would be desirable for detailed case studies, and gather such additional information for these cases as seems necessary to round out their case histories.

The program as outlined above was often complicated by the necessity of stopping to hunt up lost cases. Although the majority of our families have notified us of changed addresses whenever they have moved, a small proportion have failed to do so and have also failed to leave permanent forwarding addresses with the post office. Ingenious search through school and neighborhood channels was occasionally necessary in order to relocate these cases. If such families were found to have moved out of range of the field assistants' territories, their names were sent to the Stanford office and the cases were then followed through correspondence.

DATA COLLECTED

Every reasonable effort was made to secure complete returns. Lost cases were hunted diligently through the personal efforts of the field assistants, and through correspondence between Stanford and the schools, relatives, and friends of the members of our group. In case parents, teachers, or children did not return the data blanks promptly, duplicate copies were mailed out after two or three months with a letter explaining the importance of making this follow-up a complete one, and requesting renewed co-operation.

Children unable to attend the group tests at the times arranged were given one or more opportunities to attend make-up tests. Sometimes the field workers devoted an entire half-day to a single child in order to administer the battery of group tests which he was unable to take at an earlier appointed period.

The tabular material of Tables 2, 3, and 4 shows the status of our files on January 1, 1929, and indicates to what degree

TABLE 2

STATUS OF GIFTED GROUPS, JANUARY 1, 1929

	MAIN EXPERIMENTAL GROUP		Outside Binet Cases	Outside Group Test Cases	Special Ability Cases
	Regulars	Sibs of Regulars			
In our files in 1924.....	643	35	356	378	26
Co-operating by 1924...	637	35	250	299	21
Added since 1924......	0	2	38	1	1
Deceased by 1927......	3	0	2	5	0
Total in files, 1927......	640	37	392	374	27
Co-operating 1927–28...	587	34	273	293	14

TABLE 3

HOME INFORMATION BLANKS RECEIVED FOR REGULARS, 1921–22 TO 1927–28

	Number	Percentage
Original group	643	....
Home report received before 1924..........	617	96.0
1924 follow-up report received.............	547	85.1
1925 follow-up report received.............	558	87.2
Living in 1927 (so far as known)..............	640	
1927–28 follow-up report received..........	503	78.6
Parents refused co-operation...............	6	0.9
Family cannot be located..................	11	1.7
Others for whom Home Blank was not obtained (most of them co-operating otherwise)	120	18.8

we were successful in obtaining the data we started out to gather.

On the whole, the co-operation was very satisfactory indeed. A case was listed as "co-operative" if, through filling out our blanks or through participation of our gifted subject in the follow-up tests, the child or his parents signified willingness to assist the investigation. By this criterion nearly 92 per cent of the cases in the Regular group were co-operative.

TABLE 4

ANALYSIS OF DATA COLLECTED IN 1927–28 FOR REGULARS

	Number	Percentage
Living at beginning of follow-up	640	....
Information obtained regarding present status	619	96.7
Co-operating during follow-up	587	91.7
Home data		
Home Information Blank or abbreviated Information Blank	503	78.6
Field assistants' report on home visit	552	86.2
Child's interests		
Interest Blank or abbreviated Information Blank	517	80.8
Field assistants' report on child conference*	241	37.7
School data		
Children in school (not college)	413	64.7
School Blank for above....... 360 (87.2%)		
Transcript of record for above* 173 (42.5%)		
Field assistants' report on school visit* 163 (39.4%)		
Children in college	132	20.6
Record of scholarship for above 122 (92.4%)		
Children not in school	68	10.6
School status unknown	26	4.1
Test data		
Children eligible for tests (exclusive of Vocational Blank)	525	82.0
Above cases tested........... 467 (89.0%)		
Boys eligible for Vocational Blank	247	....
Above cases tested........... 169 (68.4%)		

* Not all the blanks and data enumerated in Table 4 were gathered as part of the routine follow-up of each child. Our endeavor was to gain a satisfactory picture of the present status of each child, and this was best accomplished sometimes through certain channels and sometimes through others.

In appraising the success of the methods used it is necessary to take account of the enormity of the task and of the limitations set by the time and funds available. These limitations have made it impossible to secure all the data that one would naturally like to have. It would have been desirable to secure for each subject sufficiently detailed information for a case analysis. There are many individual cases in our group which would repay months of observation and study. Such intensive work has not been feasible. It has been possible, however, to make contact with the large majority of our subjects and to secure information regarding the present status of 96.7 per cent of the group which was most intensively studied in 1921–22. That the serious cooperation of 91.7 per cent of the group was secured is reassuring as to the representative nature of the results reported in the chapters which follow. A retrospective view of the follow-up investigation does not disclose, to the authors at least, any major weaknesses of method which the limitations of circumstances did not render more or less inevitable.

CHAPTER III

RETESTS OF INTELLIGENCE

To some readers the data reported in the present chapter may hold more interest than those summarized in any other section of this volume. They are concerned with a problem of widespread interest and significance: Do intellectually superior children become intellectually superior adults? Opinions have varied from "always" and "usually" to "seldom" and "never."

The first large-scale scientific investigation of the problem is found in the work of Dr. Catharine Morris Cox, whose findings constitute Volume II of the present series. With 301 of the most eminent men and women of history as her subjects, Dr. Cox, consulting some three thousand biographical sources, sought to establish the nature of early mental traits of geniuses. Upon the evidence assembled from biographies, three judges[1] estimated the childhood IQ's of the subjects. "The ratings were made on the basis of the standards and norms for intelligent behavior established by mental tests." The most significant conclusion of the author is that "the extraordinary genius who achieves the highest eminence is also the gifted individual whom intelligence tests may discover in childhood. The converse of this proposition is yet to be proved."

It is the "converse of this proposition" which is on trial in our investigation of California gifted children. We start with a group of boys and girls selected on the basis of high intelligence test scores (IQ 140 or over). Some of the questions which we seek to answer regarding this group are: (1) How well does the mental ability of these children hold up on the average? (2) How many of the children later show radical changes in intelligence rating, either positive or negative? (3) How do the sexes differ from each other with respect to 1 and 2?

Other related questions of equal importance, but not dealt with in this chapter, concern the uses to which the

[1] L. M. Terman, Maud A. Merrill, and Catharine Cox herself.

children later apply their mental ability. It seems quite evident that while any person with an IQ as high as 140 may have the sheer intelligence requisite for exceptional achievement, only a very small proportion are likely to possess the total complex of mental and personality traits that cause an individual to become eminent. If it were not that personality traits and other non-intellectual aspects of endowment wield an enormous power to enhance or inhibit the individual's use of his intelligence, we might expect in ten or fifteen years, from our thousand California gifted children, such a crop of geniuses as has never before graced the population of a single state.

The present volume undertakes to present material that bears upon these questions. The majority of our subjects, it must be remembered, are still children or adolescents, but it is reasonable to suppose that the end results (i.e., the attainments of our subjects when they become adults) will be foreshadowed by the data collected six years or more after the 1921–22 survey. The data concerning the intellectual ability of our subjects will be summarized in the present chapter. Material related to the useful application of their intelligence, and to the traits that portend future success or mediocrity of achievement and social adjustment will be reported in the subsequent chapters.

STANFORD-BINET RETESTS

It will be recalled that for all the accessible children of our group of ages up to and including 13-0, our follow-up program included a Stanford-Binet test. As the mean age of the Regular group approximately six years before was 9 years and 11 months, and as only 68 cases were then under seven years of age, the number of Regulars eligible for a Stanford-Binet retest in 1927–28 was not large. To augment the numbers slightly, we are summarizing also in this section the retest results for sixteen Outside Binet cases. Outside Binet cases are included here only if the children had been first tested in 1921–22, for we wished to keep the time interval approximately constant between tests and retests.

All IQ's used in the following summaries have been "corrected" by the method outlined in Volume I, pages 42 ff. The corrections, seldom amounting to more than 4 or 5 points, allow for the fact that our older gifted children are penalized by the inadequacy of the scale at the upper end. To insure accuracy, all Stanford-Binet test booklets were scored twice by experienced examiners from the verbatim records of responses.

A comparison of mean IQ's in 1921–22 and in 1927–28 is given in Table 5. Here it is seen that the average drop in IQ for both sexes combined is 9 points. It is noteworthy that the drop is nearly five times as large for girls as for boys, the girls averaging 13 points lower than they did at the time of the original tests, and the boys only 3 points lower. The difference, 10 points, between the average decrease for the boys and the girls, has a standard error of approximately 3 points.

TABLE 5

COMPARISON OF STANFORD-BINET IQ's, 1921–22 AND 1927–28

	BOYS			GIRLS			ALL		
	Mean	S.D.	N	Mean	S.D.	N	Mean	S.D.	N
Regulars, 1921–22 ...	147	8.4	27	150	11.8	27	148	10.4	54
Regulars, 1927–28 ...	144	14.5	27	133	14.0	27	139	15.1	54
Difference	3	−6.1	..	17	−2.2	..	9	−4.7	..
S.D. of difference (approximate) ..	2	....	..	2	....	..	2	....	..
Regulars and Outside Binets, 1921–22 ..	146	8.2	38	149	11.2	35	148	10.0	73
Regulars and Outside Binets, 1927–28 ..	143	17.8*	38	136	15.4	35	140	17.0	73
Difference	3	−9.6	..	13	−4.2	..	8	−7.0	..
S.D. of difference (approximate) ..	2	....	..	2	....	..	1	....	..

* The excessively high standard deviation is here due to one case, a boy who scored 198 IQ. We have reason to believe this boy had been coached before he took the retest.

We have frequently wondered whether gifted children who score high at a very young age will fluctuate more upon retests than will children first tested at an older age. In Table 6 (p. 26), comparative data are presented for children whose ages were two to six at the time of the original tests, and eight to twelve at the time of the retests. The numbers in each age group are too small to make minute comparisons profitable, and we attach no statistical significance to the fact that the six children who were ten years old at retest actually increased a few points on the retest; but the data do seem to indicate that there is no gross tendency for the youngest children of our group to exceed the older children in average drop.

TABLE 6

COMPARISON OF 1921–22 AND 1927–28 IQ'S BY AGE

	AGE AT TIME OF RETEST			
Regulars	8-0 to 9-11	10-0 to 10-11	11-0 to 11-11	12-0 to 13-0
Mean IQ, 1921–22	145	146	147	149
Mean IQ, 1927–28	139	146	135	141
Difference	6	0	12	8
Number	5	5	15	29
Regulars and Outside Binets				
Mean IQ, 1921–22	143	145	146	150
Mean IQ, 1927–28	136	150	136	141
Difference	7	–5	10	9
Number	6	6	23	38

Of greater significance than the average tendencies noted in the data of Tables 5 and 6 are the facts regarding the total distribution of IQ changes. These are summarized in Table 7.

TABLE 7

SUMMARY OF IQ CHANGES, 1921–22 TO 1927–28

	IQ's LOWER IN 1927–28		IQ's HIGHER IN 1927–28		ALL STANFORD-BINET RETESTS, 1927–28		
	Mean Drop	N	Mean Gain	N	Mean Change	S.D.	N
Regular boys	13	15	12	10	12	8.3	27
Regular and Outside Binet boys	14	24	16	12	13	11.1	38
Regular girls	16	25	1	1	16	9.3	26*
Regular and Outside Binet girls	16	30	10	4	15	9.8	34*
Total, boys and girls.	15	54	14	16	14	10.5	72*

* One girl whose original IQ was 192 and whose corrected 1928 IQ was 173 was not included in the tabulation, because she passed every test on the Stanford-Binet scale and hence was inadequately measured.

It is seen from Table 7 that while there are no very pronounced sex differences with respect to the average amount of change in IQ, when direction of change is disregarded, the girls greatly outnumber the boys in IQ decreases, and the boys exceed the girls in number of IQ gains. The tabulation from which Table 7 was derived shows that 5 of the 27 Regular boys and 8 of the total 38 boys lost as much as 15 points each in IQ; 5 of the Regular boys and 7 of the total 38 boys gained as much as 15 points each; 14 of the 26 Regular girls and 16 of the entire 34 girls lost as much as 15 points each; none of the Regular girls and only one of the entire 34 girls gained as much as 15 points each. There were several cases of extreme change, two Regular boys and four Regular girls each dropping 25 points or more.

Table 8 shows the 1927–28 distribution of IQ's of the 54 Regulars who were retested on the Stanford-Binet. It is seen

TABLE 8

DISTRIBUTION OF CORRECTED IQ'S, 1927–28 (REGULARS)

IQ	Age 8 B	Age 8 G	Age 9 B	Age 9 G	Age 10 B	Age 10 G	Age 11 B	Age 11 G	Age 12 B	Age 12 G	Age 13 B	Age 13 G	Total B	Total G
170–179.....					1					1			1	1
169.........									2				2	
164.........					1				2				3	
159.........										1				1
154.........			1				1		2	1			4	1
149.........								1	1				1	1
144.........			1	1		1	1			2			2	4
139.........	1	1			1		3	3	2	2		1	7	7
134.........							2	1	1	3			3	4
129.........	1						1			3	1		3	3
124.........										1				1
119.........						1		1						2
114.........									1				1	
109.........								1						1
100–104.....										1				1
Total ...	2	1	2	1	3	2	8	7	11	15	1	1	27	27

that while most of the children still belong in the high levels of ability, a few now have IQ's that are not greatly above average. The inferior showing of the girls, as compared with the boys, is quite noticeable in the total columns. A further analysis of the cases dropping 15 points or more is reported on pages 43 ff.

PARENTS' ESTIMATES OF GAIN OR LOSS IN ABILITY

An interesting sidelight upon this general discussion is given by the answers of the parents to a question contained on the follow-up Home Blank.

"In general ability, is gaining, holding his own, or losing ground?" (Home Blank: II, 10). [Question answered upon 96 per cent of the blanks received.]

The responses are summarized in Table 9. As the same question was included in the 1924 Home Blank sent out to parents by mail two years after the original survey, we are including in Table 9 comparative figures upon the responses made in 1924.

TABLE 9

CHANGES IN GENERAL ABILITY AS ESTIMATED BY PARENTS

	1924			1927–28		
	Boys %	Girls %	Total %	Boys %	Girls %	Total %
Gaining	42	49	45	54	53	54
No change	57	51	54	44	46	45
Losing	2	0	1	2	1	1

An almost negligible proportion of the parents either in 1924 or during the recent follow-up have felt that their children were losing ground in general ability. A larger proportion now believe their children to be gaining in general ability than believed so in 1924. Since these judgments doubtless involve a number of subjective errors, some of which may be correlated with age of the child, we do not attach particular significance to this increased number; however, it is interesting and probably quite significant that loss in general ability has evidenced itself to the parents so rarely on both occasions. It is also a noteworthy fact that in the estimate of parents the gifted girls have maintained their level of ability as well as the gifted boys, although the test scores indicate the contrary. The parents' estimates may be based to a considerable degree upon their children's school marks in which, we shall later see, the girls are superior to the boys.

CORRELATION BETWEEN TEST AND RETEST

It was thought that a correlation coefficient computed between the 1921–22 and the 1927–28 series of Stanford-Binet scores would contain considerable interest, but the bizarre form of the correlation array resulting from the two distributions made it evident that a product-moment method was unsuitable. The artificial truncation of 1921–22 scores at 140, the arbitrary standard set for inclusion in the group, had the effect of making the regression lines violently nonlinear at the lower portion of the scatter diagram.

In lieu of a product-moment correlation coefficient, we used the following three methods:

1. Tetrachoric correlation, dichotomic lines at the medians. The formula for this correlation[1] is $r = \cos (\pi u)$ where u is the "proportion of unlike sign pairs" of scores. When the correlation surface is normal it gives a value equivalent to the product-moment coefficient. Used in the present case it eliminates in part the effect of the great disparity in form between the two distributions. However, it is lower than a coefficient that would express the true interdependence of the two series of scores, since the concentration of cases around the median in the 1921–22 series gives a range of only 5 or 6 points for cases below the median.

2. Estimate of the correlation obtaining in a population of normal variability when the amount of regression from the mean 1921–22 score of our gifted group is 9 points. The original mean IQ of our 54 retest cases was 148; the 1927–28 mean IQ is 139. Since $\bar{x}_2 = r_{12}x_1$ when the standard deviations of two series of scores are equal, the quotient 39/48 should give us the expected correlation in the unselected population from which our highly selected gifted children were taken.

3. Estimate of the correlation obtaining in a population of normal variability when the standard deviation of $(x_1 - x_2)$, the difference between first and second score, has a value equal to that found in the gifted group. The formula used in this method is[2] $\sigma_d = \sigma\sqrt{2 - 2r_{12}}$. The value of σ is taken to be 15; the value of σ_d is computed from the test data, and the equation is then solved for r. This method contains a small error that would have the effect of spuriously raising the correlation. In a normal distribution the standard deviation of the difference $(x_1 - x_2)$ would be a little larger than it would be for a restricted portion. It is unlikely, however, that this error would change the correlation by over 3 or 4 points in the second decimal.

In Table 10 (p. 30) the results of these three methods of attack are reported.

For reasons that have been discussed, methods 2 and 3 give results that represent the real facts more accurately

---

[1] Kelley, T. L., *Statistical Method*, 1924, p. 257.

[2] Kelley, T. L., *Interpretation of Educational Measurements*, 1927, p. 180.

than method 1. A correlation of .81 (method 2) or .77
(method 3) agrees reasonably well with data to be found
in the literature concerning retests after several years.
Baldwin and Stecher[1] have reported a correlation of

TABLE 10

INTERDEPENDENCE OF 1921–22 AND 1927–28 STANFORD-BINET IQ'S

Method	Correlation	S.D.$_r$
1. Tetrachoric		
Regular group	.60	.15
Regulars and Outside Binets	.65	.13
2. Regression estimate		
Regular group	.81	...
3. Estimate from $\dfrac{\Sigma (x_1-x_2)^2}{N}$		
Regular group	.77	...

.82 ± .04 in a group of thirty-six children for IQ's on Stanford-Binet tests administered about three and a half years
apart. Garrison[2] has reported a correlation of .83 for forty-
two cases retested on the Stanford-Binet after an interval of
three years. In general, the correlation between test and
retest is found to decrease slightly as the interval between
the tests is increased. When we consider that the interval
between tests of the gifted group is six years, the results
are not out of harmony with the findings of other investigations.

TERMAN GROUP TESTS

It was out of the question to give the Stanford-Binet test
to the older members of our group, since (1) the scale does
not go up to sufficiently high levels of difficulty to measure
our brighter children over thirteen or fourteen years old;
and (2) the IQ as ordinarily computed becomes a somewhat ambiguous measure for children over thirteen or fourteen years of age at any level of ability, because of the
negative acceleration of the rate of mental growth after that
time.

The Terman Group Test of Mental Ability was selected
for use with our older children. This test was chosen in

[1] *University of Iowa Studies in Child Welfare*, 1922, No. 1.
[2] *Journal of Educational Psychology*, Vol. 13, 1922, pp. 307–312.

preference to other group intelligence tests because its reliability is unusually high, considering the short period of
time required to administer it, because it maintains a higher
correlation with the Stanford-Binet than do most group intelligence tests, because it yields relatively high predictions
of scholastic success, and because the gifted High School
group, selected in 1921–22 by means of the Terman Group
Test, would provide interesting comparative data.

The reliability of this test (Form A against Form B), as
reported by various investigators,[1] lies between .87 and .95
for a single grade range. It is probable that the true value
of the reliability is .90 or higher.

The correlation of the Terman Group Test with the Stanford-Binet is not far from .80 for children of a single grade
or age group. The experimental literature would indicate
that the value of the correlation remains about the same for
children between the seventh or eighth grade, and first year
of college inclusive.[2]

The scoring of each test, as in the case of Stanford-Binet
tests, was performed twice to insure accuracy.

The Terman Group Test was administered to all accessible children of our Main Experimental group, Outside
Binet group, and Special Ability group who met the following criteria:

1. Age over 13-0.
2. Not above college freshman standing.
3. Not in school or college, but under 20 years old.

The restrictions upon the upper limit of school standing
and chronological age were introduced because (1) there are
no adequate norms for students beyond the first year of college, or for adults, and (2) the test, though having more
"top" than the Stanford-Binet, is inadequate at the upper
end to measure even the median performance of our oldest
gifted children. A few children beyond college freshman
standing were tested when this could be conveniently done,

[1] Holzinger, K., *Journal of Educational Psychology*, Vol. 14, 1923,
pp. 302–305; Johnson, O. J., *Journal of Educational Research*, Vol. 7, 1923,
pp. 458–459; Kelley, T. L., *Interpretation of Educational Measurements*,
1927; Willard, D. W., *School and Society*, Vol. 16, 1922, pp. 750–756.

[2] Avery, G. T., *Journal of Educational Research*, Vol. 7, 1923, pp. 429–
433; Johnson, O. J., *ibid.*, Vol. 7, 1923, pp. 458–459; Jordan, A. M., *Journal
of Educational Psychology*, Vol. 14, 1923, pp. 348–366; Miller, W. S., *ibid.*,
Vol. 15, 1924, pp. 359–366.

and these cases have been included in the age-by-age tabulations of scores. However, it is not known whether the gifted children tested at ages seventeen and beyond represent an unbiased sampling of our gifted group; for this reason, and because the Terman Group Test is inadequate for most of our oldest children, the medians reported for the ages beyond sixteen must not be taken too seriously. The distribution of 1928 Terman Group Test scores is given in Table 11. Medians and standard deviations are reported in Table 12. Medians were used in preference to means to minimize as much as possible the inadequacy of the scale at the upper end. For the same reason, standard deviations as reported are computed for only half of each distribution, i.e., from the median downward. The inclusion of the scores above the median, which are closely "bunched" at most ages, would give spuriously low standard deviations.

TABLE 11

DISTRIBUTION OF TERMAN GROUP TEST SCORES, 1928, REGULAR GROUP

Point Scores	AGE 13 B	AGE 13 G	AGE 14 B	AGE 14 G	AGE 15 B	AGE 15 G	AGE 16 B	AGE 16 G	AGE 17 B	AGE 17 G	AGE 18 B	AGE 18 G	AGE 19 B	AGE 19 G
216–220	..	..	..	..	1	..	..	..	..	..	1	1	..	..
215	..	..	..	1	2	1	4	..	5	..	..	1	1	..
210	..	..	..	..	6	..	5	7	7	5	6	3	2	1
205	1	..	5	3	8	1	8	6	8	9	4	1	1	..
200	3	..	5	5	7	5	9	6	8	4	2	4	..	1
195	5	2	4	5	10	8	10	3	5	5	3	2	..	1
190	1	..	5	5	5	6	9	7	5	2	..	2	..	..
185	2	3	4	7	6	5	2	4	..	4	2	..	..	..
180	2	4	3	3	5	3	3	3	2	..	..	1	..	..
175	1	2	1	1	1	3	1	..	..	1	..	1	..	..
170	1	..	1	2	..	1	1	..	1	..	..	..	..	..
165	1	3	..	..	..	1	..	..	..	1	..	..	..	..
160	1	1	1	1	..	..	..	..	..	..	..	..	..	..
155	1	1	..	2	..	..	..	1	..	..	..	..	..	..
150	1	..	..	1	1	..	..	..	..	..	..	..	..	..
145	1	1	..	1	..	..	..	1	..	..	..	..	..	..
140	1	..	..	..	..	..	..	..	..	..	..	..	..	..
135	..	..	..	..	..	..	..	..	..	..	..	..	..	..
130	..	1	..	..	..	..	..	..	..	..	..	..	..	..
125	..	..	..	..	..	..	..	..	..	..	..	..	..	..
120	..	..	..	..	..	..	..	..	..	..	..	..	..	..
111–115	1	..	..	..	..	..	..	..	..	..	..	..	..	..
Total	23	18	29	37	53	33	52	38	41	31	18	16	4	3
Grand Total														399

Table 12 shows that there is an increase in score at all ages, although the nineteen-year-olds may be properly omitted from discussion, since there are only seven of them. However, the increase from year to year becomes less as age increases; in fact the increment is already very small between fourteen and fifteen.

We do not know, of course, that the steps between points around 190 and 200 are equal in value to those between points around 150, 160, or 170, and for this reason the exact meaning of the increase of medians with age is obscured. We are sure that high-testing individuals suffer a handicap due to the inadequacy of the scale at scores above 200 (a perfect score is 220), and it is probable that this handicap begins to be effective as low as scores 180 or 190. Accordingly, the amount of the mental growth with age remains in doubt and may well be larger than the medians themselves suggest. Regardless of these considerations, it is significant that some age increment exists beyond fifteen or sixteen in age-groups known to have had nearly identical mean IQ's six years ago.

TABLE 12

MEDIANS AND S.D.'s ON TERMAN GROUP TEST, 1928, REGULAR GROUP

Median	Age 13*	Age 14	Age 15	Age 16	Age 17	Age 18	Age 19
Boys	182.2	191.5	194.8	196.0	200.7	203.5	208.5
Girls	176.0	186.5	189.8	196.0	199.1	198.5	198.5
Difference.	6.2	4.0	5.0	0.0	1.6	5.0	.....†
S.D. of dif-							
ference.	8.0	3.8	3.4	3.4	3.3	5.0	.....†
All	178.1	188.5	192.7	196.0	200.2	200.3	206.8
S.D.							
Boys	32	13	15	11	12	11	.....
Girls	22	19	10	18	14	12	.....
All	26	18	13	14	16	12	.....

* Age 13 includes children between 13-0 and 14-0, age 14 those between 14-0 and 15-0, etc.
† Too few cases for comparison.

The boys show a small superiority to the girls on the Terman Group Test scores at nearly every age. At no one age is the difference enough to be very significant in the light of its standard error, but the difference of 4.92 between the median of the entire group of boys and that of the entire group of girls is nearly three times its standard error. The difference may be due to actual male superiority in the gifted group, or it may be due to the nature of the test. It is possible that the elements of the test are such as to capitalize training that is more often received by boys than by girls. However, the sex difference found here is in line with the results of the Stanford-Binet retests already reported.

A question of major importance concerns the interpretation of the Terman Group Test scores of our gifted children in terms of the level of ability of the group at the time of the original survey. There is no wholly satisfactory way of doing this, since the norms for children beyond twelve or thirteen for this test, and, so far as we know, for all other intelligence tests, are biased by the selective process of school mortality. The average high-school senior, for example, represents a much higher level of native ability than does the average eighth-grade pupil. The pupil at the 99 percentile of high-school seniors is a far more highly selected individual than a pupil at the corresponding percentile of eighth-grade pupils.

Bearing in mind the distorting effect of school mortality, it will be interesting to examine the scores of the members of the gifted group in the light of the grade norms published in the *Terman Group Test Manual of Directions*. In Table 13 the scores are compared with the norms of the grades for which our children would be approximately "at age" if they had progressed through school at an average instead of an accelerated rate. The average age of the children constituting any one age group falls at the half-year, i.e., our thirteen-year-olds average about 13-6. Accordingly we have compared in Table 13 the scores of the gifted group with two sets of norms, one set being possibly half a grade too low and the other set possibly half a grade too high.

In Table 13 it is seen that by either set of norms, the median scores of our age groups range from the 97.5 percentile to beyond the 99 percentile. Translated into terms of IQ, such percentile ranks undoubtedly mean that the median ability of the children who were tested by the Terman Group Test, like that of the children who were retested by the Stanford-Binet, is well over 130 IQ, for the 99 percentile of unselected elementary school children is 130. The medians of our gifted subjects exceed the 99 percentiles, even of selected high school children, up to age fifteen. Because of the more and more stringent selection that affects the norms of the highest grades, it must be kept in mind that the decreases in percentile ranks after age fifteen cannot be inter-

TABLE 13

PERCENTILE RANKS, BY AGE, ON TERMAN GROUP TEST, REGULAR GROUP

	\multicolumn{6}{c}{AGE OF SUBJECTS}					
	13	14	15	16	17	18
Method A						
Grade norms used................	7	8	9	10	11	12
Percentile rank, gifted median......	Above 99	Above 99	Above 99	Above 99	98	97.5
Percentile rank, lower gifted quartile...	Above 99	Above 99	Above 99	97.5	96	95
Percentile rank, lowest gifted score.....	Above 90	Above 90	Above 85	Above 70	75	80
Method B						
Grade Norms used................	8	9	10	11	12	...
Percentile rank, gifted median......	Above 99	Above 99	99	97.5	97.5	...
Percentile rank, lower gifted quartile...	98	99	97	95	Above 90	...
Percentile rank, lowest gifted score.....	75	85	75	55	70	...

preted as meaning decrements in the ability of our older gifted subjects with respect to unselected children.

The percentile ratings of our gifted subjects are based upon grade distributions, while the IQ interpretation of these percentile ratings is based upon age distributions. However, for the rough comparison which we have made, this fact makes little difference since the variation of intelligence in a single grade is ordinarily nearly as great as the variation in a single age level.

Another way of treating the Terman Group Test scores is more direct, but can be safely applied only to the data from our gifted thirteen-year-olds (for whom ordinary Stanford-Binet IQ's would still be fairly valid measures). According to the mental age equivalents published in the *Terman Group Test Manual of Directions,* the median score, 178, of our thirteen-year-olds corresponds to a mental age of 18–0. This mental age, divided by a median chronological age of 13-6, gives a median IQ of 133.

Considering, next, the form of distribution of the Terman Group Test scores, we are inclined to believe that it represents roughly the same range of ability as does that of the Stanford-Binet retests. By the more stringent of the norms with which the scores of our group are compared in Table 13, the lower quartiles of our thirteen- and fourteen-year-old gifted subjects correspond to the 98 and 99 percentile of children of the eighth and ninth grades, respectively. Such percentile ranks correspond to IQ's of about 128 or 130. In Table 8 it can be seen that the lower quartile of the fifty-four Regulars retested on the Stanford-Binet scale falls between 130 and 134 IQ.

The percentile rank of the lowest Terman Group Test score for each respective age group fluctuates, for the most part, between 75 and 90, depending upon which norms are used. These percentiles correspond to IQ's between 108 and 116, which result again is in harmony with the distribution of Stanford-Binet IQ's of Table 8. Taking the evidence as a whole, there seems to be reason for believing that the large sample of gifted children tested in 1928 on the Terman Group Test resembles fairly closely with respect to distribution of mental ability the smaller group retested upon the Stanford-Binet.

Comparing, finally, the 1927–28 Terman Group Test

scores of the Regulars with the 1921–22 Terman Group
Test scores of the High School group, we are impressed with
the fact that the original median scores of the High School
group are fairly close to the 1927–28 median scores of the
Regulars at ages fourteen and fifteen, and are appreciably
higher than those of the Regulars at ages fifteen and sixteen. After age sixteen the medians converge again, but as
the medians are above 200 after age sixteen, it is probable
that any real differences between the groups would be covered up by the inadequacy of the scale. A comparison of the
medians is given in Table 14.

TABLE 14

COMPARISON OF MEDIAN TERMAN GROUP TEST SCORES OF HIGH SCHOOL
GROUP IN 1921–22 AND REGULAR GROUP IN 1927–28

	Age 13	Age 14	Age 15	Age 16	Age 17	Age 18	Age 19
High School Group	181.2	192.5	200.2	201.7	201.7	201.0	200.8
Regular Group....	178.1	188.5	192.7	196.0	200.2	200.3	206.8

The comparison made in Table 14 leads us to conclude
that the present median ability of our Regulars is not very
different from the 1921–22 median ability of the High School
group. Such differences as there are favor the original
scores of the High School group.

The data suggest that the standards originally set for
the inclusion of high-school pupils in the gifted group may
have been somewhat more severe for the older high-school
subjects than for the younger ones. The form of distribution of the original scores of the High School group also
supports this hypothesis (see Volume I, p. 559, Table 197).
The distributions after age fourteen show pronounced clustering near the scores set as standards for inclusion, while
the distributions below age fifteen show a gradual thinning
out of cases below the modal score, with very few cases
testing as low as the scores set as standards for inclusion.

THORNDIKE COLLEGE ENTRANCE EXAMINATION

In addition to the intelligence tests which were administered as part of our follow-up program we have an interesting series of Thorndike tests given between 1923 and
1928 to 229 members of our gifted group, 66 of them
Regulars.

It should be explained at this point that Stanford University, since 1921, has required every student who enters to take the Thorndike College Entrance Examination. Since 1924, Stanford has required every student who applies for admission to take it. Although the examination is not, strictly speaking, an intelligence test, since much of the material in it is directly taught in the high schools, it probably comes fairly close to being an intelligence test for students who have the common background of a college preparatory course. Though taking less than three hours to administer, it gives about as valid a prediction of academic success in college as do four-year records of high-school marks. Most colleges that have used it find correlations of about .50 to .60 between Thorndike scores and college grades.

The members of our High School group who took the test before 1924 possibly represent a biased selection of our entire gifted group, since they represent only those students who gained admission to a university of high standards. However, none of our Regular group were ready for college before 1924. Those who took the test during or after 1924 are less selected, since the test, by that time, was required of all applicants. It can, of course, be said that the mere fact of applying for university admission constitutes a factor of selection. This would certainly be the case among children at large, but the factor is not a serious one in our group, since the large majority of them are destined to go to college. Of the Regulars for whom we gathered follow-up information, 200 had graduated from high school or had left school, and 82 per cent of these had entered college or were planning to do so.

Another possible selective influence involves the ages of our gifted children who have taken the test. Most of the Regulars were in high school during the 1927–28 follow-up. Only 29 per cent of them had finished high school. Our selection of cases, therefore, tends to favor children who graduated from high school when especially young, and these children may represent a level of ability higher than the mean ability of the gifted group. On the other hand, it is possible that such children are penalized considerably on the Thorndike test by reason of their age. In our opinion, the two influences about cancel one another. This is ren-

dered very probable by the fact that we found the mean
Thorndike scores of the gifted boys and gifted girls to show
no clear trend with age. Table 15 shows the mean Thorndike scores for Regular and Outside Binet cases of ages
fourteen to seventeen inclusive. The populations used in
Table 15 include only those subjects who took the examination after it became compulsory for all Stanford applicants
(i.e., after 1923), and who were within four months of high-
school graduation, or had graduated within three months,
at the time they took the examination. The results reported
in Table 15 would appear to justify us in disregarding age
when dealing with the scores of members of the gifted
group who are within a few months of high-school graduation.

TABLE 15

MEAN THORNDIKE SCORES OF GIFTED CHILDREN ACCORDING TO AGE

AGE	BOYS		GIRLS	
	Mean	N	Mean	N
14............	88	2	86	3
15............	88	11	86	9
16............	86	26	83	23
17............	88	8	84	17

Table 16 (p. 40) gives essential facts regarding the distribution of Thorndike scores of Regular and Outside Binet
boys and girls of all ages combined who took the Thorndike
Examination after 1923. For comparative purposes, certain
facts are also included regarding all students who entered
Stanford in the fall quarters of 1921 and 1922. The latter
students did not take the test until after entering Stanford.
Nearly all of the gifted subjects (since we have included
only those tested after 1923) took the test before entering
Stanford, and a number, especially among the group of girls,
are included who decided to go to college elsewhere or were
not admitted to Stanford.

It should be explained that because of the rigid limita-
tion upon the number of women students accepted at Stanford, only a very small proportion of women applicants can
be admitted. Failure to be admitted upon a competitive
basis does not therefore signify that the applicant has not
submitted highly satisfactory credentials.

In Table 16 it is seen that the mean Thorndike scores of our gifted subjects exceed the means of all students entering Stanford in 1921 and 1922 by about one standard deviation of the Stanford distribution. As a matter of fact only 11 per cent of the 1921 and 1922 series of Stanford men exceed the mean of the gifted boys, and only 16 per cent of the 1921 and 1922 series of Stanford women exceed the mean of the gifted girls.

TABLE 16

MEANS, S.D.'S, AND RANGES OF THORNDIKE SCORES

Boys	Mean	S.D.	Highest Score	Lowest Score	N
Regulars	88	11	109	62	39
Regulars and Outside Binets	87	11	113	58	69
All Stanford entrants, 1921 and 1922..............	71	16	...	..	923
Girls					
Regulars	83	7	102	73	27
Regulars and Outside Binets	84	10	109	60	57
All Stanford entrants, 1921 and 1922..............	72	13	...	..	204

If a comparison were made with the more recent Stanford entrants, the superiority of the gifted group would not be so patent, since the Admissions Committee now gives considerable weight to the Thorndike scores of the applicants in making selections. As a result of using the Thorndike test in selecting applicants the mean score of entrants has been steadily rising, so that by 1928 it had become 83. It is interesting to note that of the new undergraduates entering Stanford in the fall of 1928, 11 per cent of the women and 5 per cent of the men were members of our gifted group.

We have no way of telling exactly what level of ability is represented by the average Stanford applicant, but studies that have been made of school mortality agree that few students with IQ's below 115 attempt to go to college. It is probable that in an institution such as Stanford, the average IQ of students gaining admission in 1921 was in the neighborhood of 125 or 130. If the standard deviation of the IQ's of Stanford students is about 10 points, an estimate which seems reasonable in the light of experimental studies, the

average level of the members of our gifted group who have
taken the Thorndike test could be properly estimated as
falling near 140. This result bears out the conclusions
reached from an analysis of the 1928 Stanford-Binet and
Terman Group Test data.

RETESTS OF CHILDREN WHOSE IQ'S CHANGED SIGNIFICANTLY

It has been shown that on the whole our gifted children,
who were selected six years previously upon the basis of
very exceptional mental test scores, still test far above average during the present follow-up. Particularly is this true
of the boys. As we have seen, thirty-eight gifted boys retested by the Stanford-Binet in 1927–28 show a mean drop
of only 3 points IQ. Thirty-five gifted girls show a mean
drop of 13 IQ points; but even so their mean IQ of 136 in
1927–28 is well within the top 1 per cent of unselected
children's scores. The results of the Terman Group Test and
the Thorndike Examination substantially bear out the Stanford-Binet retest data.

The mental levels of a number of children, however,
showed marked departures from the level that might have
been predicted from the earlier test scores. Such departures
are most frequently in a downward direction, but in a few
cases are upward. It is as interesting and important to
know that a certain proportion of gifted children change by
becoming more or less bright as time goes on as it is to know
that the majority remain at approximately the same level
of brightness. It seemed to us that a consideration of the
possible causes of the IQ changes found among children of
the gifted group would have so much significance that it
would be worth while to give an additional retest to the
children whose ability appeared to have changed most. It
was decided to administer the Herring-Binet test to children
whose Stanford-Binet IQ's had changed as much as 15
points; Form B of the Terman Group Test to children whose
1928 scores on Form A of this test indicated a marked
change of ability; and Form A to those whose 1928 scores
on Form B indicated a marked change.

There were thirty-seven cases whose 1927–28 Stanford-
Binet IQ's had changed by 15 points or more. It was nearly
time for the schools to close for the summer when the decision was made to give the additional retests, but it was

possible to reach and test with the Herring-Binet twenty-
seven of the thirty-seven cases. There is no reason to think
that the twenty-seven cases represent any but a random
sampling of the thirty-seven, except that a special effort was
made to reach the Regulars. A few of the cases are Outside
Binet subjects who were originally tested subsequent to the
1921–22 survey, and who consequently do not appear in the
summarized data of Tables 5, 6, and 7. Of the thirty-seven
cases fifteen were Regulars, and fourteen of these were given
the Herring-Binet.

To select the cases for the Terman Group retests, changes
of ability were estimated by a rather rough system of equat-
ing the 1927–28 distribution of Stanford-Binet IQ's to the
1928 Terman Group Test distribution in successive age-
groups. The correlation between Stanford-Binet IQ's and
Terman Group Test scores for unselected children of a
single age-group is probably not far from .80. As the co-
relation over a period of six years is possibly lower than
this, we arbitrarily selected .75, and from this value estimated the probable average regression toward the mean
for children whose original IQ's averaged 150. The result
would not have been widely different if we had used a
coefficient as low as .65 or as high as .85 instead. We next
proceeded to equate the standard deviation of retest IQ's
to the standard deviation of 1928 Terman Group Test scores
of each successive age-group, on the assumption that the
form of distribution was about the same on both tests.
Since, as was previously explained, the upper end of the
Terman Group Test provides an inadequate measure of our
older gifted children, the standard deviations both for this
test and for the Stanford-Binet were computed as though
the total distribution were symmetrical, only the scores falling below the medians being used. This done, it was a
simple matter to estimate how many Terman Group Test
points equaled one IQ unit at the various ages, and hence
to estimate the IQ of each child, knowing the amount of his
positive or negative deviation from the median of the gifted
children of his age.

It is not claimed that this method gives very accurate
results, but we feel that it is adequate for identifying children in whom gross changes in mental test level have occurred. As a check, the IQ's of the children in the gifted

group who took the follow-up Terman Group Test at the age of thirteen were first estimated by the above scheme. IQ's were then computed by using the mental age equivalents published in the *Terman Group Test Manual,* and obtaining the ratio M.A./C.A. The estimated IQ's varied from 8 points higher than those obtained by the mental age equivalent method at estimated 150, to 5 points lower at estimated 115. The difference was zero at estimated 129, and slight within the entire range that concerns us. A similar check could not be made upon the estimated IQ's of the older children because of the ambiguity of the M.A./C.A. ratio at ages beyond thirteen or fourteen.

It was decided to give an additional Terman Group Test to Regulars whose estimated 1928 IQ's differed by as much as 30 points from their 1921–22 Binet IQ's. A wider divergence from original IQ was permitted here than with the Binet retest cases because the Stanford-Binet and Terman Group Test differ sufficiently in their nature to make considerable variation probable in an individual's rank upon the two tests, even though his ability measured upon either one of the tests should remain constant. A list was made of thirty-two children to be given a Terman Group retest. Tests were obtained for twenty-six of these.

We may now consider the children who were retested on the Herring-Binet. The Herring-Binet was employed because it measures so nearly the same functions as are measured by the Stanford-Binet. Herring[1] has reported correlations of .97 and .98 between M.A.'s on the Stanford-Binet and Herrington-Binet of unselected children of single age-groups.

In Table 17 (p. 44) are reported some comparisons between the 1921–22 and 1927–28 Stanford-Binet IQ's and the 1928 Herring-Binet IQ's of the twenty-seven cases who took the Herring-Binet. No method has been worked out for "correcting" the Herring-Binet IQ when a child approaches the limit of the test. The uncorrected as well as the corrected Stanford-Binet IQ's are therefore reported, since the former provide a fairer comparison with the Herring IQ's. It is seen that the decreases in Stanford-Binet IQ's are in most cases considerably accentuated in the IQ's yielded by the

[1] Herring, J. P., *Journal of Educational Psychology,* Vol. 15, 1924, pp. 217–228.

Herring-Binet. The average decrease for the twenty cases under discussion is 22 points on the corrected Stanford-Binet. The Herring-Binet gives an average that is 11 points

TABLE 17

STANFORD-BINET AND HERRING-BINET IQ'S

IQ LOWER IN 1927–28 (N = 20)

Sex	Original Stanford-Binet IQ	Stanford-Binet Retest (Corrected)	Loss or Gain	Herring-Binet IQ	Stanford-Binet Retest (Uncorrected)
Male	171	137	34	123	137
Female	164	137	27	121	131
Female	163	148	15	133	146
Male	161	135	26	129	135
Male	156	139	17	131	133
Female	156	131	25	116	127
Female	155	140	15	146	140
Female	153	137	16	117	135
Female	151	133	18	115	133
Female	148	122	26	112	122
Male	146	131	15	119	131
Female	144	128	16	112	124
Female	142	127	15	114	123
Female	142	121	21	96	121
Male	139	106	33	97	106
Female	139	103	36	107	103
Female	139	111	28	108	111
Female	138	113	25	107	113
Female	137	120	17	111	120
Female	137	112	25	109	112
Mean	149	127	22	116	125
S.D.	10	12	7	12	12

IQ HIGHER IN 1927–28 (N = 7)

Sex	Original Stanford-Binet IQ	Stanford-Binet Retest (Corrected)	Loss or Gain	Herring-Binet IQ	Stanford-Binet Retest (Uncorrected)
Male	154	169	15	137	169
Male	149	198	49	158	188
Female	148	166	18	129	152
Female	145	167	22	153	167
Male	144	180	36	143	174
Female	142	172	30	137	162
Male	138	154	16	143	154
Mean	146	172	27	143	167
S.D.	5	13	12	9	11

lower than the average corrected Stanford IQ, or 9 points lower than the uncorrected Stanford IQ. On the other hand, the children whose Stanford-Binet IQ's showed considerable gain do not show gains on the Herring-Binet. The mean IQ for these children on the Herring-Binet is about equal to their mean on the original Stanford-Binet test.

That the disparity between the 1927–28 IQ's on the two Binet revisions can be more than accounted for by differences in the standardization of the tests is clear from a report published by Carroll and Hollingworth[1] upon Herring-Binets administered to a group of eighty gifted children. The subjects, whose ages ranged from seven to twelve, and whose IQ's on the Stanford-Binet ranged from 133 to 190, had IQ's which averaged 17 points lower on the Herring-Binet than on the Stanford-Binet. Of the 17 points, 3 or 4 points were doubtless due to the statistical regression always found in a group of deviates selected on the basis of a fallible test, but 13 or 14 points must probably be attributed to differences in test standardization.

It follows that we might have expected a mean Herring-Binet IQ of only 132 in the case of our twenty subjects whose IQ's decreased, even if their true ability had remained constant since 1922. The mean IQ, 116, which these subjects actually earned on the Herring-Binet is thus only 16 points, instead of 30 points, below the expected level. Since at least 3 or 4 points of the 22 points drop on the Stanford-Binet can be explained by statistical regression, we may say that the 1927–28 mean Stanford-Binet IQ of the twenty cases is not over 19 points below the expected level. The Herring-Binet scores thus corroborate the Stanford-Binet scores far more faithfully than the data of Table 17 suggest.

By similar reasoning the expected mean Herring-Binet IQ of the seven cases of Table 17 who gained in IQ is only 129, instead of 143 as actually found. An increment of 14 points above the expected value is equivalent to a gain of approximately 11 points (because the expected level is about 3 points below the original level). While this 11 points falls short of the gain of 21 points found in the uncorrected Stanford-Binet IQ's, the number of cases is too small to impart much weight to this fact. We may at least conclude

[1] *Ibid.*, Vol. 21, 1930, pp. 1–11.

that the Herring-Binet scores lend qualitative corroboration to the gains observed in the Stanford-Binet IQ's.

We may consider next the children whose 1928 IQ's estimated from the Terman Group Test showed a marked change from those upon the original Stanford-Binets. It will be recalled that only subjects whose estimated IQ's had changed by as much as 30 points were selected for Terman Group retests. There were no cases whose estimated IQ's had increased by as much as 30 points. All twenty-six cases here reported, therefore, represent decreases. Table 18 gives

TABLE 18

Stanford-Binet IQ's and Estimated Terman Group Test IQ's of Children Given a Second Terman Group Test

Sex	Original Stanford-Binet IQ	First 1928 T.G.T.			Second 1928 T.G.T.		
		Age	Score	Est. IQ	Age	Score	Est. IQ
Female	190	15	195	144	16	186	130
Female	186	15	188	137	15	200	148
Female	178	14	189	143	14	185	139
Female	173	16	197	140	16	197	140
Female	172	13	171	132	14	189	143
Female	171	15	187	136	15	193	142
Female	164	16	187	131	17	194	134
Female	164	13	173	133	13	191	143
Male	160	15	178	125	16	188	132
Male	159	13	161	127	14	164	120
Female	157	14	166	122	14	181	136
Male	153	13	149	120	14	163	120
Female	151	14	151	109	14	162	118
Male	149	15	165	117	15	173	124
Female	149	14	159	116	14	185	139
Male	148	16	169	112	16	177	122
Female	148	16	151	99*	16	176	121
Male	148	13	142	116	13	157	122
Male	147	14	156	113	14	156	113
Female	147	14	154	112	14	175	130
Male	143	15	147	101	15	166	118
Female	142	17	165	108	17	174	116
Female	142	13	126	107	13	163	128
Female	142	14	142	101	14	175	130
Male	139	13	111	99*	13	138	114
Female	139	16	145	94*	16	160	107
Mean	156	14.5	162	119	14.7	176	128
S.D.	14	0.5	21	14	1.1	15	11

* Obviously too low; cf. Terman Group Test mental age norms in *Manual*.

comparative data upon the original Stanford-Binet IQ's and the estimated 1928 IQ's.

It is seen from Table 18 that the Terman Group retests confirm in the main the results of the first 1928 Terman Group Tests in showing a decrease of IQ since 1921–22. To be sure, the point scores on the retest average nearly 14 points higher than upon the first test, and the estimated IQ's average 9 points higher on the retest than on the first test; but some of this increase can be accounted for through practice effect.

School Achievement of Subjects Showing IQ Drop

Having seen that our subjects who have exhibited marked changes in IQ have probably been measured with fair accuracy during the follow-up, we turn next to an analysis of their school achievement. As few of the children tested in 1927–28 on the Stanford-Binet were six years old or over when originally tested, our early achievement test data for the Binet retest group are very scanty. They are more satisfactory for those children who were retested on the Terman Group Test and who were, for the most part, in high school at the time of the follow-up.

In Table 19 the 1928 Stanford Achievement Test subject quotients of twelve children whose Stanford-Binet IQ's dropped 15 points or more are compared with the subject quotients of children of corresponding age who took the

TABLE 19

CHILDREN WHOSE IQ'S HAD DROPPED IN 1928 COMPARED WITH GIFTED
ELEVEN-YEAR-OLDS OF 1922 WITH RESPECT TO MEAN
ACHIEVEMENT QUOTIENTS

	Reading Quotient	Arithmetic Quotient	Language Quotient	Spelling Quotient	Mean Age	IQ
1928 quotients of 12 cases whose IQ's dropped ..	132	134	137	119	11-1	128
120 gifted children tested in 1922	145	138	144	139	11-6	150*
Difference†	−13	−4	−7	−20	....	−22

* Approximately.
† The differences have standard errors of about 3 or 4 points.

test during the original survey. The average age of these twelve children was 11-1 at the time of the follow-up achievement test, and their average subject quotients (Subject-Age/C.A.) were therefore compared with those of the eleven-year-olds taking the original tests. The eleven-year-olds of 1922 show some superiority in all four parts of the test, though not quite as much as the difference in IQ's would suggest. However, the number of cases in the group whose IQ's dropped is not sufficient to yield very reliable averages, and the true differences may well be 4 or 5 points greater or less than those found. The standard errors of difference are 3 and 4 points.

It may be of interest to the reader to know that four children whose 1927–28 IQ's were 120 or less had IQ's and subject quotients as follows:

IQ	Reading Q	Arithmetic Q	Language Q	Spelling Q
120	114	111	142	104
111	138	120	148	112
106	126	133	132	108
103	123	120	126	102
Mean 110	125	121	137	106

Four children whose IQ's had increased by 15 points or more had a mean IQ of 176, a mean reading quotient of 171, a mean arithmetic quotient of 126, a mean language quotient of 161, and a mean spelling quotient of 143. The corresponding mean quotient of eight children whose IQ's had remained over 140 were: IQ, 152; reading, 144; arithmetic, 134; language, 141; spelling, 130. The differences between these latter values and the standards reached by the gifted group in 1922 are not significant in the light of their standard errors.

The data regarding the 1922 achievement test records of the children selected for having lower estimated IQ's in 1928 on the Terman Group Test are summarized in Table 20. The means and standard deviations of their IQ's and subject quotients of 1922 are scarcely distinguishable from those of the gifted children with whom they are compared, although the difference between the reading quotients of the two groups may possibly be significant. That is, there was nothing in the 1922 achievement scores of this group of children to suggest that their 1922 IQ ratings were spuriously high.

TABLE 20

CHILDREN WHOSE ESTIMATED IQ'S HAD DROPPED IN 1928 COMPARED WITH GIFTED NINE-YEAR-OLDS OF 1922 WITH RESPECT TO 1922 ACHIEVEMENT QUOTIENTS

	Reading Q		Arithmetic Q		Language Q		Spelling Q		Age in 1922		IQ in 1922	
	M	S.D.	M	S.D.	M	S.D.	M	S.D.	M	S.D.	M	S.D.
1922 quotients of 26 cases whose ability dropped	146	12	137	11	153	18	144	15	9–2	1–1	156	14
1922 quotients of 92 gifted nine-year-olds	151	12	139	15	156	14	142	13	9–6		151	10*
Difference	−5		−2		−3		2				5	
S.D. of difference	2		2		3		2				2	

* Approximately.

We may consider, finally, the present educational product of these children whose estimated ability seems to be definitely lower than it was in 1922. For twenty-two of them we have Stanford Literary Comprehension Tests, and for sixteen of them we have Hotz Algebra Tests, all administered in 1928. This discussion anticipates at some points the data presented in Chapter V on the educational achievement of the gifted group during the 1927–28 follow-up.

In Tables 21 and 22 the means or medians of the Literary Comprehension and Algebra scores of the children whose

TABLE 21

CHILDREN WHOSE ESTIMATED IQ'S DROPPED COMPARED WITH GIFTED FOURTEEN-YEAR-OLDS UPON 1928 LITERARY TEST MEDIANS

STANFORD TEST IN COMPREHENSION OF LITERATURE

	I	II	III	Mean Age
22 cases whose ability dropped...	31	37	28	14-10
47 cases of age 14...............	34	38	32	14-6
Difference	3	1	4	....
S.D. of difference	1.6	2.1	1.9	....

estimated IQ's dropped are compared with those for other members of the gifted group tested during 1928. Medians were employed with the Literary Comprehension scores because the upper end of the scale is inadequate for the

TABLE 22

CHILDREN WHOSE ESTIMATED IQ'S DROPPED COMPARED WITH OTHER GIFTED CHILDREN UPON ALGEBRA TEST MEANS

	Problems	Equation and Formula	Mean Age
16 cases whose ability dropped....	6.4	8.4	14-10*
148 cases not included above.....	8.6	14.9	14-8
Difference	2.2	6.5	....
S.D. of difference	.7	1.3	....

* Approximately.

highest-scoring members of the gifted group. The Literary Comprehension Test is divided into three subtests that measure different phases of literary comprehension; hence the columns headed I, II, and III in Table 21.

On the whole, the data of Tables 21 and 22 agree with those of Table 19 in showing definite effects upon educational achievement traceable to changes in the intelligence scores. From results reported in chapter v it may be calculated that the cases showing marked decrease of IQ average roughly half a control S.D. below other members of the gifted group on the Stanford Literary Test, three-quarters of an S.D. below on the Hotz Problems Scale, and more than an S.D. below on the Hotz Equation and Formula Scale. They average 26 points below the entire group of gifted fourteen-year-olds in scores on the 1928 Terman Group Test (cf. Tables 12 and 18), this amount being in the neighborhood of a standard deviation of a comparable grade or age group. The 1928 achievement test scores of the "decreased ability" cases are thus a little higher than their present intelligence level might lead one to predict. This may mean that the decreases in intelligence test level are more apparent than real. On the other hand, it may mean that the effects of the subject's previously higher intelligence are still being evidenced in school achievement.

POSSIBLE CAUSES OF IQ CHANGES

We may now inquire whether there are any conditions of environment, personality, health, or race that are peculiar to the group whose IQ's show decreases and which might therefore account for the measured IQ changes. Our sources of information are the original and follow-up Home and School Blanks, the field visitors' home interviews, and the test data obtained during the follow-up. In the following treatment only the cases that showed marked decreases in Stanford-Binet IQ have been considered, because there are too few cases showing marked increases to make statistical treatment of them profitable, and because the significance of changes estimated from the follow-up Terman Group Test scores is not so clear-cut.

Health. In Table 23 (p. 52) data provided by the follow-up Home and School Blanks regarding the health of our subjects since 1922 are summarized. Data from the group of children whose IQ's markedly decreased are compared with corresponding data for the entire group of Regulars. We find in Table 23 no evidence that the "lowered IQ" cases have more than their share of poor health; in fact, the figures, if taken at their face value, are slightly more favorable for the "lowered IQ" subjects, though the number of cases is not sufficient to establish this reliably.

TABLE 23
CASES WHOSE IQ'S DECREASED COMPARED WITH ALL REGULARS WITH REGARD TO HEALTH SINCE 1922

General Health	IQ's Dropped (N = 26) %	All Regulars %
(Home Blank)		
Good	85	86
Fair	15	13
Poor	..	1
(School Blank)		
Good	81	80
Fair	19	17
Poor	..	3
Has Colds		
(Home Blank)		
Frequently or very frequently	19	14
Occasionally	27	42
Rarely	54	44

A further review of the Home Blanks fails to disclose any illnesses or accidents among the "lowered IQ" subjects since the original survey which have probable bearing upon the IQ's. Nearly half have had no illnesses reported since the time of the original tests; the rest have had various "children's diseases," the only uncommon ones being one case of erysipelas and one case of scarlet fever. There were no cases among them of poliomyelitis, encephalitis, or other diseases sometimes having mental after-effects. The search for health factors that would account for the apparent decreases in IQ has therefore yielded only negative results.

Personality traits. We have summarized follow-up information regarding certain traits of personality in Table 24. There is no clear evidence here for inferring that the children whose IQ's dropped have poor balance or undesirable personality traits as compared with the members of the entire gifted group. The relative excess in the former group of children showing signs of nervousness and of children whose companionship is especially sought may have some slight diagnostic significance, though the number of cases is too small to establish the excess with certainty.

TABLE 24

CASES WHOSE IQ'S DECREASED COMPARED WITH ALL REGULARS WITH
REGARD TO PERSONALITY TRAITS IN 1927–28

	IQ's Decreased		All Regulars
Signs of special nervousness	N	%	%
(Home Blank)			
Yes	6	23	15
No	20	77	85
(School Blank)			
Yes	5	19	16
No	21	81	84
Marked tendency to worry			
(Home Blank)			
Yes	3	12	9
No	23	88	91
Companionship			
(School Blank)			
Especially sought	12	46	31
Rather avoided	2	8	5
Neither	12	46	64
Conduct or personality problem			
(Home Blank and Home Interview)			
Serious	1	3	4
Slight	10	31	26
None	21	66	70
Woodworth-Cady scores			
Mean (of x/σ score)	—.5	..	—.5*
N	11	..	89

* Based upon subjects of ages 11 to 14 only.

Race. The theory is sometimes advanced that members
of certain races or nationalities are quick-maturing, and that
these individuals might have a superiority in childhood that
would soon be lost because their mental growth would begin
to slacken so early. We do not have sufficient data to test
out this theory, owing to the great paucity in our gifted
group of cases representing the races commonly thought to
mature early. We can find out, however, if a disproportionate number of our cases whose IQ's dropped represent
such races, thus establishing whether or not the IQ decreases
in our group are conditioned by factors connected with race.

The ancestry of the children in the "lowered IQ" group was analyzed by the method described in Volume I, page 55. The values in Table 25 represent the percentage of grandparents with the descent in question. In connection with Table 25 it should be borne in mind that since the number of cases in the "lowered IQ" group is relatively small (about 30), it is beyond the realm of probability that these cases should represent all the nationalities represented by the entire gifted group; also, that when a child does occur whose descent is from one of the nationalities to which few of the gifted group belong, the percentage from that nationality is greatly altered because of the small total number of cases. Thus we have only 0.3 per cent Spanish descent for the Regular group, but 4.2 per cent Spanish descent for the "lowered IQ" cases. On the other hand, we have certain small proportions of Bohemian, Armenian, Portuguese, Negro, and Indian descent for the Regular group, but none for the "lowered IQ" cases. If we lump certain nationalities occurring frequently in the Regular group which have been shown in many previous studies to be fairly comparable with respect to mental level, we obtain a more reliable result. The outcome of such grouping is shown in the last item of Table 25. It is seen that there are no significant differences

TABLE 25

CASES WHOSE IQ'S DECREASED COMPARED WITH ALL REGULARS
WITH REGARD TO RACIAL EXTRACTION

| | PERCENTAGE OF TOTAL | |
Racial Stock	IQ's Decreased	All Regulars
English	28.6	30.7
Scotch	14.3	11.3
German	12.7	15.7
Scotch-Irish	9.5	2.8
French	7.7	5.7
Jewish	6.9	10.5
Welsh	5.8	1.4
Danish	4.2	0.9
Spanish	4.2	0.3
Irish	2.4	9.0
Dutch	1.6	...
Mexican	1.1	0.1
Icelandic	1.1	0.1
English, German, Scotch, Irish, Scotch-Irish, and Welsh	73.3	70.9

in the racial extraction of the entire gifted group and that of the "lowered IQ" cases.

Environmental factors. To many readers the thought will occur, as it did to us, that the changes in IQ might be accounted for by environmental factors.

The group of cases under consideration contains Outside Binet cases as well as Regulars. The Regulars and Outside Binets represent somewhat different samples of the population with respect to environment and home status; we have accordingly gone to greater pains here than we did in the immediately previous sections to secure comparative data. In the previous sections our comparative material consisted merely of data which had been worked up for the entire Regular group and which are published in subsequent chapters of this volume. In this section data from both the Regular group and the Outside Binet group have been specially compiled for our present purposes. Moreover, we have compared the "lowered IQ" cases with a group of children whose IQ's upon the follow-up retest did not fluctuate by more than 5 points from their original values.

A full explanation of the Barr ratings of occupational status summarized in Table 26 (p. 56) is given in Volume I, pages 66 ff. These ratings provide estimates of the intellectual status of men working in a large number of varied occupations. They are very reliable when group averages are employed, even though they may contain large errors when applied to individual cases.

The environmental ratings made by the field assistants of 1928 upon the basis of home visits are explained in detail on pages 192 ff. of the present volume. It is sufficient, here, to state that a rating of 1 signifies that in the field visitor's opinion the home is an ideal one in which to foster wholesome mental and spiritual development in a child; a rating of 5 signifies that the home conditions are such as might seriously handicap a child's development.

Consulting Table 26, we fail, once more, to find anything of positive significance. There is a slight tendency for the "lowered IQ" cases to come from better homes as measured by Barr occupational ratings; but the difference, 1.7, between the mean Barr rating of the "lowered IQ" cases and the "constant IQ" cases has a standard error of 0.8 and is thus hardly significant. The environmental conditions, as rated by the field assistants, are rather well matched in the two groups. In neither of the two groups is there an appreciable incidence of "marked change in family circumstances."

TABLE 26

COMPARISON WITH REGARD TO ENVIRONMENTAL CONDITIONS OF CASES WHOSE IQ's DECREASED COMPARED WITH CASES WHOSE IQ's REMAINED CONSTANT

Parents' occupational Barr rating

(Home Blank)	IQ's Decreased	IQ's Constant
Mean	14.2	12.5
S.D.	3.0	2.0
N	28	15

Field visitors' environmental rating

	No.	%	No.	%
1	4	12.5	2	13.3
2	8	25.0	5	33.3
3	15	46.9	4	26.7
4	4	12.5	4	26.7
5	1	3.1	0	....
Mean rating	2.7		2.7	

Changes in family circumstances

(Home Visit Blank)	No.	%	No.	%
Marked change upward	1	3.1	0	....
Marked change downward	2	6.2	1	6.7
No marked change	29	90.6	14	93.3

Mental growth rate. We have found no reason for believing that conditions of environment, personality, health, or race have been responsible for the IQ decreases that have occurred. We have not, of course, eliminated the possibility that obscure factors of environment, personality, or health may have been at work to bring about the observed changes; but if obvious factors of this kind have had no demonstrable effect, the presence of mysterious subterranean influences that are undermining our children's ability seems at least improbable.

Two other possibilities suggest themselves. One is that the fluctuations in IQ may be accounted for by changes in the rate of mental growth that are congenital or at least quite normal in character. It is well known that there is a high correlation between physical stature in childhood and adulthood but that occasionally the adult's stature misses by a wide margin the value that would have been predicted in his childhood. Such deviations are not necessarily accounted for by pathological or traumatic conditions. Some children merely seem to grow by spurts and starts. The causes of the fluctuations in growth doubtless have physiological bases and may be closely tied up with endocrine secretions, but that is not saying that the physiological bases may not be congenital and normal. It is possible that an analogy exists in the mental domain. If no other theory can be made to account for the observed data, we feel that a normal-change-of-rate theory is reasonable and does no violence to established facts.

One naturally raises the question whether the congenital mental ability of the children whose IQ's decreased is best represented by the high level found at the time of their original tests or whether it is reflected more faithfully in their present scores. If the second of these two alternatives were true, we should expect to find the cultural environment of the "lowered IQ" cases more nearly average than that of the other members of the group. We should also expect to find the siblings of the "lowered IQ" cases more nearly average in ability than the siblings of the entire group. As a matter of fact neither of these expectations is realized. As can be seen in Table 26, the environmental conditions of the "lowered IQ" cases and of the "constant IQ" cases are almost indistinguishable in so far as we can estimate them. Furthermore, the siblings of the "lowered IQ" cases average a little higher, if anything, than do the siblings of the entire group. Eleven siblings of "lowered IQ" cases were tested on the Stanford-Binet during the follow-up. Eleven siblings of Terman Group retest cases (i.e., of children whose estimated ability on the Terman Group Test had dropped 30 points or more) have been included with these to augment the numbers, but the additional eleven cases had little effect upon the average score. The average IQ of 22 siblings of "lowered IQ" cases is 126; that of 179 siblings of other cases is 120. The difference, 6 points, has a standard error of about 5 points. These findings make it seem quite probable that the hereditary stock of the "lowered IQ" cases is as superior on the average as that of the entire gifted group, and support

the first of the two possibilities, i.e., that the original tests
represent more nearly the inherited mental level of the
"lowered IQ" cases.

Nature of the Stanford-Binet Test. Thus far our discussion has assumed that the Stanford-Binet scale measures the
same trait or traits at all age levels with which we are concerned. This is not the same thing as positing Spearman's
general factor of intelligence. For our present purpose it is
irrelevant whether intelligence as measured by the Stanford-
Binet test is composed simply of Spearman's *g,* or of a large
number of only partially correlated contributing factors. It
is important, however, to know whether or not the test is
measuring very nearly the same factor or factors at all
mental age levels. If the nature of the test should be such
that at age six, for example, it measured a factor A and a
factor B but at age twelve it measured factor A, a new
factor C, and no factor B, and if, further, factors B and C
were large enough to make significant contributions to the
total scores, we might expect considerable fluctuation in IQ
even though the true intellectual abilities of the subjects
remained the same over the period of six years.

C. S. Slocombe has considered this question in an article
entitled "Why the IQ Is Not and Cannot Be Constant."[1] Taking data reported by Baldwin and Stecher on Stanford-Binet
tests administered six times to a group of children at yearly
intervals, he finds that the correlations tend to be a little
higher between tests separated by short intervals of time
than between tests separated by longer intervals. Applying
the tetrad difference technique, he finds more tetrad differences of positive value than chance would account for. He
concludes that comparisons of scores at different ages "are
invalidated by the fact that the same thing is not measured
at these different ages."

It can readily be seen that while Slocombe's conclusion
is a possible explanation of the data he reports, it is not a
necessary one. The "group factors" which he detects may
be inherent in the test, as he suspects; but they may, on the
other hand, be inherent in the individuals tested. In other
words, they may be "rate-of-mental-growth" factors. These
latter, if they should exist, could account adequately for

---

[1] *Journal of Educational Psychology,* Vol. 18, 1927, pp. 421–423.

slightly higher correlations between the tests separated by the shortest intervals of time.

It was hoped that our follow-up data might afford a means of testing the hypothesis that changes in IQ are due to changes in the nature of the Stanford-Binet scale. One of the authors[1] has devised a method of investigating such a hypothesis through a comparison of the correlation between scores of siblings tested at approximately the same age with that between scores of siblings tested at ages differing by a specified amount. It can readily be seen that if the scale at two levels of mental ability measured factors that were sufficiently disparate, there would be a more favorable chance for either inherited or acquired similarities between siblings to show up when both members of each pair were tested on the same level of the scale. Just as we should expect to obtain a higher coefficient if we correlated children's reading ability with the reading ability of their siblings than if we correlated children's reading ability with some quite different trait of their siblings such as musical ability, we should expect a correlation between the IQ's of siblings differing in age to be affected by disparate factors measured at two levels of a single scale.

Adapting the method described in full in the reference cited, we have calculated the effect that a possible difference in the nature of the Stanford-Binet test at two different age levels might be expected to have upon sibling correlations. This effect, if sufficient to account for such fluctuations in IQ as were found in the gifted group, would also be sufficient to increase the difference between the mean IQ of our gifted subjects and that of their siblings by a little over half a point per year of difference in their ages. Siblings of our group tested when as much as six years apart in age would thus have a difference in mean IQ level 3 or 4 points greater than would siblings tested when at the same age.

This effect is not large, though it corresponds to a reduction of the order of .48 to .40, or .50 to .43, in a sibling correlation based upon unselected subjects. During the follow-up we obtained 143 Stanford-Binet tests of siblings of children in the Regular group. We have compared the IQ's of these siblings with the original IQ's of our gifted

[1] Burks, Barbara S., *Journal of Educational Psychology*, 1930.

children, tabulating difference in age at time of test against difference in IQ for each pair. We do not find any evidence that the IQ differences increase with age differences, but our cases are too few to establish with certainty so small an increase of IQ difference as half a point a year. Accordingly, our sibling data do not preclude the possibility of change with age in the functions measured by the Stanford-Binet scale; but they give it no support.

Sex as associated with decrease in IQ. A final line of reasoning reverts to the sex differences, reported earlier in this chapter, on the follow-up retests. It will be recalled that the twenty-seven Regular boys retested on the Stanford-Binet gave an average decrease of only 3 points, while the twenty-seven girls retested gave an average decrease of 17 points. In the Regular group the number dropping by 15 points or more was nearly three times as great for girls as for boys. We cannot reconcile such a sex difference with a theory explaining IQ changes as due to a radical change in the nature of the test. If the *test* made the IQ's of the girls decrease, why did it leave the mean of the boys within 3 points of their original mean? While it might be thought that the test is actually built out of materials that favor boys more than girls, quite regardless of their intelligence, we find this hypothesis impossible to reconcile with the fact that the average IQ of unselected girls is as high as the average IQ of unselected boys.

Conclusion with respect to cause of IQ changes. The only conclusion that we can see from the data at hand is that changes in ability found over a term of years in such a group as ours are due chiefly to "change-of-rate" factors inherent in the individuals, and that such factors are correlated with sex. Whether their effect upon mental growth is permanent or temporary we have no way of knowing at present. It is to be hoped that a subsequent follow-up may provide an answer to this question.

The conclusion has special interest in the light of the notable sex difference, found at the time our subjects were located, in the incidence of high ability. In the Regular group the ratio of boys to girls is 121 to 100; in the High School group (selected in 1921–22 on the basis of the Terman Group Test) the ratio is 183 to 100. If in the Regular group we consider just the subjects whose IQ's on the Stanford-

Binet follow-up tests are over 135, the ratio is 158 to 100.[1]
Thus it appears that boys not only are more likely than girls
to have high IQ's but are more likely than girls to retain the
high IQ's which they have evidenced in their early school
years.

If we consider just the Regulars over fifteen years of age
whose scores on the follow-up Terman Group Test would
entitle them to a place in the gifted group according to the
standard originally used in the selection of the High School
group,[2] the sex ratio is at least 147 to 100.[3]

At this point the reader may wish to turn to chapter xvi,
pages 272 ff., for an examination of case studies of subjects
whose IQ's have undergone marked changes.

Summary

1. Members of the gifted group up to and including 13-0
were retested on the Stanford-Binet. The "corrected" IQ's
of thirty-eight boys have dropped 3 points on the average
since 1921–22; those of thirty-five girls have dropped 13
points on the average.

2. No relationship is found between age at the time of
first test and drop in IQ.

3. The changes in IQ of the gifted subjects correspond in
amount (disregarding direction) to those that would be
expected in a population of normal variability if the correlation between test and retest were about .75 or .80.

4. Point scores (not IQ's) of gifted subjects upon the
Terman Group Test show an increase with age throughout
the range tested, ages thirteen to nineteen. The interval
between medians decreases with age, however, and becomes
small after age fourteen.

5. The gifted boys surpass the gifted girls on the Terman

[1] This ratio makes statistical allowance for the fact that a slightly
greater proportion of the girls than of the boys were reached and tested
on the Stanford-Binet during the follow-up.

[2] See Vol. I, p. 37.

[3] Proportionally more of the boys than of the girls were reached and
tested on the Terman Group Test. The ratio, 147 to 100, was therefore obtained on the assumption that the subjects who were tested had the same
mental level as the subjects who were not tested. The proportions of tested
boys and girls who scored up to the original standard were weighted according to the original sex ratio, 121 to 100, the resulting ratio being 147 to
100. If for some reason the subjects not reached by tests tend to be less
bright than those tested, the correct ratio may be higher than 147 to 100.

Group Test at practically every age tested. The difference
between the point score medians of the entire group of boys
and the entire group of girls is 4.9.

6. In several independent ways the average of the scores
of subjects who took the Terman Group Test during the
follow-up is estimated as equivalent to an IQ of between
130 and 135.

7. The mean Thorndike score of gifted subjects who
took the Thorndike College Entrance Examination when
applying for entrance to Stanford exceeds the mean scores
of entering Stanford students by about one standard deviation of the score distribution for all Stanford entrants.

8. Twenty-seven subjects whose IQ's on the Stanford-
Binet retest changed by 15 points or more were tested on the
Herring-Binet. IQ decreases were more than corroborated
by the Herring-Binet IQ's, but IQ gains were not. The disparity between the Stanford-Binet and Herring-Binet tests
is probably due to differences in standardization of the two
tests.

9. Twenty-six subjects whose IQ's as estimated from the
Terman Group Test showed a marked decrease were retested on a second form of the Terman Group Test. The
results of these retests confirm in the main the results of
the first form of the Terman Group Test.

10. The school achievement test scores of the subjects
whose intelligence appears to have dropped substantially
average somewhat lower than those of the remaining members of the gifted group, though not as much lower as the
difference in intelligence would lead one to expect.

11. Factors of environment, personality, health, race, and
nature of the Stanford-Binet test were investigated as possible influences upon the IQ in the case of gifted subjects
showing marked IQ change. No evidence could be found
that these factors were significant in causing changes.

12. The data point with considerable force to the conclusion that changes in ability found over a term of years in
such a group as ours are due chiefly to "change-of-rate"
factors inherent in the individuals concerned, and that such
factors are correlated with sex. Boys not only become increasingly more likely than girls to have a high IQ as they
advance in age, but they are more likely than girls to retain
a high IQ earlier evidenced.

CHAPTER IV

EDUCATIONAL PROGRESS

Following the plan adopted in Volume I, we have treated separately our data regarding the educational progress and school achievement scores of the gifted group. These constitute chapters iv, v, and vi. Chapter iv deals chiefly with data obtained from the Home and School Information Blanks or from the field assistants' Home Visit Reports, and concerns present school status, educational plans, regularity of attendance, attitude toward school, testimony of teachers and parents, etc. Chapters v and vi summarize the results obtained from the achievement tests administered during the follow-up and from the transcripts of grades furnished by the schools. In addition to the data reported in these chapters, some of the material summarized in chapter vii (Scholastic and Other Interests) is pertinent, for it includes the testimony of the children themselves regarding the school and college subjects they prefer, their fondness for study, etc.

In this chapter, as in other chapters of this volume and of Volume I, the summarized data pertain to the Regulars of the Main Experimental group unless otherwise expressly stated. The reader is reminded that while the Home Blanks from which much of the material in this chapter is summarized are representative of the gifted group as a whole, the School Blanks represent chiefly the members of the gifted group who were in grammar school or high school at the time of the follow-up, these constituting about 75 per cent of the total group. We did not attempt, except in a few special cases, to get School Blanks filled out for our subjects who were attending college, and when this was occasionally done the blanks were not included with those upon which the tabulations are based. When possible, however, we asked former teachers to fill out School Blanks for recent graduates, a number of whom had graduated after the follow-up was already in progress. Blanks from former teachers were thus secured for approximately forty boys

and girls, and data from these blanks are incorporated
with those from 342 others in the summaries of the present
chapter.

Present Educational Status

At the time of the original survey the great majority of
the children of our Regular group were in the pre-high-
school grades, though a sprinkling of cases were not yet
attending school, and a handful were attending high school.
The main search for subjects was conducted in the grammar
grades, both because it was desirable to obtain a group of
young children whose development could be followed from
pre-adolescent childhood and because it was necessary to
secure a group in which the selective process of school mortality had not yet been felt. The restrictions as to grade
location meant, however, that the complete answers to many
interesting questions regarding educational progress would
have to be deferred for some years. Do most gifted children
seek and obtain as much education as their minds can assimilate? What proportion of gifted children graduate from
high school? How many gifted children go to college? If
they do not obtain a higher education, what do they get
instead? How long does the typical gifted child take to
complete the ordinary grammar school, high school, or college course? These questions, in so far as our data now
permit, as well as a number of other questions regarding the
stability of the general educational goals, attitudes, and accomplishments of our group, are discussed in this chapter
and in chapters v and vi.

In Tables 27, 28, and 29, the age-grade status of our subjects at the time of the follow-up is given separately for the
boys and the girls. In addition to the 539 cases represented
in these tables, it is seen from Table 27 that we have four

TABLE 27

CLASSIFICATION OF GIFTED GROUP ACCORDING TO SCHOOL STATUS
(1927–28)

	Grammar School	High School (and P.G.)	Business or Eve- ning School	College	Not in School	Status Unknown
Boys	31	204	4	64	27	21
Girls	24	148	2	68	26	21
Total	55	352	6	132	53	42

TABLE 28

AGE-GRADE DISTRIBUTION OF BOYS (1927–28)

	GRADE														
	3	4	5	6	7	8	9	10	11	12	P.G.	Fr.	Soph.	Jr.	Total
Age 8	1														1
Age 9		3		1											4
Age 10			1	4		1									6
Age 11				1	5	3									9
Age 12					3	6	2	1							12
Age 13					1	1	18	10	1						31
Age 14							10	20	9	2					41
Age 15							1	5	35	23		1			65
Age 16								2	13	25	2	11	3		56
Age 17									2	16	5	22	4	1	50
Age 18										1	1	8	8		18
Age 19												4	4		8
Age 20												1	1		2
Total	1	3	1	6	9	11	31	38	60	67	8	47	20	1	303

TABLE 29

Age-Grade Distribution of Girls (1927–28)

	Grade														
	4	5	6	7	8	9	10	11	12	P.G.	Fr.	Soph.	Jr.	Sen.	Total
Age 8	1														1
Age 9		3													3
Age 10		1	1												2
Age 11			1	4	1										6
Age 12				1	10	8									19
Age 13				1		9	5	2							17
Age 14						3	17	15	3						38
Age 15							5	20	17		2				44
Age 16							1	5	23	3	9	3			44
Age 17									10	1	15	9			35
Age 18										1	6	8	3		18
Age 19											2	2	4	1	9
Total	1	4	2	6	11	20	28	42	53	5	34	22	7	1	236

boys and two girls attending business college or night school, twenty-seven boys and twenty-six girls not attending school at all, and twenty-one boys and twenty-one girls whose present grade status was not ascertained.

It was shown in the original report (Vol. I) that by the commonly employed Ayres-Strayer age-grade standards not a single child among our 616 subjects of the Regular group then attending school was retarded. By the same age-grade standards 67 per cent of the group were accelerated. By these standards a child is called "at age" if he is 7-0 to 7-11 and in the first or second grade, 8-0 to 8-11 and in the second or third grade, etc. Using a more refined method than the above, through which ages and grades were tabulated to the nearest half-year, there was still no subject retarded, and 83.5 per cent of the group were classified as accelerated (84.5 per cent of the boys and 82.5 per cent of the girls).

We have used the Ayres-Strayer standards, projected through high school and college, to compare the age-grade status of the gifted group at the time of the follow-up with that at the time of the original survey. An age-grade distribution has doubtful value when applied to college students, and begins to lose its significance in the high-school grades, owing to the many causes other than poor scholarship that may operate to retard older students. It is a little unfair to our subjects, therefore, to compare the present percentages of acceleration and retardation with those of 1921–22, which were obtained when practically all were attending elementary schools. However, some rough comparisons have been made which possess considerable interest. Of the entire 303 boys and 236 girls whose age-grade status is entered in Tables 28 and 29, 74 per cent of the boys and 84 per cent of the girls are accelerated according to the projected Ayres-Strayer standards. The corresponding figures for those who are in high school but not yet in college are 74 per cent for boys and 83 per cent for girls. Since 67 per cent of the gifted group were accelerated in 1921–22 (and the percentages were nearly the same for both boys and girls), it is seen that an appreciable number of our group who were previously attending school in grades ill-adapted to their mental level have since been given an opportunity to forge ahead at more nearly their natural pace.

By way of additional interest, the approximate average age at which the members of our group graduate from the eighth grade and from high school has been deduced from Tables 28 and 29. The average age of our subjects in the twelfth grade is found to be 16.4 in the case of boys and 16.3 in the case of girls. Because of the small numbers available in the elementary schools we have taken a weighted average of the ages of the children in the seventh, eighth, and ninth grades, after first adding a year to the mean age of those in the seventh grade and subtracting a year from the mean age of those in the ninth grade. The averages are found to be 12.7 for boys and 12.4 for girls. Since most of the blanks from which the age-grade data have been tabulated were filled out at or near the middle of the school year, we need to add approximately 0.4 of a year to the above ages in order to obtain the mean ages of graduation. When this is done we reach the result that our gifted boys graduate from eighth grade at about 13-1 and from high school at about 16-10; our gifted girls graduate from eighth grade at about 12-10 and from high school at about 16-8.

EDUCATIONAL PLANS

As a considerable proportion of the gifted group by now either have graduated from high school or would have graduated had they remained in school, it is possible to ascertain with some reliability what proportion of the group intend to secure a higher education, what fields they plan to specialize in when they take university work, and what reasons lead some of the group to discontinue their formal schooling. In Table 30 certain facts are recorded which bear upon higher education secured or planned for.

Table 30 shows that there are 104 gifted boys and 96 gifted girls who are now potential candidates for a college education. Of these, 68 boys and 64 girls are attending college; 3 boys and 4 girls have attended college but have dropped out for one reason or another. Nearly all of the 8 boys and 5 girls taking post-graduate work at high school will in all probability attend college, as the reason usually assigned by the parents for registration of their children as high school postgraduates is either reluctance to send the children away to college at too youthful an age or the necessity of making up a few college entrance units in which the child failed to receive a "college recommended" grade. There are also 9 boys and 2 girls who have graduated from high school and remain out of school temporarily but who definitely plan to go to college. Combining all of these cases, we find that there are 88 boys and 75 girls who have gone or will go to college; there are 16 boys and 21 girls who have not gone and will probably not go to college. Thus 85 per cent of our boys and 78 per cent of our girls who are in line for a college education have gone or definitely plan to go to college.

TABLE 30

HIGHER EDUCATION OF MEMBERS OF THE GIFTED GROUP

	Boys	Girls
High-school graduates	99	86

	Boys	Girls
Attending college	68	64
Post-graduates at high school	8	5
Attended college but not now attending	3	4
Out of school but plan to attend college	9	2
No plans to attend college, or doubtful	11	11

	Boys	Girls
Non-graduates, and have left school (of college age)	2	8
Attending business college or evening school (of college age)	3	2
Totals	104	96

These percentages are checked fairly closely by the answers to a question included in the follow-up Home Information Blank as to whether or not plans were being made to attend college. The question was definitely answered for 203 of the boys and 159 of the girls for whom we received blanks. A considerable proportion of those for whom the question was not answered were already attending college; hence the proportion of the total gifted group planning to attend college is probably slightly underestimated when we report a percentage of 83 for the boys and 80 for the girls.

The number planning to attend college may be contrasted with the number who, according to the answers to a related question in the Home Information Blank, desire to attend college. This question was answered for 226 of the boys and 179 of the girls. The proportions of boys and girls desiring to attend college are 98 per cent and 94 per cent, respectively.

In this connection an inquiry as to the reasons for terminating their formal education may prove instructive in the case of our subjects who are permanently out of school. It was reckoned above that 16 boys and 21 girls out of 104 boys and 96 girls of college age in Table 30 probably would not go to college. Reasons for discontinuing their schooling were indicated upon the Home Information Blanks for 7 of the boys and 17 of the girls as follows:

	Boys	Girls
To go to work	2	7
Lack of finances	1	4
Illness or accident	..	3
Illness in family	1	..
Parents opposed to further education	1	1
To study music	..	1
To enlist in Navy	1	..
Unwilling to earn part of college expenses	..	1
Loss of interest	1	..
	7	17

It would appear that only in the case of a minority of the group not planning for a college education is there evidence of lack of interest or desire on the part of the subjects. The reason most frequently given, "to go to work," is probably in most cases merely another form of the answer "lack of finances," since, as we have seen, 98 per cent of our boys and 94 per cent of our girls have expressed a desire to go to college.

We may, of course, inquire why an able-bodied gifted child should consent to forego a college education merely because his parents cannot afford to send him. Many young people, gifted and not gifted, attain an education through their own efforts. Of the gifted subjects now attending college approximately 90 per cent of the boys and 58 per cent of the girls are at least partially self-supporting. The answer probably lies partly in the fact that the particular boys and girls who are missing college because of financial reasons have in a majority of cases more difficult conditions to contend with than do those who are attending college despite financial handicaps. For example, the boy who gives "lack of finances" as a reason for leaving school is the oldest son in a family living on a ranch. His father has deserted the family. His sister is earning her entire way through college, but he is not similarly free to go to college and earn his way, for he is the manager of the ranch on which the family is dependent for its meager living. It is doubtless true, however, that some of the subjects who are remaining out because of financial reasons could have college training if they had sufficient ambition. As an example we have a girl of IQ 167 who is recorded as "unwilling to earn part of college expenses." Rather than take part time employment while attending college, she preferred not to attend. Instead she took a position as a filing clerk, in which she has rendered unsatisfactory service.

The possibility suggests itself that there may be some relationship between dropping off in IQ and failure to appreciate and secure a higher education. However, examination of the Terman Group Test scores earned by the boys and girls in question hardly bears out the suggestion. Unfortunately it proved more difficult to get tests during the follow-up of our subjects who were no longer in school than of those still in school, even though evening test sessions were arranged to accommodate those who were employed during the day. But we do have tests for seven of the boys and seven of the girls. As these subjects are about evenly divided between age seventeen and age eighteen, we have compared their scores with the median follow-up scores of our gifted eighteen-year-olds. These medians were 204 for boys and 198 for girls, while the median scores of the seven boys and seven girls are 201 and 192, respectively. The slight disparities between the the medians for the total group and for the fourteen picked cases are not significant in the light of their probable errors.

REGULARITY OF ATTENDANCE

Both the Home Blank and the School Blank asked for data on regularity of school attendance.

"Any long absences from school since 1922? .... How long? .... Reasons for irregularity. . . ." (Home Blank: II, 4; Information Blank: 4.)

The question regarding long absences was answered in the affirmative upon the blanks of 22 per cent of the boys and 19 per cent of the girls. If we include just those cases for which a definite affirmative or negative answer was given, the percentages of affirmative answers are 27 for boys and 26 for girls, but the presumption is that the latter percentages overstate the facts, for we have found a tendency among our group to omit answers more frequently when there is nothing of positive interest to report. The percentages of 27 and 26 may be compared with a corresponding percentage of 45 for boys and girls, combined, reported in the original study.

The durations of the "long" absences since 1922 have been tabulated for boys and girls combined, since the separate results for boys and girls are practically indistinguishable.

Length of Absence (months)	No. of Cases (Total 105)	Percentage of Absences
0– 2	35	33
3– 4	10	10
5– 6	18	17
7– 8	6	6
9–10	5	5
11–12	24	23
13–18	3	3
19–24	2	2
Over 24	2	2

Reasons for irregularity reported in 104 of the 105 above cases are as follows:

Reasons	No. of Cases	Percentage
Illness or accident (personal)	54	52
Traveling	19	18
Working	8	8
Illness in family	6	6
Too young for high school or college	5	5
Financial reasons	4	4
Moved during school year	2	2
Correcting speech defect	2	2
Miscellaneous	4	4

It is seen that a fairly large proportion of the "long absences" are accounted for by children who have been out of school a year or longer. Only a third of the "long absences" are less than three months, whereas the absence was less than three months in 57 per cent of the "long absences" reported at the time of the original survey (Vol. I, p. 268).

In 41 per cent of the cases the absence is over six months, whereas the absence was over six months in only 6 per cent of the cases in the original report. The differences in these proportions are probably accounted for largely by the reasons underlying the absences themselves. In the list of "reasons" only 52 per cent are now concerned with illness of the subject, whereas illness of the subject was the reason given in 76 per cent of the cases originally reported. Travel, and too rapid school acceleration, are both reported more frequently than they were originally; "working" and "financial reasons" combined account for 12 per cent of the present cases, but for none of the original cases.

"Has attendance been very regular, fairly regular, rather irregular, very irregular?" (School Blank: III, 1.) [Question answered on 95 per cent of the blanks received.]

For comparative purposes we are including with the summary of these answers a summary from Volume I of the answers given to the same question in 1922 for the gifted group and for a control group.

	GIFTED GROUP 1927–28		GIFTED GROUP 1922		CONTROL GROUP 1922	
	Boys %	Girls %	Boys %	Girls %	Boys %	Girls %
Very regular	78	70	79	80	72	74
Fairly regular	18	21	14	15	22	21
Rather irregular	3	6	5	3	4	3
Very irregular	1	3	2	2	1	2

There appears to be little significant change in the regularity of attendance reported by teachers, with the exception of a 10 per cent drop in the proportion of girls whose attendance is "very regular." It is possible that this drop is due to sexual maturation and accompanying health problems, for only a small proportion of the girls in the Regular group had menstruated at the time of the original survey.

ATTITUDE TOWARD SCHOOL

"Liking for school very strong, fairly strong, slight liking, positive dislike." (Home Blank: II, 5.) [Question answered on 98 per cent of the blanks received.]

As this question is phrased in the same way on the follow-up blank as on the original home blank, it is possible to make a comparison of the answers on the two sets of blanks.

| | 1927–28 | | 1921–22 | |
	Boys %	Girls %	Boys %	Girls %
Very strong	40	65	55	70
Fairly strong	52	33	39	27
Slight liking	5	2	5	2
Positive dislike	3	0.5	1	1

The percentages of boys having "very strong" and "fairly strong" liking for school have become very nearly interchanged since 1922, but aside from this there appear to be no really significant changes. It is conceivable that the proportion of boys actually having a "very strong" liking for school is no less now than it was in 1922. Competing adolescent interests may prevent the school from assuming as central an emphasis as it formerly did, thus leading the parents to rate the "liking for school" more conservatively.

"Describe the student's attitude toward school or college...." (School Blank: III, 2.) [Question answered on 81 per cent of the blanks received.]

Despite the subjectivity of responses to this question, it will be interesting to compare the answers given by teachers during the follow-up with those given in 1921–22. In order to summarize the heterogeneous material reported in answer to this question it was necessary to condense and categorize the replies. A key word, usually an adjective, was in most instances chosen for this purpose.

In addition to the 303 cases classified in Table 31 as having desirable or undesirable attitudes, there are four boys and three girls whose attitudes we find it difficult to classify. The attitudes in question are: "industrious if interested," 3 cases; "improving," "acquiescent," "interested mostly in social problems," "works for high grades," 1 case each.

In 1921–22 the proportions of gifted children showing desirable attitudes included 91 per cent of boys and 96 per cent of girls. Corresponding figures for the control group were 80 per cent for boys and 92 per cent for girls. If we compare these figures with the 84 per cent of gifted boys and 80 per cent of gifted girls now showing desirable atti-

TABLE 31

ATTITUDE TOWARD SCHOOL AS DESCRIBED BY TEACHERS

Desirable Attitudes	Boys	Girls	Total
Interested	46	38	84
Very good	46	36	82
Conscientious or faithful	5	11	16
Co-operative	6	9	15
Enthusiastic	5	3	8
Good attention or concentration	2	1	3
Enjoys school	2	6	8
Industrious	9	0	9
Earnest	8	0	8
Eager to learn	3	0	3
Ambitious	0	3	3
Normal or wholesome	0	3	3
Progressive	1	0	1
Appreciative	2	0	2.
Confident of success	0	1	1
Fair	3	0	3
Total with desirable attitudes	138	111	249

Undesirable Attitudes	Boys	Girls	Total
Indifferent, bored, or lack interest	14	18	32
Satisfied with fair results	3	3	6
Avoids work	1	2	3
Careless	3	0	3
Takes things lightly	3	0	3
Selfish	1	0	1
Unstable	1	0	1
Immature	0	1	1
Follower	0	1	1
Supercilious	0	1	1
Grades declining	0	1	1
Very poor	0	1	1
Total with undesirable attitudes	26	28	54

	Boys	Girls	Total
Number in each group	164	139	303
Percentage showing desirable attitude	84	80	82
Percentage showing undesirable attitude	16	20	18

tudes, the surprising thing is that the gifted girls have not only lost their lead over gifted boys and over control boys and girls but have dropped to the figure previously reported for control boys. We do not know, it is true, but that the proportions of control boys and girls showing desirable attitudes may have decreased fully as much as did the proportions of gifted subjects. Both gifted and control subjects were pre-high-school pupils at the time of the original survey. Since the majority of subjects for whom we obtained School Blanks during the follow-up were attending high school, where the school situation is different in many respects, the 1921–22 and 1927–28 figures are not strictly comparable. However, it appears to be well established that the gifted girls now compare unfavorably with the gifted boys in attitude toward school.

TIME DEVOTED TO STUDY

"About how many hours a week (outside of school hours) do you spend on school (or college) studies?...." (Interest Blank: 4.) [Question answered on 93 per cent of the blanks received.]

This question was taken from the original Home Information Blank (where it seemed appropriate to include it at the time of the original survey) and incorporated in the follow-up Interest Blank. The responses are summarized by age separately for boys and girls in Tables 32 and 33.

If the means of the number of hours of study at ages ten to twelve inclusive are compared with corresponding means for the same ages as reported in Volume I (Tables 100 and 101), it is seen that those of both boys and girls are now about half an hour to two hours greater than were reported in the original study. At age thirteen the 1927–28 means take an abrupt rise, that for the boys being two hours and that for the girls nearly three hours greater than the means for the original thirteen-year-old boys and girls, respectively. This disparity can probably be explained by the fact that nearly all our present thirteen-year-olds are now in high school, whereas our few thirteen-year-olds in 1921–22 were "selected" cases, i.e., children who were bright enough to qualify for the gifted group but were not yet in high school at the age of thirteen.

For the slight increase in the length of time devoted to study by the children under thirteen there are three possible explanations: (1) that the intelligence level of our group is not quite so high now as formerly and that a little more study is therefore necessary to cover the same ground; (2) that because of the increasing tendency of schools to section their pupils according to brightness (demanding more work

TABLE 32

Time (Hours Per Week*) Devoted to Home Study of School Lessons by Gifted Boys

Age	0	1	2	3	4	5	6	7	8	9	10	11	12	13	14	15	16	17	18	19	20	25	30	35	40	N	Mean
8			1																							1	1.50
9																										0	—
10		2		2		1	1																			4	3.75
11	2	1	1	2	1	1	1	1	1																	5	3.50
12	1	1	1	3	3	2	2	1	1	1		1														9	3.39
13	1	1	2	3	2	5	3	3	1	4	4	1	6	1	1	1	1	1	2		1	1	1			26	5.54
14	2	3	2	3	1	9	8	6	4	3	10		3	1	1	2		2	1		2	2	1			33	4.70
15	2	1	1	3	7	5	3	4	3	3	3		2	1	1			1	1		3	1	2	1		51	8.72
16	2	1		2		2	3	1	2	2	7	2	3	1	1	3		2	1		3		2	1		50	9.52
17	2	1		4	1	2	2	3	3	2	2	2	2	1	1	1			1			2				41	10.26
18				1										1		1		1	1		1	1				18	12.50
19	1			1	1	1	2				2			1		1		1	1					1		7	14.93
20		1												1		1									1	2	6.25
Total	10	12	7	20	11	27	19	16	19	9	31	6	15	5	3	8	1	4	5	0	7	6	3	2	1	247	8.31

TABLE 33

Time (Hours Per Week*) Devoted to Home Study of School Lessons by Gifted Girls

Age	0	1	2	3	4	5	6	7	8	9	10	11	12	13	14	15	16	17	18	19	20	25	30	35	40	N	Mean
8		1																								1	.50
9		1																								1	.50
10	1				1																					3	3.00
11	2		3	3	1	2	2	1	1		3	2														5	2.90
12	2			1		2	3	1	5	2	3	1	2	3	1	1			1			1				13	4.65
13			3	3	3	2	2	4	4	1	2	1	4	1		2					2	1				17	8.56
14	1			4	1	5	5	5	4	2	5	1	2	3	1				1	2	2	1				35	8.56
15	2	1		1	1	5	2	4	4	2	4	1	2	1	2	1			2	2	2	1				37	6.34
16			2	1	1	3	1	1	2				2	1	1	1					1	1				31	10.58
17	2	1		1	1	2	1	3	1				3	1	1	1	1		2			1			1	30	10.83
18	1						1		1				1	1	1				3			1				16	14.47
19													1			1					1	2		1	1	7	19.06
20																							1		1	1	21.79
Total	8	6	9	10	8	21	17	11	17	8	14	4	16	8	5	5	1	0	7	2	7	8	1	2	2	197	10.20

* Limits of groups—Zero indicates no home study; 1 indicates any amount up to and including one hour; 2 indicates from one up to and including two hours, etc.

of the brightest) and to provide extra-curricular activities that eat into the allotted "study periods," the children are actually covering more ground and are given less time at school to prepare their lessons; (3) that the number of hours of study was originally estimated by the parents but is now estimated by the subjects themselves. There may be a constant error in one set of estimates or in both.

The later ages, with one or two minor fluctuations, show a steady increase of hours of study with age, so that by the time our subjects reach college they are studying an average of ten to nineteen hours a week outside of school hours. It would appear, however, that the subjects who have reached college are really devoting little if any more time to classes and study than are the subjects who are in high school. A high-school student usually spends about twenty-five hours a week at school. If he averages about eight hours of home study a week, as our subjects do, the total time spent is approximately thirty-three hours. A college student usually spends from fifteen to twenty-five hours a week in class and laboratory. If he averages about twelve hours of home study a week, as our subjects do, the total time spent is approximately twenty-seven to thirty-seven hours.

It was noted in the original study that the gifted girls devoted about an hour more a week to home study than did the gifted boys. In the follow-up data this lead is seen to have been maintained fairly consistently at most ages, the mean for the entire group of girls being one hour greater than the mean for the entire group of boys. For some reason unknown to us the situation is reversed at age fifteen, the boys being nearly two and a half hours ahead of the girls. However, since the standard error of the latter difference is approximately one hour, the difference is possibly not a true one.

School Ratings on Scholarship

"Compared with the average student of the same school grade or college year, the quality of this student's general academic work is very superior, superior, high average, average, low average, inferior, very inferior." (School Blank: II, 1.) [Question answered on 65 per cent of the blanks received.]

This question was included in the School Blank to provide material for certain rough comparisons with scholarship ratings obtained during the original survey, and also to insure some sort of rating, general though it might be, upon the scholarship of the members of the group for whom we might fail to secure follow-up achievement tests or transcripts of records. The question was not answered on a very large proportion of the school blanks, a number of teachers, especially in the high schools, maintaining that their information regarding the pupil's academic work was limited to the courses which they themselves taught. The results, to which perhaps no great significance can be attached, are as follows:

SCHOOL RATINGS ON GENERAL ACADEMIC WORK

	Gifted Boys %	Gifted Girls %
1. Very superior	18	26
2. Superior	32	30
3. High average	24	25
4. Average	18	16
5. Low average	6	3.5
6. Inferior	1.5	..
7. Very inferior	1.5	..
Mean rating	2.72	2.40

The mean rating was obtained by assigning a value of 1 to the top rating, 2 to the next highest, etc. As it turns out, the mean ratings given above correspond very closely to the mean ratings secured during the original investigation. The latter, reported in Volume I, page 260, are 2.78 for gifted boys and 2.54 for gifted girls. Ratings secured during the original investigation for a control group yielded mean values of 3.80 for boys and 3.58 for girls.

Since the teachers were not asked during the follow-up, as they were in the original investigation, to rate the members of our group upon separate school subjects, it is not possible to make certain direct comparisons that would have considerable interest. It is, however, possible to utilize the separate ratings of 1921–22 for comparison with responses to several questions included on the 1927–28 School Blank. This has been done in connection with the following questions:

"Does the student show very extraordinary ability in any special subject or subjects?.... What subjects?.... How shown?" (School Blank: II, 2.)

"Is the student especially weak in any subjects? .... What sub-jects? .... What are the reasons, if known to you? ...." (School Blank: II, 3.)

The question regarding extraordinary ability is answered in the affirmative upon 28 per cent of the boys' blanks and 42 per cent of the girls' blanks; that regarding weaknesses upon 14 per cent of the boys' blanks and 16 per cent of the girls' blanks. The school subjects in which the special abili-ties and special weaknesses are noted are listed in Table 34. The reader should, of course, bear in mind that we have no way of knowing just what, to the teachers, constitutes ex-traordinary ability or special weakness.

TABLE 34

SPECIAL ABILITIES AND WEAKNESSES NOTED BY TEACHERS

	SPECIAL ABILITY		SPECIAL WEAKNESS	
	Boys	Girls	Boys	Girls
English	22	34	5	3
Mathematics	21	9	9	12
Languages	13	15	8	10
Science	17	4	5	4
History	11	6	3	1
Music	8	11	0	0
Art	7	6	3	1
Dramatics	2	3	0	0
Reading	1	3	0	0
Commercial subjects	0	4	0	0
Debating	2	1	0	0
Physical education	1	2	0	0
Geography	1	1	0	0
Dancing	1	1	0	0
Logic	1	0	0	0
Mechanical work	2	0	0	0
Handwork	0	1	0	0
Oral expression	0	0	1	0
Sewing	0	0	0	1
Spelling	0	0	0	1

The questions asking how the special abilities were shown and inquiring as to the probable reasons for special weaknesses elicited some material that has value from the standpoint of the case records kept on file for the individual members of the group, but the responses were too general and too brief to render their statistical treatment very en-lightening.

We have computed the ratios of number showing weakness to number showing extraordinary ability for the separate school studies. The result gives us a rough idea of the relative excellence of our gifted group in the various school studies. Unfortunately there were too few showing either extraordinary ability or special weakness in certain of the school studies to make the determination of ratios for these worth while. The ratios for six studies are reported in Table 35.

TABLE 35

RATIOS OF GIFTED CHILDREN SHOWING SPECIAL WEAKNESSES TO THOSE
SHOWING EXTRAORDINARY ABILITY, COMPARED WITH
RATINGS OF 1921–22

	1927–28 RATIO			1921–22 MEAN RATING*		
	Boys	Girls	Total	Boys	Girls	Total
English	.23	.09	.14	2.17	1.94	2.08
History	.23	.17	.21	2.02	2.18	2.09
Art	.43	.17	.31	3.72	3.43	3.60
Science	.29	1.00	.43	2.50	2.39	2.46
Languages	.62	.67	.64	....	....	....
Mathematics	.43	1.33	.70	2.53	2.51	2.52

* Mean English ratings were taken as the averages of ratings on composition and on literature; history ratings as the averages of ratings on ancient history, American history, and civics; so with the other subjects.

When we consider that the studies involved in the 1927–28 ratings differ considerably from studies called by the same name in 1921–22, and are almost always much more complex, the agreement shown in the data of Table 35 is quite striking. Mathematics, for example, consists chiefly of simple arithmetic in the grammar grades, but includes arithmetic, algebra, geometry, and trigonometry in high school. Science in the grammar grades embraces little beyond observing tadpoles and making wild-flower collections, but in high school it includes more or less thorough-going courses in botany, biology, chemistry, and physics. Despite these considerations, the rank order of the school studies in 1921–22 and in 1927–28 for the gifted group as a whole gives perfect agreement except for a shift in the rank held by art. Artistic talent often matures late; several of the members of the gifted group who showed no especially marked artistic talent at the time of the original study have now developed into artists of considerable promise.

There are several interesting sex differences which are more observable now than they were in 1921–22. The girls appear to be relatively superior to boys in English and in art; the boys relatively superior to girls in science and in mathematics. Further comparisons between the sexes will be made in the next two chapters, utilizing data from standard tests and from transcripts of school and college grades.

ABILITIES REPORTED BY THE HOME

"Ability recently noted in special fields (as music, mathematics, science, nature study, mechanical ingenuity, art, dramatics, handiwork, etc.). Give brief description of the development of specialized ability, if any . . . ." (Home Blank: II, 8.)

Although this question was included upon the follow-up Home Blank especially for the purpose of gathering case data for the individual members of our group, it will be of interest to note the frequencies with which various kinds of ability are reported by the parents. The majority of the parents indicate that their children are exhibiting some type of specialized ability; in fact, this is reported for 62 per cent of the boys and for 64 per cent of the girls. In Table 36 each ability mentioned is entered and included in the total. Since

TABLE 36
ABILITY IN SPECIAL FIELDS

	Gifted Boys	Gifted Girls	Total
Music	36	44	80
Mathematics	45	22	67
Science	43	17	60
Dramatics	16	33	49
Mechanical ingenuity	40	3	43
Art	14	27	41
Handiwork	13	16	29
Writing	9	19	28
Nature study	12	9	21
Debating or public speaking	13	7	20
Languages	7	6	13
Sewing	0	8	8
Athletics	2	3	5
Cooking	1	3	4
Dancing	0	4	4
Designing	0	4	4
Total	251	225	476

two or more special abilities are reported for a few subjects, the totals are greater than the actual number of cases involved.

Table 36 confirms the judgment of the teachers that the gifted boys more often than the gifted girls excel in mathematics and science, while the girls more often show a special bent for art and for English (as evidenced by talent for writing). Other fields in which the boys show a marked superiority are mechanical ingenuity and debating or public speaking; the girls, on the other hand, lead the boys in dramatics, in the household arts, in dancing, and to some degree in music. It would be interesting to know whether the superiority of the gifted boys in such intellectual subjects as mathematics, science, and debating is connected with their superior showing on our follow-up intelligence tests.

SUMMARY

1. By Ayres-Strayer age-grade standards, arbitrarily projected to include high-school and college years, 74 per cent of the gifted boys and 84 per cent of the gifted girls are accelerated. These figures are to be compared with 67 per cent acceleration of both boys and girls at the time of the original survey.

2. The mean age of graduation from the eighth grade is approximately 13-1 for the gifted boys and 12-10 for the gifted girls; from high school, approximately 16-10 for the gifted boys and 16-8 for the gifted girls.

3. Of the gifted subjects who either have graduated from high school or would have graduated had they remained in school, 85 per cent of the boys and 78 per cent of the girls have gone or are definitely planning to go to college. These percentages are checked fairly closely by responses to a question on the Home Blank which indicate that 83 per cent of the boys and 80 per cent of the girls of the entire gifted group plan to go to college.

4. The proportions of gifted subjects who desire to attend college are: boys, 98 per cent; girls, 94 per cent. Financial reasons often complicated by family exigencies account most frequently for termination of formal schooling.

5. There appears to be little significant change with respect to regularity of school attendance since the time of the original survey, as evidenced by home and school reports.

6. Forty per cent of boys and 65 per cent of girls now have a "very strong" liking for school, as contrasted with 55 per cent of boys and 70 per cent of girls in 1921–22. Three per cent of boys and 0.5 per cent of girls now have a "positive dislike" for school, as contrasted with 1 per cent of both boys and girls in 1921–22.

7. Classification of school reports regarding "attitude toward school" indicates that 84 per cent of boys and 80 per cent of girls show desirable attitudes. These figures are significantly less than those for 1921–22, which were 91 per cent and 96 per cent, respectively. It is difficult to interpret the drop without figures for a control group of corresponding age.

8. The time devoted to home work on school lessons shows, with one or two minor fluctuations, a steady increase with age, our subjects of college age studying an average of ten to nineteen hours a week outside of classes. Because of the different apportionment of classroom time in the colleges, however, our subjects who have reached college are devoting little if any more time to classes and study together than are the subjects who are in high school.

9. The mean ratings by teachers on general academic work are very nearly the same as they were in 1921–22.

10. According to teachers' testimony, 28 per cent of the boys and 42 per cent of the girls show "very extraordinary ability" in some special subject or subjects, while 14 per cent of the boys and 16 per cent of the girls are "especially weak" in some subject or subjects.

11. The gifted group as a whole is relatively superior and weak in the same school subjects now as it was in 1921–22; art, however, holds a higher rank than it did formerly. The girls are relatively superior to boys in English and art, while the boys are relatively superior to girls in science and mathematics.

12. Specialized abilities are reported on the Home Blanks of boys in 62 per cent of the cases; on those of girls in 64 per cent of the cases. Abilities more often reported for boys are mathematics, science, debating or public speaking, and mechanical ingenuity. Abilities more often reported for girls are art, writing, dramatics, dancing, household arts, and music.

CHAPTER V

TESTS OF SCHOLASTIC ACHIEVEMENT

The achievement tests of the 1927–28 follow-up schedule probably furnish our most significant evidence regarding the application of ability in our Regular group toward useful ends. The Stanford Achievement Test administered to the gifted group in 1922 showed that our subjects were on the average about 80 per cent as much accelerated in their mastery of school subject-matter as in their mental development itself. Has this superior achievement persisted and kept pace with the mental development of the past six years?

Before attempting an answer to the question it is necessary to mention the factor of selection which undoubtedly influences the norms for the standard tests administered during the follow-up to those of our gifted subjects who have passed beyond the elementary grades. Because of selective school "mortality" the school norms, as we pass from the eighth grade through high school and up to college, represent pupils who show successively larger positive deviations from average ability. Large allowance should be made for this fact in estimating the relative superiority of the gifted child's educational attainment to that of the strictly average child.

Another source of difficulty lies in the fact that the norms of practically all the more advanced achievement tests are given in terms of grade rather than age. When we consider the scores of the gifted in the light of grade norms, the gifted have the disadvantage of being, on the average, almost two years younger than their classmates. The effect upon test norms of selective school mortality, and the disparity in age between the gifted subjects and their classmates, should both be kept in mind when interpreting the test data. These difficulties are minimized, of course, in the case of the Stanford Achievement Test data, for here we are dealing with pre-high-school pupils, and have age norms to facilitate direct comparisons.

The majority of the tests whose results are summarized in the present chapter were administered in February or March, 1928.

STANFORD ACHIEVEMENT TEST SCORES

The Stanford Achievement Test was administered during the follow-up to our subjects who had not yet reached the ninth grade. The number in the Regular group who by 1928 were still attending elementary school was so small that we have combined the Stanford Achievement Test data for Outside Binet cases with those for the Regular group in order to make statistical treatment feasible. The Regular subjects here comprise over half of the total number. Even after combining the data, the number of cases at any one age is not large enough to make age comparisons profitable.

In Table 37 the mean subject quotients[1] are reported for all ages combined, boys and girls separately. As the children who took the Stanford Achievement Test in 1927–28 were eleven years old on the average, their mean scores have been compared in Table 37 with those earned in 1921–22 by members of the group who were eleven years old at that time.

It is apparent that the general educational level of the gifted group is still very far above average in all the school branches covered by the Stanford Achievement Test, though not quite so high as it was for the gifted of equal mean chronological age who took the test in 1922. If we consider only the first four tests of the battery (these being the only ones that are common to the Stanford Achievement Test as administered in 1922 and in 1928), the 1928 mean of the gifted boys is 6 points below the 1922 mean and the 1928 mean of the gifted girls is 10 points below the 1922 mean. In the case of the boys the disparity in achievement scores is no more than one would expect from the disparity in mean IQ's, and in the case of the girls the disparity in achievement test scores is less than might be anticipated from the IQ's of the 1922 and 1928 groups.

The decrease in IQ of gifted subjects who took the Stanford Achievement Test in 1928 is not so great as the data in Table 37 on eleven-year-olds of 1922 might have led one to expect. In fact, the boys whose 1928 achievement scores are reported dropped on the average only 3 points in IQ, and the girls, 10 points, for the original IQ's of these subjects happen to have averaged a little below those of the subjects who were aged eleven in 1922.

---

[1] The subject quotient is, by definition, the ratio of a child's "subject age" to his chronological age, and is computed similarly to the IQ. A quotient of 100 is thus average.

A direct comparison based upon Stanford Achievement Tests of the same gifted subjects six years ago is not possible because practically all of those who took it during the follow-up were too young to take it in 1922. From the indirect comparisons we have been able to make it appears that the mean achievement of boys, like their mean IQ, has dropped but little, while the drop in mean achievement score of girls is somewhat greater and is closely in proportion to their drop in mean IQ.

TABLE 37

STANFORD ACHIEVEMENT TEST SUBJECT QUOTIENTS OF 1927–28
COMPARED WITH THOSE OF 1921–22

| | 1927–28 | | | | 1921–22 (ELEVEN-YEAR-OLDS) | | | |
| | Gifted Boys (N = 24) | | Gifted Girls (N = 29) | | Gifted Boys (N = 68) | | Gifted Girls (N = 52) | |
	M	S.D.	M	S.D.	M	S.D.	M	S.D.
Reading total	143	21	139	14	145	8	145	9
Arithmetic total	129	11	127	17	139	11	137	10
Language usage	139	15	142	15	141	11	147	9
Spelling	129	14	120	12	139	14	140	13
Science,* etc.	134	12	125	11	151	..	145	..
History and Literature†	141	14	128	12	...	..	...	..
Language and Literature‡	..	..	...	..	159	..	156	..
History and Civics‡	...	..	...	..	158	..	140	..
The Arts‡	...	..	...	..	157	..	158	..
Total score	135	10	128	10	...	..	...	..
Mean of quotients on separate tests	136	..	130	..	149	..	148	..
Mean of quotients on first four tests	135	..	132	..	141	..	142	..
IQ	146	9	136	20	153§	..	155§	..

* The "Science" test as administered in 1921–22 and in 1927–28 differed on the two occasions. In 1921–22 it included geography, hygiene, and elementary science while in 1927–28 it included nature study and science.
† Included in the 1928 form of the Stanford Achievement Test but not in the original version.
‡ Included only in the original form of the Stanford Achievement Test.
§ Approximate.

THE STANFORD TEST IN COMPREHENSION OF LITERATURE

The Test in Comprehension of Literature is an outgrowth of a study completed at Stanford by Dr. Mary C. Burch on determining a content for courses in literature "of a suitable

difficulty for junior and senior high-school students."[1] As
an indispensable step in her problem of measuring the degree of comprehension necessary for the understanding and
enjoyment of literature of varying degrees of difficulty, Dr.
Burch constructed a test in two forms having three subtests.
The function of the subtests is to measure the student's attainment on each of three goals which Dr. Burch selected
as most representative of those formulated by numerous
course-of-study committees whose publications she examined. The goals, reduced to their essentials, are to prepare
children to

"(1) Enter imaginatively into and vicariously participate in the
situations and events set forth on the printed page;
"(2) Judge the character of the people written about, sense the
motives of their conduct, and share their emotional experiences;
"(3) Understand the ideas expressed in expository writing."

Each part of the test includes a number of short selections
chosen from works of standard authors as suitable for testing the ability in question, and as containing within short
limits a thought, description, or incident that is unified and
complete. The pupil reads the selections silently and writes
answers to questions of the multiple choice type which follow each selection. The time limit on each of the three subtests is twenty minutes. The maximum score on Tests I and
III is 40 each; on Test II, 48.

Reliability coefficients have been computed by Dr. Burch
grade by grade for each of the three subtests, and for the
composite, by correlating Form A against Form B. The coefficients are reproduced in Table 38. Pupils of grades 11
and 12 were combined in securing the coefficients of the last
column because only three years of English are required in
the high school used by Dr. Burch to establish norms (Watsonville, California), and the third year can be taken in
either the eleventh or the twelfth grade.

Measures of central tendency and dispersion for the
Regular gifted group and for the Watsonville pupils with
whom the test was standardized (March testing) are tabulated in Table 39 (p. 90). Because the scale is inadequate at
the upper end to measure the most superior of our group, we

---

[1] Burch, Mary C.: Unpublished Ph.D. dissertation, 1926. 112 pp., bibliography, and appendix. Stanford Library. The test is published by the
Stanford University Press.

have made use of the median rather than the mean scores of the gifted subjects. It is doubtful whether even the medians do this group justice, since the medians of the gifted on each subtest in nearly every grade fall only a few points short of the maximum or "perfect" score. It should therefore be borne in mind that our attempt to measure literary comprehension in our group undoubtedly errs in the direction of under-estimation of ability.

TABLE 38

RELIABILITY COEFFICIENTS FOR STANFORD TEST IN COMPREHENSION
OF LITERATURE

	GRADE				
	7	8	9	10	11 and 12
Test I					
r	.81	.84	.85	.90	.88
No. of cases............	122	85	148	87	78
Test II					
r	.82	.84	.88	.86	.90
No. of cases............	122	83	149	88	79
Test III					
r	.74	.82	.79	.85	.89
No. of cases............	123	86	149	91	71
Composite					
r	.92	.94	.94	.94	.95
No. of cases............	112	76	130	75	60

For the same reason that we have employed medians instead of means with the gifted group, we have computed measures of dispersion as if the distributions of scores below the median were matched by similar distributions above the median.

The follow-up testing schedule called for the Test in Comprehension of Literature in the first three high-school grades only, but we have summarized the scores of a few fourth-year high-school subjects who also took the test.

A comparison of the gifted and control levels of performance in Table 39 shows that the gifted, notwithstanding their age handicap, excel the control of corresponding grades by more than a control standard deviation on all three subtests. On the subtests I and II the tendency is for the gifted to excel the control by more than 1.5 control S.D.'s. If, making allowance for the fact that the gifted subjects are about two years accelerated in school on the average, we compare the gifted eleventh graders with the control ninth graders, we find that the gifted have well over two standard deviations advantage over the control on all three subtests. By way of

TABLE 39

MEASURES OF CENTRAL TENDENCY AND DISPERSION FOR GIFTED AND
CONTROL SUBJECTS ON STANFORD TEST IN COM-
PREHENSION OF LITERATURE
FORM A

GRADE		GIFTED			CONTROL		
		Median	S.D.	N	Mean	S.D.	N
	Test I	32	6.9	29	19	7.4	148
9	Test II	34	5.6	27	21	7.8	149
	Test III	27	6.2	22	19	6.1	149
	Test I	33	4.6	49	21	7.4	87
10	Test II	38	8.5	46	24	9.1	88
	Test III	30	3.9	46	20	6.6	91
	Test I	34	4.2	87			
11	Test II	40	6.9	87			
	Test III	33	5.6	82	26	7.2	78*
					30	9.0	79
	Test I	35	5.7	36	26	7.0	71
12	Test II	42	6.0	30			
	Test III	34	1.8	15			

* Grades eleven and twelve were combined by Dr. Burch in establishing the control norms because only three years of English was required in the high school attended by her subjects, and the third year could be taken either in the eleventh or twelfth grade.

additional interest we may also compare the scores of our gifted ninth grade subjects with the eleventh grade norms. Although our gifted ninth grade pupils are on the average about four years younger than control eleventh grade pupils, they average a little higher than the eleventh grade control on all three subtests.

A comparison of the median levels of gifted subjects of the two sexes is made in Table 40.

The medians reveal few sex differences that are at all significant, and we might perhaps conclude that the girls do not have an objectively measurable advantage over the boys in the study of literature, despite the inferences, based upon teachers' judgments, that were drawn in chapter iv. As has been pointed out, however, the inadequacy of the test at the upper end causes a clustering of scores within a few points of the top, and this fact might cause actual sex differences to be obscured. To test this possibility we have computed the proportions of gifted boys and girls whose scores

TABLE 40

COMPARISON OF MEDIANS OF GIFTED BOYS AND GIRLS ON STANFORD TEST
IN COMPREHENSION OF LITERATURE, FORM A

	GRADE 9		GRADE 10		GRADE 11		GRADE 12	
	Boys	Girls	Boys	Girls	Boys	Girls	Boys	Girls
Test I	33	30	33	34	34	35	35	34
Test II	34	34	37	40	39	41	41	44
Test III	31	26	30	32	33	35	33	34

reach or exceed the norms for the high-school grades in which they are registered. These proportions are shown in the following tabulation:

	Boys %	Girls %	Diff. %	S.D. of Diff.
Test I	93	96	3	3
Test II	93	100	7	3
Test III	90	93	3	4

By this criterion the girls are seen to have perhaps a slight advantage, though the difference on any one part of the test is not reliable in the light of its standard error.

The most important result of the application of the Test in Comprehension of Literature has been to show that in the abilities measured by this test the gifted children rate very high—at least two standard deviations above the general run of high-school students of corresponding age.

HOTZ FIRST-YEAR ALGEBRA SCALES

The two scales which Hotz believes to be the most valuable of the five algebra scales constructed by him were administered to the gifted subjects in grades nine to eleven inclusive. The two scales are the "Equation and Formula Scale" and the "Problem Scale," Series B. Each scale requires forty minutes to administer.

Separate norms are furnished by Hotz for pupils who have been pursuing a first-year algebra course for three months, for six months, and for nine months. The norms are given in terms of medians and semi-interquartile ranges. The latter we have transformed approximately into standard deviations by dividing by .6745. The norms are reproduced in Table 41.

TABLE 41

Norms for Hotz First-Year Algebra Scales, Series B

	Three-Months Group (N = 689)	Six-Months Group (N = 746)	Nine-Months Group (N = 1612)
Equation and Formula Scale			
Median	7.8	14.3	16.0
Q	1.85	3.02	3.05
S.D.*	2.74	4.48	4.52
Problem Scale			
Median	5.4	6.5	7.5
Q	1.23	1.61	1.94
S.D.*	1.82	2.39	2.88

* Approximate.

At first thought it would seem as if the scores of our gifted subjects might not be properly compared with the norms furnished by Hotz, since his are based upon pupils who were actually registered in algebra classes at the time the tests were administered. Only a small proportion of the gifted subjects were enrolled in algebra classes at the time of testing, though practically every child had at some time taken algebra. It might be that those who had not had algebra for two or three years would suffer a handicap that would show up in the scores.

We sought light upon this point by tabulating scores on the test according to the interval that had elapsed since the subject first began his study of algebra. The results rather surprisingly give no evidence that attainment has dropped off with lapse of time, although the amount of time that has elapsed since the study of algebra was begun ranges up to three and one-half years.

Another fact to be considered is that the gifted subjects are not entirely homogeneous with respect to amount of algebraic instruction received. Some have had only a fraction

of a term, some a full year or two terms, and some three
terms. It seemed to us probable that the subjects having less
than two terms of algebra would very nearly cancel the
number having more than two terms, but as a matter of pre-
caution we tested the validity of making a single report, as
we have done, of the results for all from the Regular group
who took the test. Scanning the high-school transcripts, we
selected the subjects who had had just two terms of algebra
and for whom we have Hotz tests. We found their mean
scores on the Hotz tests to be the same, within a fraction of a
point, as the mean scores of the entire group from which
they were selected. We feel, therefore, that the results reported in Table 42 can be taken as quite representative of
gifted subjects who have had algebra for two terms, and
that they may justly be compared with the norms for Hotz's
nine-months group.

TABLE 42

MEASURES OF CENTRAL TENDENCY AND DISPERSION FOR GIFTED SUBJECTS
ON HOTZ ALGEBRA SCALES, SERIES B

	EQUATIONS AND FORMULA SCALE		PROBLEM SCALE	
	Gifted Boys	Gifted Girls	Gifted Boys	Gifted Girls
Mean	15.3	14.0	8.8	8.8
Median	16.2	13.8	8.6	9.2
S.D.	5.5	5.5	2.8	2.7
N	91	73	92	72

In variability the gifted boys and girls are nearly identical on both tests; in mean or median they do not differ
significantly on the Problem Scale, but on the Equations and
Formula Scale the mean of the boys exceeds that of the girls
by about half a control S.D. or by one and one-half times the
standard error of the difference.

When we compare the medians of the gifted in Table 42
with the medians of the nine-months pupils reported by
Hotz in Table 41, we find no apparent superiority of the
gifted on the Equations and Formula Scale; in fact the median of the gifted girls is found to be nearly half an S.D.
below the norm. On the Problem Scale, however, both
gifted boys and girls do somewhat better, exceeding the
norm by nearly half an S.D. Of the gifted pupils who began
the study of algebra more than six months previous to the

tests, 60 per cent of the boys and 44 per cent of the girls reach or exceed the nine-months norm on the Equations and Formula Scale, while 71 per cent of the boys and 69 per cent of the girls reach or exceed the nine-months norm on the Problem Scale.

In interpreting the above findings it is important to bear in mind that members of the gifted group when taking first year algebra probably averaged about two years younger than the group which furnished the norms for the scale. This fact might easily be overlooked if the ages of our subjects at the time of taking the test were considered, since gifted subjects up to third-year standing in high school were tested. Considering the results in their entirety, one can say that the intellectual superiority of the gifted girls over ordinary high-school pupils of the same school grade has just about atoned for their age handicap of two years, and that the boys have done even better than this.

However, the gifted subjects make a less superior showing on the Hotz tests than on any of the other achievement tests we have given them. This may be due in large part to the selected character of the group upon whom the norms were based. It has been demonstrated frequently that pupils who elect to take algebra in high school are brighter on the average than those who do not elect it. Nevertheless, despite possible selection and despite the factor of age difference, it is extremely improbable that the level of mental ability of the subjects with whom the tests were standardized averaged as high as that of the gifted subjects who took the test. If this belief is justified, the conclusion would be that our gifted children are relatively somewhat weaker in the abilities which the Hotz test measures than they are in the abilities which enter into the scores of the other achievement tests we have given.

Iowa High-School Content Examination

The Iowa High-School Content Examination, Form A-1, was administered during the follow-up to subjects who had reached high-school senior, high-school post-graduate, or college freshman status. It was also given to a few subjects who had very recently graduated from high school and were not at the time attending any institution of learning. In our treatment of the data the high-school seniors have been tabulated as one group and the remaining cases as another group. The large majority of the second group are college freshmen.

The working time on the Iowa Examination, Form A-1 or Form B-1, is fifty-five minutes. The examination is divided into four parts designed to measure achievement in four fundamental branches of a four-year high-school curriculum, viz., English, mathematics, science, and history. The reliability of the total test as reported by Ruch and Stoddard for a large group of high-school seniors is .95. For the same group the standard deviation is 32, and the P.E. of an individual score is 5 points. The reliabilities of the four separate parts of the examination range between .89 and .93. The norms are reproduced in Table 43.

TABLE 43

NORMS FOR 2108 HIGH-SCHOOL SENIORS (APRIL TESTING) ON
IOWA HIGH-SCHOOL CONTENT EXAMINATION

	Mean	S.D.
English	37.7	13.2
Mathematics	19.3	10.1
Science	13.1	7.7
History	36.0	12.1
Total test	106.1	35.5

Table 44 (p. 96) and Figure 1 (p. 97) give results of the Iowa Examination for members of the Regular group who took it. We note little difference, on the whole, between the scores of gifted high-school seniors and gifted college freshmen on either the total test or the subtests. The gifted boys are consistently superior to the gifted girls on all except the English test, on which the girls show a slight superiority. The superiority of boys to girls is most marked of all on the science test, on which boys surpass girls by more than one S.D. of the distribution of unselected high-school seniors. The marked sex disparity is doubtless partly due to the fact that the boys have taken more science courses than the girls, but this fact may perhaps itself be accounted for by a greater aptitude for science in boys than in girls. The mean scores of the gifted girls tend to be roughly 1 to 1.5 control S.D.'s above the norm, those of the gifted boys to be roughly 1.5 to 2 control S.D.'s above the norm.

TABLE 44

HIGH-SCHOOL ACHIEVEMENT OF GIFTED SUBJECTS AS MEASURED ON THE IOWA HIGH-SCHOOL CONTENT EXAMINATION

	HIGH-SCHOOL SENIORS		COLLEGE FRESHMEN AND RECENT H.S. GRADUATES	
	Gifted Boys (N = 63)	Gifted Girls (N = 40)	Gifted Boys (N = 31)	Gifted Girls (N = 27)
Part 1. English				
Mean	55	59	59	60
S.D.	7.5	5.9	6.7	8.1
Percentile on H.S. control distribution	85	90	91	92
Superiority to norm (in control S.D.'s)	1.3	1.6	1.7	1.6
Part 2. Mathematics				
Mean	36	28	34	26
S.D.	10.0	8.2	9.7	9.6
Percentile on H.S. control distribution	90	79	89	76
Superiority to norm (in control S.D.'s)	1.6	0.8	1.4	0.7
Part 3. Science				
Mean	30	21	32	22
S.D.	8.5	6.8	7.6	7.2
Percentile on H.S. control distribution	95	87	97	88
Superiority to norm (in control S.D.'s)	2.2	1.1	2.4	1.2
Part 4. History				
Mean	54	51	59	49
S.D.	9.8	8.2	9.2	12.2
Percentile on H.S. control distribution	93	90	97	87
Superiority to norm (in control S.D.'s)	1.5	1.3	1.9	1.1
Total Score				
Mean	173	158	183	160
S.D.	27.5	21.2	21.9	21.5
Percentile on H.S. control distribution	93	89	95	90
Superiority to norm (in control S.D.'s)	1.9	1.5	2.1	1.5

Considering only the gifted subjects who are high-school seniors, the following proportions reach or exceed the norms

FIGURE 1

DISTRIBUTION OF TOTAL SCORES OF IOWA HIGH-SCHOOL CONTENT
EXAMINATION FOR GIFTED HIGH-SCHOOL SENIORS,
63 BOYS AND 40 GIRLS

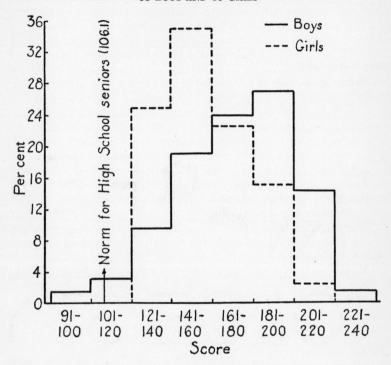

for high-school seniors, notwithstanding that the norm group
has an age advantage of about two years on the average.

	Boys %	Girls %
English	97	100
Mathematics	97	90
Science	97	90
History	95	98
Total score	97	100

If circumstances had permitted, it would have been desirable to extend the scope of the achievement testing program. It would have been especially interesting to know

what strengths and weaknesses would be brought to light for the group as a whole and for individual subjects by extensive and thoroughgoing testing in each of several fields, for example, language and literature, the physical sciences and mathematics, the biological sciences, the social sciences, and the arts. Such data, besides giving valuable information on the natural relationships of abilities, would have afforded a wealth of clinical material that would become invaluable when interpreted in the light of the later development of the subjects. However, a program of this kind was entirely out of the question. The funds were inadequate, suitable tests of proved reliability and validity were not available in all the fields named, and the amount of time which could reasonably be asked of the subjects was limited. Another obstacle to the carrying out of an ideal testing program was the wide range of ages of the subjects. At present there is hardly a single aspect of human achievement which can be measured thoroughly from the fourth elementary school grade to the post-graduate years of college.

While not claiming that the achievement testing program adopted was the best that the situation would have permitted, we believe that the findings which have been set forth give a fairly adequate idea of the general excellence of accomplishment to be expected in grades four to twelve by subjects who six years earlier have rated 140 or higher in IQ. Additional evidence to be found in several other chapters of this volume will help to complete the picture.

SUMMARY

1. The mean educational quotients of gifted subjects tested on the Stanford Achievement Test in 1928 are a little lower than those of gifted subjects of similar age who took the same test in 1922. The average discrepancy amounts to 6 E.Q. points in the case of the boys and 10 E.Q. points in the case of the girls upon the four tests which were included in identical form in the 1922 and 1928 batteries. It is not known how much, if any, of this drop can be attributed to faults in the standardization of the tests.

2. The present Stanford Achievement Test level of the gifted boys is in line with their present mean IQ, and the present achievement level of the gifted girls is a little higher than their present IQ's would suggest.

3. On the three subtests of the Stanford Test in Compre-

hension of Literature the gifted excel the control of corresponding high-school grades by more than a control standard deviation, notwithstanding an age advantage of possibly two years in favor of the control group. On subtests I and II the tendency is for the gifted to excel the control by more than 1.5 control S.D.'s. Gifted subjects in the eleventh grade excel control ninth-grade subjects, whom they match fairly well in age, by more than two control S.D.'s on all three subtests. Gifted girls do slightly better than gifted boys on all of the three subtests.

4. The results from the Hotz Algebra Scales administered to the gifted subjects attending high school indicate that there is no superiority of gifted over control on the Equation and Formula Scale; in fact, the median of the gifted girls is nearly half an S.D. below the Hotz norm. On the Problem Scale, however, both gifted boys and gifted girls exceed the norm by nearly half a control S.D.

5. The Hotz Problem Scale brings out no significant sex differences, but on the Equation and Formula Scale the mean of the gifted boys exceeds that of the gifted girls by about half a control group S.D., or one and a half times the standard error of the difference.

6. The fact that the gifted subjects appear to make a less superior showing upon the algebra tests than upon any other achievement test administered to them may be due in part to the selected character of the group upon whom the norms were based.

7. On the Iowa High-School Content Examination (which includes English, mathematics, science, and history) the mean scores of the high-school senior and college freshman gifted boys tend to be roughly 1.5 to 2 control group S.D.'s above the norm; those of the high-school senior and college freshman gifted girls roughly 1 to 1.5 control S.D.'s above the norm. Considering that high-school students are selected, perhaps representing in the eleventh or twelfth grade chiefly the upper fifty per cent of the generality of school children, the showing made by the gifted group on the Iowa High-School Content Examination must be regarded as extremely gratifying.

8. The gifted boys are superior to the gifted girls on all parts of the Iowa Examination except English, in which the girls show a slight superiority.

CHAPTER VI

ACHIEVEMENT AS INDICATED BY GRADES

Data are summarized in this chapter from transcripts of high-school grades received for 49 boys and 28 girls of the Regular group who had graduated from high school, and from college transcripts of record for 39 boys and 38 girls also of the Regular group. While the test data of chapter v are admittedly far superior to the grades from the standpoint of reliability and objectivity, the latter provide certain interesting material not contained in the former; for example they furnish information regarding a number of school studies not embraced by the achievement tests and, incidentally, regarding the frequency with which various types of studies are pursued by our gifted subjects. That grades are more subjective than test scores and more affected by the personality traits of the student renders them more rather than less interesting for our present purposes. If the test scores of the gifted group tell us what they have actually achieved, their scholastic grades tell us what their teachers think they have achieved. The latter is no less important to know than the former.

High-School Graduates

In Table 45 the high-school grades received by 77 gifted high-school graduates are tabulated.

Some of the school subjects, of course, such as English, United States history, and physical education, are required of all high-school pupils; others, while not required of all pupils, must be taken by those who wish to enter a college of good standing. It cannot, therefore, be concluded that because English, history, mathematics, and language have been taken with the highest frequencies these courses are necessarily preferred above all others by the gifted group. (In chapter vii data are given upon expressed preferences.) However, a number of facts revealed by the frequencies of Table 45 are significant, namely: that modern languages are taken more frequently than ancient languages, especially by gifted girls; that gifted boys take relatively much more

TABLE 45

SUMMARY OF HIGH-SCHOOL TRANSCRIPTS OF 49 GIFTED BOYS AND 28 GIFTED GIRLS WHO HAVE GRADUATED FROM HIGH SCHOOL

	Gifted Boys							Gifted Girls						
	A %	B %	C %	D %	E %	No. of Grades	Mean	A %	B %	C %	D %	E %	No. of Grades	Mean
Art	42	39	19	..	..	31	1.8	68	27	5	..	..	40	1.4
Ancient language (chiefly Latin)	41	46	11	2	..	133	1.7	79	14	7	..	..	73	1.3
English (including journalism)	42	51	6	1	..	322	1.7	83	17	..	..	..	209	1.2
History (including civics and economics)	51	42	7	..	..	270	1.6	68	30	2	..	..	133	1.3
Mathematics:														
Algebra	42	50	7	..	1	144	1.7	82	16	2	..	..	61	1.2
Geometry	47	41	10	2	..	107	1.7	64	28	6	2	..	53	1.5
Miscellaneous	55	27	14	4	..	22	1.7	..	..	..	..	..	5	..
Modern language	49	40	10	0.6	0.6	162	1.6	69	30	1	..	..	157	1.3
Music:														
Orchestra, band, etc.	64	34	2	..	..	47	1.4	84	16	..	..	..	62	1.2
Theoretical, harmony, etc.	..	..	..	..	..	3	..	83	17	..	..	..	18	1.2
Physical education and hygiene	36	59	5	..	..	123	1.7	70	26	4	..	..	53	1.3
Practical subjects:														
Commercial courses	39	54	7	..	..	41	1.7	74	19	6	..	..	31	1.3
Home economics	..	..	..	..	..	..	..	56	44	..	..	..	27	1.4
Shop, printing, mechanical drawing, etc.	35	46	18	..	..	82	1.8	..	..	..	..	..	..	..
Public speaking, expression, etc.	46	46	8	..	..	37	1.6	65	24	12	..	..	17	1.5
Science:														
General and miscellaneous	57	40	3	..	..	30	1.4	88	12	..	..	..	17	1.1
Chemistry	43	47	7	3	..	70	1.7	56	39	5	..	..	36	1.5
Physics	46	52	..	2	..	46	1.6	50	50	..	..	..	12	1.5
Life sciences	42	58	..	..	..	24	1.6	57	43	..	..	..	14	1.4
All school subjects	45	46	8	0.8	0.2	1,694	1.6	73	24	2	0.1	..	1,018	1.3

science and mathematics than do gifted girls; that art and music and home economics are by the criterion of frequencies "girls'" subjects; and that only a small proportion of the total high-school work is done in the so-called "practical subjects." There are a few additional school subjects that were taken by so small a proportion of our group that we have not included them in the tabulation.

If we consult the columns of means, we note that the averages of grades in the various school subjects are fairly uniform within each sex. The boys of the gifted group average between 1.4 and 1.8 on their various courses, and the girls between 1.1 and 1.5, where 1 is A, 2 is B, 3 is C, etc.

A study recently made by Dr. Nettels[1] of the Los Angeles City Schools enables us to compare the marks of the gifted with those of unselected high-school pupils in the Los Angeles system. For the year 1927–28 the scholarship average of Los Angeles high-school students, based upon 98,000 marks in all school studies, was 2.7. The marks were distributed in the following proportions: A, 13%; B, 30%; C, 27%; D, 13%; E, 8%; dropped or incomplete, 9%.

The distributions of A, B, C, D, and E marks reported by Nettels for the separate school studies (not reproduced here) show that "A" grades are received by the gifted in their separate school studies from four to eight times as frequently as by the general run of high-school pupils. Both gifted boys and gifted girls have particularly high marks in "general and miscellaneous" scientific courses, receiving "A" in such courses six to ten times as frequently as do unselected high-school pupils.

Comparing the gifted boys with the gifted girls in Table 45, we see that the girls receive higher average marks than the boys in every course, including science and mathematics, two fields in which the test scores of the boys are significantly higher than those of the girls. The superior marks of the girls invite speculation, but they are in harmony with results reported by many others[2] for pupils unselected for intelligence.

Other interesting facts to be noted in Table 45 are the

---

[1] Nettels, C. H., *Educational Research Bulletin*, Los Angeles Schools, Vol. 8, 1929, pp. 5–16.

[2] See, for example, Lentz, T. F., "Sex Differences in School Marks with Achievement Test Scores Constant," *School and Society*, Vol. 29, 1929, pp. 65–68.

following: no girls and a negligible proportion of boys have failed in any of their studies; few boys and only one girl have received a mark as low as "D" in any study; the girls receive a grade of "A" in nearly three-quarters of their school work, the boys in slightly less than half of theirs.

COLLEGE STUDENTS

In Table 46 (p. 104) the mean grades of members of the Regular group for whom we have college transcripts are given. The 77 cases entering this table might have been augmented by 45 if we had secured from the Stanford Registrar's Office transcripts of record for the members of the Regular group who have attended Stanford. This was not done because it is possible to obtain from the Stanford directory the scholarship or "grade-point" average of every student, and we felt that the extra labor involved in getting complete transcripts would not be justified at this time. The scholarship averages of gifted subjects attending Stanford are summarized in Table 47 (p. 105).

Table 46 also includes the mean grades received in the fall semester of 1927 by the generality of University of California students registered in lower-division, upper-division, and graduate courses of the departments in question. These mean grades have been computed from data contained in a Recorder's Office bulletin furnished us by the University of California. As a large proportion of the gifted students for whom we have transcripts are attending the University of California, these data provide excellent comparative material. It is seen that except for a few courses the gifted boys and girls (most of whom are lower-division students) receive significantly higher average grades than random university students in their lower-division courses. The exceptions are: (1) physical education and hygiene, in which the gifted boys, but not the gifted girls, are a shade below the mean; (2) the political science, economics, and sociology group, in which the gifted girls rate at the mean while the gifted boys rate much higher; and (3) chemistry, in which the gifted girls are somewhat below the norm. The mean for the gifted girls in chemistry, however, is based upon the grades of so few cases as to be rather unreliable. In most courses the gifted subjects average higher even than the random students in University of California upper-division

TABLE 46

MEAN COLLEGE GRADES OF 39 GIFTED BOYS AND 38 GIFTED GIRLS COMPARED WITH THOSE OF UNIVERSITY OF CALIFORNIA STUDENTS

	Gifted Boys		Gifted Girls		Univ. of Calif. Student Body 1927 Mean Grades		
	Mean Grade	No. of Units	Mean Grade	No. of Units	Lower Div. Courses	Upper Div. Courses	Graduate Courses
Art		7*	2.2	35	2.6	2.3	2.0
Ancient languages	2.4	16	1.5	71	2.7	2.3	1.4
Education		3	2.2	28		2.5	1.9
Engineering:							
Civil		9					
Mechanical	2.2	7			2.9	2.6	2.1
English	2.0	137	2.0	270	2.7	2.5	1.5
History	2.2	60	2.2	168	2.6	2.6	1.8
Mathematics	2.2	86	1.9	78	2.7	2.0	
Military	2.2	103½			2.9	2.6	1.8
Modern languages	2.2	262	2.0	331	2.5	2.2	
Music	2.3	11½	2.3	49	2.8	2.5	1.2
Philosophy	2.3	69	2.0	108	2.5	2.4	2.2
Physical educ. and hygiene	2.6	48½	2.1	54	2.7	2.6	1.8
Polit. science, economics, sociology	2.0	101	2.7	94	2.7	2.3	1.6
Psychology	2.6	20	2.0	50	2.8	2.5	
Public speaking, dramatics, etc.	1.9	61	2.2	68			1.3
Science:							
Chemistry	1.9	185	3.1	36	2.7	2.4	1.9
Geology	2.2	40	2.5	41	2.8	2.7	1.3
Life sciences	1.9	69	2.2	131	2.7	2.3	
Miscellaneous	1.7	35	2.2	47			1.7
Physics	1.7	95	1.8	22	2.7	2.6	

* Mean grades were computed only if the number of semester units recorded under a given college subject amounted to 10 or more.

courses, but it is only in a few departments that the gifted average higher than students taking graduate work in those departments.

Table 46 confirms Table 45 in the main with respect to the higher grades received by the girls in most courses. The boys have higher grades, however, in all the scientific subjects; in the political science, economics, and sociology group; and, rather surprisingly, in public speaking and dramatics. For some reason or reasons, the girls have particularly high grades in ancient languages and particularly low grades in chemistry. This may be partly because no one would be likely to take an ancient language in college unless he really liked it, while girls who take chemistry are probably in competition with boys who have more of the vocational or semi-vocational interest in it.

It is interesting to note that among the college students a larger proportion of the total work is done in modern languages than in English; that proportionately more boys than girls take scientific courses, but that the girls greatly outweigh the boys with respect to proportions taking art, English, languages, history, education, philosophy, and psychology. Of the sciences, chemistry is the one most frequently elected by the boys, while the biological sciences are most frequently elected by the girls.

TABLE 47

MEAN GRADES RECEIVED BY GIFTED SUBJECTS ATTENDING STANFORD

	BOYS		GIRLS	
	Mean	N	Mean	N
Regular group	2.4	32	2.1	13
Regular and outside Binet groups	2.4	53	2.1	28
Above groups, first freshman quarter	2.4	40	2.1	22

The data concerning the gifted subjects attending Stanford are given in Table 47. It will be of interest to compare the figures in Table 47 with the mean scholarship ratings of (1) the generality of Stanford freshmen and (2) Stanford freshmen who come from their high schools with "gold seal" diplomas awarded for high scholarship. For the generality of Stanford freshmen the scholarship average is 2.5; for the "seal bearers," 2.2. The gifted boys are seen to average slightly higher than the general run of Stanford freshmen, but not so high as the "seal bearers." The gifted girls, on the other hand, average a little above the "seal-bearers."

The showing made by the members of our gifted group who have entered Stanford may impress the reader as surprisingly commonplace. However, if the factors of age and selection are taken into account the showing is little if at all below what should have been expected. The gifted freshmen average almost two years younger than the group with which they are compared, and to have made good this handicap is no mean accomplishment. The highly selected nature of the Stanford student body is an even more important factor that must be taken into account. Few students graduate from high school who do not belong in the highest quarter of children in general with respect to intelligence; and of high-school graduates, few are admitted to Stanford who do not belong in the highest fifth of high-school graduates in scholarship, intelligence test score, and personal recommendations. The result is that the Stanford freshmen with whom our gifted group is compared represent for the most part the best two or three per cent of the general population and probably include few who are below the best five per cent. Their average Thorndike intelligence score, as was shown in chapter iii, does not fall so very far short of the average for our gifted group. Viewed in the light of these facts, the scholastic grades earned by the members of our group who have entered Stanford cannot be regarded as disappointing.

If, as may be possible, their average grade is a small fraction below that which their intelligence alone would lead one to predict, this might easily be due to a natural tendency of instructors to underrate the achievement of those students who are considerably younger than their classmates and for this reason more likely to be diffident or shy in their classroom behavior. It appears also that some of the brightest in our group have made mediocre records in college as the result of a deliberate intention to divest themselves of their reputation for intellectual brilliance and to go out for activities which are more richly rewarded in terms of social approval of their fellows. These factors, however, are minor ones. Apart from the handicap of age, the main reason why our group does not stand out very distinctly above the average of Stanford freshmen in scholastic grades is found in the highly selected nature of the Stanford student body. Since 1924 the Thorndike Examination has been required of all applicants, and scores upon this test have been given considerable weight in granting admission. As a result a steady rise has taken place in the intellectual caliber of the entering freshman classes. In 1923 the mean Thorndike score of the entering class was 71. In 1924 it jumped to 77, and by 1928 had reached 83. The latter value is only 5 points, or a third of a standard deviation, below the mean Thorndike score of our gifted boys, and is just equal to the mean Thorndike score of our gifted girls.

Graduation Honors

Another interesting comparison is that based upon graduation honors. Here the showing made by the gifted group is more favorable than in that based upon average grades. Of the 54 members[1] of our group who have graduated from Stanford in departments giving eligibility to Phi Beta Kappa membership (i.e., non-engineering departments), 30 per cent were honored by Phi Beta Kappa election. In a group of 58 gifted subjects[1] who have graduated from the University of California (where the local Phi Beta Kappa chapter elects students from engineering as well as from non-engineering departments), 28 per cent were elected. As only 10 per cent of all Stanford and University of California graduates from eligible departments are elected, the proportion of our gifted group elected is approximately three times the expected.

Other graduation honors at Stanford include graduation "with distinction" and "with great distinction." In competition for these honors the engineering departments are not excluded. Graduation "with great distinction" is limited by rule to the highest five per cent in grade-point average; graduation "with distinction," to the next ten per cent below these. Of 56 Stanford graduates from our group who enter into this comparison, 12.5 per cent have graduated "with great distinction," and 19.6 per cent "with distinction." The total is 32.1 per cent, as compared with 15 per cent of Stanford graduates in general.

[1] These subjects were not drawn from the Regular group exclusively, but included students from the gifted group at large.

The reader is referred to the section on case studies for
descriptions of several gifted subjects who illustrate superior
or inferior accomplishment in their school work. It will be
seen from the case studies that character and personality
are important factors in determining school success.

SUMMARY

1. Transcripts of high-school grades for gifted subjects
who have graduated from high school show that the averages
of grades in the various school courses are fairly uniform
within each sex. Gifted pupils of both sexes average far
above unselected high-school pupils, and receive "A" grades
in their separate school studies about four to eight times as
frequently as do unselected high-school pupils in the same
school studies.

2. The gifted girls receive higher average marks than
the gifted boys in every high-school course, including science
and mathematics, two fields in which the achievement test
scores of the boys are significantly higher than those of the
girls.

3. No gifted girls and a negligible proportion of the
gifted boys have failed in any of their high-school studies.
The girls receive a grade of "A" in nearly three-quarters of
their school work, the boys in 45 per cent.

4. The college transcripts of gifted subjects confirm the
high-school transcripts with respect to the high grades received by the gifted subjects in most courses, and with respect to the higher grades received by the girls. The boys
have higher college grades, however, in all the science
courses, in the courses which are grouped under the heading
"political science, economics, and sociology," and in public
speaking.

5. Gifted boys attending Stanford University make a
scholarship average that is slightly above that of Stanford
freshmen, but not so high as that of students who come to
Stanford with "gold-seal" diplomas. Gifted girls attending
Stanford average slightly higher than the "seal-bearers."
The selection of Stanford students is so rigorous that our
gifted subjects at Stanford are competing for grades with
students whose level of ability averages only a little below
their own and who are also not far from two years older on
the average.

6. Of fifty-four members of the gifted group who have graduated from Stanford in departments from which Phi Beta Kappa membership is drawn, 30 per cent were elected to Phi Beta Kappa, and of fifty-eight who graduated from the University of California, 28 per cent were elected, as compared with 10 per cent of all seniors who graduate from eligible departments. The proportion of our group who have graduated from Stanford "with distinction" or "with great distinction" is more than twice as great as for the generality of Stanford graduates.

CHAPTER VII

SCHOLASTIC AND OTHER INTERESTS

We have traced, in chapters iii to vi, the progress of the members of the gifted group to date with respect to intellectual and scholastic abilities. It remains to inquire rather carefully into other important aspects of the personality make-up of our gifted subjects. With their high intelligence and their demonstrated capacity to excel in pursuit of the usual scholastic goals, what have they in the way of interests, ambitions, and social idiosyncrasies that favor or hinder their accomplishment? The present chapter and the three immediately following will be devoted to a discussion of interests and personality traits.

SCHOLASTIC INTERESTS

Questions 1, 2, and 3 of the follow-up Interest Blank read:

"What studies have you liked most during the last two or three years?.... What studies have you liked least?.... Reason?.... If you are at college, what is your major subject?...."

In order to express the data in a manner that would permit for each school study a single index founded upon both likes and dislikes, a method was adopted similar to that used for combining the "special weaknesses" and "extraordinary abilities" reported by teachers (p. 81). For any given school study the number of gifted subjects listing it among studies liked least was divided by the number listing it among studies liked most. The resulting ratios, which are reported in Tables 48 and 49, give a rough measure of the attitude of the gifted group toward the several studies, a low ratio indicating that more of the pupils like the study than dislike it, a ratio of 1.00 that equal numbers like and dislike it, and a ratio greater than 1.00 that it is disliked by more pupils than like it.

Not all the school and college courses which have been studied by our gifted subjects were reported by any of them as being either "most liked" or "least liked," and some

110

courses were reported by so few as to make the determination of ratio highly unreliable. Upon some courses, however, large numbers of gifted subjects expressed themselves. For five broadly classified fields of study the numbers involved are large enough to make possible a comparison of gifted subjects attending high school with those attending college.

TABLE 48

Subjects Most Liked and Least Liked by Gifted Students Attending High School and College

| | ATTENDING HIGH SCHOOL | | | | | |
| | BOYS (N = 181) | | | GIRLS (N = 140) | | |
	Most	Least	Ratio	Most	Least	Ratio
English	75	48	.64	103	14	.14
History	68	34	.50	49	26	.53
Mathematics	100	45	.45	49	53	1.08
Sciences	128	19	.15	47	30	.64
Modern languages	46	24	.52	52	17	.33

| | ATTENDING COLLEGE | | | | | |
| | BOYS (N = 60) | | | GIRLS (N = 56) | | |
	Most	Least	Ratio	Most	Least	Ratio
English	26	5	.19	39	8	.21
History	15	8	.53	19	12	.63
Mathematics	17	10	.59	13	8	.62
Sciences	41	20	.49	28	19	.68
Modern languages	14	7	.50	21	7	.33

This is done in Table 48. We observe that the boys tend to like mathematics and science better than the girls do, although the tendency is not so strong among the college students as among the high-school students. English and history are "girls' studies" among the high-school gifted subjects, but become "boys' studies" among the group attending college, the curious reversal being due not to a decrease in the relative number of girls who express their liking for these studies but to an increase in the relative number of girls who like them least. Modern languages are better liked by the girls than by the boys both in high school and in college, though the difference is small in the college group.

Table 49 (p. 112) is based upon results from the gifted subjects of high school and college combined. Certain

courses are listed in this table which are not included in
Table 48, since the combined numbers of high-school and
college gifted subjects provide more reliable data. However,
there are still some courses, such as political science, engineering, and philosophy, offered only in colleges and universities, which are mentioned by so few of our gifted subjects
that we have not included them in the tabular summary.

TABLE 49

SUBJECTS MOST LIKED AND LEAST LIKED, GIFTED HIGH-SCHOOL
AND COLLEGE STUDENTS COMBINED

	BOYS (N = 241)			GIRLS (N = 196)		
	Most	Least	Ratio	Most	Least	Ratio
Art	13	7	.54	35	6	.17
English	101	53	.52	142	22	.15
Debating	6	..	...	3	..	...
Dramatics	8	..	...	18	1	.06
History	83	42	.51	68	38	.56
Languages	11	9	.82	3	1	.33
Ancient	29	45	1.55	33	19	.58
Modern	60	31	.52	73	24	.33
Mathematics	117	55	.47	62	61	.98
Music	13	2	.15	30	3	.10
Physical education ...	3	3	1.00	9	3	.33
Political science and civics	21	13	.62	7	13	1.86
Practical subjects (shop, mechanical drawing, typing, sewing)	29	8	.28	22	14	.64
Science (except chem. and physics) ...	66	18	.27	38	25	.66
Chemistry	64	13	.20	29	17	.59
Physics	39	8	.21	8	7	.87

Possibly the most noteworthy facts revealed by Table 49
are: the relatively strong liking of the girls for art, English,
and modern languages; the distaste of the girls for mathematics, and for civics; the relatively strong liking of the boys
for the sciences; and the distaste of the boys for ancient
languages. There is a striking parallelism between the
courses liked and disliked by the gifted subjects and the
courses in which, according to their teachers, they show
unusual abilities and weaknesses. (See chapter iv.)

It should be clear, of course, that the ratios in Tables 48 and 49 do not tell the whole story. One study may be liked and disliked by a large number of the pupils, while another study is liked and disliked by a much smaller number, though the ratios may be the same in the two cases. Another type of example occurs in the case of English. If we considered only the ratios, we would infer that while attending high school gifted girls like English better than gifted boys do, but that in college gifted boys like it better than gifted girls do, though in college as in high school a larger proportion of the girls than of the boys actually profess their liking for it. As was pointed out before, the reversal of ratios takes place because of an increase in the proportion of girls expressing a distaste for the study of English.

Another pitfall in the interpretation of Tables 48 and 49 concerns those studies which are more or less optional. While all students in a college preparatory course are required to take such studies as English, mathematics, science, and history, they are not required to take such studies as art, debating, dramatics, music, etc. Hence those who take these "extras" are likely to be pupils who have an unusual liking for them. These considerations undoubtedly account for the fact that art, music, and dramatics have the best (lowest) ratios of all the studies listed in Table 49.

To approach the discussion of scholastic interests of members of the gifted group from a different angle we have summarized in Table 50 (p. 114) the answers to another question that was included both on the Interest Blank and on the Information Blank:

"If you are at college, what is your major subject? . . . ." (Interest Blank: 3; Information Blank: 7.)

If we group the subjects listed in Table 50 according to their logical affinities, the data on choice of major become more significant. Doing this gives us the following figures:

	Boys	Girls
Physical sciences	12	5
Biological sciences	8	4
Social sciences	19	15
Language and literature	10	17
Music and art	2	6
Undecided	9	9

TABLE 50

Major Studies of Gifted Subjects Attending College

	Boys	Girls
Architectural drawing	1	.
Art	1	5
Biological sciences:		
Bacteriology	.	1
Biology	.	1
Botany	1	.
Zoölogy	1	.
Chemistry	6	.
Commerce	1	1
Economics	5	4
Engineering	4	.
English	6	12
Geology	1	1
History	.	3
Law	2	.
Pre-legal	1	.
Languages	1	.
Classical literature	1	.
French	.	4
Greek	1	.
Latin	1	1
Mathematics	1	4
Medical	2	.
Pre-medical	4	1
Music	.	1
Philosophy	1	2
Physical education	.	1
Political science	7	1
Psychology	1	1
Social science	1	3
Undecided	9	9
Total	60	56

Reading Interests

"About how many hours a week do you spend on 'general reading' (not school studies)?.... What kind of reading do you enjoy most: e.g., travel, history, essays, plays, adventure stories, science, poetry, short stories, novels, detective stories, etc.?.... Name a few books and magazines you have enjoyed recently . . . ." (Interest Blank: 5.) [Question answered on approximately 96 per cent of the follow-up blanks received.]

Answers to the first part of the question are summarized in Tables 51 and 52. The time devoted to reading shows

TABLE 51

Time (Hours per Week*) Devoted to General Reading (Gifted Boys)

Age	0	1	2	3	4	5	6	7	8	9	10	11	12	13	14	15	16	17	18	19	20	25	30	N	Mean
8						1	1																	2	5.0
9																									
10			1			1		1	1	1	1													6	7.5
11		1	2	3	1		1	1			1	1	1		1									6	14.2
12		2	5	3	3	5	3	1	2	2	2	2	1				1				1	1		10	10.3
13		4	4	6	3	4	4	1	2		3	2	1		1	1								26	6.2
14	1	3	4	6	1	8	3	4	2	1	3	2	1		1	1	1	1	2		1	1	1	32	6.5
15	1	1	3	6	7	8	5	6	3	1	6	2	1	1		1			2		2	1	1	50	6.5
16	1	1	4	5	6	5	5	4	5	1	6		2		1	6			1		3	1	1	51	6.8
17	1	1	3	4	4	4	2	1	1	1	1		1			2								44	8.3
18	1		2	2			1	1	1		1		1			1			1			1		19	6.6
19			1						1															7	8.9
20									1															1	7.5
Total ...	3	8	21	29	26	28	16	20	18	7	25	5	7	1	3	14	2	1	5		7	5	3	254	7.2

TABLE 52

Time (Hours per Week*) Devoted to General Reading (Gifted Girls)

Age	0	1	2	3	4	5	6	7	8	9	10	11	12	13	14	15	16	17	18	19	20	25	30	35	N	Mean
7		1			1	1			1																1	1.5
8			1					1	1																1	4.5
9				2	1		2		1	1	2				1	1					1				3	6.5
10	1	1	3	1	1	1		1	1	2	2	1	3	1		1	1	1	1		1	1			5	1.8
11		2	3	3	1	7	5	1	2	4	4	3	3	1		1	2	1	1			1			14	6.1
12		3	3	2	4	4	3	2	4	4	4	4	3	1	1	2	1	1	1			2			15	7.9
13		1	2	4	4	6	3	6	4	1	4	3	4	2	1		2	3	3		1		1		37	7.6
14			3	3	3	3		1	6	1	3	1	4	1	1	2		1			1				34	7.8
15			3	6	2	4	3	1	1	1		1	1	1							1	1			30	9.8
16		1	1	2	4	4	3	1	1	2	1		1						3		1	2			30	6.6
17		2	5	2	1	1																			16	6.2
18	1	1	2	1	1	1	2	1	1		1					1							1		6	8.0
19																										
20																								1		14.5
Total ...	1	6	20	18	16	24	16	16	10	4	15	4	11	4	2	6			6		5	8	1	1	194	7.6

*In each case the number of hours given in the heading indicates the upper limit of the interval.

practically no dependence upon age within the age-range for which adequate numbers of cases are available, i.e., about thirteen to eighteen years. The girls slightly exceed the boys with respect to time spent in reading, with a weekly average of 7.6 hours as contrasted with 7.2 hours for the boys. These averages are distinctly lower than those reported for the gifted subjects at any age beyond eight in Table 167 of Volume I. The averages of Volume I, however, were based upon parents' estimates, while the averages reported in the present chapter are based upon the estimates of the gifted subjects themselves. The discrepancy may be due to a constant error in the estimates of the parents or of the subjects or of both.

If we compare Tables 51 and 52 with Tables 32 and 33 of chapter iv (hours a week in home study of school lessons), we find that up to and including age fourteen, the gifted boys spend more time in general reading than in home study, but that after age fourteen they spend more time in home study. The hours of home study of the gifted girls overtake their hours of general reading at age thirteen.

The types of reading which the gifted subjects profess to enjoy most are shown in Table 53. Since about two and a half types of reading were recorded by each gifted subject on the average, the number of entries in the first and fourth columns of Table 53 exceeds the number of gifted subjects who answered the question. The percentages of gifted subjects mentioning each type of reading are recorded in the second and fifth columns, and the numbers of reading preferences falling into each type are expressed as percentages of the total number of preferences in the third and sixth columns.

An interesting comparison can here be made with Table 170 of Volume I. The figures of the two tables are not strictly comparable, since the percentages reported in Volume I represent books actually read during a two-months' period, while those in Table 53 represent stated preferences falling into each type. However, we can safely compare the rank orders of the preferred types. If we combine adventure, detective, and mystery stories, we find that this class has now fallen a little below straight fiction (novels and short stories) in popularity with the boys, although adventure and mystery stories formerly headed the list for the

boys. A combined class of history, biography, and travel
now ranks third with the boys, though formerly it was fifth.
Science has come up to fourth place from sixth with the
boys; poetry and drama have risen to fifth from last place;
and such types as legends, fairy tales, nature and animal

TABLE 53

KIND OF READING ENJOYED MOST

	Boys			Girls		
	Number Mention- ing	Percent- age Men- tioning	Percentage of Prefer- ences	Number Mention- ing	Percent- age Men- tioning	Percentage of Prefer- ences
Novels	110	42.6	17.6	124	60.2	23.9
Adventure stories	99	38.4	15.8	41	19.9	7.9
Science	93	36.0	14.9	22	10.7	4.2
Short stories	86	33.3	13.8	78	37.9	15.0
Travel	63	24.4	10.1	44	21.4	8.5
Detective stories .	49	19.0	7.8	22	10.7	4.2
History	47	18.2	7.5	36	17.5	6.9
Plays	30	11.6	4.8	45	21.8	8.7
Poetry	22	8.5	3.5	59	28.6	11.4
Essays	11	4.3	1.8	25	12.1	4.8
Biography	4	1.6	0.6	7	3.4	1.3
"All kinds"	4	1.6	0.6	4	1.9	0.8
Magazines	3	1.2	0.5	..	...	...
Religion	2	0.8	0.3	1	0.5	0.2
Comedy	1	0.4	0.2	..	...	...
Animal stories ..	1	0.4	0.2	..	...	...
"Exposition"	..	...	...	1	0.5	0.2
Nature books	..	...	...	1	0.5	0.2
Mystery	..	...	...	6	2.9	1.2
Myths and legends	..	...	...	1	0.5	0.2
Music and art....	..	...	...	2	1.0	0.4

stories, etc., have practically disappeared. With the girls
straight fiction continues to hold first place, but poetry and
drama rise to second place from sixth or seventh. History,
biography, and travel rank third, but formerly ranked
fourth or fifth, and the adventure or mystery tale falls to
fourth place from the second place which it formerly held.
Science continues to rank low, and, as in the case of the
boys, legends, nature or animal stories, etc., have practically
disappeared. The girls continue to show a greater interest
than the boys in fiction, and more than twice as many girls
as boys have developed an interest in poetry and drama.

The boys continue to show a greater interest than girls do in adventure stories; they also show a greater interest in detective stories, but the few individuals who still express enjoyment in "mystery" stories are all girls. There is no marked sex difference in the number enjoying history, biography, and travel.

In order that the type of reading which the gifted subjects enjoy at various ages may be visualized more concretely than the data of Table 53 permit, we have assembled the answers to the question regarding books and magazines "enjoyed recently." The gifted subjects were grouped by sex into age ranges of 13 to 14, 15 to 16, 17 to 20. The titles of the five books and magazines mentioned most frequently by the subjects of each age group were retained for Table 54. If two or more books or magazines tied for fifth place upon a list, more than five titles were retained upon the list. The lists are not arranged in order of frequency, but alphabetically instead, since many of the items on the lists tied for frequency.

The lists of Table 54 are extremely interesting, but we forego extended comment. The books mentioned seem to us to belong on the whole to a decidedly superior type. The magazines, however, are less impressive, particularly those mentioned by the girls.

USE OF LEISURE TIME

It is conceivable that the use made by young people of their free time may be an important indicator of their future achievements. Such, in fact, is strongly suggested by Dr. Catharine Cox's study of the early mental development of geniuses.[1] We have therefore tried to secure considerable information regarding the interests, hobbies, likes, and dislikes of each member of the gifted group.

The follow-up Interest Blank asked the subject to rate his liking for twelve "different kinds of things to do." As the question was contained in almost identical form on the original Interest Blank, a comparison can be made between the preferences indicated during the present follow-up and those of 1921–22.

[1] *Genetic Studies of Genius*, Volume II.

TABLE 54

BOOKS AND MAGAZINES "RECENTLY ENJOYED" BY GIFTED SUBJECTS AT THREE AGE-LEVELS

AGE 13-14

GIFTED BOYS		GIFTED GIRLS	
Books	Magazines	Books	Magazines
Ben Hur	Amazing Stories	David Copperfield	American
Ivanhoe	American Boy	Ivanhoe	Evergirl's
Last Days of Pompeii	Boy's Life	Old Curiosity Shop	Good Housekeeping
Royal Road to Romance	Liberty	Quentin Durward	Ladies' Home Journal
Three Musketeers	Literary Digest	Ramona	Literary Digest
	National Geographic	Royal Road to Romance	National Geographic
	Popular Mechanics	Showboat	Saturday Evening Post
	Saturday Evening Post	Talisman	St. Nicholas
			Youth's Companion

AGE 15-16

GIFTED BOYS		GIFTED GIRLS	
Books	Magazines	Books	Magazines
Beau Geste	American	Adam Bede	American
O. Henry's works	American Boy	Beau Geste	Cosmopolitan
Revolt in the Desert	Literary Digest	Ivanhoe	Harper's
Royal Road to Romance	National Geographic	Kipling's works	National Geographic
Shakespeare's works	Saturday Evening Post	Royal Road to Romance	Saturday Evening Post
		Sorrell and Son	
		Tale of Two Cities	

AGE 17-20

GIFTED BOYS		GIFTED GIRLS	
Books	Magazines	Books	Magazines
Beau Geste	American Mercury	Essays (Emerson)	American
Royal Road to Romance	Collier's	Forsyte Saga	Cosmopolitan
Sorrell and Son	Cosmopolitan	King's Henchman	Golden Book
Thunder on the Left	Literary Digest	Lord Jim	Good Housekeeping
Where the Blue Begins	National Geographic	Ordeal of Richard Feverel	Harper's
	Saturday Evening Post	Royal Road to Romance	Saturday Evening Post
		Tale of Two Cities	
		Trader Horn	

The directions are: "Below are several different kinds of things to do. On the line before each thing, put a figure (1, 2, 3, 4, or 5) to show how well you like to do that thing. Put a 1 if you like it very much; put a 2 if you like it fairly well; put a 3 if you neither like it nor dislike it; put a 4 if you rather dislike it; put a 5 if you dislike it very much." (These directions are followed by the list contained in Table 55.) [The question was answered by 99 per cent of the cases from whom blanks were received.]

Dividing the members of the Regular group into sub-groups of those attending grammar school, high school, college, and no school at all, we computed the means of the ratings made by each sex on each of the twelve items. These are reported in Table 55. It is seen that the relative placement of the twelve activities shows only minor fluctuations with age, and that only in the case of a few items is there much difference in the mean ratings of the two sexes. Both sexes prefer reading to all the other occupations; both sexes enjoy "games that require lots of exercise" but tend to feel indifferent toward "games that require little exercise"; neither sex rates "study" very high, the attitude of the boys, especially, tending to be one of indifference; both sexes give the lowest rank to "sewing, cooking, knitting, housework, etc.," the boys, especially, actively disliking such pursuits. The boys neither like nor dislike "spending time alone," but the girls tend to like it fairly well. Both sexes enjoy spending time with either one other person or several other persons, and like fairly well to be leaders and to manage other persons. As would be expected, the sexes differ chiefly in their ratings upon "practicing," "going to parties, etc.," and "using tools, etc."

Comparison with Table 145 of Volume I shows that the gifted boys and girls have made little significant change on the average either in relative or absolute ratings of the twelve activities. The girls now tend to rate "sewing, cooking, knitting, housework, etc." lower than they did originally, but the grammar-school girls assign ratings to these two items that average only a little lower than the 1921–22 ratings of girls who were then in grammar school.

"When you have an hour or two to spend just as you please, what do you like to do best?".... (Interest Blank: 7.) [Question answered by 97 per cent of the gifted subjects from whom blanks were received.]

TABLE 55

Mean Preference Ratings on Various Activities by Gifted Subjects

	In Grammar School		In High School		In College		Not in School	
	B	G	B	G	B	G	B	G
Studying	3.0	2.4	2.7	2.4	2.4	2.0	2.1	1.8
General reading (books, magazines, newspapers)	1.2	1.1	1.3	1.1	1.6	1.1	1.4	1.1
Practicing music, drawing, dancing, etc.	3.2	1.6	2.7	1.9	2.7	2.3	2.6	1.1
Games that require little exercise	2.2	2.5	2.6	2.6	2.4	2.4	2.9	2.2
Games that require lots of exercise	1.4	1.2	1.5	1.6	1.6	1.8	2.0	1.6
Spending time with several other persons	1.6	1.4	2.0	1.7	1.8	1.8	2.0	1.4
Spending time with one other person	1.8	1.6	1.8	1.5	1.8	1.5	1.6	1.6
Spending time alone	3.0	3.4	2.9	2.2	2.9	2.0	2.3	2.1
Going to parties, picnics, dances, club meetings, etc.	2.3	1.3	2.3	1.6	2.2	1.7	2.4	1.4
Using tools or working with apparatus or machinery	1.4	2.2	2.1	3.2	2.4	3.0	2.8	3.0
Sewing, cooking, knitting, housework, etc.	4.4	2.4	4.3	2.9	4.5	3.1	4.3	3.2
Being leader in a team or club and managing other persons	1.7	1.6	2.0	2.1	2.0	2.2	2.1	2.2

The answers to this question have been categorized when doing so adds to the clarity and compactness of the summary of preferred activities which follows.

Grammar-School Boys		Grammar-School Girls	
Read	12	Read	9
Athletic games	3	Games, exercise, etc.	7
Play with chum	3	Art, drawing, etc.	2
Play with Meccano	1	Practice music	1
Ride on bus	1	Make candy	1
	20		20

High-School Boys		High-School Girls	
Read	86	Read	88
Athletic games	30	Athletic games, hike, etc.	12
Make something, work with tools, etc.	10	Practice music	8

High-School Boys (Continued)

Play	6
Play on instrument	5
Draw, cartoon, etc.	5
Swim	4
Ride	4
Look over stamp collection	3
Do what every one else is doing	3
Play chess	2
Build radios	2
Different hobbies	2
Do mathematics	1
Hunt ground squirrels	1
Go to football game	1
Ride to beach	1
Go to scout meeting	1
Work with chemicals	1
Study	1
Play pool or billiards	1
Sail	1
Be with one other person	1
Experiment with music	1
Depends on mood	1
	174

High-School Girls (Continued)

Swim	6
Draw	5
Play a game	4
Ride horseback	3
Write letters or stories	2
Dance	1
Go to a play	1
Sail	1
Cook	1
Sew	1
Play with a baby	1
	134

College Boys

Read	16
Athletic games, exercise, etc.	5
Work with tools	3
Spend time with others	3
Experiment, research, etc.	3
Study	2
Think	2
See a show, hear music, etc.	2
Go to a party	1
Art work	1
Chess	1
Hunt	1
Plan machinery	1
Look at maps	1
Discuss new cars	1
Keep car in condition	1
Have no spare time	1
	45

College Girls

Read	35
Exercise, hikes, etc.	3
Draw	2
Dance	1
Sleep	1
Listen to radio	1
Sew	1
Practice	1
See movies	1
Talk with others	1
	47

Boys Not in School		Girls Not in School	
Read	11	Read	7
Games, exercise, etc...	2	Work crossword puzzles	1
Work with machinery	2		–
Draw	2		8
Study	2		
Attend Y.M.C.A.	1		
Spend time with others	1		
	21		

The preferred activities which we have just listed appear to be normal and wholesome ones. Reading is the outstanding favorite of all the activities for both boys and girls, more subjects mentioning this than all the other activities combined. Athletic games and exercise come second on the lists of both boys and girls, and other activities follow with lower frequencies. It is difficult to draw quantitative conclusions from data of this kind, but inspection of the lists suggests that the boys tend to prefer somewhat more active and objective pastimes than the girls do and that the boys more frequently than the girls display enthusiasm for hobbies or pastimes that may eventually lead to creative work.

The same tendencies are also revealed in the answers to two questions contained on the follow-up Home Information Blank:

"How has leisure time been spent during the last two or three years? (Examples: games, hiking, reading, writing, study, experiments, hobbies, exercise, making collections, working with machinery or tools, sewing, household work, etc.) .... Describe briefly any special projects or hobbies that have been carried on recently....."

We are not summarizing here the data secured in response to these questions as they would require a great deal of space and would serve only to emphasize the tendencies found in those just reported.

COLLECTIONS

"Name all the collections you have been making during the past four or five years and tell how large the collections are ...." (Interest Blank: 9.)

We have first considered all the collections mentioned by the gifted subjects, regardless of kind, and then the collections to which scientific value or interest attaches. Collections of the following kinds are included in the latter category:

> Birds, birds' eggs, nests, feathers, etc.
> Coins and money
> Flowers, grasses, leaves, etc.
> Foreign articles (pottery, ancient weapons, etc.)
> Rocks, stones, minerals, etc.
> Shells, fish, insects of various sorts
> Stamps
> Electrical instruments
> Different kinds of woods
> Data of various kinds, medical, agricultural, etc.

Separate tabulations were made including subjects between the ages of eight and twelve, thirteen and fourteen, fifteen and sixteen, and seventeen to twenty. Table 56 summarizes the results, and shows clearly a decline in collecting interest after age fourteen. The means of the number of collections reported by subjects between the ages of eight and twelve are not very different from the mean numbers reported for the gifted subjects of corresponding age in 1921-22 (see Volume I, p. 379), although the number made by the girls seems now to be a little less than it was then. It should be pointed out, however, that the question on the follow-up blank asked the subject to name collections made during the past four or five years, while the question on the original Interest Blank asked the subject to name all the collections he had made. This fact might easily account for the small drop in the number listed by the girls.

Table 56 shows that the boys rather outnumber the girls with respect to number of collections made and very greatly outnumber them with respect to number of collections having scientific interest. On the average about twice as many collections of the latter type have been made by the boys as by the girls.

In interpreting the results of this section it is of particular importance to take into consideration the form of the question which our gifted subjects were asked. There is little doubt that if a check-list of collectible objects had been placed before the children many more collections would have been reported, for children vary greatly in their conceptions of what a collection is. Several children, for example, stated that they were collecting letters which they received, but it probably did not occur to a number of the children who were preserving their letters that these constituted a collection. Witty and Lehman have shown[1] that children report about twice as many collections when a check-list technique is used as when they are merely asked to write the names of the things they are collecting. It is reasonable to suppose, however, that the latter method is more efficacious in eliciting the collections in which children are taking an active interest.

TABLE 56

COLLECTIONS MADE BY GIFTED SUBJECTS DURING PAST FOUR OR FIVE YEARS

	Age 8–12		Age 13–14		Age 15–16		Age 17–20	
	B	G	B	G	B	G	B	G
Number of subjects......	24	23	59	54	106	72	76	64
Average number of collections	1.7	1.3	1.6	1.3	1.3	1.0	0.9	0.6
Average number of scientific collections	1.2	0.7	1.0	0.5	0.8	0.4	0.5	0.2

OFFICES AND HONORS

Information regarding offices and honors won by our subjects is of special interest in two respects: it gives a clue to the interests which motivate them, and it throws light upon their social adaptability and qualities of leadership.

The question on this point was worded as follows:

"Name all the offices or honors you have held during the last five years. (Examples: class officer, scout officer, club officer, actor in plays, scholarship prize or honor, member of band, orchestra, debating team, athletic team, school committee, school paper, etc.)" (Interest Blank: 11; Information Blank: 18.)

One or more offices or honors such as the above are recorded upon the blanks of 90 per cent of the boys and 96 per cent of the girls from whom blanks were received. The discrepancy between the two proportions may be significant, but may mean only that the girls are more careful in filling out their blanks, for a number of the blanks of boys who failed to record any "honors" contained other unanswered questions.

[1] *Journal of Educational Psychology*, Vol. 21, 1930, pp. 112–127.

The proportions of subjects noting offices or honors of various types are indicated in Table 57.

TABLE 57

PROPORTIONS OF GIFTED SUBJECTS HAVING OFFICES OR HONORS OF VARIOUS TYPES DURING PAST FIVE YEARS

	Gifted Boys %	Gifted Girls %
Athletic teams or honors	35	29
Club offices	35	39
School and class offices	30	34
Participated in dramatics	30	44
Worked on school and other publications	29	32
Offices in Sunday School, Christian Endeavor, scout troops, etc.	28	16
Scholarship honors	27	33
In orchestras, bands, glee clubs, etc.	18	20
Debating teams	14	14
Managerial positions at school or college	11	3

The figures of Table 57 indicate that the gifted subjects take part in a wide variety of extra-curricular activities and that they are as likely to gain recognition in any one of several kinds of non-academic activity as they are in scholarship. We have evidence that the proportions listed are minimum figures, inasmuch as an individual sometimes forgets to record on the Interest Blank an office or honor that he has had. In general, the girls seem to show a slightly greater tendency to participate in extra-curricular activities than the boys do, this tendency being most marked in dramatics. The boys, however, hold more student body managerial positions than the girls do. The disparity between the proportions of boys and girls holding offices in church organizations or scout troops is due to the relatively large number of boys who have held scout offices rather than to the number who have held office in church organizations.

The reader may be interested in knowing specifically about some of the most unusual honors won by members of the gifted group. A partial list of especially noteworthy honors follows:

Commencement speaker or valedictorian in high school: three boys and seven girls

Commencement speaker at the University of California (for class of over 2,000) : a girl

Highest scholarship average in high-school graduating class:
two boys and two girls

Elected to Ephebian Society[1]: four boys and five girls

Eagle Scout: five boys

First Knight Eagle Scout in America: one boy

Baby champion diver of Pacific Coast: a girl

Has won eight medals and three silver cups for swimming,
before age of ten: a boy

Gold medal won in piano contest: a girl

Boy mayor of San Francisco during boy's week: a boy

Wampas Baby Star: a girl

Won prize in contest of American Chemical Society: two
boys

Won second prize in Southern California Shakespeare contest: a boy

Won national oratorical contest for his division: a boy

Won prize in *Bookman* essay contest: a girl

One of eight California finalists for Edison's national
. scholarship competition: a boy

One of New Jersey finalists for Edison's national scholarship
competition: a boy

The honors just reported are confined to those won by
members of the Regular group. If we should add to these
the honors won by other members of the gifted group, many
of whom have had broader scope for their abilities because
of being older, the list would be materially increased. As a
matter of fact, it is almost impossible at present to read a
newspaper account of any sort of competition or activity in
which California boys and girls participate without finding
among the winners the names of one or more young people
who are members of our gifted group.

INFLUENCES RECOGNIZED BY SUBJECTS

In the hope that at least some of our gifted subjects might
recognize certain shaping currents in their lives and convey
to us the significance of such influences, we included two
questions on the follow-up Interest Blank and Information
Blank designed to elicit data in point. It is possible that

---

[1] An honor society in the Los Angeles City Schools. Membership is
based upon scholarship and leadership. About one in forty graduating
high-school seniors is elected.

many vital influences, even when recognized by the gifted
subjects, have not been recorded on the blanks, and that
many other significant influences have been wholly unrec-
ognized. Nevertheless it will be instructive to learn what the
subjects say regarding various influences.

"Have any disappointments, perplexities, failures, or bereavements ever exerted a prolonged influence upon you?.... If so,
briefly describe, stating your age at the time....." (Interest Blank:
15; Information Blank: 21.)

This question was answered in the affirmative by the following proportions of subjects from whom blanks were received:

	Boys %	Girls %
In grammar school................	20	20
In high school....................	9	18
In college	22	22
Not in school.....................	4	18

Influences mentioned by subjects who answered the question in the affirmative may be divided roughly as follows:

	Boys	Girls
Death of relatives.................	16	12
Unsettled mental state.............	1	9
Poor work at school...............	4	1
Social adjustment, trouble with friends, etc.	3	1
Love affairs (including one marriage and annulment)	0	4
Family trouble, separation of parents, etc.	2	3
Physical troubles, health, etc.......	1	3
Miscellaneous	7	7

It is seen that the girls have a stronger tendency than the
boys to be influenced by disappointments and griefs, or else
a greater tendency to admit such influences. The college
boys appear to be far more sensitive than the high-school
boys to such experiences.

The second question in this connection was as follows:

"Do you consider that any single person, book, philosophy, or
religion has had a profound influence on your life?.... If so, what
was it?.... Age at which such influence, if any, began....." (Interest Blank: 16; Information Blank: 22.)

This question was answered in the affirmative by the following proportions of subjects from whom blanks were received:

	Boys %	Girls %
In grammar school	30	40
In high school	24	42
In college	39	44
Not in school	36	47

The affirmative answers are far more numerous in the case of this question than in that of the question just discussed. There is little difference in the proportions of younger and older girls answering in the affirmative, but more of the older than of the younger boys answer it so. The answers have been categorized, and are listed below:

	Boys	Girls
One or both parents	25	36
Brother or sister	2	3
Family or relatives	2	1
Teacher	6	8
Friends	..	3
"A person"	17	11
Religion, the Bible, etc.	21	25
A book or several books	10	9
A philosophy	5	5
Miscellaneous	2	5

It is seen that a large number of subjects pay tribute to their parents. The data upon which the tabulation was based show a preponderant influence of mothers, for about four times as many boys and six times as many girls mention the influence of their mothers as mention the influence of their fathers. Religion, also, receives rather frequent mention. Quite a number mention "a person" without giving any further details as to the nature of the influence.

THE WYMAN INTEREST TEST

The follow-up investigation provided opportunity for ascertaining in the gifted group the degree of permanence of certain types of interest as measured upon an objective test. The Wyman Interest Test is a test of the free association type designed to measure three aspects of interest—intellectual interest, social interest, and activity interest. The test was administered during the follow-up to 91 gifted subjects who had previously taken it in 1923 when between the ages of nine and fourteen inclusive. As there were no important sex differences with respect to the 1923 Wyman scores, we have combined the two sexes in the present treatment in order to have a sufficient number of cases in computing means, correlations, etc.

The number of subjects for whom we have 1928 Wyman scores is as follows:

Present age 13   14   15   16   17   18
N 15   25   29   29   6   2

Ninety-one of these cases are used in the correlations of Table 59.

In Table 58 it is seen that the correlation of the 1928 scores with age is negligible and that in 1923 the only part of

TABLE 58

COMPARISON OF 1923 AND 1928 MEAN SCORES ON WYMAN INTEREST TEST

Age	Intellectual Interest		Social Interest		Activity Interest	
	1923	1928	1923	1928	1923	1928
8	116	...	116	...	122	...
9	125	...	121	...	124	...
10	127	...	122	...	123	...
11	130	...	122	...	123	...
12	132	...	124	...	123	...
13	131	132	122	123	123	124
14	133	130	123	121	122	123
15	131	131	123	123	122	124
16	...	131	...	123	...	122
17	...	133	...	127	...	127
18	...	128	...	122	...	125
All ages	...	131	...	123	...	123
S.D. of distribution.	...	7.7	...	5.9	...	3.7

the test to show appreciable change with age is intellectual interest. For the ages that overlap in 1923 and 1928, the mean scores are found to be practically identical except for small sampling errors.

In computing correlation coefficients between 1923 and 1928 test results, raw scores were used. It was first thought that because of the slight correlation of intellectual-interest score with age found in the 1923 data it might be well to use standard scores in the correlation for intellectual interest. This was tried, but failed to raise the correlation, so Table 59 is based entirely upon raw scores, ages combined. The reliability coefficients employed for computing the correlations corrected for attenuation are values reported by the author of the test for 140 seventh-grade boys and girls who took the test in two sessions separated by ten days. The correlations between the two parts of the test thus separately given were stepped up by means of the Spearman-Brown formula to obtain the reliabilities of the whole.

The correlations of Table 59 suggest a mild degree of permanence in the three types of interest, especially in social interest. We believe that these correlations represent minimum rather than maximum values for the relationships in question, since the test was standardized upon children of grammar-school age and may not be wholly suitable in its present form for individuals of high-school and college age.

TABLE 59

CORRELATIONS BETWEEN 1923 AND 1928 SCORES ON WYMAN
INTEREST TEST

	r	$P.E._r$	r (Corrected for Attenuation)	Reliability
Intellectual interest	.31	.06	.38	.81
Social interest	.37	.06	.50	.74
Activity interest	.15	.07	.25	.61

SUMMARY

1. Answers given by the gifted subjects when questioned as to which school studies are liked most and least show in the case of boys a relatively strong liking for the sciences and a marked distaste for ancient languages; for the girls, a relatively strong liking for art, English, and modern languages, and a distaste for mathematics and civics.

2. With respect to time spent in general reading the girls slightly exceed the boys. Their average number of hours weekly is 7.6, as contrasted with 7.2 for the boys.

3. Up to and including age fourteen, the gifted boys spend more time upon general reading than upon home study, but after age fourteen they spend more time on home study.

The hours of home study of the gifted girls overtake their hours of general reading at age thirteen.

4. The gifted boys are more interested in fiction, history, biography, travel, science, poetry, and drama, and less interested in adventure, detective stories, and nature or animal stories than they were at the time of the original study. The girls are more interested than formerly in poetry, drama, history, biography, and travel, and less interested in adventure, mystery tales, legends, and nature or animal stories.

5. The girls continue to show a greater interest than the boys in fiction, and more than twice as many girls as boys have developed an interest in poetry and drama. The boys continue to show a greater interest than the girls in adventure and detective stories. There is no marked sex difference in the number enjoying history, biography, and travel.

6. Both gifted boys and gifted girls tend to prefer reading to all other occupations; both sexes prefer "games that require lots of exercise" to "games that require little exercise." The attitude of the boys toward study tends to be one of indifference. Both sexes dislike "sewing, cooking, knitting, housework, etc." The boys neither like nor dislike "spending time alone," but the girls tend to like it fairly well. Both sexes enjoy spending time with either one other person or several other persons, and like fairly well to be leaders and to manage other persons.

7. More than half of the gifted boys and girls prefer to read when they have "an hour or two to spend just as they please." Athletic games and exercise come second on the lists of preference.

8. Gifted boys and girls show a decline in collecting interests after age fourteen. The boys rather outnumber the girls with respect to number of collections made, and very greatly outnumber the girls with respect to number of collections having scientific interest.

9. One or more offices or honors are recorded upon the Interest Blanks of 87 per cent of the boys and 96 per cent of the girls from whom blanks were received. The gifted subjects take part in a wide variety of extra-curricular activities, and are as likely to gain recognition in any one of several kinds of non-academic activity as they are in scholarship.

10. The girls more often than the boys participate in dramatics; the boys more often hold student-body managerial positions and offices in scout troops.

11. From 4 to 22 per cent of the boys and from 12 to 25 per cent of the girls of the various age classifications state that some disappointment, perplexity, failure, or bereavement has exerted a prolonged influence upon them. The type of influence mentioned most frequently is the death of a close relative.

12. From 24 to 38 per cent of the boys and from 42 to 47 per cent of the girls of the various ages state that their lives have been greatly influenced by a "single person, book, philosophy, or religion." The type of influence mentioned most frequently is that of one or both parents.

13. On the Wyman Test of intellectual, social, and activity interest the mean scores at the time of the follow-up were practically identical, except for small sampling errors, with those for gifted subjects of corresponding ages in 1923.

14. The 1923 and 1928 Wyman scores of 91 subjects correlate with each other to the extent of .31 for intellectual interest, .37 for social interest, and .15 for activity interest, thus showing only a mild degree of interest permanency.

CHAPTER VIII

VOCATIONAL PLANS AND VOCATIONAL ACHIEVEMENTS

Though up to the present only a small, selected portion of the Regular group have left school permanently and begun the serious business of earning a livelihood, more than half of the entire group, according to their own statements, have decided what vocation they wish to follow. It will be interesting and informing to draw comparisons between the vocational choices of 1927–28 and those of 1921–22.

In addition to the subjective testimony of the gifted subjects themselves, we are able to report as a result of the 1927–28 follow-up certain objective data regarding their vocational aptitudes. The scores of 169 boys of the Regular group on the Strong Vocational Interest Blank provide valuable data which are summarized in the present chapter. We have also summarized data collected by Dr. David L. Zyve for 53 members of the gifted group who were attending Stanford University at the time he constructed and standardized his Scientific Aptitude Test.

VOCATIONAL PLANS

"Have you decided yet what life vocation you wish to follow? .... If so, what occupation? .... Under what circumstances did you make this choice? .... (e.g., what influences determined the decision —such as school or college courses, advice of relatives, teachers, or friends, reading, close-hand observation, etc.?) ...." (Interest Blank: 14; Information Blank: 20.) [Question answered on 93 per cent of the blanks received.]

The Regular group has been divided into subgroups of subjects attending grammar school, those attending high school, those attending college, and those who are not in school. For these subgroups, and for the gifted group as a whole, the proportions who have decided upon a life vocation are reported in Table 60, together with data upon the vocation chosen. When the question was not answered we assumed that a vocation had not been chosen.

134

In the case of individuals who have decided upon a vocation, Barr[1] ratings have been assigned to the chosen occupations when these are described in terms specific enough to warrant a rating. The means and S.D.'s of the ratings are reported in the last two columns of Table 60. Included for

TABLE 60

VOCATIONAL PLANS OF REGULAR GROUP

	Have Decided on Vocation %	Vocations Falling in "Professional" Class %	BARR RATINGS	
			Mean	S.D.
Gifted subjects in grammar school, 1927–28:				
Boys (20)	30	83	16.5	...
Girls (20)	65	71	14.6	2.2
Gifted subjects in high school, 1927–28:				
Boys (185)	54	83	15.6	1.0
Girls (140)	51	86	14.9	1.4
Gifted subjects in college, 1927–28:				
Boys (56)	58	91	15.8	0.9
Girls (56)	66	89	15.1	1.5
Gifted subjects not in school, 1927–28:				
Boys (25)	56	50	15.0	1.6
Girls (17)	59	50	14.5	1.6
All gifted subjects, 1927–28:				
Boys (286)	53	82	15.6	1.1
Girls (233)	56	83	14.9	1.5
All gifted subjects, 1921–22:				
Boys	..	48	15.4	2.4
Girls	..	38	13.9	1.8
Control group, 1921–22:				
Boys	..	25	12.7	...
Girls	..	38	12.6	...
Fathers of gifted subjects, 1921–22	..	29	12.8	2.8
Adult males of general population	..	3	7.9	3.4

comparison are the means and S.D.'s of Barr ratings made in 1921–22 on the "probable vocational choices" of the gifted and control groups, upon the occupations of the fathers of

[1] See Volume I, pp. 66 ff., for description of the Barr Scale of occupational intelligence.

gifted subjects, and upon those of adult males in general. At the time of making Barr ratings note was also made of whether or not the occupations fell into a "professional" classification. The proportions falling into such a classification are reported in the second column of Table 60 together with comparative data.

The figures of Table 60 show a very marked increase since 1921–22 in the proportion of subjects who plan to enter professional fields. This increase is greatest in the case of the girls, the proportion having more than doubled. About four-fifths of both boys and girls now plan to enter a professional field. In all subgroups the proportions greatly exceed the proportion of fathers of gifted subjects engaged in professional fields and very greatly surpass the corresponding proportion of adult males of the general population. It is important to note, however, that the proportion making a "professional" choice in the 1921–22 control group is considerably larger than the proportion of professional men in the population at large. The Barr ratings of the vocational choices of the control group also average far above the mean for the general population. These facts carry the strong implication that a considerable number of the control subjects have aimed much higher than they will ever reach. It is possible that some of the gifted subjects have done so, too.

We may get some light on this question by consulting the data on the vocational choices and activities of the older and consequently more "settled" members of the High School group. (See chapter xiii, pages 230 ff.) An analysis was made of certain facts concerning (1) members of the High School group who have graduated from college and (2) members of the High School group who have reached or passed the age of twenty and have gone to work without graduating from college. In the first group 88 per cent of the boys and 93 per cent of the girls who have decided upon a vocation expect to follow definite professional occupations; in the second group 35 per cent of the boys and 38 per cent of the girls expect to do so; in the two groups combined 69 per cent of the boys and 73 per cent of the girls have similar expectations. The latter two proportions are not quite so high as the proportions in the Regular group who signify their intentions of entering professional work. In both the Regular group and the High School group the proportions probably exaggerate somewhat the tendency that is characteristic of the gifted group as a whole. Our figures concern only the subjects who have decided upon a vocation; it is quite possible that the subjects who are yet undecided as to choice will not turn in such large numbers to professional occupations.

Considering next the Barr Scale ratings upon prospective occupations, we find little to choose between the mean rating of 1921–22 and that of 1927–28 in the case of the gifted boys, but the mean for the gifted girls has risen during the six-year period by over half a standard deviation of gifted girls' 1921–22 ratings. The standard deviations for both gifted boys and gifted girls have decreased, especially in the case of the boys.

It is of interest that among the entire group of gifted subjects entering Table 60 there are only six whose vocational ambitions can be ranked below the two highest grades of the Taussig five-grade classification. These are: one boy who plans to be a forest ranger and one who plans to be a printer; three girls who plan to go into nursing and one girl who plans to go into millinery and dressmaking. If these young people should eventually work up to administrative positions in their respective fields, which in view of their superior ability would rather be expected, their status would of course rise to the second Taussig grade.

Paid Employment of Gifted Subjects

The Interest Blank and Information Blank contain the item: "Name all the paid jobs you have had during the last five years." Space is provided for the subject to note what jobs he has had, how long he held them, what hours he worked, compensation received, and his age at the time. We have not attempted to summarize all this material, for much of it is not adapted to statistical treatment. However, in Table 61 (p. 138) we have indicated what proportions of the subjects at various stages of educational progress have had paid employment outside their homes. We have also reported the average weekly compensation earned in the most recent full-time jobs of these subjects. Part-time jobs have not been included in computations of average weekly compensation. Two values are given for the average weekly

compensation received by the boys and girls not now attending school. The second value in each case is that obtained
by averaging all but one of the available cases, those left out
being a boy and a girl who are each earning several hundred
dollars a week on the stage or in the movies. The figures in
parentheses refer to the number of cases for whom data are
available. Incidentally we may say that the numbers indicated in the last column do not include all the subjects who
have held full-time jobs, since in recording data from the
blanks we made note only of the most recent job of each
individual. Some of our subjects who were attending school
and working part-time when they filled out their blanks had
previously held full-time jobs.

TABLE 61

PAID EMPLOYMENT OF GIFTED SUBJECTS OF REGULAR GROUP

	Have Had Employment Outside the Home %	Average Weekly Compensation (for Full-Time Jobs)
Subjects in grammar school:		
Boys (20)	30	....
Girls (20)	10	....
Subjects in high school:		
Boys (185)	81	$16 (43)
Girls (140)	31	$13 (7)
Subjects in college:		
Boys (56)	95	$21 (23)
Girls (56)	59	$16 (18)
Subjects not in school:		
Boys (25)	96	$43 (18)
		$22 (17)
Girls (17)	88	$47 (11)
		$21 (10)

It is also possible that the proportions for whom paid
employment is reported are a little lower than they should
be, for some of the subjects who did not answer the question
may at some time have had small jobs which they did not
consider worth recording. However, the figures as they
stand show that a large proportion have had paid employment, although, as the reader may recall, only a handful of
each sex are over eighteen. More than nine-tenths of the
boys attending college have helped support themselves, and
well over half of the college girls have done so. Most of the

subjects who have left school permanently or temporarily are self-supporting. If we consider only the 35 boys and 34 girls who have reached or passed the age of eighteen, 97 per cent of the boys and 74 per cent of the girls have had paid employment.

THE STRONG OCCUPATIONAL INTEREST TEST

This is a test[1] consisting of 420 items arranged so that an individual may indicate whether he likes, dislikes, or is indifferent to various (1) occupations, (2) amusements, (3) school subjects, (4) activities more or less related to occupations, and (5) peculiarities of people. Data collected by Dr. Strong during the past few years by means of the test show that men engaged in a particular occupation have a characteristic set of likes and dislikes which distinguish them more or less from men in other occupations. The test has been standardized for twenty-five occupational fields upon the basis of the responses of men known to be successful in these fields. A rating of "A" in a given occupation means that an individual has interests decidedly like those of men in that occupation; it separates the lower quartile of the scores of men in the criterion group from the remaining scores. A rating of "B" is a doubtful rating, and indicates a score within the lower quartile of the criterion group. A rating of "C" means that 98 to 100 per cent of the criterion group scored higher in the occupation in question than the person obtaining the rating. Dr. Strong has found during the course of his investigations that few men rate "A" in any occupation except their own, and that few men rating "C" in an occupation are successful in it or remain in it any length of time.

In the spring of 1928 we mailed the Strong Blank to 247 boys in the Regular group who were past the age of fourteen. Blanks were filled out and returned to us (in time for us to score and use them in the statistical summary) by 169 of the boys, or 68 per cent of those to whom it was sent. The directions which were mailed with the blanks included a list of twenty-five occupations for which scoring keys were available at Stanford. These were:

[1] *The Strong Occupational Interest Test,* together with directions and scoring keys, is published by the Stanford University Press.

Advertiser	Farmer
Architect	Journalist
Artist	Lawyer
Author	Life insurance salesman
Banker	Minister
Certified public accountant	Physician
Chemist	Psychologist
District sales manager	Purchasing agent
Engineer	Real estate salesman
Civil engineer	Specialty salesman
Electrical engineer	Teacher
Mechanical engineer	Y.M.C.A. secretary
Mining engineer	

The subject was asked to mark "1" the occupation on the list in which he was most interested, and "2" the occupation in which he was next interested. Finally he was asked to indicate in a space at the foot of the page the occupation which he was most likely to follow whether it was included on our list or not.

All blanks were scored for the first and second preferences indicated on the list, and reports were mailed to the subjects containing information as to their letter ratings and suggestions as to interpretation. The means and standard deviations of their scores upon the two choices have been computed separately by occupation. We have considered them in the light of the norms established by members of the criterion occupational groups, and by a group of 287 unselected Stanford seniors,[1] all of whom were scored on nearly all the occupations regardless of what occupations they planned to enter. Means and standard deviations were also computed for the scores on the first choice, using only the 112 cases for whom first choice on our list coincided with the occupation "most likely" to be followed.

From Table 62 it is obvious that the gifted subjects, upon the occupations indicated as "first choice," tend to score higher than upon those indicated as "second choice" and very much higher than the unselected seniors upon the same occupations. There is little difference, however, between the mean ratings upon "first choice" and those upon the occupa-

[1] Data concerning the criterion groups and the unselected seniors were kindly put at our disposal by Dr. Strong.

TABLE 62

RATINGS OF GIFTED BOYS ON THE STRONG VOCATIONAL INTEREST BLANK

Occupation	First Choice			Second Choice			"Most Likely"				287 Stanford Seniors			
	M	S.D.	N	M	S.D.	N	M	S.D.	"A" %	N	M	S.D.	"A" %	"A" Boundary
Advertiser	58	164	11	21	189	10	54	176	12	8	−67	207	2	367
Architect	370	...	1	154	105	8	370	...	0	1	...	...	...	320
Artist	83	260	10	382	...	2	24	253	...	5	−247	301	1	560
Author	97	329	11	151	290	9	206	62	20	3	...	...	...	373
Banker	28	57	9	15	43	12	16	...	...	5	...	...	...	89
C.P.A.	15	...	1	13	105	5	15	...	...	1	−70	83	0	186
Chemist	218	119	15	151	128	19	219	130	73	11	−4	191	14	209
District sales manager	−43	...	3	−65	...	2	−147	...	...	1	...	...	...	543
Engineer	169	157	7	−112	...	1	218	110	50	6	−17	197	15	202
Civil engineer	171	96	11	92	84	6	150	96	0	9	...	...	...	320
Electrical engineer	262	83	8	96	142	8	262	83	25	8	...	...	...	320
Mechanical engineer	140	152	11	255	143	6	179	...	...	3	...	...	...	279
Mining engineer	103	...	1	141	...	3	103	...	...	1	...	...	...	227
Farmer	110	...	3	124	...	4	106	...	...	2	−10	187	8	234
Journalist	26	171	14	5	137	20	100	161	25	8	−105	171	9	153
Lawyer	84	97	23	68	81	16	87	95	11	19	−20	138	8	200
Life insurance salesman	−72	...	1	...	...	1	−72	...	...	1	−82	170	5	223
Minister	242	...	3	134	...	1	242	...	...	3	−221	208	0.4	376
Physician	106	120	12	53	63	8	116	121	27	11	−77	149	5	171
Psychologist	10	...	3	−50	37	5	10	...	...	3	−91	196	2	300
Purchasing agent	149	...	1	79	...	1	149	...	...	1	...	...	...	155
Teacher	8	99	7	44	124	16	−74	...	...	2	−68	114	4	180
Y.M.C.A. secretary	...	...	...	−32	...	1	...	...	...	...	...	...	...	319

tions which the subjects are "most likely" to choose. The
variability of the subjects' scores upon any given occupational choice is large, but tends to be about 15 to 20 per cent
less than the corresponding variability for Stanford seniors
unselected as to vocational choice.

If we consider the scores upon the "most likely" occupations, there are three occupations in which the mean scores
of the gifted boys exceed the "A" boundary (i.e., the 25 percentile of the criterion groups upon which the test was
standardized). These occupations are architect, chemist,
and engineer. As the high score in architecture is based
upon only one gifted boy we cannot take it very seriously,
especially as the mean score of the eight boys who indicate
architecture as a second choice is about a standard deviation below the "A" boundary.

In the scores of the 287 Stanford seniors upon the two
occupations, chemist and engineer, there are smaller gaps
between the means and the "A" boundaries than is the case
for any other occupation—namely, 1.1 of the standard deviation of the seniors. This fact suggests the possibility that
the relatively high scores of the gifted boys who wish to
become chemists or engineers are not due so much to unusual shrewdness on the part of these boys in diagnosing
their own vocational aptitudes as to the large common human denominator in the "characteristic set of likes and dislikes" of chemists and engineers that tends to stack the cards
in favor of any boy of college calibre choosing these occupations. The fact that 50 per cent of the gifted boys who wish
to become engineers and 73 per cent of those who wish to
become chemists score "A" in the field of their choice is
partly accounted for by a tendency among boys at large to
have the interests of those occupations. In the entire group
of Stanford seniors 14 per cent have an "A" rating in chemistry and 15 have an "A" rating in engineering.[1]

Considering the other occupations for which the scores
of the college seniors are available, we have a marked
parallelism between the rank orders of (1) mean level of
the gifted boys upon "most likely" occupations and (2)

[1] The latter figures are probably somewhat higher than they would be
for boys from many other colleges, owing to the fact that Stanford gives
strong emphasis to its science and engineering courses, thus attracting students who are interested in these fields.

mean level of unselected senior boys on the same occupations. We refer here not to the mean raw scores, but to these
scores interpreted as deviations from the "A" boundary in
terms of S.D.'s of the college seniors' scores. There are only
four occupations in which the rank orders differ by more
than one place, and in each of these (farmer, minister, psychologist, and teacher) the determination of rank in the
gifted group is based upon the scores of only two or three
boys. These results are in close harmony with the observations concerning the ratings upon chemist and engineer.
They support the hypothesis that the fluctuation in the proportion of gifted boys attaining "A" ratings on their chosen
vocation is due to variation among the vocations themselves
with respect to commonness or rarity of the associated complexes of interests.

The range of variation of the mean scores of the gifted
boys, reckoned from the "A" boundaries in terms of S.D.'s of
the seniors, is from about +.1 (engineer) to —1.8 (artist).
The tendency is for the mean scores on the "most likely"
occupations of the gifted subjects to exceed by roughly .5
to 1.0 S.D. the norms established by the Stanford seniors
unselected as to vocational choice. While there are some
gifted subjects who do not appear to have the interests of
men successful in their chosen occupations, the test scores
of the gifted subjects show a far better relationship between
vocational choice and fitness than chance alone would give.
By chance alone we might expect only 5 or 6 per cent of
"A" ratings, 25 per cent of "B" ratings, and 70 per cent of
"C" ratings.[1] The gifted boys on their "most likely" vocations received 23 per cent of "A" ratings, 50 per cent of "B"
ratings, and only 27 per cent of "C" ratings. The latter
ratings may in turn be compared with the ratings received
by the Stanford seniors upon occupations which they intend
to follow permanently, according to questionnaire sheets
mailed by them to Professor Strong six months after graduation. On the occupations for which scoring scales were available the ratings were 32 per cent "A", 50 per cent "B", and
18 per cent "C". When we consider that the gifted boys were
practically all between the ages of fifteen and nineteen, and

[1] Letter ratings were found in these proportions for the scores of the
unselected Stanford seniors upon thirteen occupations.

that many of them will almost surely change their occupational choice before reaching the educational status of the college seniors, their showing on the Strong vocational test compares favorably with that of the seniors.

To find out whether there might be an unusual tendency among gifted boys to score especially high or low in certain representative occupations, we took the test blanks of five random groups of forty subjects each, and scored them upon artist, C.P.A., farmer, life insurance salesman, and teacher. The results are reported in Table 63. The ratings of the gifted do not differ significantly from the ratings of the Stanford seniors. It is possible, of course, that if the gifted boys could be compared with a sample of the general population instead of with a sample of college youths the differences would be more striking.

TABLE 63

RATINGS OF RANDOM GIFTED BOYS ON FIVE REPRESENTATIVE OCCUPATIONS

	Mean	S.D.	N	"A" Ratings %	"A" Ratings of Stanford Seniors %
Artist	−222	262	40	2.5	1.1
C.P.A.	−69	87	40	0.0	0.0
Farmer	6	171	40	12.5	8.3
Life insurance	−146	124	40	0.0	4.5
Teacher	−40	132	40	5.0	3.8

THE STANFORD SCIENTIFIC APTITUDE TEST

In 1926 Dr. David L. Zyve completed at Stanford University a study[1] of scientific aptitude. The measuring instrument which Dr. Zyve devised in connection with this study is a test which requires between one and a quarter and two and a half hours to administer. The reliability, based upon the correlation between two forms administered to forty undergraduates, is .93.

There is good reason to believe that the test measures aptitude rather than attainment. That such is the case is

[1] "An Experimental Study of Scientific Aptitude," unpublished Ph.D. dissertation, August, 1926. 167 pages and bibliography. Stanford Library. (The test blanks and *Manual of Directions* are published by the Stanford University Press.) A brief account of the test including samples of the material used and results with certain student and faculty groups has been published by Dr. Zyve in the *Journal of Educational Psychology*, Vol. 18, 1927, pp. 525–546.

suggested by inspection of the type of material that composes the test and by the fact that it is not unknown for freshmen and others with meager scientific training to score as high as graduate research students or university professors in scientific departments. It also seems clear that the trait measured by the test is not merely intelligence under another guise, for (1) the test has a rather low correlation with the Thorndike Intelligence Examination for High-School Graduates (between .29 and .51 for various groups); (2) it has a low correlation with scholarship averages of students majoring in non-scientific departments (.02 ± .09 for 47 such students), and a higher correlation with the scholarship averages of students majoring in scientific departments (.51 for 48 members of a criterion research student group); (3) it yields a higher mean for faculty members in scientific departments than for those in non-scientific departments, the difference being equal to nearly a standard deviation of the distribution of unselected freshman students; (4) the correlations between scores on the test and ratings by professors upon the research ability of graduate students engaged in research are remarkably high. The rank order correlation between scores and ratings for twenty graduate students in chemistry, each rated by two professors, is .85 ± .04; for eight graduate students in physics, each rated by two professors, .93 ± .04; for nineteen graduate students in electrical engineering, .96 ± .01 when rated by one professor, and .89 ± .03 when rated by a second professor. If all the cases entering into these rank order correlations are grouped together and a product-moment coefficient computed, the correlation is .74 ± .04, or .82 ± .07 when corrected for attenuation.

That the members of the gifted group are somewhat superior to the average college student in the trait or traits measured by the Scientific Aptitude Test is shown by comparing the mean scores reported in Table 64 (p. 146) for certain groups who took the test. The 53 gifted subjects whose mean score is given in Table 64 are not for the most part members of the Regular group, as the tests were administered before many of the Regular group had reached college status. Nevertheless their scores are probably quite representative of the scientific aptitude of undergraduates of the gifted group as a whole.

TABLE 64

MEANS AND STANDARD DEVIATIONS OF REPRESENTATIVE GROUPS ON THE STANFORD SCIENTIFIC APTITUDE TEST

	Mean	S.D.	N
Gifted subjects	114	23.5	53
Criterion group of graduate students in scientific departments	142	28.2	50
Students in non-scientific departments	90	29.3	47
Unselected freshmen	105	28.3	244
Faculty:			
In scientific departments	153	....	21
In non-scientific departments	128	....	14

The mean of the gifted group is seen to be about a third of a standard deviation higher than that of unselected freshmen, nearly a standard deviation higher than that of students (chiefly of graduate status) majoring in non-scientific departments, but a standard deviation lower than that of graduate students of the criterion group. The gifted rank half a standard deviation below faculty members of non-scientific departments, and nearly one and a half standard deviations below faculty members of scientific departments.

The group of 53 gifted subjects contains only twelve girls, but the scores of these girls furnish an interesting contrast to those of the boys. The mean score of the girls is 95, while that of the boys is 125. The difference between the means is thus 30 points, or more than a standard deviation of the freshman distribution. The standard error of the difference is 4 points. The mean for the gifted boys is thus seen to be more than two-thirds of a standard deviation above that of unselected Stanford freshmen (about 80 per cent of whom are boys), almost as high as the mean for professors in non-scientific departments, and about two-thirds of a standard deviation below that of the criterion group of graduate students in scientific departments.

SUMMARY

1. In the Regular group somewhat more than 50 per cent of both gifted boys and gifted girls state that they have decided upon a vocation. Over four-fifths of the subjects who have decided upon a vocation plan to enter a professional field.

2. The mean of the Barr Scale rating of the prospective

occupations of the gifted boys has changed little since 1921–22, but the mean for the gifted girls has risen during the six-year period by over half a standard deviation of gifted girls' 1921–22 ratings.

3. The number of gifted boys who have had paid employment outside the home varies from 30 per cent of those attending grammar school to 96 per cent of those not in school. The number of gifted girls having had such employment varies from 10 per cent of those attending grammar school to 88 per cent of those not in school. In the group attending college 95 per cent of the boys and 59 per cent of the girls have had employment.

4. On the Strong Vocational Interest Blank gifted boys tend to score higher upon the occupations indicated as "first choice" than upon those indicated as "second choice," and very much higher than Stanford seniors, unselected as to vocational choice, upon the same occupations.

5. Scores of the gifted boys in the Strong Test on vocations which they are "most likely" to enter give 23 per cent of "A" ratings, 50 per cent of "B" ratings, and 27 per cent of "C" ratings. By chance alone we might expect only 5 or 6 per cent of "A" ratings, 25 per cent of "B" ratings, and 70 per cent of "C" ratings.

6. On five occupations upon which random gifted subjects were scored, the scores do not differ appreciably from the scores of unselected Stanford seniors for the same occupations.

7. On the Stanford Scientific Aptitude Test, the mean score of 53 gifted subjects attending Stanford exceeded that of unselected Stanford freshmen by about a third of a standard deviation of the freshmen, and that of students (chiefly of graduate status) majoring in non-scientific departments by nearly a standard deviation. The gifted averaged a standard deviation lower than research students of Zyve's criterion group.

8. The mean score of 41 gifted boys who took the Scientific Aptitude Test was more than a standard deviation above the mean score of twelve gifted girls who took it, two-thirds of a standard deviation above that of unselected Stanford freshmen, and the same amount below a group of graduate students (mostly men) majoring in scientific departments.

CHAPTER IX

SOCIAL AND PERSONALITY TRAITS

For some readers the material presented in this chapter will have more interest than the follow-up measurements of intelligence. Of what use, it may be argued, is a high IQ, unless the individual possessing it also possesses social adaptability and moral stamina?

At the time of the original survey the members of the gifted group were found, on the whole, to have personality traits superior to those of the controls with whom they were compared. The gifted subjects made a noteworthy showing upon the Raubenheimer-Cady battery of character tests, approximately 85 per cent of the gifted surpassing the average of unselected children. A modification of Woodworth's test of psychotic tendencies indicated that approximately 75 per cent of the gifted are more stable than the average child.

The common opinion that intellectually superior children are as a rule characterized by a deficiency of play interests was shown to be unfounded. The mean play-information quotient of the gifted group was 136. The typical gifted child of nine years was found to have a larger body of definite knowledge about plays and games than the average child of twelve years. Another important finding in this connection was that the play interests of the typical gifted boy were above rather than below the norm in degree of "masculinity."

Other lines of evidence, some of them of less precision, but nevertheless having significance in comparisons of large groups of children, were convergent in showing that the typical gifted child has an advantage over his fellows not only in matters of the intellect but in social and moral traits as well. The purposes of this chapter are (1) to show to what extent this early superiority has been maintained, and (2) to contribute additional personality data made possible by certain new tests developed and standardized since the time of the original study. The following tests of personality

or character were administered during the 1927–28 follow-up
to gifted subjects of appropriate age:

Woodworth-Cady Questionnaire
Watson Test of Fair-Mindedness
Masculinity-Femininity Test
George Washington University Social Intelli-
    gence Test

WOODWORTH-CADY QUESTIONNAIRE

In the Raubenheimer-Cady battery of character tests administered in 1923 to the gifted group, the Woodworth-Cady
Questionnaire is the only test suitable for children of the
ages that a majority of our group have now reached. The
Woodworth-Cady Questionnaire is described and reproduced in Volume I, pages 500–505. For the benefit of the
reader who is not familiar with the test it may be said that it
is an adaptation of a test devised by Woodworth in 1918 for
use in identifying soldiers having abnormal or unstable
emotional tendencies. The reliability of the Cady modification for 150 boys of twelve to fourteen years, one form
against another form, is .75.

TABLE 65

WOODWORTH-CADY SCORES OF GIFTED GROUP, 1927–28

Age	Boys			Girls		
	Mean	S.D.	N	Mean	S.D.	N
11	10.5	7.6	8	12.5	1.4	5
12	6.5	5.1	5	13.7	6.8	6
13	14.3	6.7	14	10.7	6.1	9
14	11.9	6.2	23	12.0	5.8	19
15	10.2	5.7	35	15.2	6.9	19
16	11.0	5.6	33	11.3	5.6	20
17	14.1	5.9	20	10.9	6.0	16
18	10.2	9.4	7	11.1	5.1	9

Table 65 presents the means and standard deviations of
the scores of Woodworth-Cady tests during the follow-up.
There appears to be no consistent trend with age, and the
apparent irregularities in mean scores are no more than the
small numbers at any single age level would lead one to expect. (The reader is reminded that by the method of scoring this test the lower of two scores is the better.)   There

are too few cases at any one age to make profitable an age-by-age comparison of the present means with the original means; instead we have combined the cases from ages eleven to fourteen inclusive and have based our comparisons upon these. By this treatment the 1927–28 mean score of the boys turns out to be equal to that of 1923 to a tenth of a point; the 1927–28 mean score of the girls exceeds that of 1923 by only .7 of a point.

The findings demonstrate (1) that the trait measured by the Woodworth-Cady is present to about the same degree in gifted subjects of all ages within the range considered; and (2) that in the gifted group as a whole the trait has remained remarkably stable over a period of five years.[1] At the time of the original survey, the gifted boys and girls were superior to the control by roughly half a standard deviation of the control distributions.

We may now inquire as to the consistency of the individual subjects in their original and follow-up scores. During the follow-up 150 members of the Regular group took the Woodworth-Cady test who had formerly taken it at age ten or over, age ten being the earliest age for which we have control norms. The correlation between their 1923 standard scores and their 1928 standard scores[2] is .42 ± .05. If we correct this coefficient for attenuation, using the reliability .75 based upon unselected cases, we obtain .56. But even the latter coefficient probably underestimates the constancy of the trait in question for the reason that the norms are not based upon enough cases to make the determination of means and standard deviations very accurate at any one age. Errors in the determination of norms would have the effect of reducing the reliability of the standard scores, and hence would spuriously lower the correlation coefficient, possibly by as much as .10. Although the true value of the coefficient must be left indeterminate, it is obvious that it is

[1] The Woodworth-Cady and other personality tests were originally given in 1923, a year later than the intelligence tests and achievement tests. The time interval between original and follow-up tests is thus a year less than was the case for tests previously reported.

[2] Standard scores for the 1928 tests were reckoned from the means and standard deviations of scores of a random sixteen-year-old group of 56 boys and 78 girls recently tested at San Jose High School. It seemed legitimate to do this inasmuch as all subjects whose 1928 scores entered the correlation were aged fifteen or over.

high enough to demonstrate some degree of predictability for a period of five years, though the consistency is much less than is found for intelligence.

WATSON TEST OF FAIR-MINDEDNESS

One of the follow-up tests not available at the time of the original study is the Watson Test of Fair-Mindedness. This was administered in 1928 to the members of the gifted group who at the time were high-school seniors or college freshmen or had left school temporarily or permanently. The results from this test are thus well representative of the members of the group who are over fifteen or sixteen years old.

The Watson test[1] is designed to measure in the field of religious and economic issues "the tendency of any individual to manifest prejudice by (a) crossing out controversial words as disagreeable or annoying; (b) accusing sincere and competent persons who differ in opinion of being insincere and incompetent; (c) drawing from given facts conclusions which are in accord with the bias of the individual but which are not justified by the facts; (d) approving or condoning in one group acts which are condemned in some other group; (e) rating all of the arguments on one side of a disputed question as strong and all those on the other as weak, regardless of the real strength of the arguments; and (f) attributing to all of the members of a group characteristics which are true of only a portion of the group."

The reliability coefficient, secured by correlating scores on odd versus even items for a group of ordinary variability and applying the Spearman-Brown correction formula, is .96. The claim of the test to validity lies, according to the author, in (1) the content of the test itself, (2) correlations of .45 to .86 of the subtests with the battery as a whole, and (3) pronounced differences in the scores of people selected by their associates as very fair-minded or as very prejudiced.

---

[1] Watson, Goodwin B., *The Measurement of Fair-Mindedness*, Teachers College, Columbia University, Contributions to Education, No. 176, 1925, 97 pages.

We are greatly indebted to Dr. Watson for the valuable assistance which he gave us in this section of our study.

The scores of the 97 gifted boys and 71 gifted girls who took the test are tabulated in Table 66. Comparisons are offered in Table 67 of the means and standard deviations found in our gifted group and those found in a number of groups reported by Watson. Of two scores the lower is the better.

TABLE 66
SCORES OF GIFTED GROUP ON WATSON TEST OF FAIR-MINDEDNESS, 1927–28

Score	Gifted Boys	Gifted Girls
0– 5	..	1
6–10	1	2
11–15	13	7
16–20	19	15
21–25	25	18
26–30	22	15
31–35	13	9
36–40	3	3
41–45	..	1
46–50	1	..
Total number	97	71

(Lower scores are "better")

It is difficult to decide which of the many groups of Table 67 our gifted subjects might be compared with most appropriately, for all the groups are selected in one way or another. The persons that possibly come nearest to being a control group are the middle-western high-school seniors, whose mean score is 34. Unfortunately, no standard deviation is reported for this group, but as the standard deviations of other groups reported by Watson vary between 8 and 10, we see that the mean performance of the gifted group is at least one standard deviation superior to that of the high-school seniors. The mean of the gifted group is only a little superior to the means of such groups as senior students in a teachers college or journalism students in a western university, and it is inferior to the means of such special groups as students in social psychology, summer students at University of Chicago, or faculty members in journalism in a western university. Other interesting comparisons made possible by Table 67 are left to the reader.

The conclusions that seem justified are: (1) that there is no sex difference with respect to the trait measured by the Watson Test among members of the gifted group; and (2) that the gifted subjects do not differ so very greatly in this trait from other well-educated groups of presumably somewhat

TABLE 67

Scores of Gifted Group Compared with Scores of Other Groups on Watson Test of Fair-Mindedness

	Mean	S.D.	N
Gifted boys	24	7.2	97
Gifted girls	24	7.6	71
Summer-quarter students, University of Chicago.	20	8.1	30
Students in Social Psychology, Eastern university	19	10.0	35
Students in an Eastern theological seminary	17	9.7	29
Senior students in Eastern state teachers' college	26	8.2	126
Newspapermen, small Western towns	27	10.5	30
Newspapermen, large Western cities	29	10.3	23
Seniors in Middle-Western high school	34	....	22
Journalism students in Western university	25	....	21
Faculty in Journalism in Western university	17	....	5
Y.M.C.A. secretaries in large Eastern cities	29	....	109
Student secretaries in Eastern Y.M.C.A. groups	19	....	...
Physical directors in Eastern Y.M.C.A. groups	34	....	...
Men's Bible class in Eastern city	41	....	6
Methodist ministers in Middle-Western state	32	....	35
Persons selected by their friends as most fair-minded	5	....	13
Persons selected by their friends as most prejudiced	55	....	5

(Lower scores are "better")

lower mean intelligence level. If we divide the gifted subjects who took the test into subgroups of (a) high-school seniors, (b) college freshmen, and (c) subjects not attending school, the differences between the mean scores of the high-school and college students are not significant, but the mean of the subjects not in school is inferior to those of subgroups (a) and (b). The mean scores of the three subgroups are 23, 22, and 26, respectively.

MASCULINITY-FEMININITY TEST

The results of this test provide an extremely interesting sequel to some conclusions reported in Volume I based upon the Plays and Games Questionnaire developed at Stanford for use with the gifted group. The gifted group and a control group were asked at the time of the original survey to rate their preferences for ninety plays, games, and amusements, and also to indicate how frequently they engaged in each. Certain of the activities were found to be preferred more often by boys, and others more often by girls. These sex differences with respect to preference were made the basis of masculinity indices which were computed for each child who filled out the questionnaire. A child received a high masculinity index if the activities which he rated high were those preferred frequently by control boys and infrequently by control girls, a low masculinity index if his preferences were similar to those of control girls and dissimilar to those of control boys. (See Volume I, pp. 407 ff.)

The most noteworthy result in this connection was that masculinity of play interests proved to have no appreciable correlation, either positive or negative, with intellectual superiority. Both in central tendency and dispersion the gifted boys differed little from the control boys, and the gifted girls differed hardly at all from the control girls. These facts do not agree with the widespread notion that the typical gifted boy is effeminate in his play interests.

Partly as a result of the interesting avenues of research suggested by the experiment just summarized, a much more thorough-going investigation of sex differences in non-intellectual traits was undertaken at Stanford under a grant from the National Research Council in 1925, and is still in progress. The first task toward which this investigation was directed was the development of a more precise instrument for measuring masculinity and femininity of interests, attitudes, and thought trends. Two forms of the resulting Masculinity-Femininity Test have been constructed and standardized.[1] The test, which has a reliability of .90 or better within the range of a single sex, includes the exercises enumerated below:

1. Free Association. A list of stimulus words each followed by four response words, one of which is to be underlined by the subject as the word that "goes best with" the stimulus word.

---

[1] The test is to be published by the Stanford University Press.

2. Ink Blots. A page of ink blots each followed by the names of three or more objects, one of which must be associated with the ink blot by underlining.

3. Information. A general information test of the multiple-choice type.

4. Emotional Response. Subject indicates his emotional response to situations tending to arouse anger, fear, disgust, pity, or moral disapproval.

5. Likes and Dislikes. Subject indicates whether he likes, dislikes, or is indifferent to certain types of books, objects, and activities.

6. Characters and Prejudices. Subject indicates whether he likes, dislikes, or is indifferent to certain historical characters; and indicates whether he believes certain widespread popular notions are true or false.

7. Personal Information. A page of questions of the general type found in the Woodworth-Cady Questionnaire.

The hundreds of individual test items composing the battery had been selected from a much larger number as showing consistent sex differences in several experimental groups of different ages.

Form A of the Masculinity-Femininity Test has been administered to 75 boys and 72 girls of the Regular gifted group. These subjects range in age from thirteen to nineteen, and in grade placement from high-school freshman to college senior. A number of subjects who left school before or after graduating from high school are included, since an effort was made to reach with the Masculinity-Femininity Test all the gifted subjects in a certain locality except those still attending grammar school. The modal age of those tested is sixteen and the modal grade placement is the senior year of high school.

As scores on the test have been shown to be affected but little by age and education, at least within the range which we are considering, we have not tabulated scores separately by age or grade, but have based comparisons upon scores of the total number of each sex. The control group is the original group upon which the norms of the Masculinity-Femininity Test were based, and consists of junior boys and girls tested in the San Jose High School.

A distribution of total scores received by members of the gifted group is given in Table 68 (p. 156). Means and standard deviations of the gifted and control groups on the total test and on separate exercises are reported in Table 69.

TABLE 68

SCORES OF REGULAR GROUP ON MASCULINITY-FEMININITY TEST, 1927–28

Score	Gifted Boys		Gifted Girls	
	N	%	N	%
181 to 200	1	1.3	..	...
161 to 180	1	1.3	..	...
141 to 160	1	1.3	..	...
121 to 140	7	9.3	..	...
101 to 120	3	4.0	..	...
81 to 100	13	17.3	..	...
61 to 80*	18	23.9	..	...
41 to 60	13	17.3	1	1.4
21 to 40	7	9.3	2	2.8
1 to 20	4	5.3	4	5.6
0 to –19	5	6.6	6	8.3
–20 to –39	1	1.3	10	13.9
–40 to –59	..	...	17	23.6
–60 to –79	1	1.3	7	9.7
–80 to –99†	..	...	16	22.2
–100 to –119	..	...	3	4.2
–120 to –139	..	...	3	4.2
–140 to –159	..	...	3	4.2

* Median for control boys falls in this interval.
† Median for control girls falls in this interval.

From the last column of Table 69 it is seen that the difference between gifted and control boys in means for the total score is not significant in the light of its standard error, but that a difference between means of gifted and control girls is established with practical certainty. The mean of the gifted girls is displaced in the direction of masculinity by 0.6 of the standard deviation of control girls, and by four times the standard error of the difference.

If we adopt a criterion of three standard errors of difference to establish a difference with reasonable certainty, there are only two exercises which meet this criterion in the case of the boys. These are Exercise 1, Free Association, in which the gifted boys are .65 of the control S.D. more feminine than the norm, and Exercise 6, Characters and Prejudices, in which the gifted boys are .47 of the control S.D. above the norm in masculinity. It is probable although not established with certainty, that the gifted boys are less masculine than the norm in Exercise 5, Likes and Dislikes, and more masculine than the norm in Exercise 4, Emotional Response, and in Exercise 2, Ink Blots.

TABLE 69

COMPARISONS OF GIFTED AND CONTROL GROUPS,
MASCULINITY-FEMININITY TEST

BOYS

Exercise	Mean Gifted	Mean Control	S.D. Gifted	S.D. Control	Difference between Means	S.D. of Diff.	Diff. / S.D. of Diff.
1	−6.14	−.93	7.73	8.02	−5.21	1.20	−4.34
2	−.09	−.27	.56	.56	.18	.09	2.00
3	8.38	6.68	5.53	8.06	1.70	1.03	1.65
4	22.16	15.19	18.88	24.16	6.97	3.27	2.13
5	34.23	49.26	36.06	31.32	−15.03	5.22	−2.88
6	5.64	1.72	6.18	8.36	3.92	1.10	3.56
7	−.27	−.09	1.58	1.75	−.18	.25	−.72
Weighted Total	63.91	71.56	45.44	51.96	−7.65	7.43	−1.03

GIRLS

Exercise	Mean Gifted	Mean Control	S.D. Gifted	S.D. Control	Difference between Means	S.D. of Diff.	Diff. / S.D. of Diff.
1	−17.83	−13.68	7.76	7.31	−4.15	1.20	−3.46
2	−1.14	−1.08	1.12	.61	−.06	.15	−.40
3	−4.91	−12.70	6.14	9.11	7.79	1.20	6.49
4	9.94	−14.73	16.98	23.34	24.67	3.15	7.83
5	−40.06	−36.40	31.28	28.50	−3.66	4.76	−.77
6	−2.06	−5.46	6.54	7.84	3.40	1.13	3.01
7	−2.06	−1.97	2.00	1.94	−.09	.31	−.29
Weighted Total	−58.12	−86.02	42.90	45.66	27.90	6.98	4.00

There are four exercises in which the gifted and control girls show significant differences. These are Exercise 1, Free Association, in which the gifted girls are .57 of the control S.D. more feminine than the norm, and Exercises 3, 4, and 6, Information, Emotional Response, and Characters and Prejudices, in which the gifted girls are from .43 to 1.06 of the control S.D. more masculine than the norm.

Figure 2, in which the differences between gifted and control means have been transmuted into fractions of the

FIGURE 2

DEVIATION OF GIFTED SUBJECTS FROM NORMS ON THE SEPARATE
EXERCISES OF THE MASCULINITY-FEMININITY TEST

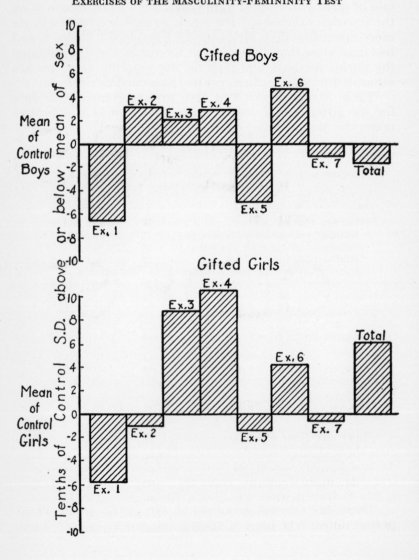

control S.D.'s and graphically represented, gives further light upon the complex trait which we have called masculinity. The representations of this figure lend emphasis to the fact that gifted boys and girls are more masculine than the norm in some exercises and less masculine in others. It is interesting to note a certain parallelism in the group of boys and of girls with respect to the direction of displacement on the separate exercises. Gifted girls as well as gifted boys are more masculine than the norms in Exercises 3, 4, and 6, and less masculine than the norms in Exercises 1 and 5, although the norms for boys and girls on the separate exercises are separated by one to three control standard deviations.

Table 70 and Figure 3 (p. 160) present comparative data for the gifted group and several other groups which have taken the Masculinity-Femininity Test.

TABLE 70

COMPARISON OF GIFTED SUBJECTS WITH OTHER GROUPS ON
MASCULINITY-FEMININITY TEST

MALE GROUPS	N	Mean and P.E. of Mean
College football men............	35	+92.6±4.8
Inferior college men (Lower Q.)..	22	+84.5±7.4
Superior college men (Upper Q.)..	20	+76.4±4.9
High-school junior boys..........	98	+71.5±3.5
Unselected college men (sophomores)	130	+67.4±2.8
Gifted boys	75	*+66.2±3.6*
Unselected unmarried men in their 20's	63	+51.6±4.6
Eighth-grade boys	100	+46.1±3.6

FEMALE GROUPS	N	
Superior college women athletes..	19	−19.3±8.5
Superior college women.........	92	−36.3±2.9
Gifted girls	72	*−57.3±3.4*
Unselected college women (sophomores)	130	−60.8±2.3
Private-school girls	28	−65.9±7.7
Unselected unmarried women in their 20's	119	−70.5±3.0
High-school junior girls..........	90	−85.5±3.2
Eighth-grade girls	98	−96.0±3.1

There are several members of the gifted group whose personalities have been of special interest to us for a number of years because they have displayed interests, hobbies, or mannerisms that have seemed so little typical of their

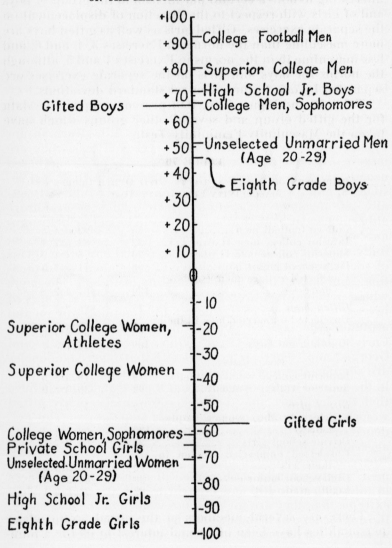

FIGURE 3

RATING OF GIFTED SUBJECTS IN COMPARISON WITH OTHER GROUPS
ON THE MASCULINITY-FEMININITY TEST

own sex and so typical of the opposite sex. It was possible during the follow-up to administer the Masculinity-Femininity Test to several of these subjects. The reader is referred to page 328 and page 330 for case descriptions of two such subjects.

The significance of masculinity-femininity traits with respect to their influence upon the total personality picture of an individual has not been fully explored. There is no doubt that individuals with ratings at either extreme stand out in the large majority of cases as different from the average person of the same sex in their behavior responses. The two case studies which are presented are in this regard typical illustrations of invert tendencies. Whether such tendencies are chiefly inborn or acquired has not yet been established with certainty, though the Miles-Terman investigation suggests that in certain cases at least they are largely acquired. Boys who have been too much mothered usually show as characteristically feminine in their test responses, and girls who have been excessively fathered usually test decidedly masculine. Such influences are probably sufficiently potent in some cases to be major determinants of the interests and attitudes which characterize an individual throughout life, affecting sexual and other forms of social behavior and the choice of vocational and avocational pursuits. There have been many historical characters whose personalities revealed more or less marked traces of inversion with respect to masculinity-femininity of mental attitudes. Among those who have been so classed are Thomas Carlyle, John Ruskin, Oscar Wilde, Queen Elizabeth, and George Sand. There is no evidence that invert tendencies are significantly more common among men of genius than in the general male population, but there is reason to believe that the incidence may be higher for intellectually gifted women than for the general female population. The evidence suggests that there is at least a little basis for the exaggerated opinion quoted from Goncourt by Lombroso that "there are no women of genius; the women of genius are all men." Between men and women of genius sex differences in interests, attitudes, and thought trends are probably less extreme than they are for men and women of the generality, the *approchement* being due chiefly to the tendency of gifted women to vary from the norm toward masculinity.

Social Intelligence

There is a widespread tradition that the intellectual prodigy is all but utterly lacking in the *savoir faire* of everyday social intercourse. The gaucheries of genius not only are universal subjects of comment among the populace, but they find frequent mention in writings of every grade of popularity from newspaper columns to scholarly scientific treatises. Everyone has heard, and no one has been able to forget, that a certain mathematical prodigy who at the age of twelve years lectured before Harvard professors on N-dimensional space later developed into a social incompetent hardly able to make his way in the world. This case, actually one of extreme rarity, is accepted by many as illustrating the rule. One can hardly expect, by any amount of evidence to the contrary, to change the popular view. For the openminded reader, however, the remainder of this chapter should prove of considerable interest.

First, the results of the George Washington University Social Intelligence Test will be given, and afterward data of a less objective kind but perhaps even more convincing than the social intelligence scores.

When we decided to include the Social Intelligence Test as one of the personality tests to be administered during the follow-up, we hoped that it would contribute data upon the social attainments of the gifted group that were more precise and more readily interpreted than those obtained by the questionnaire method. Unfortunately, data which have subsequently been reported in the experimental literature do not indicate that the test is as exclusively a measure of social intelligence as had been generally assumed. It seems to have too much in common with tests of general intelligence, and too little in common with other tests of social traits[1] or with pooled ratings of social interest, social knowledge, social conformity, or social success.[2] It may be that further experimental work will invest the test with definite significance, but for the present it seems best merely to place the results for our gifted subjects on record without attempting interpretation.

[1] See article by Pintner, R., and Upshall, C. C., *School and Society,* 1928, Vol. 27, pp. 369–370.

[2] Herrington, L. P., Master's thesis in Psychology, Stanford University.

The median scores reported for members of our gifted group in Table 71 may be compared with the following norms furnished by the authors of the test:

	Median	Q_1	Q_3	Q
High-school students	83	67	95	14.0
College freshmen	98	84	111	13.5
Upper-class college students	111	98	122	12.0
College graduates	113	99	123	12.0

It is seen that the medians for our high-school boys and girls are about two quartile deviations of the norm group above the median of the generality of "high-school students." The difference between the medians for college freshmen and the college freshman norm is somewhat less, but still very great. In whatever the test measures, the high-school seniors of our group compare favorably with the generality of college graduates.

TABLE 71

SOCIAL INTELLIGENCE TEST SCORES OF REGULAR GROUP, 1927–28

Score	HIGH-SCHOOL SENIORS		COLLEGE FRESHMEN OR RECENT HIGH-SCHOOL GRADUATES		OUT OF SCHOOL OVER ONE YEAR	
	Boys	Girls	Boys	Girls	Boys	Girls
146–150	..	..	..	..	..	1
145	..	..	1	..	..	..
140	..	1	1	1	..	..
135	3	3	4	1	1	..
130	4	2	2	4	1	..
125	4	7	6	8	..	2
120	10	7	5	10	2	..
115	9	7	9	3	2	5
110	8	7	4	2	..	1
105	4	3	6	1	1	..
100	6	1	..	2	2	1
95	4	2	1	..	1	..
90	1	..	..	..	..	..
Total number	53	40	39	32	10	10
Median	113	116	120	119	117	118

Since the items of this test have to do largely with mere knowledge of how one ought to act or what one ought to do in various social situations, we cannot infer that the actual social behavior of intellectually gifted individuals will be as superior as their scores would suggest. The score superiority is so great, however, that if the test has even a slight degree of validity, it is rendered very improbable that our gifted group would rank in social behavior below the groups with which they have been compared.

OTHER DATA ON SOCIAL TRAITS

A number of questions relating to social traits that were asked in the Home and School follow-up blanks, and in the Interest Blank filled out by the subjects themselves, were worded so that the answers might furnish data that could be compared directly with similar data obtained during the original survey. In the summaries which follow, as in the case of comparable summaries published in Volume I, the tabulated results unless otherwise stated are in terms of percentages for whom the given question was answered. It will be recalled that the data from the School Blanks represent a smaller proportion of the gifted group than do those from the Home Blank and the Interest Blank, since our follow-up schedule included School Blanks only for those members of the group who were attending high school or grammar school at the time of the follow-up. Approximately 25 per cent of the gifted group had graduated from high school at the time the follow-up was undertaken.

"Is the student's companionship especially sought, rather avoided, neither? (Underline.)" (School Blank: III, 3.) [Question answered by teachers on 90 per cent of the follow-up blanks received. Data from 1921–22 are also summarized for comparative purposes. See Volume I, p. 432.]

TABLE 72

EXTENT TO WHICH COMPANIONSHIP OF GIFTED CHILDREN IS SOUGHT OR AVOIDED

	BOYS			GIRLS		
	Especially Sought %	Rather Avoided %	Neither %	Especially Sought %	Rather Avoided %	Neither %
Gifted, 1927–28	27	5	68	34	6	60
Gifted, 1921–22	29	5	66	37	4	59
Control, 1921–22 ...	32	3	65	38	3	59

Comparing the 1927–28 figures with the corresponding figures of 1921–22 for the gifted and control groups, it is

seen that the three sets of percentages agree remarkably
well. What slight differences there are favor the control
group, but it may be pointed out in this connection, as it has
been in others, that the gifted children average about two
years younger than their classmates, with whom their
teachers naturally compare them. It is perhaps very significant that gifted children at fourteen are about as much
sought after by their classmates of sixteen years as ordinary
sixteen-year-olds are.

"Is teased by others very frequently, frequently, occasionally,
rarely, never? (Underline.)" (Home Blank: II, 13.) [Question answered by parents on 88 per cent of the follow-up blanks received.
Data from 1921–22 are also summarized for comparative purposes.
See Volume I, p. 433.]

TABLE 73

FREQUENCY WITH WHICH GIFTED CHILDREN ARE TEASED

	Very Frequently %	Fre-quently %	Occasion-ally %	Rarely %	Never %
Gifted boys, 1927–28	2	3	25	37	34
Gifted boys, 1921–22	3	8	34	38	17
Gifted girls, 1927–28	3	9	25	40	23
Gifted girls, 1921–22	3	8	31	37	21

The slight differences to be found between the 1921–22
and the 1927–28 figures are in favor of the latter. Our subjects appear to receive less teasing as they grow older. Figures for the same question, based upon school reports for
the gifted and control groups in 1921–22, showed a slight
superiority of the gifted group over the control (Volume I,
p. 433) and in view of the fact that members of the gifted
group are now even less subject to teasing than they were
originally, it is probable that they would still exhibit a slight
advantage over a control group of corresponding ages.

The evidence just presented tending to show that the
social maladjustments which characterize some gifted children grow less marked with age is in line with the observations which the senior author has made over a period of
many years. A grade of superiority represented by an IQ of
150 or higher is, for various reasons, much more likely to
attract notice and comment in the case of a child than in an
older person. For example, if we compare a typical eight-

year-old boy of 160 IQ with an equally bright boy of eighteen, the former will be seen to stand out as a much more conspicuous "case." He is probably in the fourth or fifth grade with boys two or three years his seniors whom he greatly excels in his classroom work, but with whom he cannot compete on the playground. His size at once sets him off as "different." If he is better mannered and less boisterous, he is looked upon as a "sissy." If he tries to join in the plays and games he is, because of his limited size and strength, at best tolerated. If he holds aloof he is considered queer. The gifted eighteen-year-old finds the social situation much less difficult. He is probably a junior in college and differs hardly noticeably either in size or apparent maturity from his classmates who are two or three years older. Moreover, since his classmates themselves represent a selection chiefly from the top ten per cent of school children with respect to ability, our gifted subject no longer stands out so conspicuously because of his superior intelligence. This apparent change with age is easily mistaken for actual improvement in the traits that make for social adaptability; in most cases it is the situation itself that has improved by offering fewer obstacles to normal adaptation.

"Is considered by others of the same age as queer or different?" (Home Blank II, 14.) [Question answered on 87 per cent of the follow-up blanks received.]

The question is answered "no" without qualification for 87 per cent of the boys and 91 per cent of the girls. It is answered "yes" for 5 per cent of the boys and 2 per cent of the girls, and answered in terms that might properly be interpreted as "yes" for 8 per cent of the boys and 7 per cent of the girls. The ratios of affirmative to negative answers differ but little from those for the same question as answered in 1921–22. It was answered in the negative at that time for 90 per cent of the boys and 92 per cent of the girls. (See Volume I, p. 433.) The question originally, but not during the follow-up, was included on the School Blank as well as on the Home Blank. Comparative figures from School Blanks of the gifted and control groups then showed a slight excess of gifted children who were considered queer or different, amounting to 7 per cent in the case of boys and 2 per cent in the case of girls.

"In regard to opposite sex, shows a great interest, moderate interest, indifference, aversion? (Underline.)" (Home Blank: II, 15.) [Question answered on 94 per cent of the follow-up blanks received.]

This question was not included on the original Home Blank and would have had little significance as far as our Regular group was concerned if it had been, since nearly all the members of this group were pre-adolescent when first located by us. Now that the great majority of the Regular group are in the 'teens, the question assumes greater importance. It is often suggested that the relatively low marriage rate among highly educated men and women is an indirect result of higher education. No one knows, however, but what the cause lies deeper than a hypothetical sexual insulation afforded by a few years at a university. If it should turn out that the young people from whom a large proportion of college students are recruited have a relatively high "threshold" for the opposite sex long before the colleges have had an opportunity to unsex them, the colleges would be vindicated of serious accusations. If, on the other hand, the unsexing process could be shown to be coincident with college attendance, it could justly be claimed that the colleges were exerting a dysgenic influence.

The classification of responses for the Regular group as a whole follows:

	Great Interest %	Moderate Interest %	Indifference %	Aversion %
Gifted boys	3	54	41	1
Gifted girls	10	66	24	0

The above percentages are significant in showing that gifted girls take more interest in members of the opposite sex then do gifted boys, but a far more illuminating analysis of the data can be made through the age-by-age and grade-by-grade comparisons in Table 74 (p. 168). Since a negligible proportion of boys and none of the girls show "aversion," we have simplified the comparisons by lumping together in Table 74 (1) those showing "great interest" and "moderate interest," and (2) those showing "indifference" or "aversion," so as to give the two categories: "interest" and "no interest." It is to be hoped that adequate control data may be obtained before long to compare with the material in question.

Although the columns of Table 74 show minor irregularities, especially where the number of cases is not large enough to give reliable results, certain facts emerge quite clearly. The interest of the boys takes an abrupt rise at age thirteen or fourteen, or at grade nine, while the interest of the girls shows only a small tendency to increase with age.

TABLE 74

INTEREST IN OPPOSITE SEX AS RELATED TO AGE AND EDUCATION

	GIFTED BOYS			GIFTED GIRLS		
Age	Interest %	No Interest %	N	Interest %	No Interest %	N
10 and below	22	78	9	80	20	5
11 and 12	25	75	16	60	40	20
13 and 14	55	45	62	75	25	51
15 and 16	56	44	96	82	18	79
17 and 18	74	26	69	77	23	53
19 and 20	88	12	8	78	22	9
Grade						
7 and below	29	71	14	67	33	12
8	0	100	8	71	29	7
9	70	30	27	76	24	21
10	57	43	42	74	26	31
11	47	53	49	72	28	29
12	65	35	43	84	16	44
P.G.	83	17	6	50	50	2
College 1	65	35	31	79	21	33
College 2	60	40	10	79	21	14
College 3 and over	67	33	3	80	20	5
Out of school, in business school, etc.	75	25	28	84	16	19

The interest of the girls tends to be stronger than that of the boys at nearly all ages, although the difference in the interest shown by the two sexes decreases markedly with age. Education does not appear to result in a diminution of interest in the opposite sex.

"Has the student shown any unusual or abnormal sex interests or sex behavior? .... If so, what? ...." (School Blank: III, 5.)

This question is answered in the affirmative on the School Blanks of only two boys and one girl. The testimony of the teachers certainly does not indicate that problems of sex have a prominent part in the social behavior of the members of our group, but it is probably a fact that teachers usually know nothing regarding the sex experiences of their pupils unless the results become far-reaching or disastrous. Information gained through personal interviews with the parents indicates that there has recently been a serious problem of sex behavior with at least one additional boy. For obvious reasons the replies to this question can be given little weight.

"Describe any social or moral peculiarities not listed above . . . ." (School Blank: III, 6.)

The responses which the teachers give to this question may be profitably compared with those to II, 14, of the follow-up Home Blank, which reads: "Is considered by others of the same age as queer or different?" Unfavorable social or moral peculiarities are reported on 9 per cent of the boys' School Blanks and 10 per cent of the girls'. This percentage is but slightly less than the percentages of cases who, according to the parents' testimony, are considered queer or different by others of the same age, the latter being 13 per cent for boys and 9 per cent for girls. It also agrees quite closely with the percentages of cases who, according to the teachers' and parents' testimony at the time of the original survey, were considered queer or different. (See Volume I, p. 433.)

Below are listed the social or moral peculiarities reported by teachers during the follow-up:

	Boys	Girls
Shy, quiet, or retiring..................	3	3
"Bashful, not enthusiastic".............	1	..
"Extremely timid—fear complex"......	..	1
"Very immature and childish"..........	1	..
Prefers company of older people.......	1	1
Does not mingle with others, "a lone figure," remains indoors, etc.	3	1
"Slow in developing new friendships"...	1	..
"Usually alone—odd and quaint".......	..	1
"Considered undesirable by the leaders in the school"	1	..
Conceited, shows off, self-satisfied, snobbish, etc.	4	3
"Socially retarded, morally intolerant"..	1	..
"Continually unreal—a pose"...........	..	1
"Desires to lead, not willing to make effort to gain support".................	1	..

	Boys	Girls
"Parents have not known how to deal with him"	1	..
"Stubborn and unmanageable"	..	1
"Indifferent attitude toward school work and activities"	..	1
"Eccentric mannerisms, sissy"	1	..
"Can't stand to be teased"	..	1
"Selfish and shallow—not high ideals of right and wrong"	..	1
"Very dishonest in examinations and daily work"	..	1
"Much too aggressive and self-centered".	..	1
"Very serious-minded, religious"*	1	..
"In the grip of detective and mystery stories"*	1	..
"Extremely social"*	..	1

* Not included in the percentages of "unfavorable" social or moral peculiarities.

In view of a certain degree of prejudice which many teachers entertain toward the child of high IQ, the brevity of the above list of social and moral peculiarities may be taken as valuable evidence of the rarity of extreme maladjustment in our group.

"Do you prefer to be with people who are older, younger, or the same age as yourself? .... Briefly describe your best chum .... Age of chum ...." (Interest Blank: 12.)

Preferences were expressed by the subjects in 92 per cent of the follow-up Interest Blanks. Upon 8 per cent of the blanks either the question was not answered, or the subject indicated that he had no preference as to the age of his companions. In order to find out roughly whether there might be some trend of preference with age or school status, tabulations were made for several subgroups as shown in Table 75.

There is seen to be a consistent increase in the proportions who prefer older companions as the members of our group advance from grammar school to college. Girls prefer older companions more frequently than boys do. There is a great paucity of individuals who prefer companions younger than themselves. Qualitatively the results agree with those of 1921–22, when data furnished by teachers and by parents indicated that 25 to 35 per cent of the gifted group

preferred older playmates and 4 per cent playmates who
were younger. The logical argument follows that somewhat
accelerated progress through school is desirable for gifted
children from a social as well as a scholastic point of view,
and that gifted children can better profit socially from acceleration in the later school years than in the earlier ones.

TABLE 75

AGE OF COMPANIONS PREFERRED

	N	Older	Younger	Same Age	Same or Older	Same or Younger	No Preference or Not Answered
		%	%	%	%	%	%
In grammar school:							
Gifted boys ...	20	5	...	65	10	...	20
Gifted girls ...	20	25	5	35	15	5	15
In high school:							
Gifted boys ...	177	37	0.6	44	12	0.6	5
Gifted girls ...	134	48	3	26	15	...	8
In college:							
Gifted boys ...	45	49	...	27	20	...	4
Gifted girls ...	50	52	...	18	18	...	12
Not in school:							
Gifted boys ...	20	30	...	30	25	...	15
Gifted girls ...	10	50	...	50	..	...	..
Total group:							
Gifted boys ...	262	36	0.4	42	15	0.4	7
Gifted girls ...	214	47	2	26	15	0.5	9

The responses to the second part of the question, "Briefly
describe your best chum," have considerable interest, even
though they are frequently less specific than we could have
wished. Some of the subjects indicated that they had no
chum, the proportions in the various subgroups indicating
no chum being as follows:

In Grammar School		In High School		In College		Not in School	
Boys %	Girls %	Boys %	Girls %	Boys %	Girls %	Boys %	Girls %
10	..	8	7	16	10	30	20

Many did not answer the question at all, which may or
may not mean that they have no single chum. Eleven sub-

jects answered that they have more than one chum. In Table 76 we have classified the responses of the remaining 189 boys and 179 girls so as to reveal what qualities were most frequently mentioned in describing "best chums."

TABLE 76

Traits Mentioned in Describing Chums

Qualities Mentioned	In Grammar School Boys %	In Grammar School Girls %	In High School Boys %	In High School Girls %	In College Boys %	In College Girls %
Physical characteristics	60	59	61	52	63	44
Intellectual qualities	20	35	39	34	50	63
Popularity, likableness, etc. ...	20	18	37	28	43	34
Personality traits	..	29	12	54	50	40
Athletic ability	27	24	31	14	20	12
"Likes things that I do," etc. ..	7	18	17	11	10	10
Opposite sex	..	..	..	1	3	..
Miscellaneous	..	..	14	6	7	10

Table 76 is to be read as follows: 60 per cent of grammar school boys who described their chums mentioned physical characteristics, 20 per cent mentioned intellectual qualities, and so forth down each column. The sex differences are not for the most part significant, though it is interesting to note that the boys much more frequently than the girls mention athletic ability, while the girls, except in the college group, more frequently mention personality traits than do the boys. We attach little significance to the fact that so many of our subjects mention the physical characteristics of their chums, for the wording of the question probably led a number to believe that we desired a description of the chum's appearance. If we leave physical characteristics out of consideration, it is seen that "intellectual qualities" assume major importance, and that "personality traits" come second.

The responses of the group not in school at the time of the follow-up are not included in the tabulation because so few of them described a chum.

Social Adjustment of Subjects with Highest IQ's

Many different types of data converge in showing that if the typical member of our gifted group differs at all from the average child in his social traits it is probably in the di-

rection of superiority. It has been very natural in the case
of most of the problems that have occupied our attention
during the original survey and the 1927–28 follow-up to assume without a special analysis of data that what is true of
the typical member of the gifted group is even more true of
the most highly gifted members of the group. If the typical
gifted child of IQ 150 is superior to the average child in his
school achievement, one naturally expects to find that children of IQ 170 or 180 are superior to an even greater degree.
If the typical gifted child is slightly taller, heavier, and
healthier than the average child, it seems altogether probable that children of IQ 170 or 180 tend to be still taller,
heavier, and healthier.

A similar assumption cannot be made in the case of
social traits. The distribution curve of intelligence implies
that a child of 140 or 150 IQ may find a fairly large group of
associates whose mental development and range of interests
are not hopelessly far behind his own, and who react to him
as to a congenial playfellow, perhaps elevating him to a position of real leadership. The child of 170 or 180 IQ, on the
other hand, stands in an extremely sparsely populated region of intelligence. Only one child in thousands makes so
high a score, and only one child in two hundred or more
comes within such a long-distance range as 140 IQ. If he is
promoted to a school grade in which the intelligence level
of the pupils is at all commensurate with his own, he is
likely to be so immature in size, strength, and social-emo-
tional development that there is small chance for him to
become a functioning member of the miniature social cos-
mos in which he finds himself.

In her book[1] on gifted children, Professor Hollingworth
presents case studies of a dozen children whose IQ's equal
or surpass 180. The data amassed in these studies would
appear to justify fully her generalization that the majority
of children testing above 180 "play little with other children,
unless special conditions such as those found in a special
class for the gifted are provided. They have great difficulty
in finding playmates in the ordinary course of events who
are congenial both in size and in mental ability. Thus they

[1] Leta S. Hollingworth, *Gifted Children* (The Macmillan Company,
1926).

are thrown back upon themselves to work out forms of solitary, intellectual play."

The children in our gifted group whose IQ's are over 180 tend to fall into the social pattern described by Hollingworth. We have therefore thought it worth while to summarize certain facts concerning the social traits of our subjects with the highest IQ's. Instead of limiting the cases to children with IQ over 180, we have placed the boundary at 170 IQ in order to provide a larger group, and have not confined the selection of cases to the Regular group alone.

The cases available for study include twenty boys and fifteen girls whose IQ's (corrected in the few cases needing correction) at the time they were located for the gifted group were distributed as follows:

IQ	170–74	175–79	180–84	185–89	190–94	195–99	200
Boys	7	3	6	1	2	1	..
Girls	2	3	4	3	2	..	1

In the course of the follow-up tests of 1928 the Terman Group Test was administered to sixteen of the subjects. All of them scored above the medians of scores earned by the other members of the gifted group of corresponding ages—in fact the scale does not extend far enough to measure the present ability of most of them. Seven of the subjects who took the Thorndike Examination before making application for admission to Stanford made a mean score of 100. This is 14 points above the mean earned by the other members of the gifted group who took the Thorndike.

The average age of the boys at the beginning of the follow-up was 14-10 and that of the girls 13-11. The boys ranged in age between eight and twenty-one and the girls between eight and sixteen. All the girls and all but two of the boys were accelerated in grade placement (according to projected Ayres-Strayer norms) by one to six years. The two exceptions are a boy of eight who has already skipped one grade, but was not sent to school until he was seven, and a boy of twenty-one who was entering his senior year at college with practically an "A" scholastic average. The latter had graduated from grammar school when barely thirteen, but there had been breaks in his school attendance since then.

Sufficiently detailed information was obtained through

personal interviews of the field workers with homes and schools to permit ratings upon the social adjustment of thirteen of the boys and twelve of the girls, i.e., twenty-five of the thirty-four cases. The nature of the ratings on social adjustment is described in chapter x, where ratings for the entire Regular group are reported. We may anticipate that section by the parenthetical comment that a rating of 1 indicates very marked traits of sociability and leadership, while a rating of 5 indicates either serious maladjustment or an almost complete lack of youthful social intercourse. The ratings for the twenty-five cases in question are distributed as follows:

Rating	1	2	3	4	5
N	0	2	14	7	2
Percentage	0	8	56	28	8

If we compute a "mean" rating, assuming for this purpose that the five categorical ratings represent equal steps on a scale, the result is 3.4. The mean reported in chapter x for gifted boys of the entire group is 3.0 and that for gifted girls 2.9. None of our highest IQ cases falls in the top category, and the proportion falling in the second category is less than half the proportion of the entire gifted group found in the two highest categories. The proportion of highest IQ cases falling in the two lowest categories, on the other hand, is about twice as great as for the entire gifted group.

There is a definite tendency among the highest IQ cases for those who are most highly accelerated in school to fall in the two lowest categories. Of ten cases who are accelerated by three years or more, seven are rated in categories 4 and 5, and none is rated in categories 1 and 2. Of fifteen cases who are accelerated by less than three years, only two fall in category 4 and none in category 5.

The reports on home and school interviews, the Home Blank, and the School Information Blank were next consulted to ascertain in how many instances the children of highest IQ's were described by their parents or teachers as being definitely solitary or "poor mixers." Such statements were found regarding twelve of the boys, or 60 per cent, and eleven of the girls, or 73 per cent. Mention was made of social handicap due to youthful age in the case of one additional boy and one additional girl.

These data, while showing that the special cases under consideration suffer a certain degree of social handicap, should by no means be interpreted as indicating that the majority of them are disliked or even unappreciated by their schoolmates. While none ranks as a conspicuous leader, a number have taken a creditable part in the activities of their schools. An analysis of 1927–28 Interest Blanks received from eighteen of the boys and thirteen of the girls shows that thirteen of the boys and eight of the girls have held offices of some sort within the past few years. In two cases the office was that of class president (in the grammar grades); the majority, however, were minor club or class offices. Several of the group have attained marked recognition in journalistic enterprises at high school and college.

Ratings contained on the Interest Blanks of these highly gifted subjects show that their expressed fondness for certain kinds of social activity differs but little from that of the gifted group as a whole. On a five-point rating scale (described in chapter vii), the rating 1 indicates very great liking, 5 very great dislike, 3 neither like nor dislike, etc. "Spending time with several other people" receives a mean rating of 2.0 from the highly gifted subjects, and 1.9 from the gifted group as a whole. "Spending time with one other person" receives a mean rating of 1.8 from the highly gifted subjects, and 1.7 from the gifted group as a whole. "Spending time alone" receives a mean rating of 2.3 from the highly gifted subjects and 2.6 from the gifted group as a whole.

Case studies of a boy and a girl with IQ's close to 190 are presented in chapter xiv, pages 264 ff.

While we are discussing data on social traits it would be well to refer to certain material that has been summarized in other chapters because it logically belongs there but which has, nevertheless, a direct bearing upon the social traits and social relationships of the members of our group. We have in mind, especially, material in chapter vii, "Scholastic and Other Interests," and in chapter x, "Ratings on Personal Traits." Pertinent data discussed in these chapters include offices and honors (p. 125); use of leisure time (p. 118); activity preferences (p. 118); ratings on social traits (p. 190); ratings of field visitors (p. 192).

Other related data are concerned with membership in

college fraternities and sororities. A question regarding membership in such organizations is included upon the Information Blank. As this blank was filled out chiefly by members of the gifted group who were over twenty years old at the time of the follow-up, we have information upon fraternity membership for a large proportion of the group originally located in the high schools but for a very small proportion of the Regular group. The reader is therefore referred to page 234, where data upon fraternity membership are summarized for the original High School group.

DATA ON MORAL TRAITS

"Does the student respond well to discipline? . . . . If not, explain. . . . ." (School Blank: III, 4.) [Question answered on 95 per cent of the follow-up blanks received.]

This question was also included on the School Blank of 1921–22 and that of 1924. In tabulating the results such answers as "yes," "very well," "always," etc., were recorded as satisfactory. Negative answers or qualified affirmative answers, such as "fairly well," "yes, except for occasional periods of sulkiness," etc., were recorded as not entirely satisfactory. The responses for 1921–22 and 1924 have been included in the following summary with those of 1927–28 for comparative purposes.

Response to Discipline	GIFTED BOYS			GIFTED GIRLS		
	1921–22	1924	1927–28	1921–22	1924	1927–28
	%	%	%	%	%	%
Satisfactory	92	87	87	96	92	90
Not entirely satisfactory	8	13	13	4	8	10

Neither the boys nor the girls can be said to have changed greatly with respect to the number responding well to discipline, especially since 1924. The teachers appear to find no disciplinary problems with the great majority of the gifted group. Teachers who answered the question in the negative amplified their responses with the following explanations:

Boys		Girls	
Resentful and surly	2	Character is fitful	1
An only child—adjustment difficult	2	Disagreeable to deal with	1
		Nervous, independent, self-willed	1
Resorts to forgery and deceit to avoid discipline	1	Selfish, wants own way	1

Boys		Girls	
Desires notice, limelight, etc.	2	Indifferent	1
Slightly stubborn	1	Not amenable to reason...	1
Becomes sullen	1	Disregards rules	1
Wants to entertain teachers and pupils	1	Needs repeated corrections	1
		Argumentative	1
Avoids minor school rules	1	Sulks	1
Very talkative, cannot concentrate	1	Saucy and impertinent...	1
		Takes criticism poorly ...	1

"Is very tractable, fairly tractable, rather headstrong, very headstrong regarding disciplinary matters? (Underline.)" (Home Blank: II, 11.) [Question answered by the parents in 97 per cent of the follow-up blanks received.]

	Very Tractable %	Fairly Tractable %	Rather Headstrong %	Very Headstrong %
Boys	30	42	23	5
Girls	35	42	19	5

The responses of the parents indicate that approximately three-fourths of both boys and girls are very tractable or fairly tractable, while 5 per cent of both sexes are very headstrong. The latter proportion does not seem unduly high when we consider that the great majority of the gifted group are now in their adolescent years. It would be interesting to have control data on this point, even though we do not know certainly whether it is a more desirable trait for a child to be "very tractable" or "very headstrong." Doubtless the parents have assumed that tractability is the more desirable, and although this is probably true in general, it would appear from Dr. Cox's study of the mental development of geniuses[1] that a good many eminent individuals were in childhood decidedly stubborn and headstrong.

The nature of the behavior problems encountered in the gifted group will be better understood from an analysis of responses to the question next in order on the Home Blank, and from an analysis of information ascertained from the parents in personal interviews.

"Are there any tendencies at present toward selfishness, lack of studious interests, intolerance of social customs, lack of ambition, or lack of moral integrity? .... Describe. ...." (Home Blank: II, 12.) [Question answered on 84 per cent of blanks received.]

[1] *Genetic Studies of Genius*, Volume II.

On the blanks of the gifted boys 33 per cent of the answers were positive; on the blanks of the gifted girls 22 per cent were positive. The tendencies were noted by the parents with the following frequencies:

	Boys	Girls
Selfishness	27	14
Lack of studious interests	21	10
Intolerance of social customs	13	6
Lack of ambition	11	5
Lack of moral integrity	0	2

The field assistants, when calling upon the parents of the gifted subjects, endeavored to cover certain definite ground in all their interviews. One question which was practically always brought up (except in a very small proportion of cases in which the subject happened to be present during the entire interview) concerned character traits in general and the possible presence of personality problems. Assisted by Dr. Dortha Jensen, we have gone through the Home Visit Reports of each of the field assistants and classified the information there noted so as to indicate the presence of (1) serious personality or behavior problems; (2) mild problems; (3) no problems. The problems which we have termed "serious" vary in gravity. Among the most serious are those in the cases of Alfred (reported in full, p. 310), who is serving a term in reformatory for repeated thefts culminating in grand larceny; and Joe (reported, p. 309), who accidentally killed a schoolmate and who intentionally damaged several hundred dollars worth of equipment at his school. Among problems that are less grave but still "serious" are those in the cases of Emmett (reported, p. 310), who sacrificed an opportunity to go through college because of his infatuation for a girl with whom he later lived out of wedlock; and Eva, whose attitude of coldness and antagonism is breaking the heart of her mother. Among problems that we have classified as "mild" are those of Carlotta, who is "boy struck" and who sometimes loiters in the street near the high school in order to encounter various boys of her acquaintance; and Rankin, who takes no pains to hide his scorn and intolerance of a younger brother.[1]

[1] Names throughout are fictitious.

We wish that it were feasible to add a fourth classification, instead of lumping all the remaining cases into the neutral category of "no personality problems." Many of our subjects far from having disturbing personality problems, have personalities that fairly radiate kindliness, loyalty, generosity, unselfishnes, and other desirable traits. Our methods of ascertaining and recording information during personal interviews with the parents were not so adequate, however, for distinguishing between neutral and positive character traits as they were for distinguishing between "mild" and "serious" personality problems. Accordingly we have let the classification rest as it is, though we do not wish to close the discussion without assuring the reader that the gifted group contains shining examples such as Sarah, who is earning her entire way through college, who cheerfully does "more than is asked of her" in the home of the family with whom she works for her room and board, and who helps buy the clothing of her small sister at home out of her slender earnings.

According to the threefold classification just described, the members of the Regular gifted group fall into the following categories:

	Serious Problems %	Mild Problems %	No Problems %
Boys (292)	5	24	71
Girls (237)	2	28	70

These figures provide an interesting parallelism with those reported for the responses to the question on the Home Blank regarding tractability (p. 178). The proportion reported as "very headstrong" is almost the same as the proportion showing serious personality problems; the proportion reported as "rather headstrong" nearly matches the proportion offering "mild problems"; and the combined proportions of those reported as "very tractable" and "fairly tractable" are not far from the proportions offering "no problems."

The reader may feel inclined to discount heavily the accuracy of information gained from interviews with parents regarding traits of character. A critical attitude toward such data is indeed natural and desirable. If the data given above stood alone, a considerable degree of skepticism would be justified. The fact that they are supported by confirmatory evidence from several independent sources convinces us that the results we have reported depict the situation with a fair degree of accuracy. The proportion of our group presenting character problems at all serious is probably not above five per cent of the boys and two per cent of the girls. Studies of unselected children indicate that among them the proportion is probably not far from twice as great.[1]

SUMMARY

1. In a group of gifted subjects who were given the Woodworth-Cady Questionnaire during the follow-up the mean scores of boys and girls are almost identical with the mean scores in 1923 of gifted subjects of similar age range. The correlation between the standard scores of 150 gifted subjects who took the test both in 1923 and in 1927–28 is .42 ± .05.

2. On the Watson Test of Fair-Mindedness the gifted subjects appear to differ little in the trait measured by this test from other well-educated groups of presumably somewhat lower mean intelligence level. Practically no sex differences were found on this test.

3. On a Masculinity-Femininity Test developed at Stanford, gifted boys average about .15 control S.D. less masculine than unselected boys of corresponding age, but gifted girls average about .60 control S.D. more masculine than unselected girls. The displacement of the gifted boys from the norm is not significant in the light of its standard error, but the displacement of the gifted girls from the norm is four times its standard error. The means of the gifted boys and girls on the separate exercises of the Masculinity-Femininity Test vary greatly with regard to the direction of displacement from the norm. A few cases of marked inversion in the mental traits of sex were found.

4. The George Washington University Social Intelligence Test was administered to 184 members of the gifted group. The median scores for various subgroups of those who took the test are well above the norms furnished by the authors of the test, but because of ambiguity of recent experimental

[1] See, for example, *The Estimation of Juvenile Incorrigibility*, by Dr. Vernon S. Cady, (Whittier State School, Whittier, California, 1923), p. 33.

literature concerning the significance of this test only a guarded interpretation of the results with the gifted group can be made.

5. The proportion of gifted subjects whose companionship is sought in school differs little from the proportion found in 1921–22. The latter proportion, in turn, differs but little from that found for control children.

6. Gifted subjects are teased by others to a slightly less extent than they were in 1921–22, when the figures for them were about the same as were found for control subjects.

7. The proportion of gifted subjects who are considered by others of the same age as queer or different has changed but little since 1921–22.

8. A somewhat higher proportion of gifted girls than of gifted boys have developed an interest in members of the opposite sex. One per cent of the boys and none of the girls show an aversion to members of the opposite sex. The interest of the girls tends to be stronger than that of the boys at nearly all ages, although the difference in the interest shown by the two sexes decreases markedly with age. Education does not appear to result in a diminution of interest.

9. According to the reports of teachers, only two boys and one girl of the gifted group have shown any unusual or abnormal sex interests or sex behavior. Information gained through personal interviews with the parents indicates that there have been more or less serious problems of sex behavior in the case of at least one additional boy. The data on this point are probably too incomplete to justify any conclusions.

10. The gifted subjects now show an even greater tendency to prefer companions older than themselves than they did in 1921–22, at which time many more gifted than control subjects preferred older companions.

11. There is a consistent decrease in the proportion of gifted subjects reporting a "best chum" as we advance from pupils in grammar school to students in college. The lowest proportion of all is in the group of subjects not attending school. It is not known what age differences a control group would show. The proportions of subjects mentioning intellectual qualities in describing their "best chums" vary from 20 per cent of the boys attending grammar school to 63 per cent of the girls attending college.

12. The members of the gifted group whose IQ's are in the neighborhood of 170, 180, or 190 tend to have considerably more difficulty in making social adjustments than do the more typical members of the gifted group.

13. The proportions of gifted boys and gifted girls showing satisfactory response to school discipline have not changed greatly since 1921–22. Eighty-seven per cent of the boys and 90 per cent of the girls are said to respond well to discipline.

14. Approximately three-fourths of gifted boys and gifted girls are reported by their parents as "very tractable" or "fairly tractable," while 5 per cent of both sexes are reported as "very headstrong."

15. Five per cent of the gifted boys and 2 per cent of the gifted girls present more or less serious behavior or personality problems, which is probably not more than half as great as the proportion to be found among unselected children of corresponding age.

CHAPTER X

RATINGS ON PERSONAL TRAITS AND HOME CONDITIONS

The material in the present chapter should be considered as evidence corroborative of data that have been reported in other sections of the volume. Because of the demonstrable unreliability of individual trait ratings, the data of this chapter find their main significance in group statistical treatment and are applicable only in a limited way to the study of individual cases.

TRAIT RATINGS BY PARENTS AND TEACHERS

Twelve traits sampling a fairly wide domain of personality were selected at the time of the follow-up from the group of twenty-five traits used in the original investigation. The original twenty-five traits had in turn been selected as being most important and most likely to be rated with accuracy out of an assortment of forty-six traits previously used in a preliminary study of gifted children.

The follow-up trait rating blanks contained a graphic rating scale for each of the twelve traits, these being set up in a manner almost identical to that employed in 1921–22. (See Volume I, pp. 523 ff.) The following printed directions headed the rating sheet:

> *Directions:* In each trait or characteristic, compare this boy or girl with the average for his age. Then make a small cross somewhere on the line to show how much of the trait he possesses. The ratings will be held absolutely confidential.
>
> Locate your cross any place on the line where you think it belongs. It is not necessary to locate it at any of the little vertical marks.
>
> *Examples:* In Example 1, the cross shows how one boy was rated for health. In Example 2, the cross shows how the same boy was rated for prudence and forethought.

In the statistical treatment of results the ratings for each trait were scored 1, 2, 3, 4, and so on to 13, 1 being the highest possible rating, 7 "average for age" according to the label on the rating scale itself, and 13 the lowest possible rating. It was shown in the original study (Volume I, p. 545), by analyzing teachers' trait ratings of a control group, that a "generosity factor" operates to displace the means of ratings upon a number of the traits upward by one-half S.D. to one S.D. from the "average for age" point on the graphical scale. For this reason ratings of the gifted group cannot be taken at face value, but must be compared with ratings of a control group to eliminate the "generosity factor."

In the control group for whom we obtained teachers' ratings in 1921–22, mean ratings upon the twelve traits showed no significant trends with age (in a range of eight to fourteen years) excepting a distinct downward trend for boys in the trait "desire to excel," and an upward trend for both boys and girls in the trait "freedom from vanity." We have therefore felt justified in using teachers' 1921–22 ratings of the control group to compare with teachers' 1927–28 ratings of the gifted, making allowance for the exceptions just noted, despite the fact that the gifted subjects now average several years older than the 1921–22 control group.

Ratings upon members of the Regular group were obtained during the follow-up from the teachers of 200 gifted boys and 155 gifted girls, and from the parents of 255 gifted boys and 199 gifted girls. The mean ratings for the twelve traits in 1921–22 and 1927–28 are shown graphically in Figures 4, 5, 6, and 7 (pp. 186–89).

Table 77 (p. 190) tabulates the means and S.D.'s upon the twelve traits for teachers' ratings of gifted in 1927–28, for teachers' ratings of gifted and control in 1921–22, and for parents' ratings of gifted in 1927–28 and in 1921–22. Here it is seen that although teachers' ratings of the gifted group are now lower by a small fraction of a control S.D. than they were in 1921–22 on practically every trait, they still average above the mean ratings of the control group in all but a few cases. In "fondness for groups," the mean of control boys is .14 S.D. superior to that of gifted boys, and the means of control girls and gifted girls are identical; in "popularity," the mean of control girls is .11 S.D. superior to that of gifted girls, and the means of control boys and gifted boys are identical; in "freedom from vanity," the mean of control girls is .05 S.D. superior to that of gifted girls, but the mean of gifted boys is .11 S.D. superior to that of control boys. It happens that in these traits for which the

FIGURE 4

TEACHERS' RATINGS OF BOYS ON TWELVE TRAITS

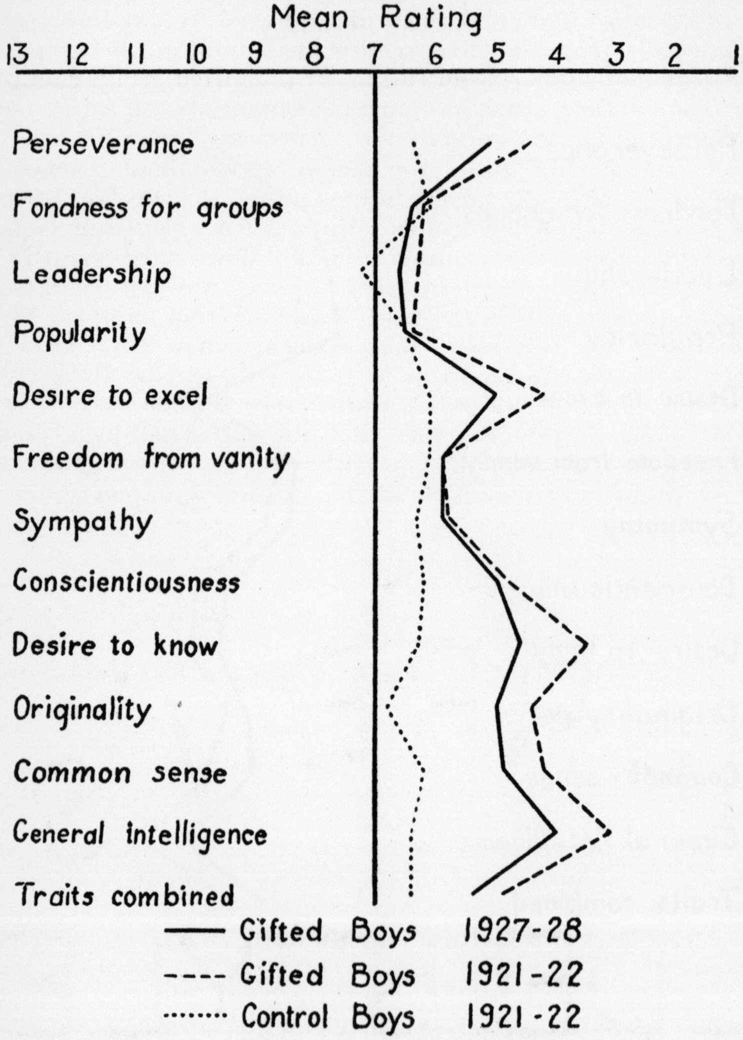

Mean Rating

13 12 11 10 9 8 7 6 5 4 3 2 1

Perseverance

Fondness for groups

Leadership

Popularity

Desire to excel

Freedom from vanity

Sympathy

Conscientiousness

Desire to know

Originality

Common sense

General intelligence

Traits combined

——— Gifted Boys 1927-28

- - - - Gifted Boys 1921-22

·········· Control Boys 1921-22

gifted means have sagged slightly below the 1921–22 control means there is really very little difference between the teachers' mean ratings of the gifted group in 1921–22 and

FIGURE 5

TEACHERS' RATINGS OF GIRLS ON TWELVE TRAITS

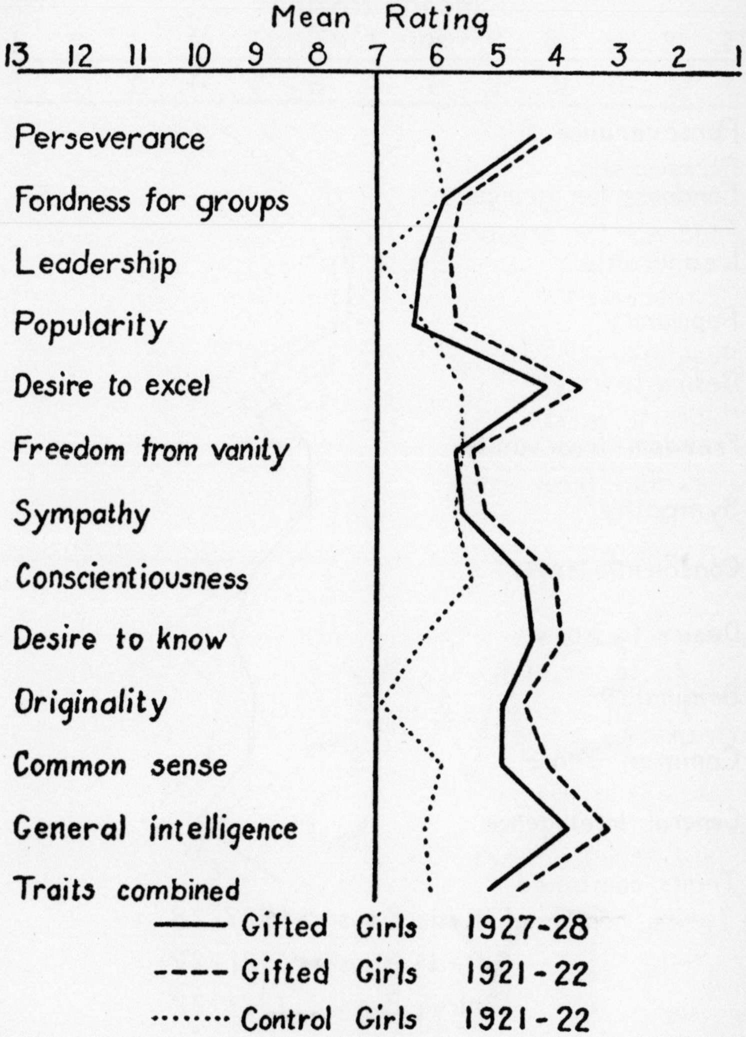

Mean Rating

13 12 11 10 9 8 7 6 5 4 3 2 1

Perseverance

Fondness for groups

Leadership

Popularity

Desire to excel

Freedom from vanity

Sympathy

Conscientiousness

Desire to know

Originality

Common sense

General intelligence

Traits combined

——— Gifted Girls   1927-28
– – – Gifted Girls   1921-22
········ Control Girls   1921-22

in 1927–28. The three traits in question ranked near the end of the list of twelve traits with respect to teachers' ratings of the gifted in 1921–22, and still do.

FIGURE 6

Comparison of Teachers' Ratings of Gifted Boys and Gifted Girls, 1927–28

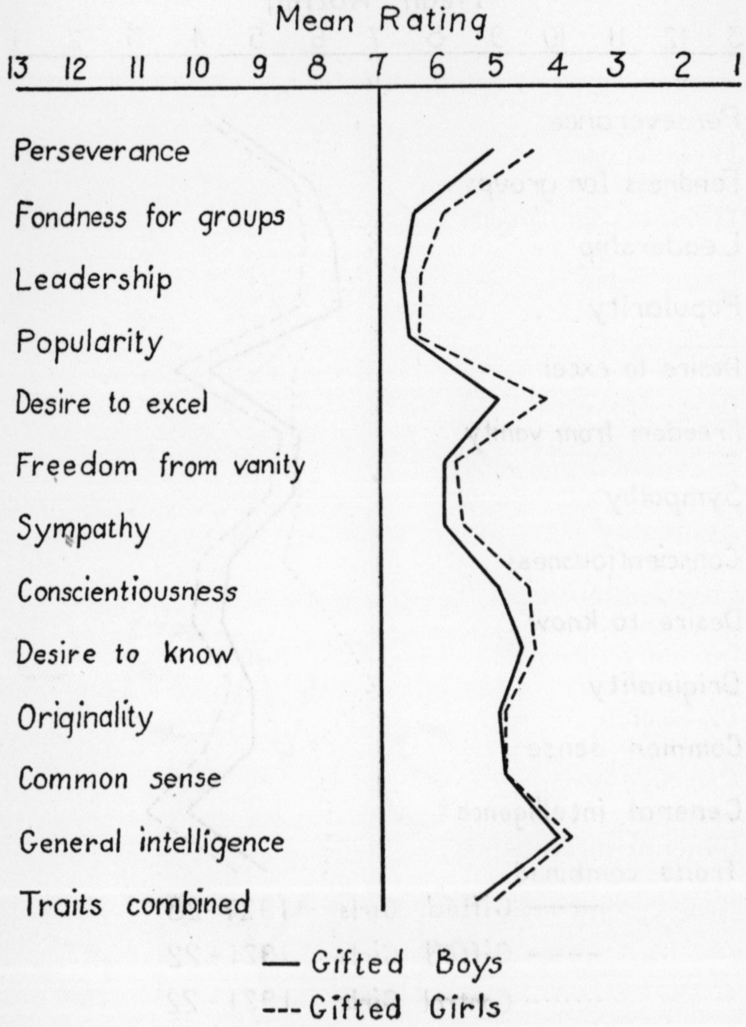
Mean Rating
13 12 11 10 9 8 7 6 5 4 3 2 1
Perseverance
Fondness for groups
Leadership
Popularity
Desire to excel
Freedom from vanity
Sympathy
Conscientiousness
Desire to know
Originality
Common sense
General intelligence
Traits combined
— Gifted Boys
--- Gifted Girls

The changes in the 1921–22 and 1927–28 mean ratings are not very pronounced in most of the traits. There are only two traits for which teachers' or parents' ratings of the

FIGURE 7

COMPARISON OF PARENTS' RATINGS OF GIFTED BOYS AND
GIFTED GIRLS, 1927–28

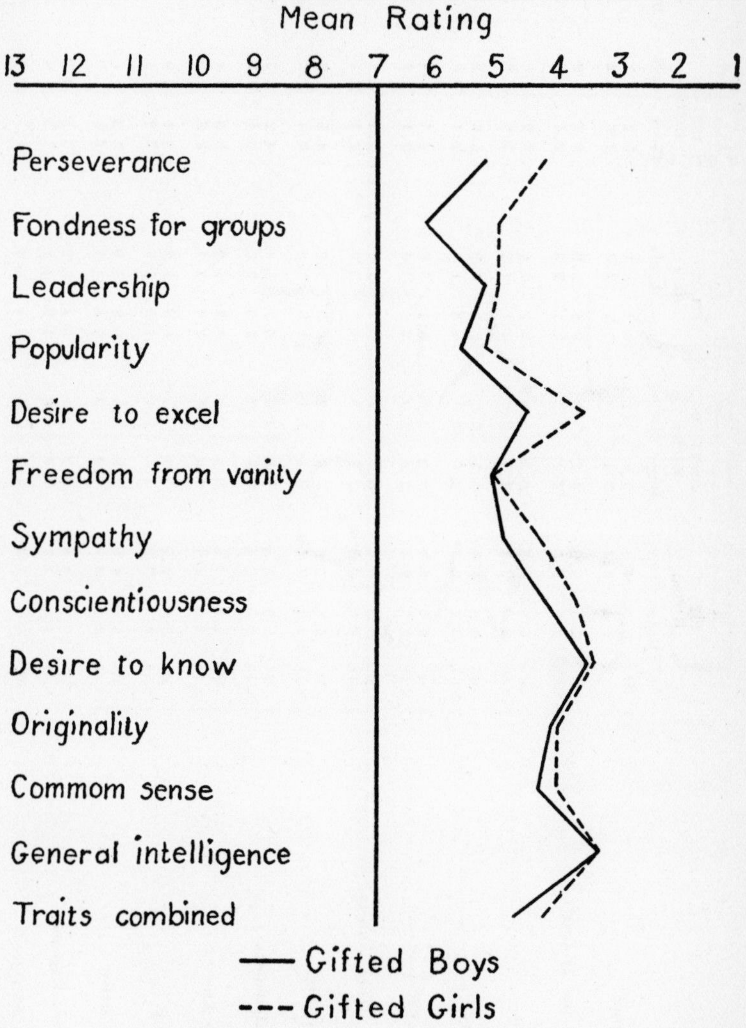

Mean Rating

13 12 11 10 9 8 7 6 5 4 3 2 1

Perseverance

Fondness for groups

Leadership

Popularity

Desire to excel

Freedom from vanity

Sympathy

Conscientiousness

Desire to know

Originality

Commom sense

General intelligence

Traits combined

—— Gifted Boys

--- Gifted Girls

gifted subjects indicate a drop as large as half a control
S.D. for either boys or girls; these are "desire to know"
(teachers' ratings of boys), and "sympathy" (parents' rat-

TABLE 77

Means and S.D.'s of Trait Ratings, 1927–28 and 1921–22

| | | Teachers' Ratings | | | | | | Parents' Ratings | | | |
| | | 1927–28 Gifted | | 1921–22 Gifted | | 1921–22 Control | | 1927–28 Gifted | | 1921–22 Gifted | |
		Boys	Girls	Boys	Girls	Boys	Girls	Boys	Girls	Boys	Girls
1. Perseverance*	M	5.1	4.4	4.4	4.1	6.4	6.1	5.2	4.2	4.9	4.1
	S.D.	2.4	2.3	2.1	1.9	2.2	2.0	2.0	2.2	2.3	2.0
2. Fondness for groups	M	6.4	5.9	6.2	5.6	6.1	5.9	6.2	5.0	5.5	4.7
	S.D.	2.2	2.1	2.1	2.2	2.1	2.0	2.7	1.8	2.6	2.2
3. Leadership	M	6.6	6.3	6.3	5.8	7.2	7.0	5.2	5.0	5.3	4.9
	S.D.	2.0	2.2	1.9	2.0	2.1	2.2	2.0	2.0	2.2	2.1
4. Popularity	M	6.5	6.4	6.4	5.7	6.5	6.2	5.6	5.2	5.5	5.2
	S.D.	2.1	2.2	2.0	2.0	1.8	1.9	2.1	1.5	2.0	2.1
5. Desire to excel	M	5.0	4.2	4.2	3.6	6.1	5.6	4.5	3.6	3.7	3.3
	S.D.	2.5	2.4	2.2	1.9	2.4	2.0	2.1	1.9	1.9	1.9
6. Freedom from vanity	M	5.9	5.7	5.9	5.4	6.1	5.6	5.1	5.1	5.7	5.9
	S.D.	2.6	2.5	2.7	2.3	1.9	2.0	2.4	2.4	2.2	2.3
7. Sympathy, etc.	M	5.9	5.6	5.8	5.2	6.3	5.7	4.9	4.3	3.9	3.7
	S.D.	2.2	2.1	2.1	2.1	1.8	1.8	2.4	2.2	2.3	2.2
8. Conscientiousness	M	5.0	4.5	4.8	4.0	6.2	5.4	4.2	3.7	4.4	4.3
	S.D.	2.6	2.4	2.5	2.2	2.3	2.2	2.4	2.2	2.1	2.2
9. Desire to know	M	4.6	4.4	3.5	3.9	6.3	6.2	3.5	3.4	2.7	2.8
	S.D.	2.3	2.4	1.9	2.1	2.0	2.1	2.2	2.0	1.9	1.8
10. Originality	M	5.0	4.9	4.4	4.5	6.8	6.9	4.1	4.0	4.0	3.9
	S.D.	2.2	2.2	2.1	2.1	1.9	1.9	2.2	2.1	2.2	2.1
11. Common sense	M	4.9	4.9	4.2	4.1	6.2	5.9	4.3	4.0	4.4	4.3
	S.D.	2.0	2.0	1.9	1.9	1.8	1.8	2.1	1.9	2.0	1.9
12. General intelligence	M	4.0	3.8	3.1	3.1	6.4	6.2	3.3	3.3	3.1	3.1
	S.D.	1.9	1.7	1.6	1.8	1.9	1.8	1.3	1.4	1.6	1.6
Traits combined	M	5.4	5.1	4.9	4.6	6.4	6.1	4.7	4.2	4.4	4.2

* The ratings for trait 1 in 1927–28 are not strictly comparable with those in 1921–22 because the description of the trait as it appeared on the trait rating blank was somewhat altered in 1927–28. Experience had shown that those making the ratings were often confused by the original wording, which combined the concepts of "will power and perseverance." The term "will

ings of boys). The trait "general intelligence" shows a drop of nearly half a control S.D. in teachers' ratings of both boys and girls. Other traits showing mean drops of less than a half S.D. but more than a quarter S.D. are: in teachers' ratings of boys, "perseverance," "desire to excel," "originality," and "common sense"; in parents' ratings of boys, "fondness for groups," "desire to excel," and "desire to know"; in teachers' ratings of girls, "popularity," "desire to excel," and "common sense"; in parents' ratings of girls, "sympathy" and "desire to know." Although there are no traits in which teachers have given a better mean rating in 1927–28 than in 1921–22, there are three in which parents have done so, namely, "freedom from vanity," "conscientiousness," and, to a very slight extent, "common sense."

Rank Order of the Traits

As might be anticipated from the fact that the changes in mean ratings by teachers and parents are for the most part only slight, the changes in the rank orders of the mean ratings are also slight. As in 1921–22, teachers and parents now tend to rate the gifted boys and girls relatively highest on the intellectual traits such as "intelligence," "desire to know," "common sense," etc., and relatively lowest on the social traits such as "fondness for groups," "popularity," and "leadership." Teachers' ratings on the latter three traits average close in value to the 1921–22 control means for the same traits, while parents' ratings average somewhat higher, especially on "leadership" and "popularity."

Spearman rank-difference correlations have been computed between rank orders of the mean trait ratings with the following result:

Teachers' Ratings vs. Parents' Ratings

1. Gifted boys vs. Gifted boys, 1927–28 90
2. Gifted boys vs. Gifted boys, 1921–22 83
3. Gifted girls vs. Gifted girls, 1927–28 91
4. Gifted girls vs. Gifted girls, 1921–22 81

Teachers' Ratings

5. Gifted boys, 1927–28 vs. Gifted boys, 1921–22 96
6. Gifted girls, 1927–28 vs. Gifted girls, 1921–22 97
7. Gifted boys, 1927–28 vs. Gifted girls, 1927–28 86
8. Gifted boys, 1921–22 vs. Gifted girls, 1921–22 93

Parents' Ratings

9. Gifted boys, 1927–28 vs. Gifted boys, 1921–22........ .81
10. Gifted girls, 1927–28 vs. Gifted girls, 1921–22........ .87
11. Gifted boys, 1927–28 vs. Gifted girls, 1927–28........ .86
12. Gifted boys, 1921–22 vs. Gifted girls, 1921–22........ .97

The outstanding facts shown by these correlations are (1) close agreement between parents and teachers in ranks of the mean ratings, especially in the case of boys (1, 2, 3, 4); (2) consistency in the ranks of the mean ratings of both teachers and parents over a period of six years, especially in the case of ratings upon the boys (5, 6, 9, 10); (3) close agreement between the ranks of the mean ratings for boys and girls, both in 1921–22 and in 1927–28 (7, 8, 11, 12).

Ratings by Field Visitors

During the 1927–28 follow-up, by means of personal interviews with parents and teachers as called for in the schedule outlined on pages 9–10, the field visitors assembled a large amount of data concerning the attainments, plans, modes of life, personality adjustments, and home environments of our subjects.

Such data are most illuminating in tracing the development of individuals in the gifted group, but are admittedly difficult to evaluate in any manner that lends itself to statistical treatment. Believing, however, that the data contained possibilities of group treatment which would be valuable even though tentative and inconclusive, we decided to subject the material to careful scrutiny and extract certain generalizations regarding (1) the achievements, (2) the social adjustment, and (3) the environmental conditions of the gifted group. The field assistants, chiefly on the basis of their home interviews, though partly on the basis of their school and child interviews, were asked to make ratings for the gifted subjects in their territories upon the three points just enumerated.

The value of the ratings would of course be increased if it were possible to obtain them also for a control group. Independently of the status of unselected children on the three factors, however, it is important to know how gifted children differ among themselves in regard to the factors in question. Intelligence doubtless correlates with all of them, particularly with the first; but in some instances high intelligence may accompany very mediocre or even low ratings on all three. The ultimate interpretation of the achievement and success of our gifted subjects in adulthood will surely gain much in richness and depth by reference to such factors as we are now considering.

Five categories were distinguished in making ratings upon each of the three factors, the top and bottom categories corresponding to sharp extremes, and the other three categories corresponding to intermediate levels. We have no reason for believing that the five categories correspond to five equidistant scaled values—indeed the forms of the distributions of ratings lead us to infer otherwise. However, they have the merit of being fairly objective in the sense that their meaning, once defined, was interpreted in very nearly the same way by the different field visitors who made the ratings. In a set of 114 ratings (38 each on achievement, social adjustment, and environment) made independently by two field assistants, 52 per cent agreed perfectly, 44 per cent differed by only one category, and 4 per cent differed by two categories. In no case did the ratings differ by more than two categories, and in no case did a field visitor rate a child in one of the two highest categories while another field visitor rated him in one of the two lowest.

The following standards were adopted for the purpose of making the ratings:

ACHIEVEMENT

Top category. The child shows outstanding achievement in some field, for example, science, music, literature, scholarship, dramatics. The achievement is of an order that would justify any impartial judge in predicting a career of distinction.

Bottom category. Viewed in terms of the standards of gifted children the child is a failure, or at least his accomplishments are of a mediocre order and characteristic of ability far below his own.

SOCIAL ADJUSTMENT

Top category. The child has many desirable friends and is a leader among them. He is successful in getting co-operation, is normal in his attitude toward those of the same and opposite sex, is fair in his dealings with people, and abides by the laws or requirements of his community—home, school, or civic.

Bottom category. The child is practically friendless or at least his friends are of an undesirable sort. He may have anti-social tendencies and run afoul of the law, or he may have such serious personality difficulties that he requires treatment from a psychiatric clinic.

ENVIRONMENTAL CONDITIONS

Top category. The environment provides every incentive for leading a wholesome and productive life, and for attaining and profiting from a higher education. A spirit of companionship exists between the parents and children. The financial conditions are adequate to finance the children through college. The cultural atmosphere and ideals of the home are such as to encourage high standards of attainment and character.

Bottom category. The environment imposes real obstacles in the child's path. The financial status may be so restricted that the child is not even free to earn his own way through college but must contribute to the family support. The attitude of the family may be antagonistic toward education so that any desire the child may have to go to college is discouraged. The atmosphere of the home may contain so much bickering or mutual hostility between family members, or laxity of moral standards, that a normal and well-ordered life is impossible for any member of the household.

The outcome of the field visitors' ratings for 301 boys and 245 girls of the Regular group is reported in Table 78. The reader is reminded that the means of the ratings, computed as they are by assigning numerical values of 1, 2, 3, 4, and 5, respectively, to the ratings falling in the five categories, are subject to some error because the boundaries of the categories are not spaced so as to divide off strictly equal intervals. It should also be emphasized that the bases for the different categorical ratings were established without regard to any hypothetical norms for unselected populations. Hence there are no grounds for assuming that the mean ratings reported in Table 78, though differing numerically very little from one another, really represent equal amounts of the three factors to which they correspond. Indeed we have reason for assigning quite different interpretations to the mean ratings and to the corresponding categorical ratings of the three factors. A rating of 3, for example, doubtless indicates a capacity for social adjustment about equal to that of the average individual of an unselected population, for evidence amassed elsewhere (see parents' and teachers' ratings on social traits in this chapter, and other data in chapter ix) suggests the conclusion that gifted children do not differ so very greatly from other children in their social traits. A rating of 3 on achievement, however, indicates attainments that are considerably superior to those of unselected children; a rating of 4 or even 5 probably corresponds fairly closely to the average achievement in a random population. Similarly there seems reason to believe that the categories of environmental conditions are scaled in such a way that a rating of 3 represents a home environment rather superior to that of the average child.

TABLE 78

FIELD VISITORS' RATINGS ON ACHIEVEMENT, SOCIAL ADJUSTMENT, AND ENVIRONMENTAL CONDITIONS

Categorical Rating	GIFTED BOYS (N = 301)			GIFTED GIRLS (N = 245)		
	Achievement %	Social Adjustment %	Environment %	Achievement %	Social Adjustment %	Environment %
1	1.7	3.7	14.1	2.4	4.6	9.5
2	20.9	18.1	23.5	17.2	20.4	20.6
3	68.4	59.5	46.3	72.7	58.3	46.1
4	7.3	12.7	13.4	6.5	12.1	17.7
5	1.7	6.0	2.7	1.2	4.6	6.2
Mean ...	2.8	3.0	2.7	2.9	2.9	2.9

It is interesting that nearly as many girls as boys are rated in the top two categories of achievement, notwithstanding the fact that the girls' mean intelligence level was not so high on the follow-up tests as that of the boys. There are differences between the two sexes, however, that fail to show up in the ratings. The girls qualify for high ratings relatively more often than the boys on the basis of high scholarship, while the boys qualify more often than the girls on the basis of achievement along the line of special interests or hobbies.

The differences between the environmental ratings of the boys and girls provide an interesting commentary on the fact that parents are more likely to encourage the educational and vocational ambitions of their sons than of their daughters. There may also be a subjective factor that accounts in part for the differences. The field visitors may have tended to give heavier weight to financial and other obstacles in the case of the girls than in the case of the boys, even when objective standards might have failed to show up any distinctions.

ILLUSTRATIVE RATINGS

Achievement rating 1. Rudolf,[1] *born in 1909, IQ 141 at age 12-7, T.G.T. point score 201 at age 18-7.* According to competent critics, Rudolf is a most promising young artist. His facility in drawing and his general interest in art were recognized very early. However, it was not until he reached the high school that he gave any adequate expression to his capacity in this direction. Here he designed complete sets for several plays and showed a remarkable ability for sketching off quickly a series of sets which took account of all the detailed effects that he desired to produce. Several outside dramatic groups demanded his attention also, and he produced for them, according to their reports, very commendable work. He quickly mastered the mechanical aspects of stagecraft and worked out the most minute details with mathematical preciseness. Much of his work is still held in the high school for demonstration purposes, and several pieces have been exhibited locally.

In addition to his theatrical designing, Rudolf has done distinguished pen-and-ink work that has been published in his high-school yearbook. He has also assisted a well-known artist in painting murals for a public building.

Achievement rating 1. Muriel, born in 1909, IQ 140 at age 12-6. Muriel was reared in the atmosphere of the theater. Both parents as well as herself were actively engaged in dramatics during her early childhood. She starred on the New York stage at the age of seven. At eleven years she played Hedwig in Ibsen's *Wild Duck.* Throughout her school career she participated in the school productions, but her gifts demanded a wider field, and she withdrew at the completion of the tenth grade to accept a large salary in moving pictures. She played with stars of international fame and then became a star in her own right. She has recently been given first place in an annual contest of moving-picture stars.

The 1928 tests given to Muriel at the age of 18-10 find her close to the median of the eighteen-year-old gifted girls on the Terman Group Test. Her point score is 194, the median of the gifted being 198. On the Iowa High School Content Examination her score is slightly above the median of ran-

[1] Names throughout the volume are fictitious.

dom high-school seniors, an excellent showing when we consider that she left high school at the end of her second year. Her score is relatively much the highest on Part I (English), in which she ranks at the 95th percentile of high-school seniors.

Achievement rating 2. John, born in 1906, IQ 156 at age 11-4, Thorndike point score 99 at time of college entrance. John is holding his own despite seemingly severe obstacles. Throughout grade school and high school he enjoyed every guaranty of social security and extended education. His father was a man of considerable wealth and the family held a prominent position in the social life of their community. Quite unexpectedly the father's wealth was depleted and his health was broken. The burden of complete self-support as well as some responsibility toward his mother and sisters was a challenge that confronted him as a college freshman.

John has been several times on the verge of withdrawing from school, but the good fortune of many jobs and excellent health has happily allowed him to continue. At college, where he has maintained a B + scholastic average, he waits on table for his meals, works for his room at the home of a professor, gives four hours a week as gardener for an elderly lady, receives a small remuneration as circulation manager for his college paper, and works eight hours a day each weekend at a gasoline station.

In high school John was editor of his class annual, and he had hoped to attain to a top position on his college paper. He had risen from cub reporter to copy editor and was in line for editor, but the burden of a heavy outside load forced him to withdraw his candidacy.

Achievement rating 2. Roderick, born in 1912, IQ 156 at age 9-9, T.G.T. point score 189 at age 16-3. At the time of our first contact with the family of Roderick, mention was made of his ability in drawing. By the age of five he could draw recognizable pictures of animals, houses, and trees. His interest in drawing persisted throughout his childhood and expanded to include architecture as well.

In the 1927–28 follow-up it was learned that by the time Roderick had reached his junior high-school year he had become the drama teacher's "right-hand man" and was even prone to neglect his other work for stagecraft, although he maintained a good scholastic record. At high school he had put in 393 extra hours upon stagecraft during a previous semester. According to his mother he went early to school and came home late; ten or eleven P.M. and even later was not unusual.

Roderick recently made free-hand sketches of lighting fixtures which were later photographed for use in a catalogue. He loves to sketch, and if not reading he is sure to be found with a pencil in his hand.

Achievement rating 2. Eleanor, born in 1910, IQ 148 at age 12-2, T.G.T. point score 217 at age 18-1. Eleanor has exhibited a high degree of versatility in her school interests as well as in leadership ability. She is a sophomore in college with a scholarship average of B +. She graduated from high school at sixteen as one of the four highest in a class of 445. She was awarded life membership in the California Scholarship Federation and was also elected to a state honor society in recognition of her activity interests and leadership. She had been a member of the high-school debating team and had placed in the district oratorical contest.

In college Eleanor has been an active officer of the Y.W.C.A. and director of its building fund campaign. Since her high-school days she has been interested in mathematics, and has chosen astronomy for her major subject in college. Curiously enough Eleanor has brought the abstruse subject of astronomy into practical play in her immediate life. Reverses in her father's financial circumstances have forced her to assist herself through college. The summer following her freshman year she was the official leader of star-gazing parties in a camp for girls. She has been offered the same position for her next vacation period.

During the school year Eleanor has been able to secure students to coach in mathematics. Her marked scholastic success coupled with her ability to meet practical situations in life should bring her success in her chosen field of work as a research astronomer.

Achievement rating 2; environmental rating 4. Marvin, born in 1910, IQ 139 at age eleven, T.G.T. point score 205 at age 17. Marvin is the younger of two boys and comes from a family who for the most part have enjoyed the privileges of higher education. Because of parental marital difficulties culminating in divorce he has been deprived of the usual cultural advantages one would expect to find in a home where the parents have had extended schooling. The only books in the house are his own, purchased since he has been old enough to earn, and cherished as treasures. They are all carefully stacked on a table and hidden behind a screen. The reason for such secrecy is hard to divine, unless the delights of ownership are more keenly sensed than if the books were offered to the public gaze. A glimpse of Marvin's books is the only relief one gets from the extreme bareness of the small box-like living room, with its worn, ingrain carpet, its two oak chairs, and sleeping couch.

Reading has been declared to be an obsession with Marvin. He no sooner crosses the threshold of the home than a book is in his hands, and in an instant he is buried deep in it, not even completely releasing it at meal time, but keeping it perched alongside him.

From such propensities one might conceive of Marvin as filling the rôle of proverbial bookworm. Actually, he would do it poorly, for he is a genial, friendly boy who loves to discuss the things he reads, and reads with such intensity only because he has very limited time in which to read. Since the age of ten (he is now eighteen) he has run the gamut of part-time jobs: newsboy, errand boy, soda fountain clerk, and theater usher. The last-named is his present position, which he has held for a year in one of the best legitimate playhouses in the city. This means working every night and Saturday and Sunday afternoons.

A course in printing in which he was much complimented for the alacrity he displayed, combined with the encouragement he received from his English teacher, tended to steer his interests toward journalism. Then came an appointment to the editorship of the junior high-school magazine. He became a reporter on his high-school paper, and from that rose to be editor of various departments and finally editor-in-chief. According to an experienced instructor in a large city school, Marvin enjoys the rare capacity among high-school students of being able to write an editorial involving sustained reasoning. Positions of honor have come to him from the student body more because of his mild, genial personality and his fairness, than from any aggressiveness on his part. The lack of aggressiveness is held by many who know him to be a lack which will seriously obstruct his progress in professional journalism. However, he is forging ahead, with study at a large eastern university as his objective when he completes his college work in the West.

Achievement rating 5. Marian, born in 1908, T.G.T. point score 178 at age 13-3. Marian graduated from high school at age 17-9. She got through "by the skin of her teeth," switched her course several times, and was the occasion for frequent visits on the part of her mother to the school because of her indifference and defiance.

Her father had hoped that she would fill a responsible office position, at least, and had secured one for her through a friend. However, she refused it and secured a position as a domestic, quite independently of her family. She held this work for four months, at which time she announced that she planned to marry. The desire for a home of her own had been one of a year's standing as far as her parents know. She had read every magazine on house planning and house furnishing that she could secure. The occasion for this intense desire for a home may be found in the relationship that existed between her father and herself. There was constant quarreling and bickering. He regarded her as lazy and careless and a poor student. There was never any overt misconduct, but she was independent, irritable, and on the defensive. The father's intense disapproval was climaxed in his adamant refusal to make her marriage a festive occasion.

Social adjustment rating 1. Mabel, born in 1910, IQ (corrected) 147 at age 11-7, Thorndike score 79 at age 16. Mabel age seventeen, is a comfort to her parents, a leader among girls, and extremely popular with young people of both sexes. She is a member of a college sorority of high standing, but does not allow her membership to curtail the range of her friendships and intimacies, for we are told that she has many different groups of friends and is happy in any group. She leads a delightful social life, attends many parties, entertains at her own home, and fits in well with grown people and young people alike. She has many friends among boys and men and has received proposals of marriage from men well able to assume the responsibilities of a home and family, but she is determined to go through college without the distraction of a serious affair.

Mabel's winning personality, versatility, and athletic prowess have brought her numerous positions of leadership. Girl Scouting has been one of her enthusiasms; she has served as an officer of her troop and more recently as counsellor at a summer camp for Girl Scouts. Upon entering college she soon became one of the most prominent freshman students. She was elected president of freshmen women students, captain of her class basketball team, and member of the governing board of the women's athletic association. She has also been a reporter on the college newspaper, and an active member of the Y.W.C.A., devoting an afternoon each week to welfare work with young children

Despite Mabel's many activities she has maintained a B scholarship average at college. The key to her personality appears to be intellectual enthusiasm, physical energy, and friendliness. In appearance she is the ideal type of wholesome outdoor girl, and in manner she is simple, sincere, and altogether likable.

Social adjustment rating 5. Ernest, born in 1912, IQ 154 at age 10, T.G.T. point score 204 at age 15. The matter of social adjustment is still a very difficult one for Ernest. When first known to us, at the age of ten, he was reported by several sources to be solitary. Our Plays and Games questionnaire corroborated these reports; he played only two games that involved more than one person, and preferred three table games that were usually played with adults. Most of his after-school hours were given to reading, with an occasional hike or game with some adult member of the household. On the school playground he stood on the outside of the circle. Forced association usually elicited from him scathing criticism of others with violent exhibitions of rage if his taunts were returned.

His parents have sent him to a summer camp, to a boarding school, and to a psychological clinic in an attempt to bring about happier social relationships. The early patterns seem, however, to persist. He is reported by home and school to be without a single friend, and still subject to temper outbursts. He has to be ordered by the highest person in authority at the school to participate in recreation, for he wants to stay in his room and read. When he plays golf and fails to send his ball in the desired direction he throws down his clubs and claws the air.

Multiple causation subtly interwoven is suggested by a review of his history. Ernest was the first child and only boy. A sister almost equally well endowed intellectually is three years younger. As a small child Ernest was considered delicate, although he suffered no organic disability; and in subsequent years he was found underweight, poor in musculature, and subject to colds.

He entered school at seven years, by which time he had acquired an outstanding fund of general information that made and continued to make in later years the ordinary procedures of the classroom dull and wearisome. His school attendance was irregular; illness, real and possibly often feigned, brought the joy of solitude and reading. By the age of ten he had read every edition of the *Iliad* and the *Odyssey* in the English language contained in the San Francisco Public Library. He had made collections of minerals, insects, and flowers.

Acceleration only partially relieved his situation, for he found himself completely outclassed on a physical basis. At no time do we find satisfactory participation in the games and sports of his peers. Boastfulness, irritability, and seclusiveness have marked his social relationships, despite all that has been done to encourage the development of normal attitudes.

Social adjustment rating 5. Ivan, born in 1910, IQ 157 at age 11-5, T.G.T. point score 193 at age 17-6. It is not because Ivan is completely devoid of friends that we might consider him in the lowest group of our gifted children from the standpoint of social adjustment, but more because he holds rigidly to outworn conceptions of social intercourse and has few assets that would cause one to predict distinction in any occupation that involves working with other people. He is strongly opposed to dancing and held out in his refusal to buy tickets for high-school dances, although the organization sponsoring the parties is one in which he is anxious to gain recognition. He selected the R.O.T.C. instead of regular gymnasium work because he considered boys' gymnasium outfits immodest. He declares he will never marry, as his mother would then have to take a second place. To the mother's knowledge he has never gone to a single social affair without her, even in his senior year at high school.

His leisure is spent on special projects of his own; he has gone far in the study of Chinese, has read extensively in the field of art, and has developed considerable technique in clay modeling. With the offer of the art editorship for his class annual came a slight change in his attitude toward school. He was less grumpy, although still holding to the idea that there was a great deal of favoritism in all the departments and that he should have been made a captain in the R.O.T.C. rather than a second lieutenant. He has maintained an average scholarship record but has not distinguished himself in the way that one might expect of so brilliant a boy. He plans to become a foreign missionary.

Ivan's score on the Masculinity-Femininity Test administered during the follow-up has special interest in the light of his unusual personality bias. His score, + 24, places him within the least masculine 15 or 20 per cent of random high-school boys. The warping of his personality seems to have resulted chiefly from excessive mothering.

Environmental rating 1. The N. family. There are six children in the N. family, two of whom belong to the gifted group. The other four all test above average.

Both parents are college graduates and take the warmest interest in providing every opportunity for their children. The home is a spacious frame dwelling set far back on beautifully landscaped grounds. The size of its living room is that of a formal salon, but its furnishings radiate an air of informality. The home is a center for the children's social life. The two older girls, now seniors in high school, as well as the two older boys, gather their particular friends at least once every two weeks for a general jollification. Even the two younger children have their share in the social life of the family. They are always included in the early evening parties and are never left out of the luncheons and dinners.

In the summer season the entire family moves to the beach, where their rambling home is open to the children's school friends. All the children are expert swimmers and Dickson, one of our subjects, has won many cups in sailing. Winter weekends are spent in the mountains, skating and skiing.

These unusual opportunities have in no way spoiled the natural grace and genuineness of the children. Their father has generously provided the bigger items, but each one has his share in building and making the home attractive and comfortable. The mother has always taken an active part in their school life. She continues as an officer in the Parent-Teacher Association and has directed many programs for the general improvement of facilities in the grade school through which all of her children have passed. The history of the family seems to demonstrate happy team work, not only within their immediate circle but beyond in whatever community the children move.

Environmental rating 1. Dalton, born in 1904, Army Alpha point score 185 at age 16-0, Thorndike point score 110 at age 18-4; Fitzhugh, born in 1906, IQ 172 at age 10-5 and 160 at age 11-8, Thorndike point score 113 at age 18-0. The commodious, old-fashioned home of these brothers is the center for frequent informal gatherings of young people. Both boys are attending college not far away and take delight in coming home for weekends and bringing their friends. The mother often acts as a tolerant and companionable chaperon for beach house parties arranged by her sons and their boy and girl friends. She takes the warmest interest in their affairs. She, as well as the father, attended college; but after a year and a half she left college to marry.

The father, a physician, has been a "perfect father" according to the mother. He and the boys often play golf together, and when they were younger he often took them with him when making professional calls.

The attitude of both parents toward the boys has been one to encourage their natural inclinations, and the financial condition of the family has been adequate to put the boys through college comfortably. Both are making brilliant scholastic records.

Environmental rating 1. Mollie, born in 1912, IQ 144 at age 7-8. Thorndike point score 89 at age 15. An unusually happy relationship exists between the members of Mollie's family. Both parents are university people, the father having taken an M.A. degree, and the mother having completed three years of college. The plans of the family include college as a matter of course for all four children. The three oldest—Mollie and her two brothers, who are two and three years older than she—are about to enter college together as freshmen.

Though living on a large ranch in the country, the children have had most of the advantages of city education. For a number of years the mother has run a sort of bus line for her brood of four, driving them five miles to city public schools in the morning and calling for them in the afternoon.

The family home itself, situated in an orchard, is a simple but ample house. A lawn with shade trees and carefully tended flowers beautifies the exterior. The furnishings inside are comfortable, and many of the recent books are to be found on a bookshelf in the living room.

In the summer, and in their spare time during the year, the older children, including Mollie, who is now a sturdy and highly vitalized girl of sixteen, help their father in the orchard. The father's hobby is experimental horticulture, and he has taught Mollie to do successful budding and grafting, an activity in which she takes much pride and delight.

The dominating atmosphere of this home is one of simplicity, good spirits, and culture.

Environment rating 5. Leland, born in 1914, IQ 147 at age 7-6, T.G.T. point score 188 at age 13-5. At age thirteen Leland is making a consistently high scholarship record in the ninth grade, and is doing especially distinguished work in science. His mother doubts very much whether he will have the privilege of going beyond high school as the financial conditions of the home are heavily strained and the father's attitude is unsympathetic. An older brother was forced to withdraw in his senior year, and the mother has little hope that the father will allow Leland to go beyond high school.

The father is almost constantly under the influence of alcohol and is harsh and critical. The mother is devoted to the boy and tries to encourage him in his school work. He has practically no money for books or extras. For the past two years he has risen early and worked as janitor in a large neighborhood store before going to school, but even this pittance has to be turned over to the father to administer. The lack of means is fully realized from a short stay in the home, which is a small bungalow in a squalid section of the city. The plaster hangs loose in great chunks, the rooms are sparsely furnished with the cheapest grade of furnishings, and despite the apparent orderliness of things, dreary grimness permeates the whole atmosphere.

The school has only favorable comments to make regarding Leland and tells us that he is always happy and intensely interested in his work.

Environmental rating 5. Dollie, born in 1910, IQ 144 at age 11-9. Dollie's physical environment is all that one might wish for in a family of moderate circumstances. She lives with her father, stepmother, and stepsister in a modern five-room flat of which her father is the owner. However, the two parents are bitterly opposed to any further schooling for Dollie and look askance on any person who they think might open the subject of college with her. They fear that by some chance her earlier desire to go on to school will be rekindled.

Dollie had been an honor pupil through high school, had taken first place in a dramatic reading contest in her city, and had frequently expressed her desire for a college education. Instead the father forced her to accept a small clerical position in a downtown business office. He pompously contends that she is not strong enough to continue in school, although he is unable to support this contention with any history of physical illness.

Dollie has no chums, and spends her time after work at home reading. "She has to be dragged to a movie with us and never evinces any interest in family excursions." The barrenness of her social opportunities makes no impression upon her boorish father's imagination.

Environmental rating 5. Delbert, born in 1910, IQ 146 at age 11, T.G.T. point score 189 at age 18. It was necessary for Delbert to leave school at the end of the tenth grade and find a job because his father was out of work and his help was badly needed. He is working as an office boy at $55 a month.

When located in the 1921–22 search for gifted subjects the family were living in abject poverty. Their home was a tiny cottage in the back yard of a three-family house in a poor neighborhood. They had come to this country three years previously from Scotland, and apparently had been about as badly off in their former home. The father was having great difficulty in finding work. He was possibly handicapped in seeking a job by his diminutive size, as he is only four and a half feet tall. The case was called to the attention of the associated charities, and the family was given assistance.

Few members of the gifted group have sprung from such plain ancestry as Delbert. The schooling of both parents is very limited. The predominating occupations of their for-bears have been of the semi-skilled labor type. The father is a machinist by trade, and the mother before her marriage was a mill worker. It is surprising that despite so unpromis-ing a family background, four of the five children test above average on the Stanford-Binet. Delbert, when first tested in 1921 at age 11-8, had an IQ of 146. His fourteen-year-old brother had an IQ of 120, and his seven-year-old sister an IQ of 114. Two young brothers tested at ages eight and six dur-ing the 1927-28 follow-up had IQ's of 85 and 112, respec-tively. At age eighteen Delbert made a Terman Group Test point score of 189. While this is 15 points below the median for the eighteen-year-old boys of the gifted group who were tested during the follow-up, it easily places him within the top 10 per cent of unselected high-school seniors.

Renewing contact with the family during the course of the follow-up, we have found them still struggling with pov-erty. They live in a shabby frame house in a slightly better neighborhood than before. A few flowers struggle in the door-yard amid considerable litter. The interior is dis-orderly and not over clean. Although the family are buying the house and feel that their circumstances have improved, they still receive occasional aid from a social agency. They manage to eke out a living by the combined efforts of the father, the mother, and the two older boys. When fortune is kind the father earns $30 a week as a mechanic; but he is frequently out of work. The mother is employed in a small cafeteria. The oldest boy works for a newspaper as a copy clerk, and Delbert, as was earlier stated, is an office boy.

Summary

1. Ratings were obtained from teachers and parents on twelve traits selected at the time of the follow-up from a group of twenty-five traits used in the original investigation.

2. Teachers' ratings of the gifted group in 1927-28 are lower by a small fraction of a control S.D. than they were in 1921-22 on nearly all the traits, but they still average above the mean ratings of the control group of 1921-22 in all but three traits. The three traits in question are social traits upon which the mean ratings in 1921-22, as in 1927-28, dif-fered but little from those of the control group.

3. There are no traits in which teachers have given a higher mean rating in 1927–28 than in 1921–22, but there are several in which parents have done so, namely, "freedom from vanity," "conscientiousness," and, to a very slight extent, "common sense."

4. The changes between 1921–22 and 1927–28 in the rank orders of the mean ratings of teachers and of parents are slight. As in 1921–22, teachers and parents now tend to rate the gifted boys and girls relatively highest on the intellectual traits, such as "intelligence," "desire to know," and "common sense," and relatively lowest on the social traits, such as "fondness for groups," "popularity," and "leadership." Teachers' ratings on the latter three traits average close in value to the 1921–22 control means for the same traits.

5. There is close agreement between parents and teachers in the rank order of mean ratings upon the twelve traits, especially in the case of boys.

6. The rank order of the mean ratings of boys agrees closely with that of the mean ratings of girls, both in 1921–22 and in 1927–28

7. By means of personal interviews with parents and teachers the field assistants collected a body of data that were used for making fivefold ratings upon the achievement, social adjustment, and environmental conditions of the individual gifted subjects.

8. Distributions of these ratings are reported, and case studies are appended to illustrate ratings of different levels in the three factors considered.

CHAPTER XI

HEALTH HISTORY AND VITAL STATISTICS

There are few questions that are raised more universally when gifted children are discussed than that concerning their health and physique. There is no estimating the effect that has been produced upon the popular mind by the abused and sickly gifted children that teem in the pages of Dickens; at any rate the belief has been persistent and widespread that through some devious mechanism of compensation the child who receives a generous endowment of mental capacity is stinted by nature in other respects, particularly in health and physical vigor.

The data assembled in Volume I presented so much evidence in contradiction of the view to which we have just referred that it was not considered necessary during the follow-up to go to the large expense of duplicating the medical examinations and anthropometric measurements that were included as part of the original schedule. It was shown in 1921–22 that in so far as the typical gifted child departs at all from the norm on physical traits he does so in the direction of superiority. While the fact seems well established that his deviation from the average on these traits is very small indeed in comparison with his deviation on intellectual and volitional traits, the traditional view certainly finds no support in our data. The typical gifted child was found to suffer from fewer headaches, to exhibit fewer symptoms of "general weakness" or of "nervousness," to mature earlier, to display more physical energy, and to be better nourished, taller, and heavier than the average child. The data on health secured during the follow-up investigation, although less reliable than the data of medical examinations, fully confirm the 1921–22 results.

FOLLOW-UP REPORTS

Several questions contained in the follow-up Home Blank and School Blank were designed to elicit data regarding the present health status of the members of the gifted group.

Some of the data can be compared directly with those se-cured in the original investigation. The responses are here summarized for the members of the Regular group.

"General health since 1922 has been good, fair, poor. (Under-line.)" (Home Blank: I, 1. Information Blank: 11.) "General health is good, fair, poor. (Underline.)" (School Blank: I, 1.) [Question answered on 98 per cent of the Home Blanks or Information Blanks of boys and of girls; upon 96 per cent of the School Blanks of boys and upon 94 per cent of the School Blanks of girls.]

TABLE 79

GENERAL HEALTH OF MEMBERS OF REGULAR GROUP

Status of Health	HOME BLANK OR INFORMATION BLANK		SCHOOL BLANK	
	Boys %	Girls %	Boys %	Girls %
Good	84	90	82	77
Fair	15	9	16	18
Poor	1	1	2	5

While the data of Table 79 cannot be compared directly with any obtained in 1921–22, they do indicate that very few members of the gifted group are suffering from evident ill health. It is perhaps surprising that the school reports are on the whole less favorable than the home reports in the case of girls. It is possible, however, that occasional irregu-larities of school attendance on the part of girls have been interpreted by teachers as signifying health that is only fair or even poor, whereas the parents may feel justified in reporting good health if the school absences are coincident with the menstrual periods and if the health at all other times is good.

The parents were also asked in the follow-up Home Blank to report any illnesses, accidents, or operations that the child had had since 1922. As similar data were asked for in 1921–22 and summarized in Volume I, and as a state-ment of the number of children who have had illnesses, accidents, or operations during an isolated period of six years has little significance unless accompanied by data for a control group, we have not included in this report any treatment of the data in question. The data were called for on the Home Blank only so that we might have an unbroken record regarding health history on file for each member of the gifted group.

"Symptoms of general weakness, if any...." (School Blank:
I, 2.)

While responses to the question just discussed cannot be
directly compared with data obtained in 1921–22, those to
the present question are comparable to data secured both
for the gifted group and for a control group at the time of
the original study. The School Blanks report symptoms of
general weakness in the following proportions of cases:

	Gifted Group		Control Group	
	Boys %	Girls %	Boys %	Girls %
1927–28	15	18	..	..
1921–22	13	10	18	14

The number of girls showing such symptoms is nearly
twice as large in 1927–28 as in 1921–22. The fact that the
great majority of girls in the Regular group have matured
since the original survey is probably significant in this connection.

"Has colds very frequently, frequently, occasionally, only rarely.
(Underline.)" (Home Blank: I, 5.) [Question answered on 97 per
cent of the blanks received.]

This question is closely allied in interest to the previous
one, for frequent colds are among the most widely recognized symptoms of run-down health or "general weakness."
The responses for 1927–28 are summarized with comparative
figures for 1921–22 in Table 80.

TABLE 80

FREQUENCY OF COLDS

	FREQUENTLY OR VERY FREQUENTLY		OCCASIONALLY		RARELY	
	Boys %	Girls %	Boys %	Girls %	Boys %	Girls %
Gifted, home reports, 1927–28	16	9	46	37	38	55
Gifted, home reports, 1921–22	16	7	47	44	37	49
Gifted, school reports, 1921–22	13	6	30	19	57	75
Control, school reports, 1921–22	9	7	35	34	56	59

There is outstanding agreement between the figures for
the home reports in 1927–28 and in 1921–22. Although the
home reports appear to be less favorable at both times than
the school data for a control group, they are also less favorable than the school data for the gifted group. The latter,
moreover, are more favorable than the school data for a
control group in the case of girls, and differ little from the
school control data in the case of boys. From these inter-
relationships we conclude (1) that the members of the gifted
group are neither more nor less susceptible to colds than
they were in 1921–22; and (2) that the gifted girls are afflicted with colds with less than average frequency.

"Organic diseases (as of heart, kidneys, lungs, etc.) ...." (Home
Blank: I, 14; School Blank: I, 6.)

A positive report is given on the Home Blank in the case
of 4 per cent of the gifted boys and 5 per cent of the gifted
girls for whom blanks were received, and upon the School
Blank in the case of 2 per cent of the gifted boys and 6 per
cent of the gifted girls for whom blanks were received. The
organic troubles reported are as follows:

	Home		School	
	Boys	Girls	Boys	Girls
Heart	6	10	2	6
Lungs	2	..	1	1
Kidneys	..	1	1	1
Sinus, or catarrh......	2	..	..	1
Asthma	1	..	1	1

"Has suffered from headaches? .... At what age? .... How
often? ...." (Home blank: I, 7.)

Data from the 1921–22 blanks are available for comparison. "Frequent" headaches are reported as follows:

	Home Blank		School Blank	
	Boys %	Girls %	Boys %	Girls %
Gifted, 1927–28	4	1	..	..
Gifted, 1921–22	2	2	2	3
Control, 1921–22	..	..	4	5

The changes in the gifted group since 1921–22 are slight
and are scarcely significant in the light of their standard

errors, which are equal to approximately 1 per cent. The figures for the gifted group both in 1921–22 and in 1927–28 indicate a slight advantage on the whole over the control group.

"Signs of special nervousness?.... How shown?...." (Home Blank: I, 10; School Blank: I, 5.)

We are including data from the 1921–22 blanks for comparative purposes. The blanks contain positive reports as follows:

	Home Blank		School Blank	
	Boys %	Girls %	Boys %	Girls %
Gifted, 1927–28	13	18	11	22
Gifted, 1921–22	25	15	16	10
Control, 1921–22	..	..	16	16

It is noteworthy that in the figures from home and school alike, fewer gifted boys but more gifted girls are now reported as showing signs of nervousness than were reported in 1921–22. It is quite possible that these changes are connected with adolescence, and that the control group would have shown similar tendencies if we could have secured follow-up data for them.

"Has shown a marked tendency to worry?.... Over what?...." (Home Blank: I, 11.) [Question answered on 89 per cent of blanks received.]

Since the Home and School Blanks of 1921–22 also contained this question, we are able to include comparative data with the summary of positive responses on the follow-up blanks.

	Home Blank		School Blank	
	Boys %	Girls %	Boys %	Girls %
Gifted, 1927–28	8	10	..	..
Gifted, 1921–22	9	10	9	12
Control, 1921–22	..	..	8	10

The excellent agreement between the proportions indicated on the Home Blanks of 1921–22 and 1927–28, coupled with the close agreement between the home and school reports for the gifted in 1921–22 and between the school reports for the gifted and control in 1921–22, leads us to the conclusion that there is still little difference between the gifted and the unselected children with respect to tendency to worry.

"Has had serious digestive trouble recently?.... At what age? .... How serious?...." (Home Blank: I, 9.) [Question answered on 96 per cent of the blanks received.]

We have summarized the responses only to the first part of the question, those to the second and third parts being significant chiefly for the clinical records of the individual children.

"Serious" digestive trouble is reported for four gifted boys and three gifted girls, or approximately 1.5 per cent of both boys and girls.

"Is vision (without glasses) normal, somewhat defective, very poor? (Underline.) .... Nature of defect, if any .... Wears glasses? ...." (School Blank: I, 3.) [Question answered on 87 per cent of the blanks received.]

"Wears glasses?.... When first worn?.... Serious eye trouble? ...." (Home Blank: I, 6.) [Question answered on 92 per cent of the blanks received.]

The percentages of gifted children reported on the 1927–28 School Blank as having subnormal vision, i.e., vision that is "somewhat defective" or "very poor," may be compared with corresponding percentages reported for the gifted and control groups in 1921–22. The percentages reported as wearing glasses may also be compared. The data are as follows:

| | Gifted, 1927–28 | | Gifted, 1921–22 | | Control, 1921–22 | |
	Boys %	Girls %	Boys %	Girls %	Boys %	Girls %
Subnormal vision	24	22	20	21	17	15
Wearing glasses	25	20	11	10	4	5

The parents report 27 per cent of the boys and 26 per cent of the girls as wearing glasses. The slight disparity between the parents' and teachers' reports may be due to the fact that the teachers' reports do not cover the members of the group who are attending college. The figures indicate that only a slightly greater number of gifted children now have subnormal vision than did have in 1921–22, although more than twice as many are wearing glasses now as previously wore them. This probably means that as the subjects advance to higher school grades in which more work is required the need for glasses to correct minor eye defects is increasingly felt. That so many more of the gifted than of the control group are wearing glasses is probably in large part a reflection of the superior parental intelligence and medical care of the gifted group. In this connection, too, it should be borne in mind that the control group is comparable in age with the gifted group of 1921–22, but not with that of 1927–28.

"Serious" eye trouble is reported on the Home Blanks for three boys and three girls, or approximately 1.5 per cent of both boys and girls. The troubles are described as:

	Boys	Girls
Extreme myopia	2	1
Hypermetropia and imperfect vision. ..		1
Congenital cataract in one eye.......	1	..
Strabismus		1

"Is hearing excellent, good, fair, poor? .... (Underline.)" (Home Blank: I, 8.) [Question answered on 97 per cent of the blanks received.]

"Is hearing normal, somewhat defective, very poor? (Underline.)" (School Blank: I, 4.) [Question answered on 92 per cent of the blanks received.]

The School Blanks report only one boy and two girls with subnormal hearing (i.e., "somewhat defective" or "very poor" hearing). The Home Blanks report four or 1.5 per cent of the boys and six or 2.8 per cent of the girls with hearing that is "fair," and none with hearing that is "poor." The figures from the Home Blanks are doubtless the more reliable, since a pupil could often have slightly defective hearing without his teacher's being aware of the fact.

It is worthy of note that the proportion of gifted subjects reported by home and school as having defective hearing is actually less now than it was in 1921–22, the figures at the earlier date for the sexes combined being 3.6 per cent for the home reports, and 2.3 per cent for the school reports. The latter figure may be compared in turn with the percentage, 5.9, of control children reported with defective hearing by the teachers in 1921–22.

"Usual hour of going to sleep? .... Of waking? .... Is sleep sound? ...." (Home Blank: I, 12.) [Question answered on 93 per cent of the blanks received.]

From the responses to this question the number of hours of sleep daily has been computed for each child. Means and standard deviations have been calculated for each age-group and compared in Table 81 with similar figures secured in 1921–22, and with norms found by Terman and Hocking for 2,682 unselected children.[1]

TABLE 81
HOURS OF SLEEP OF GIFTED AND UNSELECTED CHILDREN

Age	GIFTED, 1927–28 Mean	S.D. (Min.)	GIFTED, 1921–22 Mean	S.D. (Min.)	UNSELECTED CHILDREN Mean
8	11:00	..	10:58	41	10:42
9	10:30	8	10:38	37	10:13
10	11:08	41	10:31	44	9:56
11	10:16	29	10:27	40	10:00
12	9:40	43	10:26	43	9:36
13	9:38	37	10:15	41	9:31
14	9:24	20	.....	..	9:06
15	9:08	25	.....	..	8:54
16	9:00	40	.....	..	8:30
17	8:39	32	.....	..	8:46
18	8:28	37	.....	..	8:46
19	8:30	49	.....	..	....

The gifted children now tend to sleep somewhat less than they did at corresponding ages in 1921–22, but they still sleep more than unselected children do at all ages up to seventeen. It is possible that the decrease of sleeping hours after age sixteen in the gifted group may be explained by sleep and study habits formed by the subjects who are attending college. The irregularity in the gifted group at age ten can be accounted for by statistical unreliability, only seven cases being included at that level.

The answers to the question "Is sleep sound?" are affirmative for 98 per cent of the boys and 95 per cent of the girls. In 1921–22 sleep was so reported by the parents for 99 per cent of all cases.

VITAL STATISTICS

The members of the Regular group are, one might say, still too young to have many "vital statistics." Since the

[1] "The Sleep of School Children, etc.," *Journal of Educational Psychology*, Vol. 4 (1913), pp. 138–147, 199–208, 269–282.

members of the original High School group are on the average more than five years older than the members of the Regular group, the reader will find more of interest in the "vital statistics" section of chapter xiii than in the present chapter, as the former section includes data upon deaths, marriages, and offspring of members of the High School group.

In the Regular group three of the 643 subjects had died by the time the follow-up began (1927), and two more died during the course of the follow-up. Only two members of the group had married, both girls. Neither of the two had any offspring.

Causes of death in the deceased cases were as follows:

Boys	Girls
Measles and after-effects	Infantile paralysis
Diphtheria	Not known by us
Suicide	

SUMMARY

1. As it was not possible to repeat the medical examinations and anthropometric measurements given in connection with the original study, the health data here presented are based upon reports from parents and teacher or school principal. According to reports from home and school, between 77 per cent and 90 per cent of the gifted boys and girls have good general health. Between 1 per cent and 5 per cent have poor health.

2. The School Blanks report 15 per cent of the gifted boys and 18 per cent of the gifted girls as showing symptoms of general weakness.

3. The members of the gifted group appear to be neither more nor less susceptible to colds than they were in 1921–22; gifted boys are afflicted with colds with slightly more than average frequency and gifted girls with less than average frequency.

4. Organic diseases are reported on the Home Blank in the case of 4 per cent of the gifted boys and 5 per cent of the gifted girls for whom blanks were received, and on the School Blank in the case of 2 per cent of the gifted boys and 6 per cent of the gifted girls.

5. With respect to frequency of headaches the gifted

group has a slight advantage, both in 1921–22 and 1927–28, over the control group of 1921–22.

6. Fewer gifted boys but more gifted girls are now reported as showing signs of nervousness than were reported in 1921–22. It seems probable that these changes are connected with adolescence, and that the control group would have shown similar tendencies if follow-up data had been available.

7. The gifted group shows little change with respect to the number showing a "marked tendency to worry," the proportion of boys being 8 per cent and that of girls 10 per cent. There is little difference between the gifted and the control groups in this tendency.

8. "Serious" digestive trouble is reported in the gifted group for approximately 1.5 per cent of both boys and girls.

9. The proportion of gifted children now reported as having subnormal vision is slightly greater than that reported in 1921–22. However, more than twice as many are wearing glasses now as previously wore them.

10. "Serious" eye trouble is reported on the Home Blank for approximately 1.5 per cent of both boys and girls.

11. Subnormal hearing is reported on the School Blank for one boy and two girls. Hearing that is only "fair" is reported on the Home Blank for 1.5 per cent of the boys and 2.8 per cent of the girls. Both home and school reports indicate a smaller proportion with defective hearing now than in 1921–22.

12. The gifted subjects tend to sleep somewhat less daily than they did at corresponding ages in 1921–22, but they still sleep more than unselected children at all ages up to seventeen.

13. Parents report that 98 per cent of the boys and 95 per cent of the girls sleep soundly.

14. Of the original 643 members of the Regular group five died in the seven years between 1921 and 1928. One of these committed suicide.

15. Two members of the Regular group have married, both girls. Neither of the two has any offspring.

CHAPTER XII

FAMILY STATISTICS AND SIBLING TESTS

A complete analysis of certain vital statistics pertaining to the families of the gifted group cannot be made for many years to come. Such matters as parental mortality, divorce, and remarriage, achievements of relatives, etc., cannot be discussed with finality until death has ended the careers of the individuals concerned. However, after a lapse of six years since the original study it will be of interest to bring together family data for comparison with the material summarized in chapter vi of Volume I.

OCCUPATIONS OF FATHERS

In 1922 one of the methods by which the occupational level of the fathers of gifted subjects was compared with the average for a general population of adult males employed the Barr scale of occupational intelligence. This scale has been described in full in Volume I, pages 66 ff. and briefly in chapter viii of the present volume. We decided in 1928 to rate the present occupations of the fathers by means of the Barr scale in order to ascertain whether or not the passage of six years was associated with any significant change in level. The occupations of the fathers of 366 gifted subjects were stated upon the follow-up Home Blanks in terms sufficiently clear to warrant Barr ratings. This number is 86 per cent of the total number of fathers for whom occupations were stated. The 1928 Barr ratings of the 366 fathers have a mean value of 13.3 and standard deviation of 2.5. The mean rating in 1922 was 12.8 and the standard deviation, 2.9. This slightly upward trend might have been expected as the result of the additional years which these men have had to attain positions commensurate with their ability. The mean rating both in 1922 and in 1928 is well over a standard deviation in excess of the mean for adult males of the general population. However the fact is explained, gifted children are only rarely found in the lowest occupational levels.

Occupations of Mothers

As no data were reported in Volume I upon the occupations of the mothers of the gifted subjects, and as fully a fifth of the mothers now have paid employment we are presenting in this section a brief discussion of positions held by the mothers of the Regular group.

Approximately 16 per cent of the mothers are separated from their husbands by death, divorce, or permanent estrangement and have not remarried. (If we should include also the mothers who have remarried the proportion would be larger.) Of these widowed or estranged women 61 per cent have paid employment, while only 14 per cent of the remaining group of mothers have paid employment. The occupations in which the mothers are engaged are listed in Table 82. This table was compiled chiefly from data furnished upon the 1927–28 Home Information Blank. Each mother is entered once for each child of hers belonging to the gifted group, and thus the table really represents the number of gifted subjects whose mothers follow the occupations. Only one mother, for example, is a college president, but she has two children in our gifted group.

It is an interesting fact that 43 per cent of the mothers who are employed belong to the professional category. This proportion is considerably higher than the proportion of fathers of gifted subjects in the professional class, which was 31 per cent at the time of the original survey. The high proportion may perhaps be accounted for by a tendency among the mothers to prefer homemaking to an outside career unless the outside career holds unusual inducements in the way of interest and compensation. This possibility is supported by the fact that over half of the non-widowed mothers who have jobs are in professional fields, as compared with 32 per cent of the employed widowed mothers, more of whom are working by necessity.

Parental Mortality

Upon the follow-up blanks of the Regular group the deaths of thirteen fathers and nine mothers since the time of the original study are reported. These numbers are, respectively, 2.8 per cent and 1.9 per cent of the total number, 462, of families represented. If we add these percentages to the 8.4 per cent of fathers and to the 2.6 per cent of mothers known to be deceased in 1921–22 we find that 11.2 per cent of the families are now fatherless and 4.5 per cent of the families are motherless.

TABLE 82
OCCUPATIONS OF MOTHERS OF GIFTED SUBJECTS

	Mothers Not Widowed or Separated	Mothers Widowed or Separated
Professional		
Teacher (school, kindergarten, etc.).....	10	8
Teacher (music, voice, etc.).............	6	2
Writer	7	..
Musician	3	..
Painter	2	..
Actress	..	1
Dean of women	..	1
College president	..	2
Librarian	..	1
Semi-professional and business		
Clerical worker	16	14
Manager	4	1
Retail dealer	2	..
Insurance business	..	2
Broker	..	1
Bank teller	..	1
Interior decorator	..	1
Real estate agent	1	2
Beauty shop owner	..	1
Playground director	..	1
Skilled labor		
Dressmaking, sewing	2	4
Pastry cook	..	1
Semi-skilled to slightly skilled		
Housework	..	2
Boards children	..	1
Keeping house	341	29
Totals	394	76

DIVORCES, SEPARATIONS, AND REMARRIAGES

The follow-up blanks report seventeen parent-pairs as having separated or secured a divorce since 1921–22. This number is 3.7 per cent of the total number of families represented, and added to the proportion, 7.1, known to have been separated or divorced in 1921–22, brings the total proportion up to 10.8 per cent.

Remarriages were reported in the follow-up blanks in the case of seventeen fathers and nine mothers. As the remarriages prior to 1921–22 were not recorded on the follow-up blanks, and have never been tabulated, the complete facts regarding remarriage of the parents cannot be summarized.

TESTS OF SIBLINGS

A number of considerations led us to include intelligence tests of the siblings of members of the gifted group as part of the 1927–28 schedule. The strongest reason was the probable future usefulness of such data in comparing the life careers of individuals who qualified for the gifted group with the careers of individuals having similar environment but less ability. Another, though secondary interest, was to determine biometrically the intelligence level of children whose siblings averaged more than three standard deviations above the general mean. Still another reason was our desire to gather any and all information which might have a bearing upon the development of our gifted subjects themselves. Siblings are admittedly an integral part of a child's environment, and would merit our attention for this reason if for no other.

Our testing program called for a Stanford-Binet Test of siblings of ages three to twelve inclusive, and a Terman Group Test of siblings of the same age-range as that of the gifted subjects who were given the Terman Group Test. Tests were not planned, however, for siblings who had been tested during the original survey. Although no systematic attempt to reach all the siblings of appropriate age had been made originally, a number of siblings had been tested incidentally. Those who qualified were forthwith included as members of the gifted group. In many cases those who failed to qualify were not tested thoroughly, but were carried through the Stanford-Binet only far enough to satisfy the examiner that they could not possibly meet the standard for inclusion. If those who did not qualify had been retested during the follow-up and their scores included with the scores of the siblings tested for the first time in 1927–28, the results would have been unfairly biased in a downward direction. Accordingly the only sound procedure seemed to be the one which was followed.

During the follow-up, 130 siblings of members of the Regular group and 35 additional siblings of Outside Binet subjects were tested on the Stanford-Binet. On the Terman Group Test 35 siblings of Regular subjects were tested and 24 additional siblings of Outside Binet subjects.

The means and standard deviations of the Stanford-Binet IQ's of siblings of members of the Regular group are tabulated by age in Table 83. There appears to be no clear trend with age, and the number of cases at any one age is not sufficient to give significance to the minor fluctuations found.

TABLE 83

STANFORD-BINET IQ'S OF SIBLINGS OF MEMBERS OF THE REGULAR GROUP

Age of Siblings	Mean IQ	S.D.	N
3	132	18.4	4
4	129	7.2	4
5	124	14.9	7
6	116	9.8	17
7	123	11.4	15
8	122	14.2	19
9	123	20.4	14
10	125	13.1	14
11	125	18.6	19
12	119	14.6	17
Ages 3 to 12, inclusive:			
Boys	123	16.1	68
Girls	123	14.4	62
Sexes combined	123	15.3	130

Since the correlation between the IQ's of unselected siblings as determined in a number of experimental studies lies close to .45 or .50, we should expect the average IQ of siblings of our gifted subjects to deviate from the mean of the general population by an amount only .45 to .50 as great as the deviation of the gifted subjects themselves. As the mean IQ of the gifted group at the time of the original tests was 151, we should, therefore, expect the average of the siblings to lie between 122 and 125. This expectation is borne out by the facts, for the mean IQ of 130 siblings is 123.

The interesting fact that boy and girl siblings have exactly the same mean IQ is not entirely harmonious with the implications of the sex ratio in the gifted group itself. The ratio of gifted boys to gifted girls in the Regular group is 121 to 100, a fact which has been discussed at length in Volume I, pages 51 ff. Converging lines of evidence suggested that this ratio was not spurious, but corresponded to differential incidence of high ability in the two sexes. If, however, we increase the numbers and hence the reliability by adding, to the cases entering Table 83, thirty-five siblings of members of the Outside Binet group, the mean IQ's are changed in favor of the boys. The scores of twenty boys raise the mean of the boys to 124 and the scores of fifteen girls lower the mean of the girls to 121. Moreover, the ratio of boys to girls among the high-testing siblings is greater than in the gifted group itself. In the entire sibling group of eighty-eight boys and seventy-seven girls, twelve boys but only eight girls have IQ's above 140; twenty-four boys but only twelve girls have IQ's above 135. The numbers involved are not sufficiently large to give very high reliability to the ratios, but it is quite evident that the higher incidence of superior intelligence in boys is not contradicted by the data from the sibling tests. The fact that in the sibling group the means for the boys and girls are nearly the same, while the incidence of high-testing children is greater for boys than for girls, is accounted for by a slightly greater variability in the scores of the boys. The standard deviation of the boys' IQ's is 16.1, and of the girls' IQ's, 14.4.

With the Terman Group Test 59 siblings between the ages of thirteen and eighteen were tested—thirty-two boys and twenty-seven girls. Thirty-five of these are siblings of members of the Regular group. The mean scores by age are as follows:

Age	Mean	N
13	136	11
14	167	13
15	163	7
16	164	17
17	168	7
18	187	4

The irregularities found in the means might have been expected as a result of the small number of cases at each age level.

Comparing the mean scores with the norms for the grades in which the siblings would be "at age" if they had progressed through school at a normal rate, as was done in Table 13 with the mean T.G.T. scores of the gifted subjects themselves, we find that in the lower ages, before selection has had much opportunity to warp the grade norms, the percentile ranks of the mean scores are above 90.

Sex Ratio among Siblings

In chapter iii of Volume I the sex ratio of the siblings of the gifted subjects was discussed in connection with the sex ratio found in the gifted group itself. A higher ratio of boys to girls was found in the sibling group than in the gifted group. This fact was believed to be consistent with the hypothesis that the observed sex ratio in the gifted group corresponded to a real phenomenon rather than to obscure factors of selection, for the following reason: "If children are selected for a given trait, and that trait is more common in boys than in girls, it follows that a greater proportion of families consisting of girls only will be missed, with the result that the sibs of the children selected for the trait will also show an excess of boys." Such reasoning should only apply, of course, to siblings who were of testable age at the time of the original survey. The siblings who have sprung up since that time should have a sex ratio equal to that found in the general population.

The follow-up Home Information Blank asks the parents to note the names, sexes, and birthdays of children born during the last five or six years. A tabulation of responses shows that fourteen brothers and nineteen sisters have been born in the families of the Regular group. As these numbers are not large enough to establish a reliable sex ratio, we have increased them by adding siblings born in or since 1919 in the families of Regular and Outside Binet cases. Such siblings were under three years old at the time of the original survey, and thus were not competing for places in the gifted group. The augmented list of siblings is not complete, since in compiling it we relied to considerable extent upon the notations made by field workers upon the "guide sheets," and these were filled in only for children now living within the field workers' territories. There is no reason why the list should represent a biased selection of siblings, however. The augmented list contains sixty-seven boys and sixty-two girls, giving a sex ratio of 1.08. This ratio differs but slightly from the ratio, 1.06, computed by Nichols[1] for living births of whites in the United States. Of white living births 51.5 per cent are male, and in our sibling group 51.9 per cent are male. The latter proportion, however, has a standard error of 4.4 per cent, and many more cases are needed to establish the ratio reliably.

SUMMARY

1. On the Barr scale of occupational status the ratings upon fathers of the gifted subjects have increased slightly since 1921–22.

2. Among the mothers of the gifted subjects, 61 per cent of those who are widowed or separated from their husbands and 14 per cent of the remaining group of mothers have paid employment.

3. Of the mothers who are employed, 43 per cent belong to the professional category.

4. Of the fathers of gifted subjects, 2.8 per cent have died since 1921–22; of the mothers, 1.9 per cent have died.

5. Since 1921–22, 3.7 per cent of the parents have separated or been divorced.

6. The mean IQ of 130 siblings of members of the Regular group is 123. There is no difference in the mean IQ of the brothers and of the sisters, but more brothers than sisters test up to the standard of the gifted group.

7. The siblings who were tested on the Terman Group Test average above the ninetieth percentile for the grades in which they would be if they progressed through school at a normal rate.

8. The sex ratio of siblings born since 1919 is about equal to the sex ratio of the general white population in America. This fact supports the hypothesis that the high ratio of boys to girls found among the older siblings is due to selective factors, but is not in contradiction to the sex-ratio figures of the gifted group itself.

[1] Nichols, J. B., *Memoirs of American Anthropological Association,* Vol. I, 1907, pp. 249–300.

CHAPTER XIII

THE HIGH SCHOOL AND SPECIAL ABILITY GROUPS

THE 1921-22 HIGH SCHOOL GROUP

The account of the High School group appearing in Volume I confirmed in nearly every detail the data gathered for the Regular group; accordingly we feel justified in interpreting the findings for the High School group in 1927-28 as a sort of projection of the Regular group five or six years hence. The High School group as an experimental unit has the disadvantage of being a little less highly selected than the Regular group, of being selected under conditions less well controlled, of being measured by a group test instead of by an individual intelligence test, and of being past early childhood at the time of being located. It has the very great advantage for our present purposes, however, of providing a considerable number of subjects who have finished college and are out in the world, or who are out in the world without college training. Thus it furnishes information, of a type which we cannot obtain from the Regular group without waiting several years, regarding the status of gifted subjects who have completed their formal education, of subjects who have married, and of subjects who are earning their own living.

In the sections of the present chapter which are concerned with the High School group we shall not duplicate the data summarized for the Regular group in earlier chapters, but shall limit the discussion to those points which are invested with special significance by virtue of the age superiority of the High School group.

AGE-GRADE STATUS

Tables 84 and 85 (p. 228) record the age-grade status of the members of the High School group at the time of receipt of the 1927-28 follow-up blanks. It is seen that close to half of the group are college undergraduates—almost exactly half of the boys and slightly under half of the girls.

TABLE 84

AGE-GRADE DISTRIBUTION OF 161 BOYS OF HIGH SCHOOL GROUP

AGE	COLLEGE				POSTGRADUATE			BUSINESS COLLEGE	NOT IN SCHOOL	
	Fr.	Soph.	Jun.	Sen.	1	2	3		College grad.	Not grad.
18	1	2	2	1	..	..	..	..	..	..
19	2	4	8	4	2	..	..	2	..	1
20	..	4	9	10	1	..	..	..	2	3
21	..	4	1	5	5	..	..	..	4	5
22	..	2	2	6	2	1	..	..	6	9
23	..	2	3	6	2	5	..	..	11	8
24	1	..	..	1	1	..	1	..	3	2
25	..	..	..	..	..	1	..	..	1	2
26	..	..	..	..	..	..	..	..	..	..
27	..	..	..	..	1	..	..	..	..	..
Total	4	18	25	33	14	7	1	2	27	30

TABLE 85

AGE-GRADE DISTRIBUTION OF 87 GIRLS OF HIGH SCHOOL GROUP

AGE	COLLEGE				POST-GRAD.		Art School, Conservatory, or Bus. Coll.	NOT IN SCHOOL	
	Fr.	Soph.	Jun.	Sen.	1	2		College Grad.	Not Grad.
18	1	1	5	1	..	..	2	..	..
19	..	2	2	4	..	..	1	..	3
20	..	1	4	9	1	..	1	1	5
21	..	..	..	4	1	..	1	3	2
22	..	..	..	3	2	1	..	13	2
23	..	..	..	1	..	..	..	4	4
24	..	..	..	..	..	..	..	1	1
Total	1	4	11	22	4	1	5	22	17

EDUCATIONAL PLANS

There are 57 boys and 39 girls recorded in Tables 84 and 85 who are not attending any kind of school or college. Of these subjects, however, 27 boys and 22 girls are college graduates; 18 boys and 11 girls have attended college for various periods up to four years; and at least two additional boys and one additional girl plan to enter college. Two of the girls who are securing business or musical training have also attended college. Totaling the subjects who are now in college, those who have attended college, and those who plan to attend college, we have 151, or 94 per cent, of the entire group of boys, and 79, or 91 per cent, of the entire group of girls.

A question immediately arises as to the cause of the discrepancy between the High School group and the Regular group with respect to proportions securing a college education. The figures for the latter group, corresponding to 94 per cent and 91 per cent for the High School group, are 85 per cent and 78 per cent. (See p. 69.) The discrepancy is all the more surprising in view of the fact that the Regular group was somewhat more highly selected to start with than the High School group. It seems probable to us that the explanation lies chiefly in differential "selection" affecting the subjects of the High School group from whom we have received co-operation during the follow-up. We secured definite co-operation during the follow-up from the Regular group in 92 per cent of the cases, but from the members of the High School group (with whom we have never been in such close touch as with the Regulars) in only 80 per cent of the cases. If, as seems possible, the subjects who do not attend college are less likely than the others to appreciate the significance of scientific research and hence are less likely to co-operate with us, our figures are spuriously weighted in favor of the college-trained subjects. The resulting ambiguity of our figures emphasizes in a forceful way the necessity for securing as complete data as possible in a study of this kind if the conclusions are to represent the facts.

Of the remaining subjects who are not registered in any school or college, all but two are high-school graduates. Both of the non-graduates are boys. One of them, at least, intends to return to school and possibly to attend college after completing high school.

Of the 43 boys and 28 girls who have graduated from college, 51 per cent of the boys and 18 per cent of the girls are taking post-graduate work, and an additional 5 per cent of the boys and 25 per cent of the girls, though not now in college, have had one or two years of post-graduate work. It is possible, also, that some of the other college graduates will return later as graduate students. At any rate, the indications are that at least 56 per cent of the boys who graduate and 43 per cent of the girls who graduate take post-graduate work. This is a far larger proportion than would be found for college graduates in general.

Vocational Plans and Achievements

We have selected for comparative purposes the Information Blanks of (1) 42 boys and 24 girls who have graduated from college and (2) the 26 boys and 10 girls who have not graduated from college, who are over twenty years old, and who are not planning to secure further formal education. The two groups do not, of course, offer such a very strong contrast to one another, since the majority of the second group have attended college for at least a year or two.

Nevertheless, it will be interesting to find out whether the "certification" of a college degree in conjunction with the year or two of additional training enjoyed by the college graduates appears to be associated in any appreciable degree with their prospects of vocational success.

On the blank filled out by the gifted subjects the following question was included:

"Have you decided yet what life vocation you wish to follow? .... If so, what occupation? .... Under what circumstances did you make this choice? (E.g., what influences determined the decision, such as school or college courses, advice of relatives, teachers, or friends, reading, close-hand observation, etc.?) ...."

The proportions of subjects who state that they have decided upon their life vocations are:

	Boys %	Girls %
Group 1 (graduates)	86	63
Group 2 (non-graduates)	69	80

In the case of the boys a larger proportion of the graduates than of the non-graduates have selected a vocation. In the case of the girls the situation appears to be reversed, but the reversal is explained by the fact that seven of the ten girl non-graduates are married, and half of those who have made their decisions indicate that the vocation is that of "housewife."

Following are the vocations which the subjects intend to pursue:

GIFTED BOYS

	Group 1 (Graduates)	Group 2 (Non-graduates)
Lawyer	7	..
Educator	5	..
Engineer	7	1
Physician	3	1
Research work	..	1
College teacher	1	..
Business, foreign trade, etc.	3	6
Physicist	2	..
Chemist	1	1
Physiologist	1	..
Geologist	1	..
Naval officer	1	..
Musician	1	..
Architect	1	..
Insurance	1	1
Salesman	..	1
Clerk, bookkeeper, etc.	..	2
Broker	..	1
Farmer	..	1
Advertising	1	1
Actor	..	1
	36	18

GIFTED GIRLS

	Group 1 (Graduates)	Group 2 (Non-graduates)
Teaching	10	1
Housewife	..	4
Musician	1	..
Writer	2	1
Psychologist	1	..
Physician	1	..
Bookkeeper	..	1
Missionary	..	1
	15	8

Possibly the most noteworthy observation to be made from these lists of occupational choices is the preponderance of boys intending to pursue a business career of some sort in the group of non-college graduates. More than 50 per cent of the non-graduate boys look forward to strictly business careers, as compared with only 11 per cent of the college graduates. In the group of boys who have gradu-

ated, 83 per cent expect to take up professional careers. Our
figures would indicate that about 28 per cent of the non-
graduate boys intend to enter a profession, but the nature
of the professional ambitions of some of them makes us
feel rather sure that a few subjects have been included here
through error. We included in the non-graduate group
under consideration all subjects who did not expressly
state on their Information Blanks that they intended to return to college, and thus some subjects may have been included who really have that intention but did not say
so. This possibility is especially likely in the case of two
boys who plan to go into medicine and research.

The tendencies noted in the two groups of boys are also
found in the two groups of girls. We note that all the college
graduates who have decided on a vocation plan to enter a
profession. A rather large proportion of the non-graduates
is made up of girls who have married and do not expect to
follow any vocation outside their homes. It will be interesting a few years from now, after a number of the girls who
have graduated from college marry, to find out if a significant proportion of them combine marriage with professional careers. At the time of the follow-up only one girl
among twenty-eight college graduates had married.

In connection with the comparisons just made, we must
of course be on our guard against confusing cause with
effect. We cannot conclude that the differences found between the groups of graduates and non-graduates are necessarily due to differences in education, for the differences in
education may well be the consequence of the difference in
vocational ambitions. Certainly there is more incentive for
a young person who plans to go into medicine or law or
some scientific field to remain in college than for one who
plans to sell insurance or become a contractor.

If next we compare the graduates and non-graduates
upon the basis of present positions, the differences are still
quite marked. A number of the college graduates are still
in college, pursuing graduate studies and working part time.
In Table 86 and Table 87 occupations have been classified
as professional, business and semi-professional, etc. It is
seen from the data in these tables that proportionally many
more graduates than non-graduates are employed in professional and business callings.

TABLE 86
PRESENT OCCUPATIONS OF GIFTED BOYS

Professional	Group 1 (Graduates)	Group 2 (Non-graduates)
Teacher	3	..
Engineer	2	1
Attorney	1	..
Geologist	1	..
Lecturer and personnel work (part-time)	1	..
Naval officer	1	..
Research or teaching assistant (part-time)	4	..
Tutor (part-time)	1	..
Musician	..	1
Chemist	..	1
Business and semi-professional		
Manager (part-time)	1	..
Reporter	1	..
Publicity and advertising	2	1
Insurance	1	1
Manufacturer	1	..
X-Ray technician (part-time)	1	..
Brokerage	..	1
Clerical and skilled labor		
"Office work," clerking, etc.	2	5
Salesman	1	3
Draftsman	1	..
Chauffeur (part-time)	1	..
Electric tester	1	..
Collector (part-time)	1	..
Telegraph operator	..	1
Farming	..	2
Bank teller	..	1
Ticket agent	..	1
Carpenter	..	1
Film technician	..	1
Semi-skilled or unskilled labor		
Car loader	..	1

TABLE 87
PRESENT OCCUPATIONS OF GIFTED GIRLS

Professional	Group 1 (Graduates)	Group 2 (Non-graduates)
Teacher	11	1
Accompanist	1	..
Missionary	..	1
Semi-professional		
Publicity writer	1	..
Pharmacist	1	..
Clerical	2	2

Social Data

In chapter ix (Social and Other Personality Traits) the reader was referred to the present section in which certain data have been summarized which were not obtained during the follow-up for the members of the Regular group. These data are concerned with membership in college fraternities and sororities. The Information Blank, filled out by subjects of age twenty or over, contains the following question:

"Have you belonged to a social fraternity, sorority, or house club?.... Which one?.... If a member, are you glad you joined? ....."

The question is answered by 90 boys and 46 girls of the High School group who are in college or have attended college. The answers are divided as follows:

	Boys %	Girls %
Joined	46	48
Did not join	54	52

Of those who joined:

	Boys %	Girls %
Glad	88	77
Not glad	7	9
Uncertain	5	14

Much may be said, of course, on both sides of the fraternity question, but regardless of personal opinion regarding the possible benefit that may come to an individual through living at a Greek-letter house, it seems clear that membership in such an organization is a rough indicator of a social trait that we might term "group-mindedness" or even "social adaptability." For any given individual the reliability of such an indicator is certainly low, and the factor of financial status complicates interpretation. However, it is probably significant that nearly half of the gifted group are assimilated into social fraternities and sororities, which is probably two or three times the proportion that would be found for the generality of students in the colleges they attend. We consider this valuable evidence of the social adaptability of the gifted group as a whole.

DEATHS

Since the time of the original investigation in 1921–22, two members of the High School group are known to have died. Both of these are boys, one having died of tuberculosis and the other from a cause said by the parents to be "congenital." Although it is possible that additional subjects of the High School group have died without our knowledge, we believe that our records are complete, or practically so, for the families which have co-operated in the follow-up study. We have had such co-operation from 248 subjects belonging to the High School group; hence 0.8 per cent have died since 1921–22. If we compare this proportion with the expected proportion (computed by the use of Glover's 1910 United States Life Tables) the result is distinctly favorable to the gifted group. Among random white American boys and girls having an initial age-distribution matching that of our gifted subjects in 1921–22, 2.3 per cent die during a period of six years, i.e., between five and six cases in a group the size of ours.

Since the gifted group may owe its superior vitality partly to the admittedly wholesome California climate and partly to the environmental conditions peculiar to their superior economic status, no causal relationship between intelligence and vitality can be inferred from the comparison just made. It does seem fairly certain that the exceptional mental status of our group is not associated with an unfavorable death rate.

ENGAGEMENTS AND MARRIAGES

Of the 161 boys and 87 girls in the High School group from whom co-operation was received during the follow-up, 8 per cent of the boys and 13 per cent of the girls indicate that they are engaged; 12 per cent of the boys and 10 per cent of the girls are married. If we consider just the 79 boys and 32 girls who have reached or passed the age of twenty-two, the corresponding figures are:

Engaged, 11 per cent of boys and 12 per cent of girls.
Married, 22 per cent of boys and 16 per cent of girls.

The 19 boys who have married did so at an average age of twenty-one, the 9 girls at an average age of twenty. We may expect the average age to be materially increased when the still unmarried individuals marry.

It is interesting in the light of the many studies which have demonstrated a low marriage rate among university women that to date a slightly lower proportion of the gifted girls than of the gifted boys have married, despite the fact that the average age of marriage of unselected women is a little lower than it is for unselected men.

Offspring

Of the members of the High School group who are married, 13 boys and 6 girls have been married over one year. These subjects report upon offspring as follows:

	Married boys	Married girls
None	10	3
One child	2	2
Two children	1	..
Three children	..	1

While the number of cases is here too few to give reliable results, the evidence suggests that our subjects, like most other people of their social and economic status, are voluntarily limiting their families.

Vocational Plans

Considering next the vocational plans of the subjects who are married, we find that nine of the boys, or 47 per cent, intend to follow one of the professions. This proportion is intermediate between the proportions intending to enter a profession in the "college-graduate group" and in the "non-graduate group," but closer to the proportion in the latter than to that in the former. Only two of the nine girls who are married intend to pursue vocations outside their homes. In each case the vocation is that of teaching.

If we grant that despite many exceptions the professions demand a higher order of ability on the whole than do other vocations, and that a complete university course is beneficial to most individuals that have the requisite mental ability, then it appears that many of the gifted subjects have made serious sacrifices by marrying early. This deduction is not conclusive, however, since early marriage may possibly be a symptom rather than a cause. It may be that the individuals who find marriage attractive at a very youthful age tend to be those for whom academic and professional work is least attractive.

HUSBANDS AND WIVES OF GIFTED SUBJECTS

A "Supplementary Blank" which was mailed during the follow-up to the married gifted subjects was filled in and returned to us by 15 boys and 6 girls of the High School group. The blank was designed to elicit data regarding the vocational and educational status and the family background of the young men and women whom our gifted subjects have married.

The 15 wives for whom we received reports were between the ages of eighteen and twenty-eight, inclusive, at the time of marriage, the average age being twenty-one. Their average age at the time the blanks were received was twenty-three. The 6 husbands reported upon were between eighteen and thirty-six, inclusive, at the time of marriage, or twenty-four on the average. Their average age at the time the blanks were received was twenty-seven.

Six of the 15 wives are employed in work outside their homes, one is attending college, and the remainder are "housewives." The occupations listed for the six who are employed are:

Teacher 3
Secretarial worker 1
Typist 1
Saleswoman 1

Only one, a teacher, expects to follow an outside vocation permanently.

The education received by the 15 wives varies from four years of high school to post-graduate work in college, the average being two years of college. Four have graduated from a four-year college or university and one from a teachers' college. The average schooling is one year less than that of the gifted subjects to whom they are married.

The husbands of the 6 gifted girls who answered our inquiry are employed in the following occupations:

Teacher 1
Farmer 1
Lineman 1
Salesman and broker............................. 1
Student preacher 1
Oil engineer 1

These occupations represent fairly well the ones which the six men intend to follow permanently. The teacher intends to do "research in mathematics and physics," the lineman intends to work into "the higher branches of telephone construction," but all six may be said to have embarked upon the careers they expect to pursue.

The education received by the six husbands varies from eighth-grade to post-graduate work in college, the average being less than one year of college. Only one is a college graduate, but one is now in his senior college year. The gifted subjects to whom these men are married have had on the average over a year more schooling than their husbands.

The following occupations are recorded for the fathers of the husbands and wives of our married subjects:

FATHERS OF WIVES

High-school principal 1
Retired farmer 1
Mining engineer 1
Garage owner 1
Real estate agent.............................. 1
Merchant and contractor....................... 1
Real estate and ranching...................... 1
Accountant 1
Printer 1
Candy manufacturer 1
Small manufacturer 1
County treasurer 1
Deceased 3

FATHERS OF HUSBANDS

Rancher or farmer.............................. 2
Jersey breeder 1
Printer 1
C.P.A. 1
Carpenter 1

In only two instances is the father of one of the young people whom the gifted subjects have married in a professional occupation. This is approximately 10 per cent of the 21 cases. This proportion may be compared with the corresponding proportion of 31 per cent of fathers of the members of the High School group. It may also be compared with the proportion of 16 per cent of fathers of the married subjects of the High School group.

PRESENT SITUATION OF MARRIED SUBJECTS

The subjects who had married by the time of the 1927–28 follow-up are representative of those who marry at a particularly youthful age; consequently the data obtained from the present group of married subjects may differ markedly from those that will be obtained in the future from subjects who later marry. Nevertheless, it will be interesting to ascertain whether or not any obvious advantages or drawbacks are associated with the youthful marriages of the subjects who are now married. It is self-evident that late marriage reduces the birth rate in the long run, and that for gifted individuals to marry early is eugenic. We also wish to know what early marriage means to the gifted individuals themselves.

We have 19 boys and 9 girls who were married at an average age of twenty-one and twenty, respectively. The ages of the boys at time of marriage vary from eighteen to twenty-three, those of the girls from nineteen to twenty-one. All but three of the 19 boys and all but one of the 9 girls have attended college. Seven of the boys have graduated from college (including five now doing post-graduate work), and two more boys now attending college may graduate, but the remaining ten boys have left school or college and do not plan to return. Of the girls, only one has graduated from college and only one other plans to return. The boys have had three years of college on the average, and the girls two years. Thus we see that the early marriage of these subjects tends to be associated with curtailed education.

THE 1921–22 SPECIAL ABILITY GROUP

The Special Ability group is composed of 26 cases that failed to qualify for the gifted group on the basis of intelligence score but were unusually gifted in some special field, usually art or music. (See Volume I, p. 34 ff.) It does not contain subjects of undoubted special ability who qualified also on the basis of intelligence. In 1921–22 the special ability subjects averaged 114 in IQ and ranged in age from five to twenty-three, with an average age of twelve. Fifteen of the subjects had artistic ability, ten had musical ability, and one had mechanical ability. Co-operation has been received from 19 of the 26 cases during the follow-up, namely, from twelve with artistic ability and seven with musical ability.

Upon the basis of home interview and follow-up report blanks we have assigned to each of the 19 co-operating individuals a rating to indicate his present status in respect to his special ability. A rating of 1 indicates that the subject is making a very unusual success in the field of his talent; 2 indicates that he is moderately successful in his field and has retained a genuine interest in it; 3 indicates that he has retained only a slight interest; and 4 indicates that we find no evidence that any appreciable interest in the special field has been retained. The ratings obtained are:

Rating	No. of Cases
1	1
2	7
3	8
4	3
Average	2.7

It is seen that less than half of the special-ability subjects have retained an interest in their field that is at all marked (rating 1 or 2). If we consider the musicians and artists separately, we find that 71 per cent of the musicians but only 33 per cent of the artists receive a rating of 1 or 2. All three cases receiving a rating of 4 are in the artist group. These facts lend support to the tentative conclusion previously drawn (Volume I, chapter iv) that genuine artistic ability tends to mature considerably later than musical ability.

For the Special Ability subjects we have also made ratings upon achievement comparable to those made for the Regular group (pp. 192 ff.). In these ratings, achievements to date in any field are considered, the individual not being penalized for abandoning the field of his early talent if his achievement in some other direction warrants a superior rating. In sixteen cases for whom sufficient data to base ratings upon have been obtained, we have:

Rating	No. of Cases
1	1
2	..
3	8
4	6
5	1
Average	3.4

The average of these ratings is distinctly lower than the average for the Regular group. The one subject who receives a rating of 1 is a musical composer, whose case history is recorded on pages 322 ff. As this subject strained the limit of the Stanford-Binet scale at the age of fourteen with an uncorrected IQ of 131, we can be rather sure that his true ability was in the neighborhood of 140 IQ and that he is therefore really representative of the subjects who qualified for the gifted group on the basis of high general intelligence.

It will be necessary to wait longer before the achievements of the Special Ability group in the direction of their special talents can be appraised with finality, but the present data strongly suggest that without the support of high intelligence a special talent is not likely to mature into achievements of very unusual merit. This tentative conclusion provides a harmonious adjunct to a conclusion set forth by Dr. Cox in Volume II of this series: "The extraordinary genius who achieves the highest eminence is also the gifted individual whom intelligence tests may discover in childhood."

In our follow-up testing program ten members of the Special Ability group were reached. Nine of these were tested with the Terman Group Test. The ages of the nine range between seventeen and twenty-three, with an average age of nineteen. Their mean score on the Terman Group Test, 171, is fully a standard deviation below the mean attained on the Terman Group Test during the follow-up by members of the Regular group of comparable age-range. The original IQ's of the same nine Special Ability subjects averaged 115 with an S.D. of 11.

SUMMARY

1. Of the 248 members of the 1921–22 High School group who co-operated during the follow-up, 94 per cent of the boys and 91 per cent of the girls have gone or plan to go to college.

2. All but two members of the group have graduated from high school.

3. Of those who have graduated from college, 56 per cent of the boys and 43 per cent of the girls have taken post-graduate work.

4. Eighty-six per cent of the boys and 63 per cent of the girls who have graduated from college have decided upon their life vocations. Sixty-nine per cent of the boys and 80 per cent of the girls who have left school without graduating have decided upon their life vocations. In the latter group the vocation of "housewife" is selected in half the cases.

5. More than 50 per cent of the non-graduate boys expect to enter business pursuits, while only 11 per cent of the boys who have graduated from college expect to do so. Of the boys who have graduated, 83 per cent expect to enter a profession. Less than 30 per cent of the non-graduate boys expect to do so.

6. The same general tendencies noted in the comparison of boys who have graduated and those who have not are found in a comparison of corresponding groups of girls. All of the college graduates who have decided upon a vocation plan to enter a profession.

7. In the case of both boys and girls more college graduates than non-graduates are at present employed in professional occupations.

8. Of the members of the High School group who have attended college, 46 per cent of the boys have joined social fraternities and 48 per cent of the girls have joined sororities. Of those who have joined, 88 per cent of the boys and 77 per cent of the girls say they are glad they did so.

9. The death-rate among members of the High School group is lower than the expected rate.

10. Of subjects who have reached or passed the age of twenty-two, 11 per cent of the boys and 12 per cent of the girls are engaged; 22 per cent of the boys and 16 per cent of the girls are married.

11. A little less than a third of those who have been married more than one year have offspring.

12. The boys and girls in the group who have married were married at an average age of twenty-one and twenty, respectively. Their early marriages tend to be associated with a curtailment of education and a restriction of scope in their vocational ambitions.

13. The average amount of schooling of wives of gifted subjects is two years of college, of husbands of gifted subjects, less than one year of college. The schooling of the

wives and husbands averages about a year less in amount than that of the gifted subjects to whom they are married.

14. Approximately 10 per cent of the fathers of husbands and wives belong to the professional class. This proportion is much below the corresponding proportion of fathers of gifted subjects, but only a little below that of fathers of the gifted subjects who have married.

15. Follow-up data for members of the Special Ability group indicate that less than half of these subjects have retained a marked interest in the field of the special talents for which they were conspicuous in 1921–22.

16. The interests of the subjects originally showing artistic ability appear to be less permanent on the whole than those of the subjects originally showing musical ability.

17. The data for the Special Ability cases suggest that, without the support of high intelligence, special talent is not likely to mature into achievements of very unusual merit.

18. The Special Ability subjects who took the Terman Group Test during the follow-up average fully an S.D. below the mean of the Regular group of comparable age-range.

PART II. CASE STUDIES

CHAPTER XIV

THREE GIFTED GIRLS

INTRODUCTORY STATEMENT REGARDING THE CASE STUDIES

The case descriptions of Part II have been so selected as to give an idea of the wide variety of types of subjects represented in our gifted group. It is necessary to warn the reader, however, that no effort has been made to give the various types proportional representation. For example, the series contains a disproportionate number of those subjects who have shown undesirable traits of character or personality, also of those who have exceptional musical ability. It should especially be made clear, however, that we have purposely avoided including in the series only those subjects who would rate as among the most interesting.

We debated for a time whether or not we should include case studies of all the subjects, but decided against it because of the limitations of time and funds and because an additional volume would have been necessary. There was also the question whether the preparation of so large a number of case studies of bright subjects still for the most part in their teens would reward the reader in proportion to the work the task would involve. We feel that after ten or twenty more years have elapsed the value of such individual reports will be incomparably greater than it could possibly be at the present time.

Although the present list might profitably have been extended considerably, we feel less regret in regard to numbers than in regard to the degree of completeness which has been possible for the subjects included. Perhaps only the scientifically minded student of biography is in a position to appreciate the difficulties which beset one who undertakes to set forth the high lights in the development of anything so complex as a human being. So rarely does one know exactly what events and circumstances, of the myriad that might be brought forward, are really the most important for the picture. It is difficult enough to report even the bare facts, undistorted by observation; and when one draws in-

ferences with respect to relationships between facts, one en-
counters all the dangers that beset the path of the author of
a biography. Just as no two biographers agree in their in-
ferential uses of the documented facts relating to the life of
Napoleon or Lincoln or Goethe, so would no two phycholo-
gists agree fully in their interpretation of the facts that could
be assembled for the case description of one of our gifted
children. In the present series our attempt to furnish little
interpretation is perhaps less to be regretted than the relative paucity of the factual material we have presented in
connection with each individual case. There are many of
the subjects who would repay years of intensive study. For
that matter, perhaps any child would.

The names used in this section are all fictitious except in
the case of Henry Cowell, the musical composer, who has
become so widely known that a disguise of name would have
been both ineffective and pointless. In a few cases it has
been deemed necessary to take additional precautions to
conceal identity by altering one or more of the less essential
facts, such as place of residence, occupation of father, etc.
We have been careful to make the alterations in a way that
would not detract from the essential truthfulness of the
description given.

A Phenomenally Early Reader

Millie. This girl probably holds the world's record for
early reading. At the age of 26½ months her reading vocabulary was above 700 words, and as early as 21 months
she read and apprehended simple sentences as connected
thoughts rather than as isolated words. By that age she
could distinguish and name all the primary colors.

An extremely interesting account of Millie's early training, entitled "An Experiment in Infant Education," was
published in 1918 by the child's father in the *Journal of Applied Psychology* (with an introduction by Terman). In his
article the father relates how he initiated a course of systematic instruction when Millie was 19 months old, and described in detail the progress she made and the methods he
devised to hold the interested attention of the baby mind.

Through the use of picture books and cards upon which
he printed letters and words, through ingenious little games
that provided an incentive for learning, Millie's father was
able to teach her to recognize and to pronounce all the

capital letters by the time she was 19 months and 13 days old, and all the small letters by the time she was 20 months old. He then began to teach her to read by the word method.

By the time she was 23 months old she began to experience evident pleasure when she read. At 24 months she had a reading vocabulary of over 200 words, which had increased to more than 700 words two and one-half months later. Her speaking vocabulary at 26½ months was in the neighborhood of 2,000 words. The father makes the comment in his article that her pronunciation "has not kept pace with her reading, but her expression leaves little to be desired." When she was 25 months old she read fluently and with expression to one of us (Terman) from several primers and first readers that she had never seen before. At this age her reading ability was at least equal to that of the average seven-year-old who has attended school a year.

It is of particular interest to follow Millie's subsequent progress in the light of her extraordinary babyhood. The father, on a Home Information Blank which he filled out for us when Millie was six, stated that between the ages of five and six she spent about twenty hours a week reading for her own pleasure. When she was seven and one-half, and completing the high-third grade, her teacher graded her as "very superior" in reading, and recorded "reading" in answer to the question "In what subject is child most interested?"

Despite the fact that Millie had read so extensively, and was consequently accustomed to seeing words correctly spelled, the Interest Blank which she filled out at that time contained several amusing examples of unconventional spelling: e.g., she wrote that she had recently read "The Little Prinsess" and "Little Womon," and had had the honor of being "Capton" of the baseball team. However, in studying spelling as a class subject she did excellent work. She was quite able to learn the spellings of lists of words given in daily assignments. The fact that her spelling was poor for words not directly studied is perhaps additional evidence that Millie, from the time she first read, learned her words as unit "pictures," never analyzing them into their components.

Six months later, when Millie was just eight, we received another school report which again mentioned her superiority in reading. This report also informed us that she had skipped a half-grade because "the work of low fourth had become very easy for her." As this was just a month before regular school promotions, Millie passed within a short time into low fifth (age 8-1). Her promotions through the grades have been at the normal rate since that time. She is thus two years accelerated. At this writing she is in grade H9 at age 12-8. In the previous semester she was the only pupil in a L9 class of about 40 to make the high-school honor roll.

In our 1927–28 follow-up, the first thing the field visitor asked Millie's teacher was what subject she excelled in. The answer was "Millie reads beautifully." In a chat with the field visitor Millie said she "would like to read five books a day if it weren't for going to school." She also admitted, simply and without self-consciousness, that she could read very fast, had read through Markham's thirteen volumes of *The Real American Romance* in a week. Her father, doubting whether she could read these books so rapidly and still assimilate them, asked her questions about the material read. She was able to answer them to his satisfaction.

Millie's present vocational ambition is to be an authoress. She has written several little books of imaginative adventure, one of which was shown to the field visitor by her mother. The little book appeared to be the charming product of an intelligent and mentally vigorous child, but it did not seem to show any very unusual talent for literary expression. It is interesting to note that in rating her liking for various school studies, Millie, at the age of seven, gave to "composition" a rating of 4 on a scale of 5. This was next to the lowest of any of her ratings, the lowest being given to music.

The question arises as to what effects, if any, the "Experiment in Infant Education" has had on Millie's interests, personality traits, and physical status. It is, of course, not possible to say just what turn her development would have taken if she had not received such special stimulation in babyhood. However, there is no evidence that she has been harmed; certainly the data suggest that her present intense love for reading and extraordinary facility for rapid digestion of reading matter may be accounted for in part by her early training.

Obviously Millie is not a case of an infant prodigy that bloomed too soon and wilted on its stem. Except for her unusually strong love for reading and a disability in music which amounts almost to tonedeafness, her mental development has been even and regular. Her first Stanford-Binet test, given by one of us (Terman) when her age was 3-11, showed an M.A. of 5-6 and an IQ of 140. She was tested again when she was 6-0 by Miss Elizabeth Kellam, a psychology student at Stanford, who found her IQ to be 142. At the time of the present follow-up we found for her, at age 11-10, an IQ of 139.

In physique Millie is strong and vigorous. She has rarely been ill, but when she was six there was an interval when she suffered from indigestion, vomited at night, and slept badly. She matured at eleven. In the report of a careful medical examination made by a pediatrician when she was six, a slight inflammation of the eyes was noted, but no other unusual condition. When she was nine her eyes were examined and found to be astigmatic. She was fitted with glasses and has been wearing them ever since. It is impossible to say whether or not Millie's early instruction and persistent devotion to reading have any causal connection with the few positive data in her medical history. However that may be, her ailments have never been very serious, nor of a kind not common among children.

In social adaptability Millie is quite normal. She is large for her age, verging upon plumpness, and thus suffers no handicap due to size even though her classmates are two to three years her seniors. Her teachers have rated her about average in social adaptability from the time of our earliest reports to the present. Her eighth-grade teacher, interviewed in 1927, stated that Millie's chief characteristics were "quiet reserve and determination," adding that, while Millie never antagonized other children, she was a little too dignified to be a "real mixer." She is not without social initiative and leadership, however. She is an enthusiastic Girl Scout, and plans and directs plays for her troop. Not long ago she and a school chum organized a group of four older classmates who were having trouble with arithmetic into a special class that met outside of school hours. Millie and her chum assigned daily examples and corrected them, and the four older girls followed humbly in the lead of the younger ones until the arithmetic improved.

To conclude this case history, a few words regarding Millie's family and home background are pertinent. Both parents came of Midwestern farmer stock. The father graduated from college at twenty, and has been at various times a lawyer, a rancher, and in a small way a manufacturer. The mother was a teacher before her marriage. Millie's brother, nine years older, is also a member of our group, having earned an IQ of 171 at the age of seven. He, too, was taught by his father to read very early, but not nearly so early as his sister. He graduated from college with honors at age twenty, earning all of his expenses for the four years except board and room.

The financial circumstances of the family are rather modest, but the family group is rich in the finest kind of companionship, mutual affection and admiration, gaiety, and active mental life. The family is the hub of the social activity of its members. As the mother put it, "we enjoy each other so much that we don't seem to care about having others along, but I'm afraid it is rather selfish of us!"

Except for the few months during her babyhood, Millie has never been subject to hot-house "forcing." Indeed, the father feels that even during his experiment, no real "forcing" was done, and explains in his published account that if learning to read had not occupied the baby's active mind some other less fruitful activity would have. He also states his conviction that a baby's mind is its own best protection, citing the fact that it was impossible to gain Millie's attention when she was tired or sleepy, and observing that it is "impossible to drive the baby mind beyond that which gives it pleasure."

A Typically Normal Gifted Child

Dora. In the gifted children survey Dora was selected by her teacher as the brightest child in her class. At that time she was less than nine years old and was doing outstanding work in the low-fifth grade. On the Stanford-Binet she earned an IQ of 168.

There is nothing in Dora's family background to suggest that she has enjoyed unusual opportunities. Her parents both died from influenza when she was an infant, leaving her and two younger brothers to the care of their paternal grandparents. Both parents left school during their second year in high school. The father was engaged in a feed and supply business, and found amusement in athletics and club activities. The mother interested herself in religious activities and in music, and was considered a very accomplished musician. None of the grandparents had more than grammar-school education, although all were said to be of superior intelligence. Dora's two younger brothers earned IQ's of 129 and 155, respectively.

Dora gave evidence of superior intelligence at a very early age. She talked in simple sentences "very young," could recite Mother Goose rhymes at thirteen months, and could sing simple songs as soon as she could talk. She entered school in the second grade at the age of six, having taught herself to read at five. Her work was consistently good; she stood first in her class each year, and could have skipped several grades if her family had not felt it inadvisable. No especial incentive was held up to her to keep her work at this high standard other than the gratification of her grandparents at her success. It is interesting to note that her reading at ages eight and nine included *St. Nicholas* and *National Geographic Magazine,* in addition to a number of series, such as the *Oz* books, the *Little Colonel* books, and the books of Louisa M. Alcott.

At the age of nine Dora was described by a maternal aunt as being unusually prudent and conscientious, with a strong intellectual curiosity, good judgment, and a keen sense of humor. She also showed very exceptional musical appreciation. The aunt wrote: "She seems to have adult intelligence. She is absolutely dependable, and her judgment can be relied upon. She is quiet and reserved and learns through observation. Has very high ideals, and is refined and affectionate." Dora was rated as outstanding in personal attractiveness by the examiner, who described her as extremely pretty, well-groomed, sweet-voiced, and unaffected.

On the educational tests given in 1922, Dora did work worthy of children three or more grades in advance of that in which she was enrolled. An extra promotion was indicated, but because of her youth was not given. Her play interests were normal, with a preference for quiet or sedentary games. She was doing a great deal of reading of superior type, including *The Swiss Family Robinson, Gulliver's Travels,* and *Tanglewood Tales.*

Six years later we find Dora at the age of fourteen in her third year of high school getting excellent grades and showing an especially strong liking for Latin and Greek. She has decided to prepare herself to teach these languages. She enjoys reading, playing the piano, and playing tennis. She dislikes housework and sewing, but will do her allotted task if she can have a book propped up beside her while working. Fortunately her aunt can sympathize with this attitude.

Dora is a very pretty girl, but is small for her years. This last has proved somewhat of a handicap, as her classmates think her "cute," and try to baby her. She is not allowed by her family to go to many evening affairs, but she does not consider this a hardship. Her class teacher reports that she has a rather ungenerous attitude toward her fellow students and enjoys the discomfiture of a rival. However, as he rates her as popular with other children and a decided leader the criticism may not be as severe as it sounds. At any rate, she served as class representative and class president during her first year in high school, and as a member of the staff of the high-school weekly and journal.

Dora's case is interesting because of its normality. She is a thoroughly wholesome, likable girl from a middle-class environment. No unusual influences have been brought to bear upon her; the public school, the public library, magazines of general circulation, and a few piano and dancing lessons have formed her character and interests. The loss of her parents has been made up for by the devoted and intelligent care of her maternal aunt.

She probably exemplifies as nearly as any subject in our group the achievement and traits of character which one may normally expect of a girl of IQ 150 or 160.

A Superior Scholastic Record

Verda. The scholastic record of this girl is one of the highest to be found in our gifted group. Through four years of high school she received an "A" grade in every academic subject with the exception of one semester of French and another of biology. In each of the latter her grade was "B" for the first semester but "A" for the second. She graduated from high school at age 16-9.

If Verda's record should suggest to the reader a stoop-shouldered, hollow-eyed burner of midnight oil, let us dispel that specter immediately. According to Verda's own report her usual amount of study during her senior year was only six hours a week outside of school hours. She is fond of parties and dances and is very active in the student life, particularly through her literary contributions. As a matter of fact she rates herself (in the follow-up Interest Blank) as rather disliking study. She would rather read, play the piano, compose music, stories or plays, or spend time with her friends. She has written many plays, skits, and songs that have been used in the programs of school organizations.

Verda's exceedingly high IQ (186 at the age of ten) explains in part why she is able to maintain a solid line of A's with little apparent effort. On the occasion of our follow-up tests she was the only subject in our gifted group to make a perfect score, 220, on the Terman Group Test. On the Iowa High School Content Examination her score was within 5 points of the highest score made by any high-school senior in a test survey of a large city. On the Thorndike Examination she earned a score of 109, this being the highest score that any girl in the gifted group has made thus far, and one that has not been materially exceeded by any woman entering Stanford University in the last seven years.

The ability of this subject is manifested in many attainments other than earning high grades. When she had been at college only a few weeks she was made a feature writer on the college newspaper, an honor almost never accorded a freshman at her institution. Her plays, music, and lyrics abound in originality and humor. She has taken rôles in a number of dramatic productions, and recently won a high place in an oratorical contest.

Among the group of our gifted subjects whose scholastic grades have been as high as those of Verda there are several whose IQ's represent fairly closely the median level of the gifted group. It is not necessary, of course, for a child's IQ to be in the 180's if he is to make a flawless high-school record. It seems fairly clear, however, that it is partly the wide margin of Verda's ability over the scholastic demands placed upon it that has made it possible for her to engage in many more creative projects than the usual "straight A" student finds time or energy for.

Verda is one of the most talented writers of our gifted group. One of her poems written at the age of 10, "The Mountains," is probably as meritorious as any juvenile production we have found that had been written by any English or American poet before the age of eleven or twelve years. This poem, with others by Verda, was included in Dr. Jensen's study of literary juvenilia and is reproduced elsewhere in this volume.[1]

[1] See Part III, pages 434, 435, and 436.

CHAPTER XV

SCHOOL ACCELERATION AND SOCIAL ADJUSTMENT

One of the questions most frequently asked regarding bright children whose progress through the grades has been faster than normal is: Hasn't he been socially handicapped by his youth? Hasn't he lost much more through his rapid acceleration than he has gained?

This question cannot be answered in the abstract; we must refer, instead, to particular children. Beyond doubt, extreme acceleration in school works a grave injustice upon some children, particularly upon those whose emotional, social, or physical development is not so accelerated as their mental development. On the other hand, some children appear to thrive on extra promotions, and to function both in the classroom and out of it as would normal individuals two or three years older.

In the main, children who are accelerated mentally tend to be somewhat accelerated socially, although it is perhaps a very rare child in our gifted group who is happy if promoted to the grade to which his mental age, considered alone, would actually entitle him. However, there is such enormous variability in the social adaptability of gifted children that one is not warranted in generalizing. Some gifted children have adaptable and harmonious traits of personality that would make them favorites with children of any age; while some gifted children, like some average children, have personalities that would handicap them in any group with which they were thrown. The reader cannot be too often reminded that gifted children are not all alike, and that the educational treatment suitable for one may not be at all suitable for another.

The following three case studies deal with boys who were all fourteen or fifteen years old at the time of our follow-up and considerably accelerated in school. One of them finished his senior year of high school just before he was sixteen; one finished his first year of Junior College the month of his sixteenth birthday, and the other his junior year of high school before he was fifteen.

A Case of Brilliant Achievement Combined with Social Balance

Donald. Fourteen years old and in the third year of high school, Donald presents a picture of a happily functioning boy. Not only is he superior mentally and scholastically but he is also in excellent physical condition and well adjusted socially.

He comes from fairly well-educated people of superior stock on both sides. His paternal grandfather had a year of college and his maternal grandparents were both normal-school graduates. His father, a most successful business man, is a college graduate, and his mother attended college for one year. The prevailing occupations of his forbears have been farming and business on the paternal side, and law and teaching on the maternal side. The family live in a delightful home in an excellent residential section where Donald, who is an only child, is surrounded by every cultural advantage.

Donald showed a marked interest in drawing at three and a half years, learned to read with little help at four and a half, and at five years composed his first story. He entered school at eight years of age, beginning in the fourth grade. It was less than a year after he entered school that he was located by us in the 1921–22 survey. His IQ was 157, and he was making an excellent school record. His scores on the achievement tests given then showed him capable of doing work about three grades in advance of the one he was in. He stood out particularly in history and civics, literary knowledge, and all-round information. On the basis of the Plays and Games questionnaire, his play interests were rated as more than ordinarily social and as rather masculine. The teacher reported that his companionship was especially sought by other children.

At the time of the follow-up study he was fourteen years old and was making practically a "straight A" record in the third year of high school. His early interest in cartooning does not appear to have persisted to any extent, but his fondness for reading and his literary interests have grown rapidly. He has a real love for books, has read extensively, and is collecting a library of his own. One of his favorite occupations is writing stories, of which he has a great many to his credit. He recently won the first prize in a short-story contest sponsored by a well-known bookshop. In this contest he also took third prize for an essay and received honorable mention for general reading. He is an enthusiastic collector and during the past few years has accumulated in addition to his library about 3,000 stamps, 1,000 lead soldiers, 50 rare coins, 25 toy dogs, 800 baseball pictures, and 600 bottle tops. His lead soldiers have been a persistent hobby, and he spends many hours arranging them in battle array and maneuvering them. Donald is physically active, and fond of playing football, baseball, and tennis. He is a great "fan" of all the sports, always following in season scores of teams, standing of the colleges, names of players, and technicalities of the game. At high school he is a member of the R.O.T.C., a sergeant in rank, and soon to be a lieutenant. (A later report informs us that he was advanced to captaincy by his senior year.) A short time ago he won a medal for the best work in sergeant's individual drill in an annual, city-wide, R.O.T.C. competition.

On our 1927–28 Interest Blank Donald lists as his favorite pastimes reading, playing with other children, and playing with his soldiers. His taste in companionship is illustrated by his own description of his best chum, a fifteen-year-old boy who is athletic, fond of reading good books, an Eagle Scout, sociable, and good-natured.

Donald's most notable achievement was his selection, at the age of eleven, as Boy Mayor of one of the largest cities of California. The judges made their choice by examining the candidates on city government, current events, and affairs in general. Two outstanding boys from each school were chosen by the principals to compete, there being 150 boys in all. During his week as Boy Mayor, Donald was of course featured in all the papers; he was fêted, called on for many speeches, and otherwise made much of, but he came through it unspoiled.

At the age of fourteen Donald was 6 feet 1 inch in height and weighed 155 pounds; otherwise he was the same healthy, wholesome, freckle-faced, red-haired lad that he had been six years before. His manner was poised and unassuming, and he spoke of his achievements as interesting experiences, with no taint of bragging. He mixes well with his schoolmates and is much interested in school affairs. He is out for debating and baseball, and also holds a position as assistant in his school bank. (A later report has been received to the effect that he was made head of the school bank in his senior year.)

Though his family is in most comfortable circumstances, Donald likes to work and earn money. When he was only thirteen and a half he spent his Christmas vacation as clerk in a bookshop. The following Christmas vacation he again worked as a clerk, this time in the book section of one of the large department stores. His vocational ambition is to enter law.

On the tests which he was given in the follow-up study he made excellent scores. At age 14-8 his Terman Group Test point score was 203, or 12 points higher than the median for our fourteen-year-old gifted boys. His scores on the educational tests were correspondingly high.

We have in Donald a rather extreme case of acceleration which has had none of the unfavorable results so commonly believed to be inevitable. Size and mature appearance, as well as natural social gifts, have probably contributed to this happy outcome. No better illustration could be given of the necessity of considering each case as an individual problem when the question of extra promotion arises.

A GIFTED LEADER

Gordon. At age 15-2 Gordon entered his senior year of high school. Though he was one of the youngest of an extremely large class in a metropolitan high school, he had been far from lost in the shuffle during his three years of attendance. By the time he graduated, his record of scholarship, while adequate to gain him admission to the scholarship honor society and to a university of high standards, had been almost eclipsed by his record of activities as business manager of the school paper, athletic manager, member of the Board of Directors of the school self-government, captain in the R.O.T.C., secretary of the R.O.T.C. officers' club, and manager of the school band. The fact of his managership of school athletics is the more remarkable because Gordon is not himself an athlete. At his school, until his own recent election, the position of manager had always been meted out to the brawn of the athletic field.

When Gordon was first located by us, his social capacities were not developed to so satisfactory a level as they now are. At the time of the original survey his age was

9-10 and his IQ 164 (corrected IQ 167). He was in the low-fifth grade, and thus only a year to a year and a half accelerated in grade placement. His teacher, in filling out our School Information Blank, made the comment: "Is learning habits of idleness. Grade too easy. Other pupils not up to his ability." The results of the Stanford Achievement Test which he took at that time corroborated the teacher's judgment, for his score on the various subtests varied from high-school standard in arithmetic to above twelfth-grade standard in history and literature.

In answer to questions in the original School Information Blank, the teacher indicated that Gordon was a solitary child whose company was "rather avoided" by the others. She remarked that he would "rather read or talk with some one at recess" than to play, and that "children do not care to play with him." Nevertheless she rated him average on the trait "popularity." The Home Information Blank filled out by his parents at approximately the same date gave no hint of any difficulty in social adjustment, and assigned him an average rating both on "popularity" and on "fondness for large groups." Gordon himself, on the Interest Blank filled out concurrently, indicated that he would rather play with one other person than with several other persons. "Going to parties, picnics, dances, club meetings, etc.," he rated as a type of activity which he neither liked nor disliked. Thus there seems to be no evidence that Gordon was a serious misfit at this period of his development, though it seems that his qualities of leadership developed to considerable extent after he was first known to us.

By the time of our next reports from home and school, when Gordon was 11-7, he was in the high-eighth grade and president of his class. He had completed the sixth and seventh grades in one year. His teacher wrote: "Gordon seems to be a well-developed, thoroughly normal child in all respects. He is not selfish, and seems to mix very well with other children. He is well liked and the children recognize his uniformly satisfactory class work." It should be noted that although Gordon was at this time two or two and a half years accelerated in school, his social adjustment appeared to be notably better than it had been two years previously, when he was less accelerated by one year and was working in a grade "too easy" for his ability. Whether his improvement in social adaptability was due in part to his extra promotions, and the consequent shrinkage of the gap between ability and effort expended at school, it is impossible to say, but it seems reasonably certain that his personality suffered no injurious effects as a result of the extra promotions.

Gordon's record of high-school activities has already been reviewed, and speaks for itself. On the School Information Blank filled out by one of the teachers during the present follow-up, it is stated that his companionship is "especially sought," and that his attitude toward school is "highly satisfactory," though he is also rated as "rather vain." Now, as earlier, he is rated as having less than the average "fondness for large groups"; nevertheless he is rated above average in leadership and popularity. He tells us on the Interest Blank filled out by himself that his best chum is a boy of eighteen who is "mathematically and socially inclined."

Gordon is an avid reader and has been throughout the period we have known him. On our 1928 follow-up Interest Blank, he indicated that he preferred reading to any other occupation when he had an hour or two to spend as he pleased. He estimated that he spends 15 to 25 hours weekly on general reading and only three and a half hours weekly on home study. He has between 150 and 200 books of his own, and his parents tell us that he buys the *Bookman* every month at the news stands in order to keep up on the criticisms of the newest books.

Another of Gordon's hobbies has been photography. At the age of thirteen he fitted up a photographic dark-room in his home so that he could develop his own pictures. He is also interested in agriculture and as an occupational choice is considering this as a possible alternative for civil engineering, the profession for which he has long intended to prepare himself. Shortly after graduating from high school he had a practical test of agricultural life, spending several weeks working in a vineyard and earning a wage of $24.00 a week.

Before Gordon graduated from high school he debated whether it might be best to stay out of school for a year before entering college. He was anxious to take as substantial a part in the student activities of his college as he had in those of his high school, and he feared his youth might stand in his way. However, his record of success at high school, coupled with the fact that he is a large, well-developed boy who could be taken for two years older than he really is, caused him to decide in favor of immediate college entrance. However, he and his parents are considering the advisability of his taking five years of undergraduate work instead of four, in order that he may be able to include in his program more cultural electives than would be possible in the rigid curriculum of the engineering course he plans to follow.

A Case of Unwise Acceleration

Roger. For a fifteen-year-old college boy who has been continually in boarding school from a very tender age, Roger presents an astonishing picture of profound childishness. The *savoir faire,* the self-reliance and manliness that tradition would have develop in boys who leave the protection of the parental roof to live among strangers, are all lacking in him.

Roger was nearly eleven years old when first tested by us, and was finishing the seventh grade in an exclusive boarding school for boys. The Stanford-Binet test gave him at the age of 10-10 an IQ of 149 (corrected, 152). A Stanford Achievement Test administered a few weeks later showed him to be advanced in most school subjects to the standards of grades several years beyond that in which he was located, although his precocity in this respect was not so marked as in many other cases of our gifted group. In language and in arithmetic, for example, his scores corresponded to the norms for H7 and L8 respectively. In history and civics and in literary knowledge his scores were relatively highest, corresponding to the norm for L11. According to the teacher who filled out Roger's School Information Blank at that time, the boy was doing very mediocre school work. The teachers who had him in class attributed this to laziness and lack of application. Whether or not the school felt that stiffer course requirements would stimulate him to put forth more nearly the effort he was capable of, we do not know. Our records at this point show merely that Roger skipped the eighth grade, and entered the ninth grade at the age of 11-3. His progress after that time was at the normal rate. At 15-3 he entered the junior college department of the school that he had attended most of the time since the age of ten.

The wisdom of placing a boy of Roger's type in the ninth grade when he was barely eleven seems to us at least questionable. When still in the seventh grade he was said by his teacher to be a solitary child, "decidedly less popular than the average," though his mother, in filling out the Home Information Blank, was inclined to be more liberal, assigning him an average rating upon popularity and leadership. However, the mother, a widow who had remarried, became absorbed in her new family and solved the problem of the eldest child of her first marriage by sending him away now to one boarding school and now to another. She possibly knew too little about her son to appraise his social adjustment correctly; at any rate we were told by his teachers after he had been in the ninth grade for several months that he was still below normal in social adaptability. As in the first school report, the poor impression made by Roger in most of his classes was also mentioned.

At the time of our recent follow-up, Roger's situation was rather pitiful. At an age when most boys are in their second year of high school, Roger was finishing his first year of junior college. He was thus three years accelerated. At this time he not only did not look or act like a college youth, but looked and acted several years younger than he really was. There were transparent attempts to assume the rôle of collegian, but with his round, childish face, short stature, and wistful expression, his stiff dancing-school bow when he acknowledged introductions, and his naïve conversation, the effect produced was that of a young child playing grown-up. He was courteous and responsive, but ill at ease in the presence of the other members of the group with whom he took our follow-up tests. The fact of his precocious school advancement was evidently a source of both gratification and chagrin to him. At one instant he told the examiner with childlike relish that he was a freshman in junior college, "though I won't be sixteen till this summer, and haven't done a bit of studying since I entered the college." A little later he was confessing that he found life very dull. "You get so sick of going to movies twice a week, playing bridge, and then doing the same thing all over again. There's nothing to do, and I'm left out of everything." And he added plaintively, "I can't go out with girls the way the other fellows do because they would all say the girls were cradle-snatchers."

The head master of Roger's school tells us that the older boys in his dormitory are very kind to him, in fact "baby him to death!" This is doubtless easier for him to bear than teasing or hazing would be, yet his failure to be accepted upon a footing of equality weighs upon his mind. If Roger were a boy who had true intellectual enthusiasms, who could be happy in following out his "drives," his situation would be quite different. It might then be argued that the social deprivations incident to his accelerated progress were justified. But—we have here the evidence of the Interest Blank which he recently filled out—he dislikes study, he dislikes spending time alone, and reading he likes only "fairly well." In addition to the recurrent statements of his teachers that he lacks application, and in addition to his own statement that he "never studies" and dislikes to study, we have objective data from the Iowa High School Content examination which he took during the follow-up. Though his total score was well above the norms for high-school seniors or college freshmen, it was not so exceptional as to indicate that he had exhausted the possibilities of the high-school curriculum. The score, which was at the 80 per-centile of unselected college freshmen, was a third of a standard deviation below the median made by the college freshmen of our gifted group. He was relatively low in mathematics and English, his score on the latter being only a little above the norm for high-school seniors.

In our judgment, Roger has neither the maturity, the interests, nor the attitudes to make him a successful and happy college student at present. His case is one of the clearest in our entire gifted group of unwise haste in school advancement.

THE SOCIAL HANDICAP OF HIGH IQ

Someone has said that genius is of necessity solitary, since the population is so sparse at the higher levels of mental ability. However, adult genius is mobile and can seek out its kind. It is in the case of the child with extraordinarily high IQ that the social problem is most acute. If the IQ is 180 the intellectual level at six is almost on a par with that of the average eleven-year-old, and at ten or eleven is not far from that of the average high-school graduate. Physical development, on the other hand, is not likely to be accelerated more than 10 per cent, and social development probably not more than 20 or 30 per cent. The inevitable result is that the child of 180 IQ has one of the most difficult problems of social adjustment that any human being is ever called upon to meet.

The situation is indeed so difficult that one may well wonder how it is ever possible for such a child to develop into a socially normal adult. He cannot hope to be accepted by ordinary children of his mental level. However well he may know their games, he is too immature for them physically and finds no welcome in their play groups. There is no scorn like the scorn of older boys for the younger and weaker who aspire to equality with them, especially if they are conscious of their own relative inferiority to the latter in intelligence. In both sexes, although possibly somewhat less with girls than with boys, the natural reaction of average children is to enhance their own self feelings by advertising whatever weaknesses they find in the one who is responsible for their sense of intellectual inferiority. The physical and social immaturity of the younger child offers the desired opportunity for evening up the score.

If the gifted child attempts instead to make his social adaptations on his own age level, the situation may offer fewer inherent difficulties, but the outcome can hardly be satisfactory. He speaks a language which average children of his age literally do not understand. Their stupidities render him impatient; they are interested in nothing that he is interested in. A considerable number of gifted children would probably find a solution of a sort on this level if they were given opportunity, but after entrance to school the child of 180 IQ is soon cut off by multiple promotion from association with others of his age. Whether this is a less or a greater evil than holding the child to school tasks that make no demand upon his intelligence depends upon the individual case. In all probability a compromise between the two evils is the wiser course in the large majority of cases.

The two following cases offer fairly typical examples of the difficulties involved. When the child of 180 IQ develops as normal social traits as we find in either of these subjects one may well feel gratified. It would take a child of very superior social endowment to make the adjustments more satisfactorily than they have made them.

A Bachelor of Arts at Sixteen

David. This boy was tested by one of us in 1917. At that time he was seven years and four months old and earned a Stanford-Binet IQ of 184.[1] He had not yet attended school, but had acquired a vast fund of information at home, could read fluently, and could perform complicated arithmetic processes. He entered junior high school at nine and senior high school at ten, graduating from high school at age 12-3 and winning a scholarship to an eastern university. The Thorndike Test which he took at this time yielded a score cf 106, this being 18 points above the mean for our gifted boys, most of whom were at least four years older than David when they took it. At age twelve David passed the state examinations for high-school graduates with an average above 90, thus qualifying for a state scholarship carrying $100 a year for four years, in addition to his college scholarship.

Graduating from college at sixteen, with honors, he transferred to another university, where he registered as a graduate student in the physical sciences. He was awarded a graduate fellowship after his first graduate year, and intends to remain to get his Ph.D. He had had little work in the physical sciences as an undergraduate, and accordingly it has been necessary for him to take a number of undergraduate courses before beginning research. However, one of his teachers says that in making reports before a graduate seminar David shows a command of the intellectual aspects of his subject like that which one would expect of a college professor. He intends to make research his life work. (Since the foregoing was written David has accepted a position in the technical research department of a motion-picture industry in order to get some practical experience before completing his work for the doctorate.)

From the time that David was first known to us he has lived more or less to himself and has rarely sought the companionship of other young people. In early childhood he invented an imaginary land which he elaborated in the utmost detail. He also compiled a dictionary of words composed by himself, devised games, including schemes for three-handed and four-handed checkers (age ten), com-

---

[1] For another account of David see Terman, L. M., *The Intelligence of School Children*, 1919, pp. 251–260.

posed stories, plays, and music, compiled statistics, made countless mathematical computations, and kept notebooks of observations upon natural phenomena. Our records show that few of our gifted subjects have combined such intensity of mental life and such versatility of intellectual interests.

Professor Leta S. Hollingworth, who has been in close touch with the parents of David, includes a number of significant facts pertaining to his infancy, his parents, and his ancestry, in a case history which she has recorded in her book, *Gifted Children,* from which the following paragraphs are quoted.[1]

D. could stand, holding to chairs, at nine months of age, and walked alone at eleven to twelve months. He could say words at eight months, and could talk in sentences at eleven months. At eight months he said "little boy" when his shadow appeared on a wall. He cut his first tooth at four months. At the age of eighteen months he learned to read, sitting in his mother's lap at the typewriter, and looking at the letters. . . . .

D. is descended from Russian Jews in the paternal branch and from English Jews in the maternal branch. The father immigrated to America at an early age. He is a high-school graduate and was a student of engineering, but abandoned these studies in the third year to do newspaper work. He is now in the advertising business in a large city. His leisure is spent in writing. He has recently published his fourth book, a philosophical drama dealing with religion. The three preceding books were novels, the first of which was published when he was twenty-one years of age. . . . .

D's mother went to school only a few years. She has been largely self-taught. Before marriage she was statistician and registrar of a large philanthropic organization. She has published stories, reviews, and poems, and recently published a book on education. She has always taken part personally in the education of D. . . . .

D. is an only child. Conspicuous relatives beyond the first degree of kinship include a chief rabbi of Moscow, who was exiled for aiding the nihilists, a distinguished lawyer, a man who by his own efforts became a millionaire, a concert pianist, a composer and virtuoso, a writer, and a relative decorated for science in Poland. The maternal great-grandfather was a famous rabbi who compiled and published a Jewish calendar covering the period of 414 years. . . . . This rabbi was also the great-grandfather of the four first cousins of D. whose intelligence quotients have been taken. These cousins yielded IQ's of 156, 150, 130, and 122, respectively. A second cousin in the maternal line yielded at the age of six years an IQ of 157.

David, age eighteen at the time of the follow-up, and in his second year of graduate work, is a tall, slender boy

[1] The Macmillan Company, 1926, pp. 241–248.

whose somewhat stooped shoulders and pale complexion suggest a sedentary mode of life. He keeps long hours in the laboratory and library, and professors and students alike recognize his ability. Unfortunately, his human contacts are confined very largely to the laboratory and classroom. He is well liked by those who know him, even though they consider him a little "different," but he makes few acquaintances and takes only passing interest in many of the things that stir so deeply the emotions of the average college student. David is not and has never been maladjusted in the ordinary sense of that term; he is merely inclined to be solitary. The indications are that he will develop into a man without eccentricity other than the retiring disposition that often characterizes scientists and scholars.

Brilliant and Well Adjusted

Madeline. When she was located during the original survey Madeline's IQ proved to be one of the two highest in our entire main experimental group. At age 6-7 her M.A. was 12-8, yielding an IQ of 192. She was then in the high-third grade, but her Stanford Achievement Test scores corresponded to fifth- and sixth-grade norms.

According to Dr. Yates, who tested her, Madeline was a pretty child with a mature manner and quaint, old-fashioned ways and speech. Her responses upon our Plays and Games questionnaire indicated play interests that were socially normal and ordinarily active, and revealed a knowledge of plays and games that was far wider in extent than that of the average six-year-old child. She was precocious in reading, and the quality of the books she preferred was very superior. A letter from her father written a few months after she turned seven told us that her parents' chief concern was "to keep her doing something else than reading."

Her score on the Wyman Association Test designated her as a child with decidedly intellectual interests. This rating is fully corroborated by her developmental history, for she gave evidence of her superior intelligence and of spontaneity of interests at a very early age. At seven months she was able to point out all the pictures on the walls of her home when they were named to her. She could identify the pictures of six American poets when she was a little over a year old. She knew the common flowers before the age of three.

At three she learned to read with very little help other than telling her the words she asked about. "Reading seems to be born in her," her mother reported. "The maturity of her interpretations and expression in reading has always been a subject of surprise and comment by others."

She could count to 100 by three years, learned to play parchesi at four years, and carried the powers of 2 mentally to the 20th as a Sunday afternoon pastime before the age of six. The parents reported regarding her arithmetical ability, "She visualizes combinations, and in mental operations uses many expedients and short cuts." At seven years she was writing poetry of a rather religious nature.

At age 4-3 Madeline entered kindergarten, and despite the fact that she could read, her parents kept her there a term. They felt that she needed manual training, for she had always been slow and awkward about any sort of hand work.

She entered the first grade at age 4-11 and completed the first two grades during her first year in school. Since this double promotion, however, she has been held back to the lock-step pace, at her parents' suggestion, because of her age. For a time she was something of a problem because of her listlessness and lack of interest in school. At home she bothered her parents by chronic habits of time wasting and procrastination — traits which had arisen, no doubt, from her ability to master things so quickly and easily that there seemed to be no incentive for haste. However, her indifference to school was replaced by enthusiasm when she entered junior high school and later high school. The study of mature subjects is much more interesting to her. We find her at the time of the 1927–28 follow-up finishing the ninth grade at the age of 12-9 and making "A" grades in all except an occasional course which she regards as uninteresting or purposeless.

Madeline is now of about average size and looks like a healthy, normal child. Other children feel that she is different because of her youth and seriousness and mature attitude, but her parents and teachers report that she is overcoming an earlier shyness and becoming much better adapted socially. There is apparently not the slightest feeling of superiority on her part toward other children, but rather one of inferiority as far as personal attractiveness, dress, and wealth are concerned. She is attending a public high school in a wealthy, exclusive district, and feels herself inferior to the others because she has not so much money.

Madeline is very slow and deliberate in her actions, and her tendency toward procrastination has persisted. She lingers over her dishwashing and other duties as much as over her studies. Often when she is sent out to the back yard at night to dispose of kitchen refuse she fails to return until her mother goes in search of her. Her mother always finds her studying the heavens. Madeline has recently developed a strong interest in astronomy, has devoured several books on the subject, and is planning to become an astronomer. Her health has always been good. She has had the usual children's diseases and is susceptible to colds, but has never been seriously ill.

At the age of 10-9 Madeline visited Stanford with her parents. A Stanford-Binet test administered to her on this occasion gave an IQ (corrected) of 190. When, at the age of 12-5, she was retested during the follow-up, she "broke" the Stanford-Binet Scale by passing every test. On the Terman Group Test her score was 196, but here, also, she came so close to the limit of the scale that she was not adequately measured.

Madeline's heredity is decidedly superior. For at least two or three generations on each side the ancestors were American-born. On the paternal side the grandfather was of English and Irish descent. He graduated from college and became first a high-school teacher and later a school superintendent. He was a prominent leader in the crusade days of the prohibition movement. The paternal grandmother was of Scotch and French descent. She was a graduate of a state normal school and a teacher previous to her marriage. A paternal great-grandfather was a preacher, a great uncle was president of a state university, and a great aunt was a teacher, author, and literary critic. This side of the family is also related to William Cullen Bryant. Teaching and preaching have been the prevailing occupations.

On the maternal side the grandfather was of German and Dutch descent. He held the degree of A.B., A.M., and M.D., and was successively a teacher, high-school principal, superintendent of schools, and physician. He later held the chair of Physiology and Pharmacology in the medical school of a university. The maternal grandmother, who was of remote English descent, was also a university graduate. A great-grandfather on this side was a college graduate and teacher.

The parents of Madeline are both university graduates. The father, after completing his undergraduate work, obtained a graduate degree in forestry. He has been for a number of years in the United States Forestry Service and is now on a university faculty. His interests are wide and include philosophy, religion, botany, photography, astronomy, and city planning. The mother also followed the undergraduate college course with post-graduate study, almost completing the work for an M.A. degree in Greek. She was a high-school teacher before her marriage and occasionally does substitute teaching now. She is also active in church and club work.

Madeline has two younger sisters whose IQ's are 167 and 162.

The family is in only moderately good financial circumstances, having had considerable responsibility in the care of relatives. The home, however, is large, comfortable, and well-located, and many books are in evidence.

CHAPTER XVI

DETERIORATION OF IQ OR ACHIEVEMENT

Two Outstanding Cases of Decrease in IQ

Bertha. At the age of 6-0 Bertha earned a Stanford-Binet mental age of 8-3 and an IQ of 138. Bertha's sister had already qualified for the gifted group with an IQ of 141. As it was our practice to include in the group any sibling who tested with IQ 135 or above, Bertha became one of our subjects even though her score was two points below the regular boundary, 140.

Dr. Goodenough, who administered the Stanford-Binet test, obtained also from Bertha a drawing which was later scored according to standards ascertained through her extensive investigation of intellectual factors in children's drawings.[1] The mental age and IQ upon this test agreed exactly with those upon the Stanford-Binet, i.e., M.A. 8-3 and IQ 138, thus furnishing valuable corroboration of the validity of the Stanford-Binet rating. At the time of the examination Dr. Goodenough made the following notations: "A charming child, very chatty, but not forward. Responds readily. Shows good knowledge of her own abilities and inabilities."

In the 1927–28 follow-up we find Bertha entering the fifth grade of the Los Angeles schools at age 10-6. The Stanford-Binet test given her in 1927 yields the following result: C.A. 10-9, M.A. 12-2, IQ 113. The rating represents a drop in IQ of 25 points, and accordingly Bertha was included with the group of "lowered IQ" cases to whom a Herring-Binet was administered. The latter test yielded the result: C.A. 11-7, M.A. 12-5, IQ 107.

The 1927–28 Binet scores are corroborated by group intelligence tests administered by her school, and by the judgment of her teacher. Her IQ computed from her score on N.I.T., Scale B, Form 1, taken at age 10-7 is 106, and com-

---

[1] Goodenough, F. L., *Measurement of Intelligence by Drawings*, World Book Company, 1926.

puted from her score on N.I.T., Scale B, Form 2, taken at age 11-8, is 104. When her teacher was interviewed and a follow-up School Information Blank was given her to fill out, the teacher asked the field worker in genuine surprise, "Why is Bertha included in the gifted children group?" She added that it would never occur to her to select Bertha as having more than average ability. While conceding that she was imaginative in English work and that she read with good expression, the teacher thought her poor in spelling, and quite without "arithmetic sense."

Looking into Bertha's background and development, we fail to find anything of very clear significance that might shed light upon her change in mental status. She is an attractive child, full of motor energy, vivacious in speech, and most social in her interests. The mother tells us that at home Bertha is very tractable and easy to manage. She is good at taking responsibility and co-operative in household tasks. She is very sensitive, however, almost morbidly so, and "constantly refers remarks and jokes to herself as slights when none are intended."

Several positive facts are found in her medical history, but their bearing upon her mental development is entirely speculative. She has since babyhood been subject to fainting, particularly at the sight of blood, although her general health is good. Her physicians have diagnosed the trouble as non-epileptic. There had been a bladder infection which had cleared up. A year before the retests the subject had suffered a severe emotional shock which made her hysterical for a few hours, but it seems unlikely that this experience could have materially affected her intelligence rating.

If we look to Bertha's home environment for an explanation of her 1927 IQ we are entirely at a loss. The father is an engineer and the family lives in comfort, though not in luxury. A fine spirit of companionship exists between the parents and the children, and the members of the family usually take their recreation together. In every way Bertha's environment appears to be a wholesome one in which to rear a child.

Jerome. When tested on the Stanford-Binet at age 5-2 Jerome made an IQ of 139, this being within one point of the standard for inclusion in the Regular gifted group. Because of his strong musical appreciation, he was included as a member of the special ability group which has been followed by us since 1922 by the same techniques as those employed with the Regular group.

At age 11-1 Jerome's M.A. on the Stanford-Binet was 11-9 and his IQ 106. The decrease of 33 points in IQ was more than corroborated by his IQ of 97 on the Herring-Binet taken at age 11-10. On the Terman Group Test administered by his school when he was 12-10 he made a score of 112, which corresponds to M.A. 14-11 and IQ 116. The differences in IQ as calculated from the three tests may be due to unreliability of the tests themselves, or to incomplete overlapping in the functions measured by the tests, or to a change in the rate of Jerome's mental growth between ages 11-9 and 12-10. The three tests agree, however, in pointing to considerable deterioration in IQ since the time of the first test.

The original examiner found the attention of the subject "hard to hold," as did also the examiner who tested him during the recent follow-up. His kindergarten teacher at that time reported his attitude at school to be one of "intense interest," and gave him extremely high ratings on originality, intelligence, and common sense, all of which might cause us to discount the impression which he conveyed when taking the Stanford-Binet test if it were not for subsequent reports from his teachers and parents. His second-grade teacher described the quality of his work as superior, but indicated that he was indifferent to classroom discipline. She added the following notation: "Is heedless. Does not realize any sense of obligation." When eight years old and in the fourth grade he received school marks ranging from 1— to 3; the following year he caused his parents concern because he "made no effort to do anything except play."

Jerome was placed in a military school as a day pupil when he reached the sixth grade (age 10-10). He enjoyed this school, did fairly creditable work (B average), and completed the sixth, seventh, and eighth grade in two years. Toward the end of the eighth grade (at age 12-4) he took the New Stanford Achievement Test, Form B; his composite score corresponded to an educational age of 14-8 and EQ of 119, but was no more than average for his grade (as he was about two years accelerated in grade placement).

Jerome has now been in high school for one semester, where he has received grades ranging from 2 (composition, algebra, typing) to 4 (history). He is reported by the school to have displayed "infantile" judgment on one or two occasions, and to be a little aloof with the other pupils, but, in the words of his instructor in physical education, "He is all right after you get to know him."

Other than the indifference to study that has character-ized the subject during the greater part of his school career, and the fact that his spontaneous interests lack the intellec-tual cast so often typical of the child of high IQ, there are few positive data in Jerome's history that appear to have special significance in the light of his change in intelligence rating. His health is excellent, and there is no record of serious illnesses. We have no information upon his heredity, for he is a foster child adopted in infancy. We know, how-ever, that his home environment is rather ideal (unless the fact that he is being reared as an only child is a disadvan-tage). His foster father is a well-to-do professional man; both foster parents take a keen interest in his development and show a sympathetic understanding of his problems.

In social relationships Jerome appears to be fairly well adjusted, though no traits of leadership are evident. He prefers the companionship of a single chum rather than that of a group of boys, and has shown little interest in athletics or in organized play.

The musical ability that was clearly evident at age five (and earlier, according to home reports) is still one of his marked traits. He is fond of playing the piano for his own amusement, but is reluctant to apply himself to serious practice. It is somewhat surprising that even in this field of genuine and long-standing interest, the motivation is not strong enough to overcome his characteristic indifference to standards of accomplishment.

A Case of Moderate Deterioration of IQ and Achievement

Clara. In the hazy shadows of a clairvoyant's home—a dingy dwelling in a run-down district near the heart of Los Angeles—Clara has developed from a beautiful, charm-ing, intelligent, and studious child into a still beautiful and charming but somewhat less intelligent and studious young woman.

At age 10-6 Clara's IQ was 148. She was in grade H5, and was reported by her teacher to have a great desire to excel in her work, to be decidedly original, and to be very well-adjusted socially. By accepted age-grade standards Clara was only slightly accelerated in grade placement, but her scores on most of the separate subjects of the Stanford Achievement Test equaled the norms for the seventh, eighth, or ninth grades.

At the time of the follow-up her mother and teachers were unanimous in their opinion that Clara was a poor student, lazy, and lacking in ambition. Her score of 151 on the Terman Group Test (at age 16-3) fell at only the 65th percentile of eleventh-grade scores, this being so low as compared with the performance of the majority of the gifted group that the result was checked by retesting her three months later upon a second form of the test. This time she made a somewhat better score (176), which raised her above the 80th percentile of eleventh-grade students, but was still 20 points below the median score of our sixteen-year-old gifted subjects who took the test.

Clara's scholastic grades have been almost consistently mediocre since she entered high school (at age 13-2). The predominant mark is C, but there are some scattered B's as well as several D's. On the Burch Test of Literary Comprehension she made scores of 32, 43, and 29 upon the three parts, scores which were not conspicuously different from those of our other eleventh-grade gifted subjects and which were in harmony with a strong fondness for reading that has been one of her characteristics from early childhood. Her scores on the Hotz Algebra Scales were absurdly low: score of 1 on the Equation and Formula Scale, and 2 on the Problems Scale, although she had completed an algebra course two years before with semester grades of B and C.

Apparently Clara is as popular as ever with her schoolmates, for the reports both from her home and her school describe her as a girl with many friends. She has not taken much leadership in student activities, but has been a member of several athletic teams and has twice represented her registration room in minor offices.

There is no record of the subject's having suffered any serious illnesses since the time of the original survey, but she received "injuries to her face and hand" in an automobile accident that necessitated her absence from school for two months.

It is not, of course, possible to say what relationship Clara's unconventional environment, complicated by Italian parents who became intermittently divorced and reconciled, may have had to do with the rather disappointing turn which her development has taken. From our knowledge of the home background it seems reasonably clear that individual ambition among the three children of the family is not encouraged by their domineering, clairvoyant mother. On the other hand, several members of the gifted group have shown deterioration under extremely favorable environmental conditions. The cases of Bertha and Jerome summarized in this chapter are examples in point.

Superior Intelligence with Inferior Scholarship

The fact that a child has superior intelligence is far from being a sure guaranty that he will find interest and pleasure in school work. In general there is undoubtedly a positive correlation between mental ability and interest in the tasks which the school provides, but the correlation is so far from perfect that it is possible to find every grade of scholarship associated with the higher grades of intelligence. The causes of the indifferent school work which we sometimes find among gifted children are as numerous and varied as those which are involved in the inferior accomplishment of average children. Ill health and irregularity of attendance are perhaps not often primary factors, since the gifted child is usually located in a school grade one to three years below that which corresponds to his mental level. If there are no other complicating factors, the loss of several weeks or even months in attendance need not seriously affect the end-term grades. To be sure, there are some teachers who in such cases award low marks or even refuse promotion as a matter of principle, but an objective test will nearly always show the gifted child far in advance of the majority of his classmates in all his school studies. If justice were always done, hardly any child of 140 IQ would fail of promotion because of irregular attendance.

The factors most often responsible are those of emotion, temperament, and personality. Sometimes poor scholarship is due to bad feeling between the child and his teacher. Unfortunately, there are a good many teachers who get a certain satisfaction out of humbling the pride of their brightest pupils. We have considerable reason to believe that even university teachers find it hard to deal justly with the fourteen-year-old college freshman. Such personality faults as contrariness, stubbornness, and lack of pride are occasionally involved. Some gifted children are anything but docile, and, like Sir Walter Scott in his youth, have a natural dislike of doing any task that another has laid down for them.

Perhaps the most frequent single cause of poor scholarship on the part of intellectually superior children is lack of interest. For this the school is sometimes to blame, but not always. The correlation between interest and ability is at best only moderately high. One finds very gifted children who seem to be utterly lacking in intellectual drive. They have no zeal, no pride of accomplishment. They may busy themselves with other activities or just loaf and daydream.

Several of our subjects, after leading their classes for years, have awakened to the fact that greater recognition among their fellows may be won in other ways and have voluntarily abdicated their scholastic leadership. Weary of the reputation they have earned for brilliance, and perhaps smarting under the jibe of being bookworms, they may even go to the opposite extreme of neglecting their work and flaunting their lack of interest in it. This change is especially likely to come at the time of admission to high school or college, as this offers a favorable opportunity to turn a new leaf.

The shift of attitude may be radical and reckless or it may be moderate and deliberately reasoned. Changes of the latter sort are not always to be condemned. The college youth who looks forward to a career in business, politics, or law, may well derive more benefit from mediocre class work, plus wide participation in student activities, than he could get from a higher grade of scholarship without the training in social leadership. In a few cases we have not hesitated to give this advice to gifted subjects of the too bookish type who have asked our opinion. Such advice would perhaps be questionable in the case of a youth who proposed to devote himself to a career of scholarship or scientific research, but for those whose success in life is likely to be influenced greatly by their ability to deal with people we feel it can be fully justified. The student whose score on the Thorndike Intelligence Examination was by a considerable margin the highest that has been made by anyone entering Stanford since the tests were first instituted, graduated (for the A.B. and J.D. degrees) with a scholastic

record that was only a little above average, but with a record for popularity and leadership rarely equaled. On his
leaving the University one of us informed him of his Thorndike score and asked what was responsible for his indifferent scholastic record. The answer was that he knew he had
a better mind than most men, that in high school he always
earned A's, but that when he entered college he decided he
ought to study people if he was to make a success as a
lawyer. Viewing the matter retrospectively he said he was
entirely satisfied with the choice he had made; that he had
taken care to learn enough law to know what he was about,
and that he knew when the time came to take the position
which had long been promised him in a leading law firm
he would have no difficulty in working up his cases. His
judgment seems to have been borne out, for within three
years after completing his professional training he was
made a partner in the law firm which he entered.

One of our gifted subjects, a high-school student, suffered
so acutely from his reputation for being a bookworm that
he went to the extreme of counterfeiting ignorance and stu-
pidity in his class recitations.

However, as we have already emphasized, the inferior
scholastic records in our group of subjects have had many
causes. More often it was not a matter of deliberate choice
of other ends. Love affairs, personal griefs, financial wor-
ries, overwork in self-support, dislike of teachers, ill-health,
psychotic tendencies, and mental inertia have operated.
In a few cases the deterioration of school work has been
paralleled by a corresponding deterioration of IQ and is
doubtless explained by the latter. A few typical cases are
described.

A CASE OF INFERIOR SCHOLARSHIP DUE TO INDOLENCE

Edwin. When sixteen, and classified as a high-school
junior, Edwin was requested to withdraw from the high
school he had entered four years earlier at the age of
twelve. He had completed sixteen credits with a low C
average. Eight failures were recorded against him, four in
Latin, two in geometry, one in American literature, and one
in hygiene. He was failing in three additional subjects when
asked to withdraw.

The school believed that it had done all in its power to
encourage better scholarship; conference after conference

had been held, but Edwin's promises bore no fruit. He was never rebellious, and frequently wept; his only explanation was that he did not like to study. The proposal of a transfer to another school was met with scorn; he liked the school, had many friends, and went out each successive year for football, only to be disqualified at the announcement of grades. He was happy and active in the general social life of the school, even though his academic record prevented any opportunity for leadership.

A search for an explanation brings many interesting facts to light; but just what combination of factors really accounts for this outstanding failure is difficult to say. Edwin comes from a home of superior cultural opportunities and ambitions; on both sides of the family professional occupations have prevailed. The baffled parents have run the gamut from gentle reproof and advice to stern denouncement, but with little success. A summer at manual labor brought Edwin back with a seemingly sincere determination to succeed. Actual evidence of application followed for a time, only to vanish in less than two months.

If one were predicting future school adjustment and achievement on the basis of Edwin's grammar school record, it is very unlikely that one would conceive the full extent of his present difficulties. His IQ in 1921 was 141. In the sixth grade he was reported by his teacher to be accurate, painstaking, and brilliant in written work, although timid and self-conscious in verbal recitations and in his play with other children. In the eighth grade a similar report was made except on the score of written work, where poor penmanship tended to lower his former rating. A basis for self-consciousness might well be found in the boy's size. When examined for the Stanford gifted group at the age of ten he was thirty pounds overweight, which is 35.6 per cent above the norm for his height and age. From subsequent reports, however, it seems that the tendency to obesity has grown less marked. The large number of his boy friends was an explanation offered by his parents for school failure.

From a medical standpoint the excessive weight suggested glandular disturbance. Support was also found for this theory in a tremor of the extended fingers. A similar diagnosis was advanced by a private physician two years later, but a school physician believed there was little if any relationship between Edwin's increasingly poor school work and his rapid growth. Mere laziness was the explanation offered by several of his teachers.

Edwin's score on the Terman Group Test administered during the follow-up shows striking agreement with his score on the earlier Stanford-Binet; at age 16-8 it was 191— within five points of the median for our fifteen-year-old gifted boys.

INFERIOR SCHOLARSHIP DUE TO COMPETING INTERESTS

Thomas. There is little or no evidence that the IQ of this subject has deteriorated, but his record of school accomplishment is far below the standard attained by the majority of the gifted group. At age 7-6 his IQ on the Stanford-Binet was 142, while at age 13-6 he made a score on the Terman Group Test of 169, which corresponds to an M.A. of 17-6 and IQ of 130. The difference of 12 points IQ is not very significant when allowance is made for the fact that the functions measured by the two tests are not completely identical.

From an early age Thomas has been a mediocre student in the traditional school subjects. He was two years accelerated in grade placement at the time of the original survey (possibly because of extra coaching which his parents had provided for him), but was reported by his teacher to show inferior application and to do only average work. His scores on the subtests of the Stanford Achievement battery (taken at age 7-8 when he was in L4) corresponded to the norms for an exceedingly wide range of grades, viz.:

Reading	H5	Nature study and science	H5
Arithmetic	L3	History and civics	L2
Language usage	H2	Literary knowledge	L8
Spelling	H5	All-round information	L5

A report received a year and a half later from his fifth-grade teacher rated his work as actually inferior to that of the average pupil. It is not impossible, however, that the teacher was unduly influenced by the character of his written work, which she described as "messy and untidy."

At the time of our 1927–28 follow-up Thomas was completing the ninth grade, and had made a poor scholastic showing during his entire three-year sojourn in junior high school. The predominant mark was C, but he failed arithmetic and English in H7, history in H8, and algebra in L9, and had been obliged to clear his record by repeating these subjects at a vacation school.

In contrast to his low marks in academic work, his marks in music and orchestra have been consistently of A grade. It is in music that the boy's interests and energies have always lain, and certainly his accomplishment in this field is unusual enough to demand at least some indulgence for his apathy toward schoolroom obligations.

According to his parents he "loved music" by the time he was two years old. At four he could sing and improvise on the piano, and had about ten musical compositions to his credit. At five he played in public recitals. By the age of seven or earlier he had absolute pitch. In reports which we have received from his school from time to time the teachers have never failed to mention his musical gift. As a small child he was permitted by his parents to appear on various occasions as a professional entertainer, and recently (age 13) a motion picture theater has bid for his services as a musician. His parents, however, are anxious to have him complete his education before accepting such employment. This attitude on their part, as far as we can tell, is a new and favorable development, for at the time of our original survey they were featuring him as an entertainer and loading him with a heavy outside program of music, dancing, and elocution lessons to the probable detriment of his health and his school work.

Thomas is an attractive boy in appearance, and is successful in his social contacts, but has never displayed any talent for leadership. He belongs to a Boy Scout troop, enjoys parties and gatherings of young people, and is said by his parents to be an affectionate and considerate son. His health is now reported as good. One seeks in vain for any maladjustments in his personal relationships or physical status that could account for his failure to adapt himself to the school curriculum. There is little question in our minds that he is quite capable of making an excellent school record, but that his low standing as a student has been determined by his whole-hearted allegiance to a competing interest.

In closing this series of case descriptions we would refer the reader to the accounts of Joe, Emmett, Alfred, and Patricia in chapter xix, and to that of Marian in chapter x.

CHAPTER XVII

THE CONQUEST OF OBSTACLES

Although the handicaps of poverty, illness, and other untoward circumstances are encountered less often in our group than in the generality of children, they are by no means absent. One of our girls has been a bedfast invalid for nearly ten years. One is severely crippled as a result of infantile paralysis. Another is recovering from a two-year siege of tuberculosis. Several, both boys and girls, are struggling for an education against the odds of poverty or other discouraging home conditions. Several are handicapped by bad heredity, and several by their racial origin.

That the victims of such unfavorable circumstances carry on bravely and hopefully does not make the spectacle any less touching to the sympathetic observer. In a majority of cases, we believe, the fight will be won, though sometimes at heavy cost and not without suffering and scars. In other cases the obstacles may prove too great to surmount. The theory that "genius will out," no difference how oppressive the environment, is just nonsense. In any community at any time one can find genius that is being starved or warped or killed by influences that are too powerful or too insidious to be combated successfully. The cases presented in this chapter illustrate only a few of the many types of obstacles which have been encountered by one or more members of our group; additional types will be found in the case studies of other chapters.

A Case of Frailty, Lameness, Poverty, Bad Heredity, and Sordid Environment

Marshall. This case affords an example of superior intelligence struggling to overcome great physical, environmental, and financial handicaps. Ability of high order is found in the family stock, though Marshall's own parents are among the less successful of the line.

This boy comes from Russian-Jewish parentage. The paternal grandfather was a rabbi, and a paternal great-uncle was a noted musician who played music of his own composition for the Russian czars for twenty-five years. The maternal grandfather and a maternal great-uncle were also rabbis. The latter was also the author of a Hebrew book on history. In the mother's immediate family there is a history of epilepsy, insanity, and feeble-mindedness, Marshall's grandmother being insane and an aunt both epileptic and feeble-minded. Nothing is known by us of the more remote ancestry on either side.

Marshall's father was born in Russia and had only a meager education—four years at a Hebrew school. He went to work in a tailoring shop at the age of eight and has continued in that trade ever since. He passed the United States Civil Service examination for inspector in tailoring, and during the World War held a position for the government supervising three factories. In personality he is uninformed, unsympathetic, and aggressive.

The mother was born in the United States and had a seventh-grade education. She is an uncultured, emotional, neurotic woman, but devoted to her children. She is centering all her hopes and ambitions on Marshall and is giving him every encouragement to go ahead. She is well known to the Jewish social agencies, whose aid she seeks frequently in getting money from her husband. The family receive medical treatment from a free clinic but have not had to ask any material assistance other than occasional loans, which were always repaid. The mother is looked upon as more or less of a nuisance by the local social workers, who tire of hearing about her troubles.

In 1922 the family was living fairly comfortably over the father's small tailoring shop, in which the mother helped. Things were disorderly and upset, customers' clothes frequently getting misplaced, and everywhere the odor of cooking permeated. The parents constantly quarrelled and the father was always threatening divorce. The children had to work hard and were beaten by the father. Marshall resented these conditions and busied himself with books as a mode of escape, often reading until late in the night.

The Stanford-Binet test administered to Marshall at age 10-11 in 1922 resulted in an IQ of 144. He was in the high-sixth grade at that time, but his school achievement tests showed him above the average of eighth-grade pupils in most subjects. He was under par physically, being a frail, delicate boy, and lame as a result of infantile paralysis at eighteen months of age. In spite of his lameness, however, he had to work. He delivered papers, caddied, and did various odd jobs, with the result that he was tired most of the time.

When seen again at the time of the follow-up study, Marshall was living with his mother, two brothers, and a sister in a dark, musty, basement apartment, a squalid, untidy, ill-kept home of four or five rooms. The father had recently had financial reverses and lost his business, and the parents had separated. They were in serious financial straits, the father contributing almost nothing to their support and the mother earning only a little by doing housework.

Marshall is in his first year at college, having entered at age sixteen. He commutes from home, leaving about 6:00 A.M. and returning about 6:00 P.M. He is paying his expenses out of the savings in a childhood bank and his present earnings as a caddy on weekends. He continues to sell papers on Saturday nights, but gives the money thus earned to his mother. An older brother, who completed only two years of high school and is working as a driver of a delivery truck, also contributes his meager earnings to the family support.

The mother reports that Marshall had a nervous breakdown at the age of fifteen and was in the hospital several months under a regime of rest and quiet. He is now, at seventeen years, a tall, loose-knit, ungainly youth, poorly groomed and untidy in appearance. He has a lean and rather sharp-featured face, and looks several years older than he is. He walks with a very noticeable limp.

Marshall made a superior high-school scholastic record and was much interested in school activities of an intellectual sort. He was very active in debating, and was also the founder and president of a chess and checkers club. He is completing his first year of college with a B+ record, despite his outside work, his extra-curricular activities, and various hardships. He immediately joined the university chess club and was soon playing in a tournament, as first man on the freshman team. He is also a member of the freshman debating team. He does everything thoroughly, and often overdoes because of his desire to excel in whatever he undertakes. His recreation is not all of an intellectual type, for he is fond of golf, tennis, and swimming. He usually spends his Sunday afternoons playing ball in the street or swimming with his brother.

On the Terman Group Test in 1928 Marshall made a score of 190. This score is 11 points below the median of the seventeen-year-old gifted boys who took the test, but places him within the upper 10 per cent of random high-school seniors. The Watson Fair-mindedness Test showed average freedom from prejudices, but the Woodworth-Cady questionnaire indicated a tendency toward emotional instability, which may be significant in view of his heredity.

A younger brother was given a Stanford-Binet test in 1927 at age 14-8 and earned an IQ of 86. He is now in the eighth grade. The sister, with a C.A. of 12-6 and an IQ of 109, is also in the eighth grade.

Marshall plans to be a lawyer and does not intend to take a short-cut method. The full seven-year university course is his goal, and he says with an optimistic smile, "It isn't so very expensive; I think I can manage it." Fortunately, a scholarship has been awarded him for his sophomore year.

A Gifted Negro Girl

Harriet. Because of the exceptional and appealing problem offered by a gifted individual striving under the handicap of prejudice against her race, we have selected for special study one of the few Negro members of the gifted group.

Harriet, located in 1922 at the age of 12-8, earned an IQ (corrected) of 147 on the Stanford-Binet. The field assistant who administered the test made notations to the effect that when Harriet came for examination she was "terribly anxious to do well" and extremely nervous and apprehensive until assured that the result of the test would not influence her class standing. Her anxiety on this occasion may have been indicative of race consciousness, as may also her rating on the Raubenheimer Overstatement Test administered the following year. On this test she showed a marked tendency to overstate, although the remaining tests of the Raubenheimer-Cady battery gave more favorable ratings, showing social attitudes that were desirable and average emotional stability.

Harriet's play interests were described by her eighth-grade teacher as being fully normal; she took an enthusiastic part in games on the playground. According to her mother she had shown a distinct talent for dramatics since the age of five. Her ambition was to become a professional elocutionist. At the time of the original survey Harriet was living with her parents and three sisters in a lower middle class white neighborhood. The home, which the parents were buying on time payments, was an old-fashioned, unpretentious, two-story dwelling. It was rather in need of paint on the outside, but it was neatly kept, and an atmosphere of thrift and well-being pervaded the interior. It was sparsely and plainly furnished, but there were a piano and a small bookcase containing several reference books and encyclopedias and various novels of superior quality, such as works by Scott and Thackeray.

Not a great deal is known to us regarding Harriet's ancestry. The paternal grandfather was a Negro, but the paternal grandmother was of mixed Indian, German, and Negro descent. The maternal grandmother was a Negro, but no record has been given us of the racial descent of the maternal grandfather. It is possible, however, that he is of mixed or white descent, for Harriet's mother looks more like a Spanish woman than like a Negress. Harriet's father, now deceased, although having only eighth-grade schooling and holding the position of Pullman porter, appears to have been a man of wide interests. He was active in the affairs of the colored community, and, according to his own statement, writing was one of his hobbies. He once studied law at home through extension courses but never got anywhere with it. He was for a time a newspaper correspondent and later associate editor of a paper. One of his brothers has recently achieved considerable success as a playwright. The mother had only sixth-grade education and had worked as a housemaid and cook from the age of thirteen until her marriage at twenty-three.

Changes have come to the family since 1922. The father died four years ago and the mother and her daughters are in very straitened circumstances. The three older girls, including Harriet, the third in the family, have finished high school and gone to work. The oldest is doing clerical work, the second girl is an elevator operator, Harriet is a child's nurse, and the youngest girl is in high school. The mother does housework. The girls all contribute half or more of their salaries to the home, on which there is still considerable debt.

Harriet, in addition to her work during the day, is attending night school several times a week. She is active on a

Negro newspaper, for which she writes a humorous column
—a difficult task, she says, as the things that seem funny to
her do not always seem so to others. She also belongs to a
choir of Negro-spiritual singers which has achieved recognition in local musical circles.

During the past few years Harriet's early desire to go
into dramatic work has become eclipsed by an ambition to
enter social service. At present, however, her prospects of
attaining to either of these vocations are far from bright.
The immediate need of money has become so pressing in
the family that no further schooling is being planned for
her. While the financial problem might be overcome with
the aid of scholarships, the family feels rather hopeless of
turning to professional advantage any further education.
There is little opportunity in the social service field, the
possible openings for colored people being very few and
quickly seized upon when they occur. The teaching profession is practically closed to colored people in California.
The solution would seem to be for her to go East where the
opportunities are greater, but there seems to be no hope of
saving enough money to finance such a venture very soon.

The mother feels the situation keenly and is rather
bitter about it. All her daughters are bright and capable of
filling responsible positions, but are forced because of their
race to accept menial jobs at low wages. The race problem
constitutes a source of controversy in the family, the mother
feeling that the attitude of the whites toward the Negro is
unchristian and that it places her girls under an unfair
handicap. The daughters, particularly the second eldest,
who attended college for a short time, excuse the whites on
the ground that they are sincere in their attitude.

In view of the question that is often raised as to whether
members of "quick-maturing" races may reach the limit of
their mental development earlier than those of "late-matur-
ing" races, the score of Harriet on the Terman Group Test
administered in 1928 has exceptional interest. This score
was 180 at age eighteen. While this score places her in the
top 15 per cent of high-school seniors, and at the upper quartile of a distribution reported for freshmen attending a
teachers college in Iowa,[1] it is 19 points below the median

---

[1] Nelson, N. J., and Denny, E. C., *School and Society*, Vol. 26, 1927,
pp. 501–502.

score of the eighteen-year-old gifted girls who took the test during the follow-up, and but 4 points above the median score of gifted thirteen-year-old girls who took the test.

Harriet's score on the Watson Test of Fair-mindedness also derives special interest from her racial status. Her score on this test is 22, which compares favorably with the mean score of the gifted group as a whole and with the mean scores of various college groups reported by Watson. Despite conditions that might well arouse in Harriet a serious complex of emotional prejudice, her performance upon the Watson test is entirely normal.

THE OFFSPRING OF A JAPANESE-AMERICAN MARRIAGE

The A. family. Only a small proportion of the total space in Volume I was devoted to material of a clinical type, but of the selected families there reported individually, the Japanese-American A. family is possibly the most interesting of all.

In the brief account of this family (Volume I, pp. 107–108) note was made especially of the parentage and ancestry of the children, four of whom are members of our group. The father is a Japanese who had the equivalent of a high-school education in Japan, later studied silk culture, and before coming to America lectured on this and other subjects. His family had excellent standing in their community. The mother is an intellectual American woman who comes from exceptionally superior colonial stock. The marriage of these parents, which took place about twenty years ago, caused a storm of publicity at the time. Without entering into the question of the sociological aspects of the union, we can regard it as most successful from a biological point of view, for all five of the children are very superior indeed.

When first located by us the family, as far as the field assistant could observe, was a happy and united one. The father was at that time a florist and nurseryman, and the mother assisted in the business. Dr. Yates, after visiting their home, reported: "All adult members of the household have made it their aim to bring up the children in the best possible way. The father as well as the mother is much loved by the children. Mrs. A. says that 'he has a way with the children.' . . . . The mother and the maternal grandmother (who resides with the family) are much interested in such organizations as the Parent-Teacher Association, mothers' clubs, etc."

The mother, filling out the 1921–22 home information blanks, reported that the entire family was in the habit of tramping in the country to collect wildflowers, caterpillars, and cocoons. The caterpillars were fed at home and eagerly observed by the children as they went through their different stages and finally emerged as butterflies or moths. Mrs. A. also described the delight which the children took in dramatics. They often composed charades and playlets which they produced for the family, even the baby taking small parts by the time she was two years old. Another project was a family newspaper and family magazine for which the two oldest girls were chiefly responsible. We have copies in our files of several numbers of the newspaper and find them sparkling with a spontaneous humor and facility at parody that is rarely found in juvenile literary productions.

When the family was visited by us six and a half years later, some important changes had occurred in their manner of life. They had moved from their home in a suburb of a large California city to a remote ranch. Soon after this move the parents had separated—a development which certainly could not have been anticipated on the basis of our earlier knowledge of the family.

The father is now definitely out of the family picture and professes to be unable to contribute anything to the family support. He is making a modest living as a "character reader" and insurance agent. However, in a recent interview he told us that his character reading was not bringing in much income and that he finds it difficult to sell insurance because he doesn't greatly believe in it.

The ranch has proved to be a poor financial investment, and the mother, children, and maternal grandmother are living on it in real poverty. However, there is an atmosphere of good cheer, affection, and gaiety in the home, which, despite the absence of the father, is in full harmony with our early picture of a happy family group. The ranch is two miles from the nearest town, and the town itself is only a small hamlet boasting little besides a school, garage, general merchandise store, and motion picture theater. Conditions are such as to make a natural social unit out of the family, and as there are enough members of it for evening games of bridge and amateur dramatics, they find great enjoyment in their own pursuits.

It may be that the striking social unity of the family is partly the result of their unusual racial status. A strong racial prejudice against the Japanese exists among many Californians. The children, through their brilliance, attractiveness, and fine traits of character, have won a loyal circle of friends, but they have not been untouched by racial prejudice, especially since their move to a small rural community. Regarding this point the mother says: "In —————— (the city where the family earlier resided) the children early formed a small, select circle of friends who advanced with them from grade to grade through grammar school and into high school. In a large community there was no occasion for them to be brought into contact with any who were violently antagonistic. In —————— (their present community) the situation was different. New contacts had to be formed in a community sufficiently isolated to be extremely reserved in its attitude toward all newcomers. The children had reached an age when they had come to recognize the fact that prejudice might and probably did exist. Young children are usually happily ignorant of this. Their very recognition of this fact probably affected (quite involuntarily) their own attitude toward their new associates." In another connection the mother wrote us of an exhibition of racial prejudice which occurred when the oldest boy and girl were high-school seniors. "Both were selected for the two principal parts in the senior play. This was resented rather bitterly. The children were unconscious of this for some time, but when it was brought home to them they resigned from the cast."

Though the experience just related grieved the children at the time, Mrs. A. feels that on the whole the children's social contacts have been happy and successful. She says the two older girls "believe that whatever prejudice exists has worked somewhat to their advantage. It has been a test which has divided the sheep from the goats. The more ignorant, the narrow-minded, the prejudiced ones who were repelled would have been poor material for friends, so it has been an advantage to have a certain amount of selection done automatically."

When the children were located by us in 1922, they earned the following IQ's on the Stanford-Binet:

	Age	IQ
Sarah	12-6	143 (corrected)
Joseph	11-2	154 (corrected)
Doris	9-6	140
Daniel	7-4	147

In 1928 three of the children were given a Terman Group Test with the results:

	Age	T.G.T. Point Score
Joseph	17-11	204
Doris	16-4	183
Daniel	14-1	179

As the oldest girl was away at college when the tests were administered, we are not able to include a test record for her. We secured, however, a Terman Group Test of Mrs. A., who was much interested in our follow-up program and consented to take the test with her children. Her score was 213 out of a possible 220, and her performance was remarkable not alone for her high numerical rating but for the phenomenal speed with which she worked through each subtest.

Charlotte, the little girl who was an infant at the time of our original survey, was tested for the first time. Her IQ at age 7-1 was 133.

On the achievement tests which the children took in 1922 and in 1928, they all made very superior records.

Three series of personality tests administered during the follow-up have special interest in the light of the unusual ancestry and environment of these children. One is the Watson Test of Fair-mindedness (as applied to religious and economic issues); one is the Masculinity-Femininity Test developed at Stanford, and the other is the Woodworth-Cady questionnaire. On the Watson Test Joseph and Daniel scored almost exactly at the median for our gifted group; Doris, however, exhibited considerably less "prejudice" than our median gifted subjects. On the Masculinity-Femininity Test Joseph scored at the top quartile of unselected high-school boys toward masculinity; Daniel scored close to the median; Doris scored almost within the most feminine third of high-school girls. The Woodworth-Cady results would indicate that Daniel is emotionally extremely stable, that Joseph is about average for his age and sex, and that

Doris is possibly somewhat less stable than the average girl of her age (scores of 1, 9, and 21, respectively).

We shall conclude this account of the A. family by a characterization of the developing personality and capacity of each of the children. The reader will doubtless find it as interesting as we have to speculate as to whether the unusual creative drive of several of these young people owes any of its force to unconscious compensatory reactions resulting from their experiences with race prejudice. By way of preface it may be said that all five of the children are in appearance just what their heritage would suggest—half Japanese and half American.

Sarah. Sarah was nineteen years old at the time of our follow-up. The entire family is whole-heartedly proud of her, for she has recently entered college and is earning all her expenses. Her character has been marked by independence and initiative since infancy. Her mother, filling out our original Home Information Blank, wrote: "As a young child she was extremely willful and quick tempered. She would throw herself on the floor and scream with rage. We found that the best plan was to put her in a room by herself or in a large closet (with the door open) until she was quiet and then go on without taking any further notice of her outbreak. Before she was two years old she had learned to go into the closet by herself when she felt the need of it— which we all thought rather wonderful." The child who learned to control herself before she was two years old was at twelve "very honorable, disdaining subterfuges of any kind." Her mother wrote: "In the family we always want to do whatever she wishes us to. There has been a temptation to spoil her, she is so lovable."

Sarah graduated from high school before she was seventeen, remained at home for a time, next took some special subjects as a post-graduate high-school student, and then entered college. Now, at nineteen, she is "on her own" a hundred miles from home, and is making a success both in her college course and in earning a living. She earns her board and room by working an average of three hours a day in the home of a charming family who take a warm interest in her progress. They tell us that Sarah is always anxious to do more than is asked of her. Her other expenses have been earned in such varied ways as taking orders for Christmas cards and selling a blood transfusion.

Sarah has been interested both in art and in literature since early childhood. When she was first known to us her vocational ambition was to be a decorator. At the age of sixteen she took fourth place in a scholarship competition conducted by a well-known art school. The emphasis of her interest has now shifted to literature. She has had a number of her poems published in local papers, and her work in her English class at college is finding delighted recognition from her professor. As a special honor she is being permitted to take an advanced course in verse writing from which freshman students are almost invariably debarred.

Sarah would like to have a career as a writer, but realizing that it takes time for a writer to become established, and that her financial help would mean a great deal to her family, she is taking a teachers' course. It is possible that she may later work over from teaching into the field of creative writing. We are reproducing one of her recent poems.

THE VIRGIN

Her pride subdued by shyness, or by art,
The maiden walks; the whispers of her heart
Only betrayed by the elusive rose
Upon her cheek. Through all her being flows
A consciousness of happy innocence
And youth more sweet for its impermanence.

Eager to live, yet fearing to be caught
In life's rude turbulent flood, wise though untaught,
Aware of all she is designed to be,
She savors and delays her destiny.

Joseph. This boy was seventeen at the time of our follow-up. As the oldest son in a family without a father, he feels his responsibilities very keenly. "Life is a serious business to Joseph," his mother told us, and after talking with him we are of the same opinion.

He graduated from high school at age 15-6, and with the exception of four months away from home, during which he worked hard and saved about two hundred dollars, he has remained on the family ranch ever since. Fortunately he is a tall, well-set boy, and a tower of strength, for he has had a man's work to do. The ranch comprises sixty acres of hilly land. Only a portion of it is under cultivation, but

Joseph has the responsibility of several acres of fruit trees, of a modest beginning in live stock, and of attempting to expand the ranching enterprise to a point where it can be run on a paying basis. So far the ranch has been a financial liability rather than an asset.

Since early boyhood it has been Joseph's ambition to go into scientific stock breeding, a goal from which he has never wavered. He hopes to go to the agricultural college of the state university and specialize in animal husbandry, but is uncertain whether he can arrange it. Though undoubtedly capable of earning his way through, and willing to do so, he feels loath to abandon his home responsibilities. Perhaps when his younger brother, who is now a high-school sophomore, finishes high school, Joseph can be spared for a time. He says he is not particularly interested in a liberal arts course, and that he does not wish to work for a degree. His sole purpose in going to college is to secure the technical training necessary for success in his chosen work.

Doris. This girl was sixteen at the time of our follow-up. She, like her older sister, is talented both in art and in literature. Up to the present she has cared more for drawing and painting than for writing, though she has turned out some very creditable pieces of work of both kinds. Her vocational ambition is to be an illustrator or designer of women's clothes, and she has told us that art work "is what I love to do above all else . . . . I draw practically all my spare time." When she graduates from high school, which will not be until she is eighteen, for she was obliged to remain out of high school a year and a half because of precarious health, she hopes to win a scholarship in an art school. So far her art training has been of an indifferent and desultory sort.

Doris is a ladylike young person who meets strangers with a quiet reserve, without embarrassment. However, her mother tells us that it is extremely easy to hurt her feelings, and that she suffers acutely when teased by her brothers. The reader is reminded that of the three A. children for whom we obtained scores on the Woodworth-Cady questionnaire, Doris was the only one whose performance indicated any tendency toward emotional instability.

There is an unusual degree of rapport between Doris and her little sister Charlotte. When Charlotte was of kindergarten age Doris taught her to print and to use crayons and scissors—in fact she conducted a real kindergarten enterprise with Charlotte as her one pupil. She has kept a little scrapbook with Charlotte's progressive literary and artistic efforts carefully arranged and pasted in it.

Daniel. He was fourteen at the time of our follow-up. One notes a heartiness, gaiety, and friendliness about him that are most appealing. Life has not yet become a serious matter for him. His mother admits that he has a quick temper, but tells us that he "will quarrel and make up and forget it. . . . . He can be very naughty, but if left to himself is quick to apologize and own his fault."

Daniel has not yet chosen a life vocation, but he is anxious to go to college and plans to earn his way by draughting. He has done superlative work in draughting courses at high school and at present is trying to persuade the instructor of this subject to inaugurate a third-year course. Daniel shares to some extent the literary gift of the family, though writing is not a hobby with him as it is with his two older sisters. When he graduated from grammar school at the age of twelve he was class prophet. His prophecy was well wrought out and full of humor, and was published in the local paper. He is an enthusiastic stamp collector and makes his collection pay for itself by selling and trading duplicates.

Charlotte. This girl was seven at the time of our follow-up. She is a radiant child and shows no sign of being spoiled despite the adoration of her mother, grandmother, brothers, and sisters. Two and a half years prior to our follow-up her mother wrote us that Charlotte, the baby, "is dear but very shy. . . . . She will not make friends with strangers." She was less than four years old then. Now, possibly as a result of attending school, she is completely at ease with strangers, though not at all forward or bold. She is well able to hold up her end of a conversation and takes an almost grown-up interest in providing for the entertainment of family guests.

Charlotte's IQ of 133 is just under the standard which we have used for the inclusion in the gifted group of siblings of gifted subjects. However, we feel that the IQ obtained for her rather underestimates her real ability. There were several tests which she failed by only a narrow margin, and the quality of a number of her responses was typical of a mental age-level of ten or twelve years. In defining the word "rule," for example, she showed a capacity for conceptual thinking most unusual in one so young. "It is like a law, but a law is bigger than a rule." In our clinical judgment Charlotte's quality of mind is at least equal to that of the typical child of 140 IQ.

One naturally awaits with eagerness and some anxiety the outcome of the struggle which these children must wage against the handicap of poverty and the yet greater handicap of race prejudice. That such children should not have a fair chance in a country which boasts of its democracy is enough to bring the blush of shame to anyone who is not utterly lacking in fair-mindedness.

As typical of the ignorance and prejudice which exists in regard to race mixtures, an incident may be related which occurred at the time the A. family was discovered by us in 1922. It happened that one of the teachers in the city school which was then attended by the A. children allowed herself to be interviewed by a newspaper reporter regarding the showing they had made in our tests, with the result that a news item appeared in the local papers and was widely copied, giving the remarkable results of this Japanese-American marriage. A former United States Senator, seeing this news item, wrote to the President of Stanford University, protesting violently against the peddling of such nonsense by a university professor and suggesting that the President should do something to put an end to it. He added that this entire question regarding the results of race mixture was settled long ago by Herbert Spencer, who "proved" that hybrids from race crossings were always inferior to either of the parent races!

CHAPTER XVIII

SOME TWINS AND OTHER SIBLINGS

A PAIR OF IDENTICAL TWINS

Barbara and *Marguerite.* These thirteen-year-old twin girls are so much alike in appearance as to be almost indistinguishable, even by old friends. In their developmental history also they are very similar. Psychological, educational, personality, and physical measurements obtained at the time of the original survey and the recent follow-up may be briefly summarized as follows:

1921–22

Stanford-Binet Test

	Barbara	Marguerite
C.A.	7-0	7-0
M.A.	9-11	9-2
IQ	142	131

Stanford Achievement Test

Standards reached

	Barbara	Marguerite
Reading	L4	L4
Arithmetic	L4	L3
Spelling	H4	H4
Nature-study and science	L3	H3
History and civics	H2	H3
Literature and information	L4	L4
General information	H3	H3

Personality tests

Overstatement; marked tendency to overstate (both girls).

	Barbara	Marguerite
Resistance to temptation	Average	More than average
Social attitudes	Average	Average
Emotional stability	Average	Average
Physical measurements:		
Height	50.4 in.	49.8 in.
Weight	70.8 lb.	64.8 lb.
Breathing capacity	96 cu. in.	84 cu. in.
Width of shoulders	12.2 in.	11.8 in.

1927-28

Terman Group Test

	Barbara	Marguerite
Point score at age 13-6..........	126	144
Point score at age 13-8..........	163	166

Stanford Literary Test

Test I	27	23
Test II	29	31
Test III	25	24

Masculinity-Femininity Test

Score	−115	−109
Percentile femininity rating....	70–75	65–70

In the entire list of psychological measurements there is not one in which the twins show a statistically significant difference. Viewed in the light of their probable errors the scores of the two subjects may be considered identical. The differences shown in the physical measurements, however, are real. On the more elusive traits, attitudes, and desires reported over a six-year period by both home and school there appears to be complete resemblance between the twins. Each looks forward to doing secretarial work.

Fully as interesting as the likeness of the twins is the high intellectual fiber of their Roumanian-Jewish immigrant parents and the evidence of ability reflected in their siblings. There are five older brothers, one of whom has recently completed college with an outstanding scholastic record and has received a scholarship for further study in the East. Another has risen to a position of distinction in industry despite his limited education. A sister, the only girl besides the twins, is a member of the gifted group.

The parents have held themselves and their children to high standards of accomplishment, and industry has been a family motto and practice. Both parents have labored early and late and with the gradual release of the mother from the more confining duties of family life they have extended their business to two detached and independent stores, one managed and operated by the mother, the other by the father.

The parents' pride in their children's accomplishments is accompanied by the closest surveillance. Each child has borne his share of household work, and school studies have always come before recreation. The immediate family is the center and source of the children's social life. Barbara and Marguerite are permitted by their mother to play with only two girls in the rather heterogeneous neighborhood in which they reside. The twins and their older sister are never allowed to leave their home in the evening even to make a short trip to the public library without the escort of one of their brothers.

Fraternal Twins of Unequal Brightness

Merrill and *Wendel.* These twin boys of seventeen years are in their senior year in high school. Both are so well endowed intellectually that the most successful school careers might be expected of each one independently of the other, but a marked difference between them in intelligence which places Merrill relatively lower than Wendel has given rise to a problem of serious consequence.

There were few appreciable differences in early development, even their weights at birth differing by only half a pound. Wendel, however, talked about two months earlier than Merrill, according to the mother's record.

At the time of the original Stanford investigation a medical examination found Merrill to be a boy of large physical development, weight 43 pounds above the norm, thyroid gland slightly enlarged, fine tremor present in outspread fingers, and several nervous symptoms, including twitching of eyelids and stuttering. The evidence all pointed to considerable endocrine disturbance. Wendel, on the other hand, was found to be well-developed, normal in nutrition, and without nervous disturbances.

The Stanford-Binet gave Wendel an IQ of 167 and Merrill an IQ of 136, at the age of 10-8. Only 5 or 10 in 100,000 children equal or exceed the rank of Wendel, while that of Merrill is reached by about 1,500 in 100,000 children.

The achievement test records also showed a significant disparity. Wendel had skipped three half grades and was in L7; Merrill had skipped only half a grade and was in L6. On the Stanford Achievement Test the scores of the two boys fell close to the extrapolated norms for the following school grades:

	Wendel	Merrill
Paragraph meaning	H11	L10
Arithmetic	H11	L10
Language usage	L11	L10
Spelling	H8	H7

At home everything possible had been done to provide the boys with the same material things, and even in the matter of affection the parents made a conscious effort to have them share alike. However, it was evident very early that Wendel would get the greater amount of attention and approbation from visitors because of the quickness of his response and his general affability.

At about eight years of age Merrill began to stutter, which coincides with the time when Wendel was allowed to skip for the third time. For three years stuttering and twitching of the eyelids continued with recurrent intensity until Merrill reached the seventh grade. Here, because of his high general ability in relation to the average in his classroom, his large size, and his often expressed desire to be nearer his brother, he was allowed to skip a half grade. Improvement followed, and he was consequently again doubly promoted (to the eighth grade) in order that the two boys might complete grammar school together. The mother's report in 1924 makes this interesting note: "Merrill shows great improvement as far as his nervous symptoms are concerned. Stuttering and twitching of the eyelids have almost completely disappeared." The school report for the same year reports no nervous symptoms.

The simultaneous entrance of the twins into high school augured well as far as Merrill's nervous habits were concerned. He took several of the same courses as his brother. However, although maintaining a satisfactory record, he did not shine in any subject, while Wendel was consistently an honor student. Out of forty-two grade marks recorded for Merrill at the close of the junior year, twelve were A, twenty-seven were B, two were C, and one was D; of the 40 recorded for Wendel, twenty-seven were A, twelve were B, and one was D. Wendel had become prominent in the high school. He was manager of the debating team and its champion debater. The attempts of the parents to bring out Merrill's powers and to spur him to excel in physical education in which they were confident Wendel could not excel brought little results. Merrill compared himself constantly with Wendel, and hung on his very words.

The parents finally advised Merrill to enroll in debating, believing that what he needed was an opportunity for trained expression and a common interest with his brilliant brother. Merrill did well the first semester in the theoretical discussion of procedures and forms, but as soon as the course demanded actual participation in platform work he went to pieces and was forced to drop out. The stuttering returned worse than ever; each statement was prefaced by the most agonizing twitchings. The advice of a nerve specialist for speech-correction work was not followed, and aside from a greater effort on the part of all the members of the household to alleviate as best they could Merrill's feeling of failure no special therapy was used.

Merrill and Wendel will soon be ready for college. The problem might be solved by having them attend different colleges, a plan which their parents are considering. An older brother whom Merrill resembles more in general appearance and intellectual endowment than he does his twin is a successful student of medicine. The recent follow-up tests show Merrill to be intellectually well above the average college student and capable of a kind of scholarship which should bring considerable satisfaction. The follow-up test scores of the two boys are as follows:

	Wendel	Merrill
Terman Group Test	213	194
Iowa High-School Content Examination	212	161

Two Sisters of Unequal Brightness

Myrtle and *Katherine*. The disparity in the mental abilities of these gifted sisters differing in age by two and a half years gives the basis for a situation mildly approaching that found in the cases of Merrill and Wendel just described.

The Stanford-Binet tests administered when Katherine was 11-5 and Myrtle was 8-5 gave the former an IQ of 139 and the latter an IQ of 173. On the follow-up tests Katherine, at age 17-4 in grade H12, made a Terman Group Test point score of 189, while Myrtle, at age 14-9 in grade L11, made a score of 202 on the same test.

The girls have enjoyed every opportunity that a home of comfortable means can provide, in addition to the most intelligent guidance from their parents. Katherine, the older, has been a good student but has never distinguished herself in the way her younger sister has. She has considerable sensitiveness to the fact that Myrtle receives remarkable school grades with little effort. The attempts of the mother to minimize the significance of school marks have done little to reduce Katherine's feeling that she is falling short of her younger sister. Certain special privileges have been given her and certain deferences to her have been required because she is older, all with the design of enhancing her confidence in herself. The younger sister has been definitely made to feel that Katherine must be recognized and deferred to.

This curious and subtle conflict was also revealed in the school follow-up when Myrtle described in a charmingly written autobiography her disappointment in falling short of complete acceptance by her older sister. Myrtle has a very distinctive style and is considered by the head of the English department to have most unusual literary ability. Although in attendance at her high school only one year she has already distinguished herself, and is looked upon in all of her classes as having a very keen mind. The other children are a bit in awe of her although, according to the teachers, she is a gracious, sweet-mannered little girl. In junior high school she was valedictorian of her class, and has since maintained a solid A record in all subjects. She is an accomplished violinist and was chosen to play a solo at the junior high school graduation exercises, which is considered an exceptional honor in a large city school.

A Prize Family

The five children of this extraordinary family are all members of our gifted group. The list of subjects is as follows:

	Year of Birth	IQ
Floyd	1911	155
Stanley	1912	144
Charles	1914	153
Robert	1916	135
Albert	1919	137

While a sibship in a family of very ordinary ability may occasionally provide a gifted child by chance, the mathematical probability of this occurring by chance five times in a single family is infinitesimal. The ancestry of the boys, however, shows that in this case it has not been a matter of chance. The father and mother are both university graduates. The father is also a graduate of a theological school, and has been a minister for many years. He recently gave

up his pastorate to become executive secretary of a national
social service organization, a position of large responsibilities. He has been extremely active in social service, religious,
and educational work, and has held numerous administrative and honorary offices in connection with church organizations, boards of missions, etc. The mother, who is
greatly interested in education, lectures and writes magazine articles. She has a long record of community leadership, having held numerous offices in college organizations,
in clubs, and in welfare organizations. She was a high-school
teacher of mathematics before her marriage. In the more
remote ancestry, we find superior American stock on both
sides. The paternal relatives have been mainly farmers and
merchants, while many of those on the maternal side have
been teachers.

The family life is exceptionally harmonious and marked
by unusual unanimity of interests. Although the financial
status of the family is modest and the home is not large, a
room has been set aside for a library and study in which
there are many books. The parents take a keen interest in
all the children's activities and have a filing cabinet devoted
to them where their school reports, clippings regarding activities with which they have been connected, etc., are filed.
The environment is religious and the interests of the family
center around the church, but the atmosphere is far from
being the pall of gloom and sanctimoniousness often associated with religious households.

All the boys are athletic and active in sports. Floyd, age
seventeen, was on three championship basketball teams last
year. He is very social, with a decided tendency to leadership, and holds high offices in the clubs and organizations to
which he belongs. He teaches a Sunday School class, and
serves the Sunday School as assistant superintendent. He
is in his senior year at high school and is earning college
recommendations in his courses, but his scholastic work is
not very unusual, probably because of his many other activities. These activities, except for basketball, are outside the
school, so that he is not conspicuous there except as an athlete. For two years, in addition to all his other enterprises,
he has worked in a dry goods store after school and on
Saturdays. He will stay out of school for a year after graduation and work full time at his present job to earn money
for college. His vocation is not fully decided upon, but he is

inclined to some kind of work with boys, either in the Y.M.C.A. or as a boys' adviser or dean of boys in a school.

Stanley, who is sixteen and in the third year of high school, is a little different from the rest of the family. He has less self-confidence, is shy, and is inclined to depend a bit on Floyd. However, he is overcoming these traits and developing very satisfactorily. He, too, is athletic, and rates high in basketball. His interests are along the same line as Floyd's and he will probably go into boys' work. He plans to go to college and work his way for the most part.

Charles, who is thirteen, is active as a leader in junior church organizations and in athletics. He has distinguished himself to a greater extent as a student than his older brothers, making a straight A record. He has shown decided leadership and a high degree of dependability. He is in the ninth grade.

Robert, eleven years old and in the seventh grade, attends the same school as Charles. He is an excellent student, shows a strong sense of responsibility, and is very highly thought of by his teachers. Like his brothers he is fond of sports and is active in church organizations.

Albert, eight years old, is in the third grade. He is an excellent pupil and promises to follow in the footsteps of his brothers. Like each of his brothers, he holds a high office in the church organizations for his age group.

In the tests given in the follow-up study the boys all made scores comparable to those made six years ago when they qualified for the gifted group. Floyd, at 17-0, made a Terman Group Test score of 212. This is 11 points higher than the median for our seventeen-year-old gifted boys. Stanley, at 15-11, made a score of 183. This is 12 points lower than the median for our fifteen-year-old gifted boys but places him within the top 10 per cent of unselected eleventh-grade pupils. Charles, at 13-6, scored 188 or 6 points above the median for our thirteen-year-old gifted boys.

Robert and Albert were tested on the Stanford-Binet. Robert at 11-9 earned an IQ of 142 as compared with 135 in 1922, while Albert at 8-11 earned an IQ of 137, exactly the same as that received six years ago.

They are a thoroughly wholesome, healthy, active group of boys—"too busy to have problems" their mother says. They are encouraged in all their interests and projects by their proud and intelligently interested parents.

CHAPTER XIX

BEHAVIOR AND PERSONALITY PROBLEMS

In the general population, about one person in twenty or twenty-five becomes at some time in life a mental patient under either private or hospital care. Among unselected boys about an equal proportion show definite tendencies to delinquency. There is no evidence that psychotic tendencies are more common among the intellectually gifted than among average people, and there is a great deal of evidence that the incidence of delinquency is much lower among the brightest children of the school population than among the average or dullest. Nevertheless, in a group of a thousand gifted subjects one finds a few marked cases of character and personality defect. The most serious of those in our group are here described. Only one, so far as we can learn, has been sentenced to a correctional institution.

A DISHARMONIC PERSONALITY

Ronald. At sixteen Ronald represents a curious entanglement of contradictions. His IQ in 1921 was 143. His Terman Group Test point score six years later was 174, this being 22 points lower than the median for our sixteen-year-old gifted boys, and falling at the 80th percentile of random high-school seniors.

Ronald's 1928 Terman Group Test score may possibly reflect the specialized character of his present interests. He is ingenious in the field of electrical invention and has devised improvements for automatic dial telephones which have been so highly valued that a large telephone company offered him a permanent position whenever he wished it. He has held several positions in which he showed great ingenuity at radio work. Working for a police department of a southern California city he installed a radio system connecting the central office with the police on their respective "beats."

However, the very police department which so highly prizes his services has had to deal with him as an offender on numerous occasions. By the time he was sixteen years old he had twenty-three counts against him on the police court records, all for minor offenses such as speeding, trespassing on a vacant lot, dynamiting rocks and so breaking neighborhood windows, setting flares on a mountain road that were part of an experiment but frightened motorists, etc. On two or three occasions the charge was theft, but in each case tools were involved which Ronald claimed only to have borrowed and which he later returned.

Until recently Ronald's offenses were of a type that might be committed by any boy, but because of agitated neighbors and his long-standing reputation as a "bad boy" his escapades were always reported to the police. A short time ago, however, he got into more serious trouble. With another boy he entered vacant houses and carried away telephone and electrical equipment for use in his experimental work. He was brought before the juvenile court and put on probation, his father agreeing to send him to a military school. Ronald felt badly to have betrayed the trust of the Chief of Police who had befriended him, but aside from this the episode seems to have affected him very little.

Ronald's school life has been stormy and full of vicissitudes from the beginning. When he was only six or seven years old he was accused of having placed some dead cats in the school building. The principal, instead of handling the matter herself, called in the police, who grilled the child until in terror he confessed. Two years later he was found to be innocent. There were other similar happenings at this school. On one occasion he was accused of taking scratch paper, chalk, etc., and was later found innocent, but not before the police had been called in again. He was early branded as a "bad boy" and a school problem, and the reputation has stayed with him.

Ronald has never been outstanding at school either scholastically or in extra-curricular activities. His work at high school has been of irregular quality, but he has succeeded nearly always in making college recommendations. When he was in his third year at a public high school he was discovered to have cheated by copying a fellow-student's notebook, and as punishment was not allowed to hold office in the Camera Club in which he was much interested. Angered at this, he left the school and went to a private preparatory school. Here he did very satisfactory work and was recognized as having considerable ability.

Ronald has been much interested in the Boy Scouts, and has become an Eagle Scout and a member of the Central Examining Board of Scouts. Here, too, his career has been fraught with difficulties. When he first made application to become an Eagle Scout his mother appeared before the Board and said he was unworthy because of his rudeness and lack of docility in the home, with the result that he was turned down. He finally became an Eagle Scout, despite his mother's opposition and that of some of the Board of Directors, partly through the support of his friend, the Chief of Police.

Photography has been another of Ronald's strong interests. He is very skillful at it and has done photographic work for his father on engineering projects which, according to his father's report, equals that of experts.

In Ronald's family background we find a history of neurotic relatives and parental incompatibility. Both parents are cultured and well-educated, but between the two there was a complete lack of harmony which culminated in a divorce attended by considerable scandal. Ronald was about twelve years old at this time, and was placed in the custody of his mother. The mother wishes and tries to do her best for Ronald, but she is sorely handicapped by her own neurotic tendencies. Ronald is her only child, and because of her fondness for him she was inclined to spoil and pamper him as a small boy, but in spite of this there is a great lack of sympathy and mutual understanding between them. The mother has spent the greater part of her time travelling or devoting herself to the Girl Scouts, and has frequently boarded Ronald with a cousin. The father is very fond of the boy and extremely proud of his ability. He gives him a liberal allowance and furnishes him with a car, to both of which the mother objects on the ground that they are making Ronald spoiled, extravagant, and "wild."

Ronald's paternal grandfather is reported to have been mentally unstable to the extent of needing care and protection to keep him from harming himself. The conduct of the mother and the testimony of the greater number of those who are familiar with the family indicate that she is neurotic and unstable. Nothing is known by us of her family history from this angle.

As a child Ronald was physically below par, but as he has grown older he has improved. Now, at sixteen, he is sturdily built, above average in height, and in appearance every inch the modern youth. He has many friends, and is much interested in girls, but is slow to mix in a group.

The men who know him best—the scoutmaster of his troop, and his friend, the Chief of Police—feel that Ronald is not nearly as bad as he has been painted, that he has real genius, and should turn out well if given proper direction. Fortunately the boy's father has awakened to a serious interest in his welfare, and seems now to be doing all in his power to give him the needed guidance.

EMOTIONAL INSTABILITY, POSSIBLY OF GLANDULAR ORIGIN

Joe. He is seventeen years old and classified as a junior in high school. His home is one of superior standing from the standpoint of order and general hygiene, nevertheless Joe comes tousled and dirty to school. His written work, whether done in the classroom or outside, is illegible, not particularly from the standpoint of writing but because of its general disorder and dirt. He may begin anywhere and scrawl in any direction. Further, he seems unable to give sustained attention to class work, though at times portraying unusual brilliance in his verbal responses. He has attended three different high schools and has done equally erratic work in each. His general average so far is a low C. When reproved he is never recalcitrant but instead is pathetically tenacious in his request for another chance.

Joe's general conduct in the schoolroom is friendly and playful, but other children seem neither to like nor to dislike him. In the past he has held positions of responsibility in two different high schools for a short time when first admitted, but his home regards him as friendless. He is solicitous about his sister's participation in school activities but has done practically nothing himself. When urged about the matter he has contended that he was too young and too light for athletics and therefore had no chance. Since a very early age he has been interested in science, and it is in this field that he has done his best school work. His leisure time is spent reading scientific books and magazines.

When first known to us Joe was reported as nervous, talkative, a disturbed sleeper, argumentative, quarrelsome, and domineering with other children. He preferred children younger than himself for playmates. A complete medical examination showed him to be somewhat underweight, hyperkinetic, with hands that trembled, and with thyroid easily palpable. He was subject to a habit spasm of tagging objects, first with one hand, then with the other.

Successive reports at two-year intervals describe the boy as nervous, restless, and incapable of application. On two occasions he has been brought before the public gaze with immeasurable distress to himself and his family; first as the result of accidentally causing the death of a classmate, and again as a result of maliciously damaging high-school property to the extent of several hundred dollars.

Joe's original IQ, 156, appears to have suffered no decline, for his point score on the follow-up Terman Group Test, 214, strained the top limit of the test.

The family history is negative for insanity. The mother had a nervous breakdown during the first four months of pregnancy, but otherwise the pregnancy and birth were normal. The mother now holds a secretarial position of considerable responsibility. The father, who is Italian born and is subject to moods, is a mail carrier.

Unfortunate Heredity and Environment at Its Worst

Emmett and *Alfred E.* It is probable that no other children in our gifted group have had an early home environment comparable in sordidness to that of Emmett and Alfred E.

The father has been successively a copper smelter, a motorman, and a carpenter. The mother, after bearing four sons to her harsh, tyrannical, Austrian husband, died of blood-poisoning following an abortion when Emmett was nine and Alfred was seven. About a year later the father married a kindly woman who had been a practical nurse. This woman married him because of her interest in his children, especially Emmett, whom she described as "far the best and brightest in every way." For four years she strove against "absolutely no co-operation from the father in intelligent training of the children." She finally gave up, took up her residence elsewhere, and sued for divorce on the grounds of cruelty and infidelity. She has explained that the only reason she deferred the separation as long as she did was that she was loath to abandon the children, for whom she had a strong affection.

For their sake she had put up with the cruel and insulting treatment of Mr. E. as best she could, and frequently had interceded for the boys when their father was unjust to them. She attempted to make a real home out of the small, inadequate dwelling in which they lived, buying silver and linen out of her own savings, encouraging the boys to read books from the public library, and trying to arrange for their evenings so they would not be on the street. Her husband had scant patience with her efforts. He thought tablecloths were quite unnecessary, and objected to having the boys trained in table manners. He dictated what food should be bought, and ordered the cheapest kind, with no variety. He complained if books were brought into the house and scolded if he found the children reading. He insisted upon having the boys' earnings turned over to him when they worked after school hours.

Soon after Mrs. E. left, the father imported a widow and her two children from the East. The woman was a foreigner, knew nothing of American customs, and consented to living illicitly with Mr. E. Later, at the instigation of Mrs. E., an investigation was made by a child welfare organization of the home conditions. Mr. E. agreed to marry his "housekeeper" as soon as Mrs. E. divorced him, but the housekeeper, although pregnant, at first refused to marry him because of his vile temper and abusive language. Two years afterward, however, she did marry him.

The foregoing paragraphs provide a brief sketch of the conditions under which the E. brothers were reared. How have Emmett and Alfred fared, thus handicapped? An outline of their development to date will be presented. Who can say what part of the instability and weak moral fiber that have been exhibited by these boys is due to an early environmental handicap, and what part is due to the inheritance of inferior moral traits?

Emmett was first located and tested by us in 1922, within a few days of the date when his stepmother left the father. He was then in grade H8 at age 13-6. His IQ was 148. On the Stanford Achievement Test, which he took soon afterward, his ratings on the individual tests ranged from high-school junior standard to "beyond high school," with the exception of spelling, which was up to L10 standard. His ratings on the interest and personality tests which we administered a year later were also unusually high.

Both his stepmother and his teacher were enthusiastic in

what they wrote of Emmett on the Home Information Blank and School Information Blank shortly after we first tested him. The teacher gave him extremely high ratings upon intellectual, social, and moral traits, and spoke of him as a boy who particularly delighted in looking up information on special topics. "Several times during the day," she wrote, "he will give some information that he has gained which bears directly on the subject." She mentioned that he was president of the student self-government in his room, captain of an athletic team, and squad leader in physical training. She summarized her report by saying, "He is fair and honorable," and made special note of the fact that he "always emphasizes good spirit in room and on grounds." The stepmother also accorded him very high ratings on social and moral traits, and described him as "far the best and brightest" of the four boys.

Except for a slightly defective posture, a one-hour medical examination found him in excellent physical condition.

A few months after the installation of his father's "housekeeper," Emmett, then fourteen years old, ran away from home. The friction between him and his father was bitter. Unlike an older brother, Henry, not followed by us, Emmett was unwilling to mollify his father's unreasonable temper by an ingratiating attitude. He sought refuge at the home of his stepmother's sister, and explained to juvenile authorities who investigated his case that he would not tolerate conditions at home any longer. However, the stepmother and the welfare association interested in his case urged him to return to his home and remain there until he could support himself. As it later appeared, the wisdom of this procedure was doubtful. Emmett stayed at home for five months, and then ran away again (age 14-5). No one knew where he was until his stepmother happened to meet him on the street. She was instrumental in having him removed from his father's home permanently and placed in a boarding home with a woman and her daughter, both of whom were kind and interested. The daughter, who was musical, gave him piano lessons.

A year later his stepmother reported that he was "living in a fine home atmosphere," and had "come to realize the need of an education and the better things of life in a most remarkable manner." A report sent from his high school at the same time indicated that he was doing superior work,

that he responded well to discipline, that his deportment
was excellent, and his social adaptability average.

A report the following year from the welfare association
that had Emmett under its supervision told us that he was
"honorable and reliable in every way," though showing a
"tendency not to value money." He had been an honor
student ever since entering high school, and had recently
been elected president of the Honor Society. At that time
he was about to enter his senior year.

While attending high school, Emmett worked part time
in the laboratories of a motion-picture studio, earning $10
to $20 a week. His employers, wishing to help him obtain
a technical education, gave him money at the end of this
period for a year of college.

Up to this point, the prognosis for Emmett's future was
bright indeed. His history since that time has some very
discouraging features. He went to college (age 18-1), registered for a technical course, joined a fraternity, and cultivated an infatuation for a girl. At the end of the year he
had made a very mediocre scholastic record and had got
himself in debt to a number of his fraternity brothers as a
result of buying expensive presents for the girl. He did not
return to college. His fraternity expelled him from membership. We were told by the college authorities during the
present follow-up that Emmett lived with his girl companion
out of wedlock after leaving the institution. A still more
recent report from his former boarding mother, however,
informed us that the girl had dropped out of the picture,
that Emmett had had difficulty in finding work, but that
after working for a time as a common laborer he had found
a technical job in a motion-picture studio. On the heels of
this information came an "Information Blank" from Emmett
himself, with whom we had tried in vain to make connections all year. He is now (age 19) working as technical
assistant in a studio at a salary of $30 a week, and says he
plans to become a moving-picture director or producer.

Alfred and his oldest and youngest brothers, Henry and
Winton, were tested by us about a year after we first tested
Emmett. Alfred was then in grade L7. His age was 12-4,
his IQ (corrected) 143. Winton, age 8-7, had an IQ of 101.
Henry, at 16-8, had an IQ (corrected) of over 120, possibly
over 130. We have not followed the progress of Henry and
Winton.

Alfred was not given an achievement test, but the teacher rated his standing on his various school subjects from very superior (reading and debating) to very inferior (arithmetic), with a slightly superior median rating.

Although the teacher gave him a high rating on such intellectual traits as originality, common sense, and general intelligence, she graded him down severely upon social and moral traits. She indicated that he invariably avoided groups, that he took no pride in accomplishment, that he "acts before his class so as to gain attention . . . . kicks his near neighbors . . . . shows a lack of team spirit." She rated him below average on generosity, conscientiousness, sympathy, and truthfulness, and remarked, "If he is not interested, he will do what he sees fit to do, which may be to crawl on the floor, punch his neighbor, or read. . . . . His work is untidy and dirty. . . . . He has been sent out to comb his hair four or five times. He is not responsible. He loses his books, his papers, and his report cards. . . . . He has gone home at 11:30 to get his arithmetic and returned at 1:00 without it."

A Home Information Blank, sent us by his stepmother, who had already been separated from his father for more than a year, was not made out in full detail. It is interesting to note, however, that the stepmother's judgment concurred with that of the teacher in assigning him low ratings on moral and social traits. We also learn, from this blank, that at the time the stepmother took charge of the family (when Alfred was eight) he was thin, nervous, and in poor health. His condition improved under her care, and at the time of the medical examination given under our auspices when he was 12-4 was reported as fair except for defective vision.

We do not have a consecutive record of Alfred's difficulties after his stepmother left his father. However, we do know that he ran away from home not long afterward, that he was truant from school the following year, and that before he was fourteen he had spent several months in a foster home found for him by a welfare association. Apparently this experience in the foster home was unfortunate. He was fond of his foster mother, but it was his claim, later, that the foster father drank, gambled, and attempted acts of sex perversion with him.

About this time he became associated with a boy who taught him to steal and he ran away from his foster home.

Not long afterward he was brought into the Juvenile Court
with a companion who had stolen a bicycle. Alfred denied
having stolen anything himself except watermelons, but
claimed that his companion had stolen some watches and
that he, Alfred, had helped dispose of them.

Provision was made by the juvenile authorities for Alfred
to spend the summer on a ranch, where he was reported as
being very happy and contented. Presumably he was returned to his father's home at the end of the summer (his
father, by that time, had married the housekeeper), for a
communication from his ex-stepmother the following spring
informed us that "Alfred disappeared in February from his
father's home, and no one knows where he is." At this time
Alfred was 14-3. We were told by the association that held
him in legal guardianship that he was "showing great interest in his school work before leaving, and was making
good progress."

During our present follow-up we ascertained the following facts. Nearly a year after his disappearance he was
found by the police in an eastern city, but when neither his
father nor local authorities would send for him, he was
released. For the next four months he beat his way through
the South, occasionally working as a laborer, finally reap-
pearing in his home city and reporting directly to his legal
guardians.

Through the influence of some Juvenile Court workers,
Alfred was now given the finest opportunity he had yet had
to redeem his past record, start anew, and profit from intelligent and sympathetic guidance. He was placed in the
home of a young unmarried instructor who taught in the
college which Alfred's brother Emmett planned to enter in
a few months. He was sent to school, was helped with his
lessons by his new guardian, and was "mothered" by a
kindly woman who lived next door and who had a son of
about Alfred's age. Alfred was now 15-5.

For a time it seemed as if the change of environment were
going to bring about the desired results. Though at first he
did poorly in school and had an especially hard time with
his algebra, his work slowly improved. However, he was
consistently weak at taking responsibility; he broke things
that were lent to him and took no initiative about getting
them fixed. He expressed a desire to study engineering
when he should finish high school, but according to his

guardian he was weak in the preparatory work which he took at school, had no interest in mechanics, and could not put things together that were broken.

It was thought by the university people who became interested in Alfred that the final catastrophe in his life might not have occurred if his brother, Emmett, "had treated him half way decently." Alfred, it was said, hero-worshipped his older brother; Emmett, although living within a reasonable distance, totally ignored the younger boy and did not want to be bothered with him. It was suggested that Emmett's indifference may have preyed on the youngster's mind. However, it is impossible to say how much of this neglect may have contributed to Alfred's final downfall. Emmett himself was having difficulties at the same time.

When Alfred was 16-4 he slipped quietly away from the home of his guardian for no obvious cause, leaving no message. For nearly a year no word was heard of him. It was then learned, through a Superior Court in a California county several hundred miles away, that Alfred had been arrested at about the time of his seventeenth birthday in the company of a companion who, with Alfred, had stolen an automobile. Alfred was sentenced to a reform school, where he is to remain until the age of twenty-one unless paroled.

A recent report from the school where Alfred is serving out his sentence describes him as an "indifferent" boy who "doesn't want to follow directions." We are also told that "figures seem to worry him. He doesn't like to study them." He was given an opportunity to serve as editor of the school paper, but he "has not proved his ability, despite a certain ability to ingratiate himself with people interviewed. He is being replaced shortly. . . . . He is mentally erratic."

One hobby is mentioned by his present teacher which suggests the high mental ability he has squandered so woefully. "He has a mania for looking up new words. He makes a list of new words and looks them up in the dictionary." It is interesting to note in this connection that the one possession in addition to his clothes that Alfred took with him when he left the home of the college instructor was a dictionary which this guardian had given him for Christmas.

An Unstable Girl

Patricia. Frequent outbursts of temper and periods of silent moodiness, utter rebelliousness against restraint or advice, craving for adventure, fondness for trashy literature, and a vehemently expressed aversion to school work are high lights in the personality of this subject. At age 14-6 Patricia recently began for the third time the work of the ninth grade, in which she is earning marks of barely passing standard. She is a trouble-maker among the other students, inciting them to acts of defiance against the authorities. In her own home she is quite unmanageable, smokes incessantly, and is subject to frenzied rages on trivial provocation. She has run away with the intention of leaving school and earning her own living, but returned without protest when found without funds or a job in a neighboring city.

Although Patricia's maladjustment to her home and school environment has reached its present acute stage only within the last two years, she has exhibited since early childhood, in mild form at least, the traits which are now causing so much difficulty. When she was tested on the Stanford-Binet at age 6-10, the examiner made note of the fact that she was "very restless and active." Her teacher, in filling out the School Information Blank shortly afterward, wrote: "Patricia lacks ability to concentrate unless the work is especially interesting to her. . . . . She needs more severe control — is apt to give way to temper." On the Stanford Achievement test her scores were but little above the average for her age.

A communication received several months later from her parents rated her as "decidedly more selfish than average," stated that she was nervous, easily irritated, and subject to crying spells, and reported her worst faults to be stubbornness and contrariness. By the time she had reached age 10-5 the parents noted an "improvement in kindliness and self-control," but this improvement, if such it was, appears to have been short-lived.

In the reports made to us upon Patricia's relationships with other children, a curious contradiction stands out. At age seven she was rated by her parents as being rather less popular than average, though decidedly social in her interests. Her teacher corroborated the rating on social interests, but rated her as rather more popular than average, indicating that her companionship was especially sought by other children, and that she was "a good boss." When she was nearly nine years old she was said by her parents to be improving in her ability to get along with other children. A few months later her teacher wrote: "She is looked upon by the other children as odd, but is liked by them. . . . . She is very mature in judgment and most decidedly individual." Possibly the explanation offered by one of her present teachers accounts for the seeming discrepancies. In the teacher's opinion the girls have acquired the habit of obeying Patricia. Her influence over them is therefore enormous and she has the reputation of being popular, but she is not always liked by the very girls to whom her word is law.

Because of the special interest attaching to her case Patricia was given the Terman Group Test three times during our recent follow-up. She made scores as follows:

Age	Form	Score
13-1	A	160
13-3	B	179
14-9	B	195

The first two scores correspond to IQ's of 131 and 136, respectively, which suggests some deterioration in ability since the time of the original survey. Her corrected IQ on the Stanford-Binet taken at age 13-1 was 136, this being 16 points below her original IQ. Her Terman Group Test score at age 14-9, however, is 6 points above the median score of the fourteen-year-old gifted subjects who took the follow-up tests, and corresponds to an estimated IQ of over 140.

The etiology of Patricia's baffling personality traits, as so often is the case, appears to be overlaid with inseparable hereditary and environmental factors. As far as her parents and teachers know, she is suffering from no sexual maladjustment. The child's own explanation that she is "nagged too much at home" doubtless sheds some light on the situation. Our information regarding the home, however, discloses no condition which by itself would be likely to account for the twisted pattern into which her temperament has fallen.

From the age of 2½ to 5 she spent most of the time with her mother alone on a remote ranch. During this period she had no child playmates, although her mother reports that she learned to make satisfactory companions of animals, and that her love of animals has persisted to the present day. The fact that stands out as significant, however, is that for over two years of Patricia's early childhood mother and daughter were dependent almost entirely on each other for human companionship. One can only conjecture whether this close association fostered habits of mutual dependence which the subject has ever since striven unconsciously to sever.

In our opinion the emotional instability that has always colored Patricia's behavior is partly innate, for her negative traits have developed amid surroundings that could scarcely have had so dire an effect upon a child whose personality was normally well-balanced. No cases of insanity are reported among near relatives, but a member of the immediate family is prone to temper outbursts much like those of Patricia—a fact which lends support to a hypothesis of inherited instability, possibly aggravated by environmental conditions.

A Broken Reed

Blake. The short life history of this subject is heavy with pathos and hopelessness. The hereditary background on the maternal side is streaked with insanity and "constitutional inferiority." The mother, who is the youngest of eight children, spent several months in a state hospital for the insane, but was paroled after the diagnosis, "Constitutional inferiority, but no psychosis." One of her sisters is in the violent ward of a hospital for the insane, one of her brothers died in such a hospital, another brother spent eight years in one, and still another brother, said to have been erratic and irascible, met his death in a brawl. Almost no information is available regarding the mother's remaining three siblings, nor regarding the father and his family. The father and mother were divorced when Blake and his sister were aged only three and five, respectively. Collateral branches on the maternal side include individuals who are immoral, criminal, and feeble-minded. One normal couple is reported, however, with a daughter who is said to be a very talented violinist.

When tested by us at age 11-9, Blake earned an IQ of 154 (corrected IQ 165) on the Stanford-Binet. He was enrolled in grade L7, and made scores on the various parts of the Stanford Achievement Test that equaled ninth- to twelfth-grade standards. According to his teacher he showed intelligence in all his school subjects but was lazy and less conscientious than the average pupil. This may have been partly because the work of the seventh grade was far too easy for him.

From the time when he was first known to us, Blake's personality traits have been unpromising. The Superintendent of the orphanage in which he lived confirmed the low rating in conscientiousness assigned by the teacher, as did also the personality tests administered by our staff. The results of the latter indicated a marked tendency to overstate. His score of 22 on the Woodworth-Cady questionnaire was not so very extreme, but foreshadowed the psychotic tendencies that were to become more and more evident during the next few years.

Blake entered high school at age 13-7, receiving grades during his first semester that ranged from A to D. He had shown ability in music and had been allowed to take music lessons for six months the previous spring, but according to the orphanage Superintendent his application had been "too poor to warrant continuation of lessons." A communication received from the Superintendent during Blake's third year of high school reported the same uneven quality of school work as before, and described Blake as a "putterer" who began many things, finished few, and seldom stuck to assigned tasks in school or at home. He was said to be "fond of attracting attention," but to dislike taking part in games or associating himself with a large group.

Though Blake was rather unsocial in his interests, he was not unacceptable to other children. He was rated both at school and at home as being above average in popularity and in leadership, and in his junior year at high school his class voted their confidence in him by making him class treasurer. This confidence proved to be badly misplaced, for Blake misappropriated some of the class funds. About the same time he was found to have made sexual advances to a small girl in the orphanage and was returned to the Juvenile Court, whose ward he had been since the divorce of his parents. "He escaped, was found in another city, escaped from the Detention Home there, and has been heard from in various parts of the country as destitute. He has appeared occasionally, in very bad odor, and borrowed money from his hard working sister; he is now probably on the high seas as a common seaman."

These last sketchy facts, which were furnished us by the Superintendent of the orphanage, brought Blake's history up to date when he was seventeen. The following year we learned, through a terse newspaper dispatch, of his death. He had committed suicide in an Eastern city by swallowing poison because of despondency over an unsuccessful love affair.

This tragic instance is unique among our cases. The possession of a high intellectual endowment played little or no part in the unfolding of Blake's brief tragic career. His inherited emotional instability determined the course of his life and its early close. A more striking example could hardly be found of the valuelessness of merely fine mental ability which is not supplemented by at least a normal emotional endowment, wholesome attitudes, and sufficient power of inhibition. Blake's career suggests that of a high-powered car capable of the most perfect performance which is run by an intoxicated driver, courting destruction.

CHAPTER XX

FIVE MUSICIANS

It is a common belief that musicians are likely to be ignorant and even stupid in everything except their special field of accomplishment. The fact that scores on the Seashore tests of musical talent have been found to correlate only about .30 with intelligence test scores might seem to lend support to this tradition. However, it must be remembered that the Seashore tests measure only the most elemental constituents of musical ability, such as tone discrimination, sense of rhythm, musical memory, etc. One could hardly expect such traits as these to have very much in common with general intelligence. The assumption to be questioned is that the possession of these elemental traits in high degree offers any guaranty that one can become a high-grade musician. They may be quite necessary, but far from all that is necessary. It is possible that higher mental capacities in large measure are needed to synthesize the raw materials furnished by the kind of elemental musical traits we have mentioned. We believe this to be the case, especially for musical composition. We doubt whether there has ever been a musical composer of note whose general intelligence was not very superior. Noted performers may offer more exceptions, since their task is less creative, but we doubt whether even they are anything like as mediocre intellectually as they are often supposed to be. All the musicians in our gifted group have high IQ's. The five cases which follow are typical. The one of these whom we know best is a composer, Henry Cowell, and we would unhesitatingly rate his general intellectual endowment as equal to that of men who achieve distinction in scholarship or scientific research.

A Musical Composer

Henry Cowell.[1] Here is one of the original "charter members" of the Stanford gifted group who was tested by one

[1] In this case the name is not fictitious.

of us in 1912 on an old form of the Stanford-Binet scale. His age was then 14-10. The IQ obtained was 132, but the limit of the scale was inadequate to measure his ability. There is little doubt that in actual intelligence he was well within the range of our gifted group.

Henry's history up to 1919 was reported in *The Intelligence of School Children* (pp. 246–251) but will be reviewed briefly here. His formal schooling ended before he was seven years old, but before he was twenty-three he had served as an instructor in a large university. At fourteen he "had never touched" a piano, and had had no musical training, but he has since played his own compositions to audiences throughout the United States and in England, France, Germany, and Russia. He has published many musical compositions, and has created a new piano technique which has attracted wide attention among American and European musical critics. He is founder and editor of *New Music,* an important musical journal devoted to modernistic music, and between concert tours he attends to the duties of offices which he holds in a number of musical associations and guilds. It is a matter of special interest that Henry was composing music of an extreme modernistic type when he was a mere boy and ignorant of the very existence of such a school of composers.

When Henry was fifteen and living in the direst poverty, he scraped together enough money to buy an old piano and taught himself to play on it. By the time he was seventeen, friends in his community, recognizing his talent, subscribed to a fund that enabled him to receive competent musical instruction. From that time on, his progress has been crowded with dramatic episodes. He was sent to New York at the age of nineteen or twenty for several months to "hear some good music," and while there he made connections with a number of musical critics and composers. One of America's leading modernists at first refused to take the time to meet him when a critic who was convinced of Henry's promise attempted to arrange an introduction. The composer was finally persuaded to grant a reluctant two-minute interview, and to accept several of Henry's compositions to look over. The result was that after spending several hours playing over the boy's compositions for himself, this composer, who made a practice of holding himself aloof, invited Henry to study with him.

Henry has given concerts in European cities where the audience, unused to his original form of art, have boo-ed him off the stage, and on his return a year or two later has been awarded ovations of applause by the same audience. In 1929 he visited Russia on the invitation of the Soviet Committee on Cultural Relations and as a result several of his compositions have been translated into Russian.

Besides a book, *New Musical Resources,* published by Knopf in 1930, Henry has written many articles in leading popular magazines (including *Century* and *New Republic*) on newer trends in musical composition. Several of his articles have also been published in various European periodicals. His article on "The Process of Musical Creation" was published in the *American Journal of Psychology* (1926, pp. 233–236). Recently he has completed a book on rhythm.

Henry combines musical genius with scientific talent of no mean order. He is intensely interested in the musicological investigations in Russia and Germany, and has lectured on the subject at several American universities. It remains to be seen whether his original and rather heretical type of musical composition will finally meet general approval.

A complete biography of Henry ought sometime to be written, for it would be replete with psychological interest. The story of his rapid rise to international fame, despite the handicap of the most crushing poverty, and despite the utter lack of formal schooling, would read more like a fairy story than like the simple recital of fact that it would be. It is interesting, however, that Henry himself is thankful for these "handicaps" and believes that he owes to them whatever originality he possesses. It is his opinion that an orthodox musical training would have hindered rather than fostered his creative ability. He even regards it a favorable circumstance that during childhood he had no musical instrument of any kind on which to play, as this turned him to an inner world of music of his own creation in which he sought for effects that one never gets in musical compositions of the orthodox and traditional types. We are inclined to suspect that there is ground for this opinion.

A PIANIST AND COMPOSER

Donaldine. At age sixteen Donaldine is a musician and composer. The piano was for her a very early source of interest and exploration. Although her efforts in babyhood were not unlike the annoying thumping and banging of most young children and her parents frequently removed her from the coveted piano stool, she persisted in her efforts to play. At four she was given instruction, and from then on music made increasing demands upon her program. She learned to read music with unusual rapidity. Because of her insistence she was often given selections beyond her physical powers to perform, but the more difficult the assignment the happier she was. Along with what local critics consider exceptional ability in sight reading Donaldine has great powers of retention. At fifteen she could memorize in two or three sittings a forty-page concerto.

While she finds no embarrassment in appearing before large audiences, she has always been distinctly modest about her ability. She was enrolled a whole year in high school before her classmates or teachers knew that she played, and then it was by mere accident that her teachers learned of her accomplishments. For the past two years she has been piano accompanist for the high-school boys' glee club, accompanist for a teacher of voice, a weekly radio soloist, and soloist with the Philharmonic Orchestra in a large Western city. The composition of music has also claimed some of Donaldine's energies and interest, with results that suggest considerable promise. Two of her compositions have been published.

Donaldine has completed twelve years of school work in nine, has maintained a high record of scholarship, and in addition has participated frequently in student affairs. From her activities as tennis enthusiast, musical director of the senior play, and president of the German Club, one gains a cross-section picture of the interests to which she devotes her leisure time. Enthusiastic co-operation, friendliness, self-reliance, and industry are traits attributed to her by her teachers.

On the original intelligence test Donaldine earned an IQ of 138. Now, at age sixteen, her Terman Group Test point score is 171, or 25 points lower than the median for our sixteen-year-old gifted girls. On the Iowa High School Content Examination she scored at the 75th percentile of unselected seniors. However, her score on Part I, English and Literature, reached the 95th percentile of high-school seniors.

A Pianist

Sabina. With an IQ of 142, Sabina is a talented pianist. An interest in music was shown very early. The appearance of an equally strong interest in reading caused the mother to ignore the advice of music critics who favored early specialization in music. Sabina very soon read everything she could lay her hands on and she discussed the content with such clearness that the mother looked to school teaching as a vocation for her and one that would lead quickly to self-support without as much financial outlay.

Sabina pursued school work and music together for eight years and made a brilliant record in both, although she was forced to forego several lines of extra-curricular activities in order to have more time for practice. A review of her participation in activities, however, reveals a rather rich experience in her associations with other pupils. She was vice-president of a literary society, accompanist for the boys' glee club, a member of the staff of the class annual, secretary of the senior scholastic society, and a member of a national music sorority. She was recognized for her academic achievement with continuous membership through high school in the scholarship society, and at graduation she was awarded life membership in the California Scholarship Federation.

Sabina graduated from high school at the age of 14-11 and entered college in the following fall, but remained only one term. She recognized that she had come to a parting of the ways, and decided to concentrate in the field that gave her greatest satisfaction. She was awarded a $500 scholarship for musical study, having previously won six weeks' instruction with a visiting New York master. Sabina hopes for an opportunity later to study in the East, and her ambition is to become a concert artist.

A Violinist with Masculine Interests

Rhoda. This girl, IQ 147, is a violinist of considerable promise. An ear for music and a talent in reproduction were shown by her at a very early age. She received her first instruction from her mother, herself an accomplished musician. At three years she had a repertoire of thirty songs, at five she began composing for the piano, and before the age of six she had made several public appearances.

At eight years piano instruction was discontinued and she was placed under a noted Russian teacher of violin. Within two years she played before an internationally famous virtuoso and executed a difficult concerto so well that she received flattering notice in several musical magazines. Her progress continued steadily and rapidly, and at thirteen she made her New York début at Aeolian Hall. Now, at eighteen, she has completed a year as a scholar in a leading conservatory of music, one of fifteen among 580 contestants to be awarded this honor.

Early in childhood and continuously through high school, Rhoda presented a problem to her parents and teachers. She combined with her remarkable gift for poetic expression in music a rebelliousness against the lady-like pursuits deemed suitable for a young girl. She wanted to play marbles and football, to box and to wrestle. She had a passion for tools and carpentry and her adeptness in the use of tools was clearly shown in toy construction and in the general repairs she undertook in the house and yard. In the Plays and Games questionnaire given her at the age of twelve she doubly marked marbles, wrestling, baseball, boxing, and football, and was consistent in her expressed preferences in three independent lines of inquiry.

A very definite mannishness characterized her attitude in high school. She preferred and insisted upon lines and cuts of clothing severely masculine. She abhorred teas and the usual feminine functions of the school, but despite her idiosyncrasies she was very popular with other girls. The Masculinity-Femininity test which she took during the follow-up placed her at the upper quartile of girls in masculinity—not an extreme score. Whether the masculine trend of interests reflects a deep-seated personality twist that will impose difficulty in social adjustment and achievement remains to be seen. We hardly think it does.

Rhoda's school life was marked by rapid progress and fairly high scholarship notwithstanding the abbreviated attendance to which she was limited in order that her music practice might fall well within a child's work day. She entered school at eight and was placed in the fourth grade. She skipped half of the eighth grade, remained out of school one term in preparation for her musical début, and finished high school previous to her seventeenth birthday. In her senior year in high school she was consistently an honor pupil, second in an inter-school oratorical contest, and second in a Browning contest. From her varied activities as captain of a basketball team, captain of a baseball team, and holder of a silver cup in tennis for two successive years, one gleans some idea of her broad interests and versatility.

A Musician with Marked Femininity of Interests

Renwick. With an IQ of 150, Renwick presents the most extreme case of feminine personality bias among our gifted boys. That this tendency should in the present instance be associated with musical ability is perhaps not altogether accidental, for it has been found that male musicians and artists average decidedly less masculine on the Masculinity-Femininity Test than unselected males.

Renwick is a successful boy organist. His interests have been musical from early childhood. At the age of two years he recognized the names and melodies of sixty-four phonograph records; at two years five months he read the printed names of a hundred records; at three years he insisted upon pumping the pedals of the player piano with his hands. Definite instruction on the piano was begun at four years and has been continuous to the present time with the exception of several interruptions during the first two years. The parents encouraged him in every way and gave him opportunity for a broad musical training. At nine years he had heard most of the leading operas and the great concert singers then touring the country. When he was eleven his parents installed a pipe organ in their home, and Renwick quickly showed remarkable facility on this instrument. In less than two years he appeared as a concert organist, and at fifteen he was awarded the position of church organist and choirmaster.

Paralleling Renwick's early musical interest was an intense interest in playing "dress up." Here he inclined definitely toward the feminine. He composed playlets and operas, always casting himself for the leading feminine rôle. He played with dolls and amused himself by dyeing clothes and designing feminine garments. He refused to play with boys, notwithstanding punishment at home and merciless criticism at school.

Our Plays and Games questionnaire given him at the age of nine, in which he consistently declared his feminine preference, corroborated his unusual history. Six years later he took the Masculinity-Femininity test and earned a score which places him at the zero percentile of boys and at the 48th percentile of girls. His interests and attitudes as revealed by this test are as feminine as those of a typical girl.

The etiology of his feminine tendencies is not clear. It may be significant that he has been closely associated with his mother and that the father was past middle age at the time of his birth. A medical examination given him at the age of ten years revealed an unusual distribution of fat and some enlargement of the thyroid gland. With the onset of puberty, however, a negative thyroid is reported.

Renwick has never had much free association with mixed groups of his own age, nor any specific interest in athletics or sports. His recreation has been generally with adults and in some connection with music or drama. A brilliant future in music is the forecast of professional critics, for at fifteen he is not only a popular artist but a serious student of counterpoint and composition. He has had considerable success already in staging moving-picture prologues.

Renwick's school record gives evidence of exceptional achievement. He entered school at five years, but attended irregularly because of his parents' attempt to guard him against fatigue and to provide time for music practice. He skipped four half grades in the public school. When eleven he was placed under a private tutor and has continued his academic training with tutors. Now, at fifteen, he has completed what is equivalent to the third year in high school, and has done special work in languages. His Terman Group Test score, 194, is within one point of the median score of the fifteen-year-old gifted boys who took the test.

At this point the reader may wish to turn to chapter xxii for a somewhat fuller account of another young musician, P. J. B.

CHAPTER XXI

YOUTHFUL ZEALOTS

OUR MOST MASCULINE GIRL

Roberta. This girl has shown unusual interest in and aptitude with mechanical materials. The persistence of this interest along with a certain clustering of other traits and tendencies makes the speculation as to her vocational choice and also her social adjustment a very interesting one.

Roberta was recommended for the Stanford study at age 7-5 on the basis of a score of 88 upon the National Intelligence Test, giving her an estimated IQ of 160. Now, at age 13-4, her Terman Group Test score is 186, or 10 points above the median for our thirteen-year-old gifted girls.

Both parents were college graduates. The father, who died when Roberta was three years old, had been a structural engineer by profession. The paternal grandfather was a carpenter and is reported to have been very superior in his trade. On the maternal side the occupations cited for near relatives were storekeeper, chemist, and engineer.

At three and a half years Roberta was exceptionally dexterous with crayons and play tools. At four and a half she constructed a toy airplane that was subsequently exhibited at a university. When first reported to Stanford she was able to construct complicated devices from written plans without any assistance. Subsequent follow-up reports from home and school made note of her mechanical ability, with special reference to the building of toys such as wagons, scooters, and the like. One of her most recent pieces of work is an airplane carefully constructed, painted, varnished, and mounted on wheels.

Perhaps even more interesting than the actual nature of her mechanical output are the many angles of her personality which have been reflected in tests and personal reports. In the Play and Games questionnaire given six years ago, she consistently preferred masculine games, e.g., spinning tops, flying kites, fishing, using tools, and riding a bicycle. On the Masculinity-Femininity Test recently administered, her masculinity score was at the 49th percentile for high-school boys, while in femininity she was below the lowest high-school girl represented in the norms for the test. Roberta's voice and abrupt manner are quite unlike those of a little girl, and her desire to be attired in boy's clothes is even further unlike what is usually considered typical of girls. She has a sailor costume, a boy scout outfit, and a naval officer's outfit, all improvised, yet very effective in producing the desired rôle.

The Interest Blank filled out in 1928 tends to corroborate this tendency toward masculinity. The school subjects which Roberta likes best are general science, physical education, and orchestra; the kinds of books she prefers to read are adventure and science; the list of books and magazines given as having been recently enjoyed are: *Boy's Life Magazine*, West Point series, *Hans Brinker, Boy Scouts*, Tom Swift series, *The Trade Wind*, and *We*. On a scale of five, she labels using tools, general reading, and playing games as 1 (liked very much); while the more distinctly feminine occupations, sewing, cooking, housework, and dancing, are scored 5 (disliked very much); other occupations are scored at intermediate positions.

In a statement regarding playmates Roberta indicates that she prefers children who are younger, and describes her chum as "boyish and likes the same things I do." The mother says that in neighborhood group play Roberta is always the leader, with the others following in some form of an army or navy. Every moving picture about war, West Point, or Annapolis she is eager to attend. The mother finds this strange military interest distressing.

From a scholastic standpoint Roberta has maintained the high promise of her early tests. She is a member of the high-school Scholarship Society, and this past year stood highest in her entire city in a general science test.

What one would most like to know about Roberta is whether her masculine and scientific bent is the result of an early fixation on the father, perhaps accentuated by his death when she was still a young child, or whether it is but the manifestation of a physiological endowment that predisposes her to masculine pursuits.

Two Zealous Collectors

Walden. Here we find a collector of rather unusual versatility. At age ten, when he was first known to us, he had begun collections of flowers, rocks, books, insects, stamps, and coins. Of this original list he has continued with the stamps, which now number about 5,000, and coins, which number about 300. Phonograph records of the classics, to the number of about 1,500, and 150 opera libretti are more recent collections. Notably enough, the mere aggregation of objects does not terminate his interest. His history reveals him to be a student of the field of knowledge typified in his collections. When he was fifteen years old he sold an article on "Stamps and Music" for eight dollars. Now, at sixteen, he is president of a Philatelic Club in his city. His intense interest in opera has spurred him to private study of foreign languages; he reads libretti in French, German, Italian, and Spanish, and now has under compilation a list of all operatic records.

One immediately asks what factors have stimulated such unusual interests in collections. Do they demand, in addition to a high degree of intellectual capacity, wealth, time, and adult guidance? In this case an inquiry reveals only moderate expenditures, for Walden buys his records when music stores are clearing out their stock, and friends who know of his interests present him with their cast-offs. Even as a small child, his early collections were heavily contributed to by neighborhood boys who hunted up rocks, stamps, and insects for him. Walden has undoubtedly had more time for the pursuit of his interests than the average boy. Since the age of two he has suffered with serious and protracted attacks of asthma, which have prevented anything more than a vicarious interest in athletics. Sedentary activities were perforce encouraged. On the point of adult guidance, he unquestionably received generous quantities of time during his early childhood as well as a superior quality of assistance from his widowed mother, a woman of broad education and professional experience. Granting these predisposing factors, intellectual interest and persistence have undoubtedly determined the present size and nature of his collections. On the other hand, the exhausting nature of his chronic ailment and the frequent changes in residence that it necessitated may have curtailed the pursuit of his hobbies.

Walden might easily have become a disconsolate hypochondriac. Instead he is reported to be a friendly, somewhat vain, enthusiastic student, eager to participate in the activities of the school. He has been continuously a member of the Honor Society and has been contributor to the school paper, author and director of the Spanish Club play, and winner of a $15 prize in a Spanish essay contest. He is regarded as one of the most capable students in the physical science department of his high school.

The lure of physics versus the attraction of music and literature presents the difficult problem of deciding on a college. A technical school of high standard will be his choice if the field of physics should be elected as a vocation. To become a music critic, however, has been an ambition of two years' standing. On the paternal side Walden has two aunts who are musicians, one a violinist, the other a pianist. Although he has had less than a year's piano instruction and plays no other instrument, Walden has developed an unusual appreciation of music from his study of opera and symphony.

At the time of the original survey Walden was found to have an IQ of 164. His Terman Group Test point score is now 218, within 2 points of a perfect score. His score of 230 on the Iowa High School Content Examination is 9 points higher than the top score in a group of 623 seniors tested in an Eastern city. On the Masculinity-Femininity Test his score of +10 places him within the least masculine 10 per cent of high-school boys. His tendency to mental femininity is probably an outcome of his artistic interests, his physical illness, and his close association with his widowed mother.

William. This boy is a stamp collector of distinction, and despite added responsibilities with his increasing years he pursues the many angles that his collection has taken on with the enthusiasm of an artist. He carries on an extensive correspondence with foreign collectors, searches out information for them relative to American supplies, and tries always to fill their orders.

The collection was begun when William was seven years old at the instigation of his mother, whose office work gave access to used foreign stamps. Participation in vigorous physical exercise was barred to him because of a tubercular diathesis, and partly for this reason the collection became a major interest during his adolescence. It occupied much of his leisure time and gave him a somewhat distinguished status among the neighborhood boys, many of whom were stimulated to begin collections of their own. Now, at eighteen, he has four partially filled volumes of carefully selected stamps—7,000 varieties. He discusses with remarkable fluency their comparative art values and their historical symbolism, as well as the shifts in money values which they reflect.

The enthusiasm and thoroughness evidenced in William's stamp collection are characteristic of his entire school history. He entered kindergarten at five years, skipped five half-grades, and graduated from high school with honors at sixteen years despite extended absences due to illness. He was a member of the Honor Society throughout his entire high-school course and was awarded life membership in the California Scholarship Federation. Because of limited finances the problem of partial self-support had to be met very early. From the age of nine he assisted in the gardening and marketing of flowers. In his senior year in high school he was made student manager of the school cafeteria, from which he netted $50 a term. After graduation he secured an office position in a large financial house and has held it continuously since then. His employers have offered to retain him on a part-time basis when he enters college, which he plans soon to do.

William, whose IQ at age 12-3 when he was first located for the gifted group was 140, made a score of 217 out of a possible 220 on the Terman Group Test given at the time of the 1928 follow-up (age 18). On the Iowa High School Content Examination he reached the 95th percentile of random high-school seniors. On the Masculinity-Femininity Test his score was +9, which places him within the least masculine 10 per cent of high-school boys. The low masculinity score probably reflects in part the restrictions which his somewhat delicate health has imposed, and in part his close association with his mother, who was widowed before the birth of William, her only child.

FOUR DEVOTEES OF SCIENCE

Wallace. A senior in high school, Wallace has shown very exceptional ability in chemistry. He has not only maintained a high rating in regular course work, but has done independent research of such a quality that the science department has allowed him a full laboratory period each semester to present and discuss his projects. An elementary study of colloids and work with molecular motion and with spectra from the standpoint of chemistry are samples of his independent study.

Insistence on knowing has prompted careful and assiduous work. Wallace spends long hours in the school laboratory as well as in one that he has fitted up for himself at home. All his spare money, though he has very little, is spent for chemicals and apparatus. His stock of chemicals includes the common acids and bases, common metals, some of the common salts of these metals and some of their oxides, and a few organic chemicals, in all about 75 different reagents. His equipment, although limited and crude, has allowed experiments which are considerably in advance of what one ordinarily expects of high-school pupils.

In anticipating the future, Wallace considers nothing short of a Ph.D. degree, and although such a program will demand extreme frugality, there is little doubt that he will see himself through. Since Wallace was four years old his mother, an unschooled woman, has supported herself and the boy by hard physical labor. The boy's father died long before he could set aside money for his son's education. Apparently he was a man of high intelligence, for despite his foreign language handicap and limited schooling, he prepared himself for office work after coming to this country from Sweden. A small collection of books which remains as evidence of his intellectual aspirations is practically the only cultural facility that the humble home affords. The mother has always wisely elected to live near a public library, which for Wallace is a favorite haunt second only to his laboratory.

Wallace's singleness of interest, coupled with his limited finances, has meant a very definite circumscribing of his social life. He has attended few "parties" and has never in his life seen a moving picture other than those shown under the auspices of his school. He has attended only one dance. According to three independent sources of information he finds his sole group recreation in the high-school R.O.T.C. and in the friendship of two classmates who are considered equally bright and who are interested in the natural sciences.

To the fact that he was not well known socially was ascribed his failure to secure a $350 college scholarship. This prize went to a boy who stood somewhat lower in class marks but who was better known by the general student body, on whose vote the award was made. This was a very real disappointment, but he took his defeat graciously and conceded the worth of his opponent. Two honors in addition to the usual ones awarded by the school at graduation are indicative of his capabilities: the Paddock Trophy for highest standing in military efficiency, scholarship, and athletic activities, and the Harvard Prize, a book given by the Harvard Club of Southern California to the boy rating highest in scholarship in the senior class.

At the age of eleven Wallace earned an IQ of 138. His Terman Group Test point score at the age of seventeen was 205, this being four points above the median for our seventeen-year-old gifted boys, and at the 99th percentile of random high-school seniors.

Richard. At the time of the original survey Richard was in grade H7 at age 11-6. His Stanford-Binet IQ (corrected) was 141, and his scores on the Stanford Achievement Test were all of tenth- to twelfth-grade standard with the exception of that for spelling, which was close to the norm for grade H7. Now, at age seventeen, Richard is doing creditable work at a technical college the student body of which represents a highly selected group. His score on the Terman Group Test is 203, two points higher than the median for our seventeen-year-old gifted boys.

Richard has specialized in chemistry. Ability to draw and skill in manipulating tools were shown as early as five years. Successive years showed a steady increase of interest in science to an exclusion of other things. He spent his after-school hours setting up experiments suggested by current magazines. In high school he was a star student in the science department, and although making college recommending grades in other departments, he devoted most of his efforts to his major interest, chemistry. With money he saved from selling papers and magazines he built a small laboratory in the rear of his home. In the past four years he has accumulated over 130 different chemicals, which he has carefully bottled and labeled. According to his own statement in our 1927–28 Interest Blank, he prefers, above all things, an hour or two of quiet work in his laboratory.

Such intensity of interest would naturally make for curtailment and selection in the wide range of special activities available to the modern youth. Richard's reading of pure fiction is comparatively limited, and he rarely indulges in strictly social affairs. A natural tendency toward solitude and contentment with his own accomplishments may have been enhanced by frequent changes of school (six schools in five years). However, he enjoyed the free association with others that is incidental to athletics, for all along he swam and played ball and golf. This year he made his college class football team. Music has been an additional source of recreation, and membership in both a high-school and a college orchestra has given him desirable social contacts.

In Richard's family history we find a distinct mechanical and scientific bent. His father, with only a partial high-school education, has risen to a position of security in the field of architecture. His mother had several years' experience in drafting before her marriage. His maternal grandfather and his only maternal uncle were construction engineers.

Grenville. Here is another boy who stands out particularly because of his interest in chemistry. A general interest in mechanical and scientific things was evident in the grade school, where he consistently chose to read books and magazines of a scientific nature. At home he amused himself with his father's electrical materials and spent much time reading old textbooks that his father had used in high school. Even his play was colored by his scientific interest. A chemistry show was his usual proffer to the boys of the neighborhood in return for bottles, pieces of lead, copper, zinc, etc. His shop became the rendezvous of other twelve-year-olds who were interested in wireless. By this time he had made a receiving- and sending-set that worked well.

General science in high school crystallized his interest. The little shop, 7 x 5 feet, was henceforward called a laboratory. The shop is entirely homemade, but has a cement floor, a sink, electric lights, and a half-dozen well-filled shelves. In his senior year Grenville was made president of the Chemistry Club, and at its close he was awarded a scholarship in chemistry to one of the best technical institutions in the country. Here for a year he made a distinguished record, but because of lack of money did not return the second year despite offers of assistance made when the college discovered that he was not enrolled. He

THE PROMISE OF YOUTH

had found work in a large wholesale chemistry house and believed that with careful management he would be able to return when he was nineteen, better able to enjoy the social as well as the academic advantages of the institution. Although Grenville has always been a friendly boy, he has enjoyed little social life, being handicapped in this respect by his small stature and by the fact that he has always been among the youngest in his class. Grenville's present leisure-time activities indicate that his interests are not likely to be seriously diverted by his industrial experience. He continues to attend the evening lectures on chemistry at his college, and chemistry and German books predominate in his weekly selection at the public library.

Grenville was originally selected for membership in the gifted group on the basis of a high Terman Group Test score. At the age of 12-9 he earned a score of 176, which corresponds to an M.A. of 17-11, or IQ of 141. His score on the follow-up Terman Group Test taken at age 18-8 is 207. On the Iowa High School Content Examination he reaches the 95th percentile of high-school seniors, but on Part I of this examination (English and Literature) he reaches only the 25th percentile.

Francis. This boy is one of a small group of superior children who have been followed by us since 1910. He was born in 1900. The tests which he was given between 1910 and 1912, on such versions of the Binet Scale as were then existent, yielded results which would now be interpreted as corresponding to an IQ of 140 to 145. His score at seventeen on Examination *a*, the original form of the Army Alpha test, was one of the highest two or three found in a class of several hundred university students.

Francis was not permitted to learn to read until he was eight years old and was not sent to school until he was nine. Nevertheless, he completed the eighth grade at twelve, high school at sixteen, and was graduated from a university at twenty with the best scholastic record in his class of several hundred seniors. At twenty-four he received the degree of Doctor of Science from one of the country's leading universities and was immediately offered an instructorship in this institution. A serious illness, which came near proving fatal, prevented his acceptance and caused the loss of almost two years. He is now (1930) Associate Professor in a great university, with work in one of the physical sciences. He has published a dozen or more research contributions in technical periodicals, is co-author of a college textbook in science and has another large textbook almost ready for press. We are informed on the best authority that he is one of the country's most promising young men in his research field.

Since childhood Francis has been characterized by an intense interest in and vigorous pursuit of hobbies, chiefly of a scientific sort. At the age of fourteen he announced his choice of a career, the vocation named being substantially that which he later entered. He has always been reliable and studious, and independent in his thinking. His social development was entirely normal. He is perhaps a little too inclined to live to himself, but he is highly regarded by all who know him and was a leader in the fraternity to which he belonged in college.

The father of Francis is a member of the National Academy of Sciences.

CHAPTER XXII

THE PROMISE OF BABYHOOD AND THE FULFILL-
MENT OF YOUTH

For several of our subjects who are now almost adult, baby records of greater or less completeness were kept. Such records are naturally of very great interest when viewed in the light of later performance in standard tests and later achievement in school and life. In chapter xiv an account is given of the later development of Millie, who probably holds the world's record for early reading. Here, unfortunately, the early record is limited almost entirely to progress in learning to read. Somewhat more extensive data are on record for Beatrice, the gifted young poet described later in chapter xxvi. However, our best comparison of babyhood and youth is offered by the record of P. J. B.

P. J. B. has been included in our folio of individual studies chiefly because of the special interest attaching to a detailed account of her development from birth to the age of twenty-five months prepared by her father. For this period he kept an accurate record which he has organized in dissertation form, and which rivals in completeness the infant biographies published by Shinn, Major, and others. The father has condensed the dissertation into a relatively brief summary, which constitutes the major part of the present chapter.

So far as we know, this infant biography is the only one of comparable completeness to be followed by a quantitative appraisal of achievement in adolescence. Additional interest accrues in the fact that at age fifteen P. J. is not only a young person of general ability high enough to entitle her to a place in the gifted group, but a musician of promise and recognized attainment as well.

An individual study has also been included of P. J.'s younger sister, M. In M. we find a juvenile poet who is perhaps as talented in a literary direction as P. J. is in music. Seldom, in the same family, have we had opportunity to make a comparative study of two individuals whose talents are so unusual and at the same time so different in nature.

The First Twenty-five Months of P. J. B.'s Life

By her father, Verne B. B.

Early infancy. P. J. was born in 1913, and weighed 7¾ pounds. She was well matured at birth, with a head of heavy black hair. The nurse reported that P. J. shed tears within two hours of her birth, and her mother observed them when she was but eight hours old. At about the same time, P. J.'s eyes turned toward a light as the nurse was arranging a piece of paper over it. From the first she was sensitive to sounds or to vibration, for she would stop crying immediately when someone entered the nursery.

On the fifteenth day, as she lay on her stomach, P. J. lifted her head with no apparent effort. She first smiled between the ages of five and six weeks. In her ninth week[1] when two girls came to see her she looked several times from one to the other and regarded each attentively. In her eleventh week she "discovered" her fingers, and began to experiment with them.

She moved herself about in her bed in her fourteenth week, and vainly tried to sit up. At this time she would grasp two fingers offered her and pull herself energetically up to a sitting position. Her toes she first experimented with during her seventeenth week, after which time she spent hours at a time playing with the tassels on her booties.

The ability to roll over alone face down was acquired during the twenty-second week. A few days later, when P. J. pulled her knees up under her, the position for creeping had been assumed. She continued to roll, however, whenever she wanted to cover any distance. From the position on her hands and knees she soon began to reach for something with which to pull herself up. Next she began hunching herself about in a sitting position.

Seventh month. P. J. learned to stand up and help herself along by the fence around her pen.

Ninth month. The syllable "da," started during the eighth month, developed into "da da," and was applied to her father. Added to this was "bye bye," which meant a journey or a walk.

---

[1] Ninth week refers to the period when P. J. was eight weeks old but not yet nine weeks; likewise, eleventh week refers to the period when she was ten weeks old but not yet eleven weeks, etc.

Tenth month. P. J. first walked alone. Seven words were definitely fixed in her vocabulary.

Eleventh month. In the beginning of this month when her father at the piano sang some scale exercises, P. J. cried in a plaintive manner. With each succeeding scale he had raised the tonic half a step, lending a sad effect.

The trick of balance in walking was perfected. Three new words were added to her vocabulary. She found and recognized on her own initiative her first picture, the trade-mark, "His Master's Voice." The dog was unmistakable to her, for she rushed to her mother crying "wow, wow, wow."

Twelfth month. P. J. discovered a cow's head on a salt carton, and excitedly pointed toward it, exclaiming "boo-ba, boo-ba." This paved the way to her enjoyment of a home-made scrapbook whose pages became alive with representations of her known world.

By the end of this month her talking vocabulary consisted of twenty-two words.

Thirteenth month. When her father sang vocal exercises P. J. would also sing in her own sweet, soft manner, but to herself only; attention embarrassed her. "Here's a Ball for Baby" she distinguished as her particular song. She would leave her play at once and run with a pleased smile to the piano when her mother played or sang this song.

Fifteenth month. For a number of months members of the family had sung nursery songs to P. J. During the fifteenth month she learned to participate in Mother Goose song-plays. The rhyme "Barber, Barber, Shave a Pig" would elicit a sneeze on the last line, "Give the poor barber a pinch of snuff." At the last line of "Sing a Song of Six-pence" she would expect her nose to be tweeked at the words "nipped off her nose."

Sixteenth month. P. J. had developed great facility in selecting known objects from the pages of a picture book. That pictures, however, were still a part of her real world was evident when she sniffed at a highly colored picture of a flower, and shook the picture as though to see the petals fall.

She was taken often during this month to song services at a camp meeting near by. Standing on a seat she would sing "la, la, la," and in imitation of the conductor would beat time in perfect rhythm. Before the month was over she was correctly humming the tunes, "Holy Night," and "Oh, Moon in the Night."

Seventeenth month. The song, "My Heart Is Like a Singing Bird," a rather intricate tune, was learned from hearing her mother sing it about the house. The words to "How do you like to go up in a swing?", "See-Saw, Marjorie Daw," and a part of "Sail-Ho, Hail-Ho" were also learned. P. J. pronounced the words fairly accurately, although she did not know the meaning of them all.

Eighteenth month. Three new songs were learned. P. J. often sang songs to her dolls as she pretended to put them to sleep in their bed.

Nineteenth month. Selections from Eugene Field were read to her. "Did you ever hear the wind go, Yoo-oo-oo?" she particularly liked. After dinner she would get the "Wind-Book," as she called it, turn to the page through some mark that she recognized, and ask for the poem. One evening Dunbar's "Boogah Man" was read to her. When asked later what the Boogah Man said, she replied, "Wate'-tess [water cress]"; the eeriness of the poem must have suggested to her a weird Chinese vendor who often passed the house calling, "Water cress." One new song was learned this month.

Twentieth month. Six new songs were learned.

Twenty-first month. P. J. watched butterflies and tried to imitate their motions. Her mother improvised words to the tune, "Here We Go Round the Mulberry Bush," as follows: "This is the way we butterfly dance..... On Christmas Day in the morning." P. J. sang it, waving her arms and prancing up and down the room.

During the month P. J. composed the germ of a song, crude and simple, but perfect in rhythm. Jumping up and down from the springs of a cot, she sang, *"la - la - la; la - la la; la - la - la - la; la - la - la."* With each accented syllable, she sprang into the air. She had no definite tune except a maneuvering of the voice up and down.

Three finger plays were learned this month from Émile Poulsson's book, *Finger Plays.* P. J. now became occupied with Florence Holbrook's *Hiawatha Primer* and listened attentively to stories that her aunt told her from it.

Christmas Day fell at the close of the twenty-first month. P. J. was taken to see the outdoor municipal Christmas tree, and appeared engrossed in all the splendor and action. When a prelude to "Holy Night," her good-night song, was played softly by the band, P. J. looked thoughtful at first, then her mouth began to pucker, her tears began to fall, and she cried softly and appealingly, "Mama, mama." Then she broke into such sobs that she had to be taken home. Later in the evening when a strain from that song was sung, she ran to her mother crying.

P. J. learned nine new songs during the month. The sight of Christmas bells would release the impulse to start the song, "Merry, Merry Christmas Bells." When the Christmas candles were lighted, she at once started the song, "See the Christmas Candles."

Twenty-second month. The repertoire of songs was increased by two.

Twenty-third month. The Christmas presents, among them a book from a little friend, Dorothy, had been put away one at a time by P. J.'s parents to prevent their becoming too common. On February 15 this particular book was brought out after seven weeks in hiding. P. J. at once recognized it and shouted gleefully, "Tank 'ou, Do'ot'y, fo' book [Thank you, Dorothy, for book]."

Imaginary characters began to develop in her mind. She pretended to eat from little dishes in which there was no food. She developed a fear of the dark, projecting into it animals that existed only in her mind. A fear of the wind seized her, and as she saw the treetops wave she would exclaim, "No, no; wind hurt a-baby." When a dog barked near, she shied from him in an excited manner crying, "No, no; dog hurt a-baby." These fears seemed to manifest themselves first when she saw a picture of a boy striking a lion. That night, as she looked out the door into the dark, she said in a very cautious way, "Lion out doors." The bedtime stories were now selected carefully by the family so that no disturbing flight of imagination would interfere with her sleep.

In the last week of this month she surprised the family by singing "Goodnight, Ladies," a song which the members of the family agreed she had not heard more than five times. Often now when she was playing in her father's room he would softly hum one of the tunes familiar to her and note how quickly and unconsciously she would catch it up. Again he would strike softly a note, then the octave above, and she would imitate the notes with perfect accuracy.

Twenty-fourth month. P. J. learned to play ball, catching her big indoor baseball in her hands and arms and throwing it with accuracy to a second person. Often she spent a half hour buttoning and unbuttoning her shoes.

She had learned the story of "Goldilocks and the Three Bears," and during the twenty-third and twenty-fourth months began to act the bear parts. Then she assumed the rôle of a growling and roaring lion, running about the house pretending to bite different members of the family, and finding great amusement in their feigned confusion.

At her play she sang much of the time. Many of her songs she sang with improvisations in the way of substituted names.

From the first time P. J. saw a pencil and watched the line that followed it, she was eager to get a pencil in her hands. During her fifteenth month she observed drawings made with colored crayons, but her own scribbling was aimless. At the beginning of the twenty-fourth month she was watched carefully and was found to be producing representations intentionally. Several of her drawings made during this month are reproduced in Figures 8A and 8B. At this time she conceived of definite objects for portrayal. The "water-cress" man seemed to call for the biggest share of her effort. The reproduction of rain (not made till her twenty-fifth month) was an entirely original idea. The parts of the pictures named in the illustrations were named by her, which is convincing proof that her work was purposed.

The drawings of Figures 8A and 8B (pp. 346–47) are all remarkable for a child of two years, especially those of 8B. Unfortunately, norms are not available for scoring the drawings of the fish, chicken, rain, candles, etc.; it is extraordinary enough that a two-year-old would even attempt to draw such objects. The drawings in 8A we have attempted to score on the Goodenough Scale for Measuring Intelligence by Drawings.[1] There are some points of uncertainty, but the scores for the four drawings of the "Water-Cress Man" seem to be 3, which is slightly better than the norm for three and a half years. The drawings of 8B are probably at least equal to average four-year performance.

During the last week of the twenty-fourth month P. J. attended a circus, particularly enjoying the animal acts. Upon her return home she told many things that she had seen, as follows: "Monkney swing by tail"; "lion wode on kee-tap an' jump fwoo hot-hot [lion rode on horse and

[1] Goodenough, Florence L., *The Measurement of Intelligence by Drawings*, World Book Co., 1926, p. 177.

FIGURE 8A

Drawings of P. J. B. in Her Twenty-fourth Month

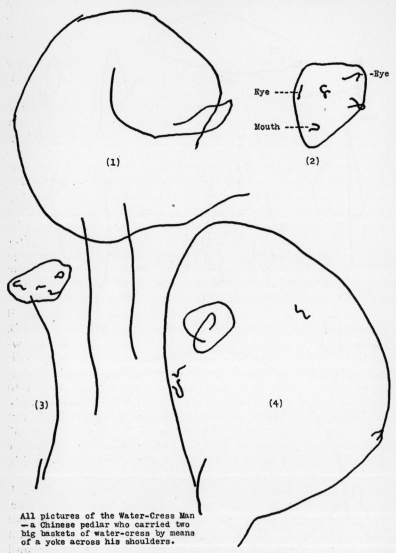

(1)

(2)

Eye ----
-Eye

Mouth ----

(3)

(4)

All pictures of the Water-Cress Man
—a Chinese pedlar who carried two
big baskets of water-cress by means
of a yoke across his shoulders.

jumped through a blazing hoop]"; "dahdy fed ahm [ele-
phant] peanuts in his long, long, nose"; etc.

FIGURE 8B

OTHER DRAWINGS OF P. J. B. IN HER TWENTY-FOURTH MONTH

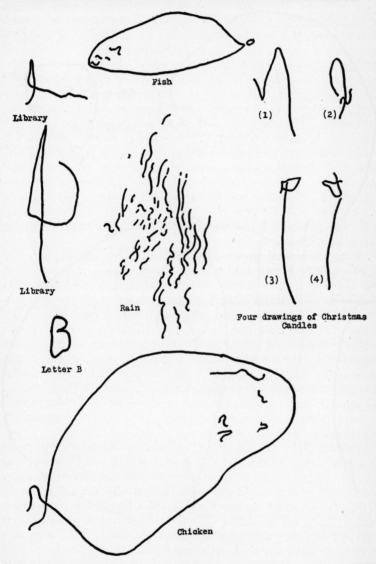

Fish

Library

Library

Letter B

Rain

(1)

(2)

(3)

(4)

Four drawings of Christmas Candles

Chicken

At the close of the second year P. J. was able to distinguish the colors: red, white, black, yellow, orange, green, blue, and brown. When asked the colors she appeared to be ignorant of what color is, but a red book, or a blue bead, or a green light, or a brown shoe was seldom named in the wrong way. She knew color as part of the object on which it appeared, but not as an abstract thing. Another abstraction was a name, and when asked her name, she seemed confused. She was told the names of her dolls and of Teddy, and she called them all by name; but if asked what their names were, she seemed not to comprehend.

P. J. now had 69 jingles or rhymes and 41 songs at her command. The tunes of all these songs and most of the words were sung correctly. Words which she did not understand, however, were often filled in with the syllables "ah" and "la." When given a large dictionary to play with she would turn the pages and look at the pictures. Finding a picture of a fish, she would repeat the rhyme, "Little Fishy in the Brook." When she turned to the illustrations of different national flags, she sang, "There are many flags in many lands."

Many services previously rendered by others for her were rapidly being taken over for her own performance. She gave up most things readily when her attention was turned to something else, but she wanted to dress and undress herself, button and unbutton her shoes, sweep the floor, dust the furniture, wipe the dishes, water the paths with the hose, and carry on the pursuits of an adult. There were particular doors through which she wanted the members of the family to go. She was insistent upon particular streets and ways of getting to town, special methods of caring for her various notions, and whims. "Udder way," "Udder door," "No, no, no; baby do it," were commands that sprang from this new phase of self-assertion.

Twenty-fifth month. P. J. showed considerable persistence with play materials, and would string beads or buttons for a long period at a time. She found a clothing sample book, and given a needle and thread she set to work to string the samples on the thread. She worked for an hour, tearing from the book the seventy-two samples, pieces about an inch square, and sewing them together. She was not contented until she had gathered them all.

Music was coming to have increasing importance in her emotional life. While playing and singing to herself one day, she started a song, but pitched it too low. She made an effort to get it higher, but failed. In an irritated manner she said, "No, no, no, baby." Then she succeeded in pitching it in a key suited to her needs. One evening she asked to have "Autumn Lullaby" sung. As soon as it was begun her eyes filled with tears and she sobbed bitterly, yet when her mother stopped singing P. J. begged her to continue. On one occasion her father sang to her the song, "Goodnight, Lena," and substituted P. J.'s name. She at once broke into sobs, asking her father to wipe her tears and not to sing that song. Another evening she was heard to sob to herself in bed. When her father went to her and asked why she was crying she replied that the sad song she was singing to her dolly made her cry. Asked why she sang that song if it made her cry, she answered, "Well, I like to cry."

P. J.'s mother had repeated many jingles for her, permitting her, after hearing them a few times, to fill in the last words of lines that contained the rhyme words. Early in the twenty-fifth month it suddenly occurred to the observer that an experiment could be made that would test the rhyming sense. A number of simple verses were improvised. These were recited to P. J. with the omission of the rhyming words; the latter she supplied herself without hesitation.

As a stringent test, several verses in which the rhymed words were distinctly not implied in the content itself were devised by the observer, as for example:

> Here's a boy from Petalama,
> And he hasn't any MAMA.
> Here's a little Kewpie laddie,
> And he does not have a DADDY.

The capitalized words were supplied by P. J., and proved in the mind of the experimenter that the rhyme words were being furnished with conscious intent.

At what age P. J. first conceived of rhyme it is difficult to say. Perhaps the same experiment could have been successfully made before the end of the second year, for her accuracy in determining the rhyme words and the zest with which she entered into it suggest that she appreciated the appropriateness of rhyme long before this time.

Her means of verbal expression were now changing and improving noticeably. Some of her used sentences were: "Look ak a-baby's needle"; "Stwawberry pie fo' din-din"; "Lots of books down to libwary"; "Budder Jim and Baby

Doll keel over"; "Baby's hands all keen [clean]"; "Tomorrow Daddy'll wix [fix] Baby's fwag [flag]"; "Soap makes Baby's hands wough [rough]." It is interesting to compare these with the following sentences which she used less than two months later (at the end of the twenty-sixth month) when her pronunciation and sentence structure had made still further advances: "Baby can blow it up just a little bit" (referring to a toy balloon); "Daddy, do ostriches lay big, big eggs?"; "I'm going to go down town with Daddy"; "Baby's going to have stwawberries for dinner tomorrow."

At the close of her twenty-fifth month her vocabulary consisted of 987 words and symbols that had been listed. These were distributed as follows:

	Number	Percentage
Nouns, common	419	42.5
Nouns, proper	246	24.9
Verbs	181	18.3
Adjectives	70	7.1
Adverbs	23	2.3
Interjections	17	1.7
Prepositions	14	1.4
Conjunctions	11	1.2
Pronouns	6	0.6

Among the 246 proper nouns are the names of 126 songs, rhymes, and jingles that she had learned during her first twenty-four months, 8 tradesmen, 60 characters, 3 animals, 3 books, and 4 dolls. The names of songs and jingles might be excepted, but she had always had a special name for each one. The list includes none of the imaginary characters invented by her, such as members of families purely fictitious.

P. J. B. AT AGE FIFTEEN

By Barbara Burks

P. J. B., age fifteen, is the oldest of a family of five children. She is a musician and composer who has achieved a well-founded local reputation and her strong musical bent has been apparent from babyhood.

In preparation for her vocational choice of concert pianist or accompanist P. J. expends a large amount of time outside of her regular school program. She tells us that her favorite occupations are playing the piano and composing music. The devoted application to music has not been at the expense of her intellectual, scholastic, social, and physical development, however, for her activities are those of an unusually well-rounded individual. During her first two years of high school she attained a number of scholastic honors, took prizes in an essay contest and a declamation contest, and won the girls' tennis championship of her school. As a high-school junior she is editor of the school paper, assistant editor of the school annual, class secretary, member of a tennis team, and member of the student-government commission. She also teaches a Sunday School class and takes an active part in the Campfire Girls' organization.

At the age of three P. J. learned to read, and at four and a half she read current events on the war and reported on them at kindergarten. At four she composed her first piece of music, going to the piano and playing a chord accompaniment while she sang a melody to "The alder by the river shakes out her powdery curls."

At age eight and a half definite piano instruction was begun. Up to the present she has had between four and five years' instruction on the piano, about a year on the violin, and very recently instruction on two brass instruments, baritone and cornet, which she plays in the high-school band. She has also had private instruction in harmony and orchestration, and she frequently assists the high-school music teacher in arranging and harmonizing compositions for various instruments. She devotes about two hours a day outside of school hours to her music and has a large number of musical compositions to her credit, some of which she has played at public programs. She played several for a small group at Stanford, including Professor Paul R. Farnsworth, a student of the psychology of music. It was the opinion of Professor Farnsworth and the others who heard her that her compositions held much promise. Her rendition of other technical compositions was also exceptionally artistic.

Professor Farnsworth kindly co-operated with us by administering the Seashore-Kwalwasser battery of music tests. P. J. made high scores on all but one test of the battery. Her percentile ranks according to the adult norms are:

Pitch	94	Harmony	82
Intensity	45	Memory	87
Rhythm	98	Consonance	97
Melody	97	Time	94

Professor Farnsworth found P. J. to possess absolute pitch on piano and organ for single tones and dyads. The timbre of forks and pipes caused errors of approximately a half-tone.

Various musical honors have already come to P. J. She has given two recitals, one at age twelve and one at age fourteen. At twelve she was selected to play for the state convention of high-school principals, at which she gave two of her own compositions. At fifteen, competing in a contest open to all school and college students in her county (in which is located a college with a conservatory of music) P. J. won a prize that had been offered for the best song commemorating an occasion of great local interest.

P. J. has taken the Terman Group Test on several different occasions, the last being at the time she took at Stanford a five-hour schedule of intelligence, achievement, personality, and music tests. The scores on the Terman Group Test are as follows:

	Age	Score
Form A	12-8	168
Form B	13-10	202
Form A	14-8	192
Form B	15-7	197

The score at age 12-8 corresponds to an M.A. of 17-6, and that at 13-10 to an M.A. of 19-1, from which IQ's of 139 and 138 may be computed. The scores at ages 14-8 and 15-7 are both above the median scores earned by our gifted subjects of corresponding ages during the 1927–28 follow-up.

Achievement tests which she took at age 15-7 indicate a superior mastery of high-school subject-matter. Although just beginning her third year in high school (with, however, several extra credits), she scored at the 85th percentile of graduating high-school seniors on each of the three parts of the Iowa High-School Content Examination which were administered—mathematics, science, and history. On the Burch Test of Literary Comprehension her scores on the three parts were 33, 41, and 39—from one to one and a half standard deviations above eleventh- and twelfth-grade norms.

In addition to the tests which have been enumerated P. J. was given the Watson Test of Fair-Mindedness, the Masculinity-Femininity Test, and the Woodworth-Cady questionnaire. On the Watson her score, 25, was about equal to the mean score of our gifted subjects and of representative groups of university students; on the Masculinity-Femininity Test she scores at the 45th percentile of high-school girls—a far more feminine rating than the typical rating received by our gifted girls; on the Woodworth-Cady questionnaire her score was 19, which would indicate possibly a little less emotional stability than that of the typical gifted girl.

The home environment of P. J. has been one to encourage her interests and talents, as well as to foster high ideals of conduct and wholesome leisure-time activities. The family group is most congenial, and the father tells us that "P. J. seems very proud of the accomplishments of the younger children of the family; the wranglings and quarrels that one sometimes sees among brothers and sisters seem lacking."

An inquiry into P. J.'s ancestry reveals abundant evidence of musicality on both sides, although there are no close relatives who were professional musicians. However, a cousin of the maternal grandfather was an opera singer, and a maternal great-uncle did considerable composing. A cousin on the father's side was a pianist and became head of the piano department of a midwestern college.

Both parents are musical and have taken lessons in instruments and voice, and both sprang from families in which music has been much appreciated and valued.

In the clearness with which later development is foreshadowed this case is most remarkable. Superiority in intelligence was noted long before the end of the first year, and she was hardly started upon her second year when her precocious interest in music became evident. By the end of her second year her vocabulary and general behavior suggest a mental level of at least three years, and her drawings a mental level of three and a half or four. She learned to read at three years and at four and a half could read accounts of current events. At four she was composing melodies and playing them on the piano. At age fourteen we find her scoring near the upper limit of the Terman Group Test for General Ability, and when half-way through high school she scores in the best fifteen per cent of graduating high-school seniors in her information on high-school subject-matter. Similar agreement between infancy and young womanhood is to be seen in her social adaptability and likable disposition. The early proficiency in drawing is to be considered as an indication of superior general intelligence, not of artistic promise.

The case of P. J. raises insistently the question whether detailed objective records for infancy and youth would usually reveal such similarity of intelligence, interests, and personality. At present there is no answer, but we much doubt whether P. J. is particularly exceptional in this respect.

M., POET AND SISTER OF P. J.

The second daughter in the B. family, M., is two years younger than P. J. She has entered upon her sophomore high-school year at age 13-5. She began school in the second grade at five and a half years, and was placed at once in the third grade, as she had been reading since the age of three and a half. Her interest in school was keen from the first. At the age of six she spent a summer at Play School at the University of California. She was put in charge of the bulletin board, and when others of her class failed to hand in enough material she would herself write little stories or poems to post.

M. took three parts of the Iowa High School Content Examination with her sister, and while she had only begun her sophomore high-school year, she scored at the 55th percentile of graduating high-school seniors in mathematics and science, and at the 65th percentile in history. On the Burch Test of Literary Comprehension she scored about two standard deviations above the tenth-grade norms, with scores on the three parts of 35, 36, and 34, respectively. On Part I the score is 2 points higher than that of P. J., and on Parts II and III, 5 points lower.

Like her sister, M. was given piano instruction. She took lessons between the ages of 6-6 and 8-6 and willingly practiced overtime, but in spite of hard work she did not accomplish much. Her playing was quite mechanical, according to her father, although her rhythm was good. Her scores on the Seashore-Kwalwasser battery of music tests are in marked contrast to those earned by P. J. At age 13-6 her percentile ranks according to eighth-grade norms are:

Pitch	78	Harmony	76
Intensity	41	Memory	59
Rhythm	88	Consonance	84
Melody	94	Time	6

She does not possess any degree of absolute pitch.

Since the age of seven M. has won numerous prizes and
honors in children's literary competitions. When she was
only two and a half her sayings often contained a poetic
touch, as when she ran to her mother with eucalyptus bud
caps to "give to the Bwonies [Brownies] fo' caps fo' dere
dollies," or remarked while viewing a sunset, "Mamma, God
sent His Son, and He sent His sunset, too." She was able to
compose childish rhymes at age 2-8.

M. has written about thirty complete poems and many
other incomplete ones. She began a drama at the age of
twelve, and has now started a novel. Her early work in
poetry (age eight or nine) showed considerable facility, but
was far below the level of quality established in poems
which she has composed within the last year and a half. It
is an interesting fact that her present enthusiasm for composing poetry did not reach large proportions until she was
twelve, M. later explaining to her parents that she had grown
tired of being known merely as P. J.'s sister and wished to
create something of worth herself.

Three samples of M.'s recent work are reproduced below.

MEMORIES (AGE 12)

Oh, golden memories are sweet roses
To be laid away in a rose jar.
The roses can never bloom again,
   No—never.
But their sweet fragrance can flow out,
And you can look back
On their withered petals.

SANCTUARY (AGE 12)

Published with two other of M.'s poems in a city newspaper.

Trees in the fog are like nuns
Somber and severe,
With hoary vestments vainly trying
To soften their barren faces.
The rustle of black,
The murmur of low voices
As with their shadowy fingers
They tell over their beads.

DUSK (AGE 13)

Like a bird's
Feathered wing
Dusk softens
Everything.

> Tall black trees
> Sharp as blades,
> Dark mountains,
> Brilliant glades;
>
> Old houses
> Fenced in,
> Sad hearts,
> Strident din.
>
> Like music
> Children sing
> Dusk softens
> Everything.

M. is as fond of reading as she is of writing, and her preference is for books of modern poetry. Her father tells us that "night after night she reads poems, and she has spent her birthday checks for modern poetry for the past three or four years. . . . . She has made a modern writers' notebook and saves pictures and clippings and also writes her own reaction to different authors' works. . . . . She sees colors and flavors in words, and judges her own writing in a rather masterly and critical way." M. herself feels that Untermeyer's *This Singing World* given to her by her father when she was eleven did much to arouse her interest in reading and writing poetry.

Drawing has also been one of M.'s hobbies, and she often has the children in the family pose for her. Although she plans a full college course, she will be so young when she graduates from high school (16-2) that she would like to spend a year or two at an art school before attending a university. She recently made about a hundred Christmas cards for the family, designing a linoleum cut, coloring the pictures, and printing them.

At Sunday School M. helps her mother in the beginners' department of twenty to thirty children, and it was recently necessary for her to take entire charge for six months. M. greatly enjoys this responsibility and spends several evenings a week outlining the lesson, learning new songs, and hunting up pictures and stories. She is a natural storyteller, and comes home each Sunday full of humorous incidents which she recites to the family. According to her parents she is "so full of prankishness, burlesque, and imitation that she is the life of the family group." Many of her young Sunday-School pupils come to see her at her home.

"She and they seem the same age when together; she does not act grown-up with them." At school M. is very generally liked, and is friendly with many more girls than is P. J., who is inclined to specialize in a small group of girl friends.

M. has taken the Terman Group Test several times, earning scores as follows:

	Age	Score
Form A	10-7	132
Form B	11-9	150
Form A	12-8	192
Form B	13-6	174

The scores on these tests correspond to IQ's of 150, 142, 147, and 131. The discrepancies between IQ's can probably be accounted for by unreliability of the test scores.

M. took several personality tests at age 13-6. On the Woodworth-Cady her score was 16, 3 points superior to that of P. J., but indicating a slight tendency toward emotional instability. Her score on the Masculinity-Femininity Test placed her within the most masculine fifth of unselected high-school girls; it indicated, however, only slightly greater masculinity than that of the typical girl of our gifted group. On the Watson Test of Fair-Mindedness M.'s score, 29, corresponded to a slightly more prejudiced attitude than did P. J.'s score, but not more than that of the average high-school pupil.

SIBLINGS OF P. J. AND M.

Two siblings of P. J. and M. have been tested, a third being too young to test.

C., a boy of twelve, earned a score of 136 on the Terman Group Test at age 10-2. The corresponding mental age, 16-0, yields an IQ of 157. C. entered high school at age 12-6 where he has maintained a consistently high record. He excels in two such varied avocations as tennis and declamation.

Cn., who has recently entered fifth grade a month before her ninth birthday, has a Stanford-Binet IQ of 137. When tested on three tests of the Stanford Achievement battery, her score in paragraph meaning equaled the L8 norm, in arithmetic computation the H5 norm, and in nature study and science the L6 norm. On the Woodworth-Cady questionnaire her score was 8, which indicates rather better than average emotional balance.

PART III. A STUDY OF LITERARY JUVENILIA

CHAPTER XXIII

DERIVATION OF A TENTATIVE SCALE FOR RATING LITERARY JUVENILIA*

PURPOSE OF THE STUDY

The writings of average children have been extensively studied by those who have constructed composition scales. These scales, however, are entirely inadequate for rating the merits of exceptionally superior literary juvenilia. Most of them in fact stop not far from the level of merit where a suitable scale for gifted children would have to begin. The purpose of the study to be described was (1) to derive a scale with steps high enough to measure the best writings of the most talented children, (2) to compare the productions of California gifted children with the juvenilia of eminent writers, and (3) to study the environment and early development of those who have evidenced precocious literary ability.

The field of this research represents a nearly virgin territory, for few efforts have been made to investigate promising juvenile writings in the light of objective standards. The publication by Terman and Fenton in 1921[1] of their study of Beatrice represents, as far as the writer is aware, the first reported attempt to evaluate the juvenilia of a highly gifted child. Five of Beatrice's poems, selected by twelve judges as her best (up to 1921) were compared with twelve other juvenilia (by Tennyson, Blake, Longfellow, Blanden, Wordsworth, Shelley, and three by Stanford students). These seventeen poems were ranked in order of literary merit by forty-six advanced students in English. In the composite rank order, Beatrice's poems rated eighth, ninth, tenth, eleventh, and fourteenth.

Mearns, in 1925, reported the results of a four-year experiment in encouraging high-school pupils to literary production. Among the examples of the pupils' writings in-

---

* Part III is a Doctor's dissertation by Dortha Williams Jensen.

[1] Terman, Lewis M., and Fenton, Jessie C., "Preliminary Report on a Gifted Juvenile Author," *Journal of Applied Psychology*, Vol. 5, 1921, pp. 163–178.

cluded in the appendix of Mearns' *Creative Youth* are some which students of literature and well-known writers have considered to be of exceptional quality. Mearns did not attempt, however, to evaluate these juvenilia in any objective manner, or to study the relationship between mental ability and the production of meritorious works.[1]

SELECTION OF SUBJECTS AND OF JUVENILIA

There were available three groups of gifted children whose literary juvenilia could be obtained and evaluated without a disproportionate expenditure of time and effort:

1. The 1,672 children of the California gifted group, for whom Dr. Terman has secured extensive and definite information.

2. The 271 of the 301 men and women of eminence studied by Dr. Catharine M. Cox who were rated as having childhood IQ's of 140 or over.

3. Ten other eminent authors, some of whose childhood writings were available and who were rated by Terman and Cox as having had childhood IQ's of 140 or over, the ratings being made in a manner comparable to that described in Volume II of this series.

It is not argued that these groups have produced the best literary juvenilia available in English. It is claimed, however, and is shown by the data, that they were exceptionally endowed with respect to both general intelligence and literary ability. For these subjects extensive information was available, thanks to the painstaking work of Terman and Cox. It seemed probable that sufficient numbers of superior juvenilia could be found in these two groups to make possible valid group comparisons. Greater numbers could have

---

[1] In correspondence with the present writer, Dr. Mearns mentioned that Dr. Harold Rugg had made a study (unpublished) of the relation between intelligence and literary achievement in these children. The correlation between Dr. Mearns' ratings of the excellence of the productions (the ratings were on a scale of 5) and the Binet test scores of the authors was almost perfect. When the Binet test scores of the poets, essayists, and fictionists were scrutinized, it was found that the poets had the highest IQ's, the essayists next, and the fictionists lowest.

Through the courtesy of Dr. Jesse Newlon, Director of the Lincoln School, a list of the Binet mental ages and IQ's of children mentioned in *Creative Youth* was sent to the writer. The range of uncorrected IQ's is from 100 (a girl aged 15-10) to 157 (a girl aged 11-6); that of the corrected IQ's would probably be 10 to 15 points higher, as most of the subjects were above the age of eleven and were therefore inadequately measured by the Stanford-Binet scale.

been secured, but the increased value to the study would have been disproportionate to the labor involved.

It would, of course, have been impossible to examine carefully the juvenile writings of all the men and women of eminence rated as having had IQ's of 140 or over. In the first place it was discovered that a fair sampling of juvenile writings was available for only a limited number of men and women so rated. One would naturally expect that the greater wealth of juvenilia in literature would be available for those eminent individuals whose writing had brought them fame. Such was found to be the case. Accordingly, the individuals with whom, and with whose writings, this study is concerned, may be said to belong to two groups of subjects whose actual or estimated IQ's in childhood were 140 or over: (1) Dr. Terman's California gifted children; (2) child writers who later attained eminence in literature, and for whom some juvenilia were available in the Stanford libraries.

The criterion of eminence in English and American letters was separate discussion of life and works in each of two widely used histories of English and American literature: Pace, *American Literature with Readings;* Pace, *English Literature with Readings;* Long, *Outlines of American Literature with Readings;* Long, *Outlines of English Literature with Readings.*

Examination of other books covering the same fields indicated that this is a fair criterion, since agreement between them is virtually complete with respect to the authors used in the present study.

It was found that ten individuals who met the standard of eminence in literature, and for whom juvenile writings were available, had not been rated in connection with Dr. Cox's study. Hence these ten were rated as to IQ by two of Dr. Cox's three judges. The estimated IQ's of these ten and the quality of their juvenile writings warranted their inclusion with those previously selected for intensive study.

From these two groups of gifted children (1,953 *in toto*— 1,672 plus 271 plus 10) it was necessary to select those who had produced juvenile writings of exceptional merit. A preliminary sifting of cases was therefore carried out, with a view to eliminating those gifted children who could not possibly qualify as child writers on the basis of available records. Because of the great mass of material to be considered, the preliminary selections were made by the present writer working alone. The data concerning each of the 1,672 members of the California gifted group included from 50 to 100 pages of data concerning heredity, school progress, general mental ability, educational level, character and personality traits, reports of progress, etc. Copies of writings were available for many of the subjects, but not for all. The preliminary selections yielded the following groups:

1. Twenty-four California subjects, some of whose works impressed the writer as being of superior or very superior quality.

2. Twenty-eight writers of eminence for whom there were available literary juvenilia which seemed to be superior or very superior in quality.

Now that the groups had been reduced in size, it was possible to ask the assistance of other individuals in a further sifting of cases. Dr. Barbara Burks, Dr. Milton B. Jensen, Dr. Terman, and the writer examined the productions of the 52 (24 plus 28) subjects who had survived the preliminary selection and agreed unanimously that 42 of them had written sufficiently well as children to justify further study of their writings. This tentative selection of cases yielded the following groups:

1. Fourteen members of the California gifted group whose names (fictitious), IQ's, and ages at time of testing are given in Table 88.

2. The 28 writers of eminence who were chosen in the preliminary selection of cases. The names and estimated IQ's of these English and American men of letters are given in Table 89 (p. 366). The IQ's of the 18 whose names are marked with asterisks are taken from Dr. Cox's study. The IQ's of the other ten were rated for the present purpose by Drs. Cox and Terman.

The next step was to secure a quantitative estimate of the merits of the juvenilia of these subjects. The task presented a number of difficulties. In the first place, there was available no measuring device which was suitable for use with productions such as these. Secondly, to secure evaluations of all the juvenilia of these children would have been an unprofitable, if not an almost impossible task.[1] It was

[1] As the most extreme example of the great mass of material which would have had to be rated, consider the case of Beatrice. When she was 14 years and 6 months old, there were 380 poetical and 107 prose selections

therefore decided to attempt the evaluation of only the "best works" of each subject, these works to be selected on ratings by three of the judges assisting in the tentative selection of cases.

TABLE 88

IQ's OF 14 CALIFORNIA GIFTED CHILDREN TENTATIVELY SELECTED AS OF OUTSTANDING LITERARY ABILITY

Name (Fictitious)	IQ	Corrected IQ	Age when Tested
Beatrice	188	...	7-10½
Edith	138	148	13- 0
Ethel	172	...	8-10
James	144	152	12- 3
Jeanette	153	...	10- 4
Juanita	134	145	13-10
Margaret	166	...	8- 4
Pauline	143	155	12-10
Ralph	152	...	6- 5
Ruth	141	157	13- 2
Verda	170	186	11- 7
Vivian	140	...	8- 6
Walter	144	148	11- 7
Wanda	172	...	9- 0

In selecting the best, it was desired that the writings chosen should be representative of as long a developmental period as possible. Hence the three judges choosing the "best works" were instructed to select and rank the three or four best writings of each child at each age at which productions were available. Writings which appeared from these ratings to be the most meritorious, age considered, were chosen for final evaluation by methods to be described later. In most instances this procedure resulted in the inclusion of not more than two selections for any child at any one age. The notable exception to this is Beatrice, who, in the opinion of the judges, had written so much as to merit more numerous ratings. Because of the length of some of the works of the eminent authors, a slight exception to the usual procedure was made in selections such as "Queen Mab," "Pauline," Hawthorne's journals, Thoreau's journals,

---

with other materials concerning her development filed at the Psychology Department at Stanford. As these selections comprised in all about 1,000 pages (double-spaced typing), the impracticability of evaluating her entire output is at once seen.

etc. Instead of including the whole selection for evaluation, the judges in such cases chose a fairly long unitary part of apparently representative quality. This procedure was unnecessary with the writings of the gifted children of Dr. Terman's group, since no extremely long selections were

TABLE 89

ENGLISH AND AMERICAN MEN OF LETTERS RATED AS HAVING HAD
CHILDHOOD IQ'S OF 140 OR OVER, FOR WHOM
JUVENILIA WERE AVAILABLE

Name	Estimated IQ (Based on Data to Age 17)
Browning, Robert	165
Bryant, William C.	170
*Burns, Robert	140
*Byron, Lord	160
*Coleridge, Samuel T.	180
*Cowper, William	150
*Dryden, John	160
*Emerson, Ralph W.	155
*Franklin, Benjamin	160
Freneau, Philip M.	160
*Hamilton, Alexander	150
*Hawthorne, Nathaniel	150
Holmes, Oliver W.	155
*Jefferson, Thomas	160
*Johnson, Samuel	165
Keats, John	165
*Longfellow, Henry W.	160
Lowell, James R.	165
*Macaulay, Thomas B.	185
*Milton, John	155
Poe, Edgar A.	165
*Pope, Alexander	165
Shelley, Percy B.	165
*Tennyson, Alfred	160
*Thackeray, William M.	145
Thoreau, Henry D.	155
Whittier, John G.	155
*Wordsworth, William	160

chosen as their "best works." Excerpts were used for only a few productions by eminent authors. In a few instances the only juvenile works available for an author at certain ages were unitary parts of longer selections. In no case were works of eminent authors included when it was impossible to ascertain the age at which they were written.

The selections rated are listed in chapter xxv by age, with name of author, title, and average rating which each received from the judges.

It seems reasonable to believe that the selections used are fairly representative of the best work of the gifted children at the various age levels, so far as it has been possible to secure their juvenile writings. It was of course impossible to determine whether the child, in all instances, had worked with absolute independence of help from others. In the opinion of the writer, any assistance which the California gifted children may have received has been small and indirect. Few of the parents seem to have considered the accomplishments of the children unusual, and in many instances the child had very early outstripped the parent in literary appreciation and production. The following scores on the Abbott-Trabue Exercises in Poetic Appreciation made by the seven California gifted children included in the final selection of cases, together with the scores of one or both of their parents secured at the same time, give some indication of the relationship between the appreciative powers of the children and their parents. A marked superiority on the part of the child is evidenced in a majority of cases.

Name	Age when Tested	Score	Mother's Score	Father's Score
Beatrice	15- 4	13 (perfect)	8	6
Edith	18- 4	11	11	11
Ethel	14- 2	8	7	..
Jeanette	16- 0	13	8	..
Ruth	18- 3	7	2	..
Verda	15- 8	12	8	12
Wanda	14-11	11	12	6

THE RATERS AND THEIR INSTRUCTIONS

The next problem was to derive a quantitative estimate of the literary merit of the writings selected. The building of a scale for evaluating purposes, and the evaluations themselves, were made possible through the generous co-operation of the following individuals:

Dr. John C. Almack, Professor of Education, Stanford University, who has had considerable teaching and administrative experience in the grades and high school as well as in college and university. His ability as a writer is indicated not only by his textbook and journalistic contributions in the field of education, but also by published poems and short stories.

Dr. Margery Bailey, Assistant Professor of English, Stanford University, who has had extensive experience in high-school and university teaching. She has published several collections of stories for young people, and has made other literary contributions, including the editing of an important two-volume work by Boswell.[1]

Dr. Mary C. Burch, now Professor of Psychology and Education, Mills College, who has had several years of experience in high-school and college English work. Her graduate studies were in the fields of education and psychology, and her Ph.D. dissertation dealt with both these fields in connection with high-school English.

Dr. Parley A. Christensen, then Assistant in Instruction, Department of English, Stanford University, and now Professor of English, Brigham Young University, who has had several years of experience in teaching English in the grades, high school, college, and university.

Mrs. Wellford D. Seay, Instructor in the Department of English in the Summer Session and Extension Department, University of California, who has had several years of teaching experience in high school and university.

The late Mr. Walter Willoughby Snyder, formerly Assistant Professor of English, University of Oregon, who had had secondary school and university teaching experience, and was also a writer of fiction.

Dr. Marion R. Trabue, Director, Bureau of Educational Research, University of North Carolina, whose teaching experience includes both high-school and university work. He is joint author, with A. A. Abbott, of the Abbott-Trabue Exercises in Poetic Appreciation, and is carrying on further research in the testing of literary appreciation.

It is at once apparent that the writer was most fortunate in securing the co-operation of judges such as these. They represent a variety of training and experience, and yet an acquaintance with the fields of literature and child development intensive enough to make their ratings exceptionally valuable.

Each of the seven judges named was given a copy of the following scale and set of directions:

[1] *The Hypochondriack*, Stanford University Press, 1927.

INSTRUCTIONS FOR RATING

FOREWORD: It is intended on the basis of combined judgments of persons familiar with literary productions and developmental psychology to construct a scale of literary merit, and at the same time secure a composite of judgments as to the literary merit of certain selections enclosed herewith.

Proceed as follows:

I. Read the Tentative Scale, immediately following. If, in your judgment, it is representative of a progression of literary merit, as you understand literary merit, rank the steps in descending order, using the designation "A" for the most meritorious from a literary standpoint, "B" for the one second to "A" in literary merit, etc. The present arrangement of the scale is merely tentative. Feel free to rank in order as your judgment dictates. Should you feel that there is no difference between some of the steps, indicate it by giving the same rank to each.

II. (*a*) On the scale resulting from your rankings, select some step with which you are particularly familiar. It may be at either end of the scale, or at any place between.

(*b*) Assign a value of 10 to the difference between the two rankings at this point (e.g., the difference between the literary merit of rank "G" and rank "H" equals 10).

(*c*) Using this as a unitary base, assign values to the differences between the other successive rankings; e.g.,

Rank

Rank		
A		
	20	Suppose the difference between C and D is selected as a
B		unit. The value assigned to this difference becomes 10. Sup-
	5	pose that, in your judgment, the difference between B and C
C		is only one-half as great as that between C and D. The value
	10	then assigned to the difference between B and C is 5. Sup-
D		pose further that the difference between A and B, in your
.		estimation, is twice that between C and D. The value as-
.		signed to the A–B difference would be 20.
.		
N		

III. Assign to each of the selections accompanying this scale an alphabetical rank (A, B, C, etc.) according to where you would place it on the scale of general literary merit resulting from your judgments in ranking the steps on the Tentative Scale of Literary Merit. Should you desire to make discriminations finer than indicated by the raw rankings, add or subtract numerical values according to the point of merit with respect to the preceding or succeeding rank; e.g., suppose a selection is judged as falling midway between ranks A and B in the example above. The proper designation would then be A — 10 or B + 10.

IV. Place the ratings given each selection on the sheet provided and affixed to the front page of each selection. An attempt has been made to eliminate all prominent marks of identification. Should you recognize, or think you recognize, a selection as one with which you are familiar, kindly indicate it in the space provided on the rating sheet.

V. It may simplify the problem of rating for you to place selections in rank order prior to assigning values on the scale. In order to make this practical, poetry and prose are appended separately, and may be ranked and rated separately, though this is not necessary.

VI. The Tentative Scale of Literary Merit follows.

TENTATIVE SCALE OF LITERARY MERIT

(Rank and evaluate as directed)

Rank

...... As good as the best work of the 10 best authors in the English language

...... As good as the average work of the 10 best authors in the English language

...... As good as the average work of authors considered good but not the best; i.e., the 30 or 40 next to the 10 best

...... As good as the average work appearing in modern literary magazines, such as *Poetry, Atlantic Monthly, Bookman,* etc.

...... As good as the average work appearing in modern popular magazines (*Good Housekeeping, American, Saturday Evening Post,* etc.)

...... As good as the average work of college seniors

...... As good as the average work of college sophomores

...... As good as the average work of twelfth-grade pupils

...... As good as the average work of tenth-grade pupils

...... As good as the average work of eighth-grade pupils

...... As good as the average work of sixth-grade pupils

...... As good as the average work of fourth-grade pupils

...... As good as the average work of second-grade pupils

...... As good as the average work of children below school age

TREATMENT OF RESULTS

As will be noted from the directions, each judge assigned quantitative values to the indicated levels of literary merit, thus permitting the construction of a composite scale expressed in numerical values.

Best averages of the numerical values of the various steps on the scale were secured by means of the formula:[1]

$$\bar{a} = \frac{\dfrac{1}{\sigma_1{}^2} a_1 + \dfrac{1}{\sigma_2{}^2} a_2 + \dfrac{1}{\sigma_3{}^2} a_3 + \ldots \dfrac{1}{\sigma_n{}^2} a_n}{\dfrac{1}{\sigma_1{}^2} + \dfrac{1}{\sigma_2{}^2} + \dfrac{1}{\sigma_3{}^2} + \ldots \dfrac{1}{\sigma_n{}^2}} .$$

[1] Kelley, Truman L., *Statistical Method,* p. 325, formula 309.

For the sake of convenience in treatment, all values assigned to the steps on the scale by the various judges have arbitrarily been made cumulative from the step "average work of children below school age," which is taken as a zero point. The ratings of the judges on the various steps of the scale are given in Table 90 (p. 372), together with the standard deviations of the ratings of the judges and the best weighted averages of the ratings for each step on the scale. The seven judges are designated alphabetically in the caption. The steps on the scale are likewise designated in the stub, and will be referred to by their alphabetical ranks throughout the study. The rather close agreement of the judges in evaluating the steps on the scale is evident by inspection. The marked differences in variability are indicative only of differences in range used in expressing opinions, and in no way invalidate the judgments.

Simultaneously with the evaluation of the various steps of the scale, the seven judges were asked to pass judgment on the literary merit of the juvenile works of the gifted children previously selected. Each selection was rated by five or seven judges, the average number of judges for each selection rated being 5.7. The poetry and prose were grouped separately and presumably so judged. (This was not necessary, but was suggested as more convenient.) The judges were instructed to rate on the basis of general literary merit, and to grade in terms of the scale which they had previously evaluated. They were asked to indicate whether or not they recognized the selections rated. They were also asked to express opinions relative to specific points of merit or lack of merit when they felt so inclined.

The 151 selections were all typed uniformly, without names of authors, dates, comments, or other means of identification, except serial numbers distributed at random. In the case of a few such well-known selections as "Queen Mab" and "Pauline," the title was simply omitted. This procedure was followed in order to minimize any "halo" effect which otherwise might have influenced the ratings. The judges were told that some of the works were those of members of the California gifted group, but were given no further information as to the authors of the selections they were asked to rate. The very small percentage of the juvenile writings of eminent authors recognized as such by the

TABLE 90

NUMERICAL EVALUATIONS OF THE THIRTEEN STEPS ON THE TENTATIVE SCALE OF LITERARY MERIT

Step		Best Average	JUDGE						
			A	B	C	D	E	F	G
A	Best work of the 10 best authors in the English language	133	137	200	195	170	150	125	91
B	Average work of 10 best authors in the English language	119	117	180	180	155	140	105	86
C	Average work of 30 or 40 authors next in rank to ten best	107	97	165	150	135	125	95	83
D	Average work in modern literary magazines	101	87	155	120	125	125	90	83
E	Average work in modern popular magazines	88	67	130	100	105	105	80	80
F	Average work of college seniors	73	47	145	80	80	90	60	68
G	College sophomores	64	37	105	70	70	85	50	63
H	Twelfth grade	54	31	90	60	60	75	35	58
I	Tenth grade	45	21	80	50	50	60	25	50
J	Eighth grade	36	16	55	40	40	45	20	44
K	Sixth grade	27	12	30	30	30	40	15	34
L	Fourth grade	18	8	20	20	20	30	10	22
M	Second grade	9	3	10	10	10	15	5	10
N	Average work of children below school age	0	0	0	0	0	0	0	0
	Standard Deviations	..	45	65	61	54	46	38	29

judges was surprising. Only 25 individual judgments were made on this point, resulting in the correct placement of 12 selections.

The next problem was to determine the proper method of weighting the ratings in order to secure best estimates of the literary merit of each selection. An examination of the intercorrelations of the judges' ratings reveals that they are of such nature as to preclude the use of reliability coefficients obtainable from these ratings by any method now available. It was thought that the method devised by Dr. Eugene Shen[1] might be used in determining the reliabilities of the judges' ratings, and that these reliabilities might be used in weighting them. It was discovered, however, that the judges differed so greatly in their opinions as to what constitutes literary merit, or else as to how these elements should be weighted, as to invalidate the use of Dr. Shen's procedure, which assumes that the judges, in rating, rate the same, or virtually the same, elements.

Tables 91 and 92 (p. 374) give the intercorrelations between the ratings of the various judges, the former the raw correlations, and the latter the correlations corrected for attenuation. The estimations of the reliability were obtained by the formula:

$$r_{11} = \frac{(a-2)r_{1p}{}^2}{ar_{pq} - 2r_{1p}}$$

where a refers to the number of judges, r_{1p} to the average intercorrelation of one judge with the others, exclusive of himself, weighted according to populations; r_{pq} to the average of the intercorrelations, weighted according to the populations; and r_{11} to the reliability of the judge in question. In the tables the letters in the stub and caption refer to the various judges (alphabetical order), and σ to the standard deviations of the ratings of the various judges. The numbers in parentheses in Table 91 refer to the populations involved in the intercorrelations.

An examination of Table 92 shows certain intercorrelations for Judge G much above 1.00. This is presumably due to the fact that the reliability coefficient for this judge, .09, is much too small, which in turn is probably due to the method

[1] Shen, Eugene, "The Reliability Coefficient of Personal Ratings," *Journal of Educational Psychology*, Vol. 16, 1925, pp. 232–236.

TABLE 91
INTERCORRELATIONS OF RATINGS

Judge	A	B	C	D	E	F	G	σ	r_{1p}	r_{11}
A		.46	.63	.49	.49	.44	.10	28.2	.47	.47
		(86)	(120)	(120)	(84)	(120)	(53)			
B	.46		.66	.52	.68	.43	.25	43.2	.51	.57
	(86)		(85)	(84)	(55)	(85)	(53)			
C	.63	.66		.53	.62	.55	.06	42.0	.53	.63
	(120)	(85)		(151)	(120)	(151)	(84)			
D	.49	.52	.53		.57	.42	.46	24.0	.50	.55
	(120)	(84)	(151)		(120)	(151)	(84)			
E	.49	.68	.62	.57		.54	.39	22.0	.55	.69
	(84)	(55)	(120)	(120)		(120)	(84)			
F	.44	.43	.55	.42	.54		.07	19.5	.43	.38
	(120)	(85)	(151)	(151)	(120)		(84)			
G	.10	.25	.06	.46	.39	.07		6.3	.23	.09
	(53)	(53)	(84)	(84)	(84)	(84)				

$$\text{Average} \ldots \ldots \begin{cases} r_{pq} = .47 \\ r_{11} = .48 \end{cases}$$

employed in getting it. This method is valid in case the various judges do in fact judge the same thing. The divergence from 1.00, both above and below, of the coefficients corrected for attenuation indicates that the judges did not have the same idea as to what constitutes literary merit. This is

TABLE 92
INTERCORRELATIONS CORRECTED FOR ATTENUATION

Judge	A	B	C	D	E	F	G
A		.64	.85	.69	.64	.67	.71
B	.64		.85	.69	.86	.62	1.78
C	.85	.85		.70	.77	.79	.43
D	.69	.69	.70		.73	.62	3.28
E	.64	.86	.77	.73		.76	2.29
F	.67	.62	.79	.62	.76		.50
G	.71	1.78	.43	3.28	2.29	.50	

probably due to differences in weights assigned to various phases of literary merit; for example, diction may have been weighted most heavily by one judge, originality by another, smoothness by another, etc. Under these conditions it is impossible to obtain throughout fair values for the reliability coefficients of the ratings of the various judges. Since it was not possible to utilize the reliability of judgment in combining ratings, what has seemed the next best thing has been done, and every rating has been assumed equally reliable with every other.

In order to secure best estimates of the values of the ratings of the selections, that is, estimates possessed of minimal standard errors (not involving reliability coefficients), the ratings of the judges on the selections were averaged by the method used in averaging their ratings of the steps on the scale. The standard deviations were determined for each judge for those of his ratings entering into each combination of ratings: that is, when averaging ratings on selections rated by any five of the seven judges, the measures of variability used were only for selections rated by all the five judges. These standard deviations are given in Table 93. The letters in the caption refer to the

TABLE 93

STANDARD DEVIATIONS OF THE JUDGES' RATINGS FOR VARIOUS
COMBINATIONS OF JUDGES

Judge	Seven Judges	Judges ABCDF	Judges ACDEF	Judges CDEFG
A	24.6	22.5	20.7	....
B	26.7	23.4	....	....
C	26.7	25.8	23.1	24.3
D	16.8	22.2	18.9	15.3
E	22.5	....	18.3	17.7
F	19.2	13.8	11.7	15.0
G	10.2	....	....	10.5
No. of selections rated by each group.....	53	33	35	30

combinations of judgments on the selections. Before determining these measures of variability, however, the original ratings of the judges were translated into units of the composite scale (expressed in the "best average" column of Table 90). Thus when Judge A gave a raw rating of 67 ("as good as the average work in modern popular magazines"), the value assigned this rating was 88—the best average for the numerical value of this particular degree of literary merit, in the opinion of the seven judges. Judge B in rating a selection as of the same quality would have assigned it a numerical value of 130; Judge C, of 100; Judge D, of 105; Judge E, of 105; Judge F, of 80; and Judge G, of 80; each of which translated into terms of the composite scale would receive the same numerical value as the rating of Judge A, namely, 88. In all instances this process consisted merely in reading across in Table 90 from the original rating of each judge to the best average numerical value for that particular degree of literary merit. This is permissible in view of the fact that the best averages of the values for the steps of the scale from the ratings of all seven judges are better estimates of the true values than are obtainable by any other combination of these ratings.

The ratings of the selections thus translated into terms of the composite scale, together with the best averages of these ratings, are given in Table 94, the judges being designated alphabetically in the caption. The serial numbers of the selections, distributed at random and used only for identification purposes, have already been explained. To interpret the numerical values in the table one should refer to Table 90.

TABLE 94

Numerical Values of Ratings of 151 Juvenilia

Serial Number	Best Average	Judge						
		A	B	C	D	E	F	G
1	83	64	64	54	88	88	77	93
2	66	54	36	54	88	36	50	79
3	75	73	50	73	95	64	61	79
4	81	..	..	101	64	64	73	78
5	81	73	65	64	95	64	73	88
6	63	64	45	59	88	..	61	..
7	65	64	42	54	59	48	69	73
8	51	37	..	36	54	45	61	..
9	78	64	119	73	73	64	50	88
10	79	73	59	69	104	73	54	80
11	73	64	59	59	88	73	45	80
12	78	45	59	64	104	73	64	79
13	102	88	107	107	104	104	81	104
14	46	54	18	45	54	..	50	..
15	68	..	..	64	54	64	77	73
16	42	27	..	41	50	41	45	..
17	74	54	42	64	104	64	50	77
18	72	88	66	64	73	..	69	..
19	67	..	..	54	64	64	57	77
20	50	45	..	54	69	36	50	..

TABLE 94 (*Continued*)

Serial Number	Best Average	JUDGE						
		A	B	C	D	E	F	G
21	86	101	50	64	101	73	73	88
22	66	73	50	54	64	..	73	..
23	72	101	59	101	64	..	84	..
24	82	..	..	73	88	59	61	99
25	56	45	27	36	45	39	54	73
26	68	64	..	54	69	59	77	..
27	56	88	64	45	64	64	73	45
28	56	45	18	41	45	..	81	..
29	64	..	..	45	64	45	54	80
30	72	36	64	64	69	54	61	88
31	78	45	..	64	88	78	88	..
32	63	45	..	54	73	75	57	..
33	63	64	27	54	54	..	81	..
34	83	..	..	107	101	73	73	79
35	66	64	..	64	81	45	69	..
36	78	101	59	73	101	..	69	..
37	88	..	..	73	88	88	73	99
38	47	73	..	27	32	46	50	..
39	53	54	35	59	73	..	50	..
40	67	..	..	45	64	48	61	83
41	80	64	..	54	113	78	73	..
42	71	45	54	54	81	64	73	77
43	77	101	46	88	95	42	61	80
44	87	101	88	59	95	64	81	93
45	77	64	..	64	104	78	73	..
46	93	107	104	109	95	113	88	86
47	81	..	..	73	101	88	64	78
48	96	107	83	107	107	96	101	88
49	99	107	85	111	113	88	107	93
50	66	45	33	54	81	48	54	77
51	89	101	73	109	88	64	101	73
52	91	73	88	107	101	73	69	83
53	74	54	45	64	81	54	54	76
54	110	101	105	111	113	73	107	104
55	84	101	71	106	88	59	101	64
56	86	101	83	73	81	91	69	76
57	99	107	71	124	107	104	101	78
58	105	107	119	124	119	104	107	80
59	54	18	0	27	40	12	36	73
60	58	88	37	64	54	..	50	..
61	95	101	..	101	104	88	101	..
62	76	..	..	54	88	64	88	73
63	84	84	92	88	73	88	88	68
64	79	101	58	106	101	..	61	..
65	80	64	..	88	104	104	64	..
66	83	..	..	54	88	104	54	93
67	86	107	100	107	95	..	64	..

TABLE 94 (*Continued*)

Serial Number	Best Average	A	B	C	D	E	F	G
68	93	73	..	107	104	88	88	..
69	83	54	33	73	81	48	69	93
70	80	..	..	73	101	64	77	79
71	90	107	93	111	107	..	69	..
72	73	45	33	106	81	31	49	76
73	84	64	..	88	95	104	77	..
74	98	107	51	107	113	78	73	93
75	94	..	..	73	88	88	101	99
76	83	73	52	91	95	54	73	78
77	88	88	53	101	88	69	88	79
78	45	54	33	45	45	..	45	..
79	84	64	..	73	104	88	84	..
80	85	..	..	88	88	54	54	109
81	77	88	40	88	95	54	54	67
82	79	101	86	111	64	..	64	..
83	104	101	101	125	104	88	107	86
84	94	101	..	101	95	88	84	..
85	96	101	58	106	95	96	88	86
86	81	..	..	64	88	73	77	86
87	77	64	38	107	73	..	88	..
88	88	101	..	88	81	104	81	..
89	94	101	55	119	104	104	101	83
90	60	..	..	36	64	27	54	78
91	102	107	99	101	101	..	101	..
92	76	45	..	45	88	78	88	..
93	84	..	..	88	64	88	88	88
94	87	101	73	107	95	104	96	74
95	104	107	45	107	107	..	88	..
96	63	45	27	50	69	48	50	78
97	90	88	88	109	104	64	84	86
98	71	36	..	54	81	68	84	..
99	91	..	..	119	107	54	101	86
100	61	54	33	64	88	..	61	..
101	89	64	..	73	104	88	96	..
102	82	..	..	45	88	64	81	93
103	89	107	59	101	101	..	84	..
104	92	88	..	101	104	88	101	..
105	64	..	..	54	88	51	81	50
106	86	101	101	113	81	104	88	77
107	81	101	36	88	81	88	69	86
108	56	73	36	64	54	..	54	..
109	89	73	..	88	104	88	88	..
110	86	..	..	73	107	88	81	79
111	65	64	27	45	88	54	77	68
112	99	101	107	133	104	88	81	99
113	84	101	54	101	101	..	84	..
114	66	64	..	54	95	78	54	..

JUDGE

TABLE 94 (*Concluded*)

Serial Number	Best Average	JUDGE A	B	C	D	E	F	G
115	77	..	..	54	88	54	69	88
116	48	54	36	88	54	..	61	..
117	69	54	..	64	101	88	54	..
118	86	..	..	88	88	88	81	86
119	75	64	101	64	101	..	64	..
120	82	54	..	54	95	104	84	..
121	85	..	..	54	88	54	101	80
122	80	107	50	107	101	..	64	..
123	95	88	..	101	104	104	88	..
124	90	73	66	109	104	104	96	84
125	70	..	..	36	73	54	57	88
126	67	54	36	73	88	..	73	..
127	89	54	..	88	104	104	88	..
128	86	..	..	119	101	96	64	79
129	90	64	61	119	107	..	96	..
130	92	64	..	101	104	104	88	..
131	82	73	..	107	88	78	77	..
132	73	..	..	45	88	54	54	88
133	64	54	59	50	88	..	64	..
134	72	64	..	64	104	73	64	..
135	75	..	..	54	88	64	54	86
136	94	107	101	119	104	96	69	88
137	86	107	105	88	88	..	69	..
138	91	101	..	101	104	104	84	..
139	79	79	57	64	107	..	81	..
140	87	107	34	95	104	78	54	83
141	83	88	72	115	101	..	69	..
142	82	107	..	107	103	88	57	..
143	87	..	..	107	101	88	54	93
144	86	101	54	91	101	..	84	..
145	89	101	..	73	113	88	81	..
146	88	..	..	101	107	88	77	83
147	65	45	27	64	59	..	88	..
148	93	101	60	69	95	73	88	99
149	81	73	..	101	104	73	73	..
150	81	64	85	88	88	54	57	84
151	69	54	..	88	73	54	73	..

VALIDITY AND RELIABILITY OF RATINGS

We may pause to consider the validity and reliability of these composite ratings. That the ratings have validity is insured by the fact that those making them were possessed of superior qualifications for such a task. Their acquaintance with child development and with literature, both as students and as producers, assures an excellent representation of reasonably expert opinion. The number of judgments on each selection (5 or 7, average 5.7) is large enough to establish a reasonably high degree of accuracy when combined as best averages. An estimation of the average reliability of the combined ratings was secured as follows:

Best averages for the ratings of Judges A, B, and C were correlated with the best averages for the ratings of Judges D, E, and F on the same selections (the 53 selections rated by all the judges). This procedure involving the ratings of six judges may be said to be consistent and representative of the ratings on the literature taken as a whole, since the average number of judges per selection rated is 5.7. The correlation coefficient (product-moment) was found to be .77 ± .02. When treated by the Spearman-Brown formula, this becomes .88. In view of the fact that the judges had somewhat different concepts as to what constitutes literary merit, this value, .88, is undoubtedly below the true reliability of the composite ratings. It is probably not under .90.

The evaluations of the "best works" of the 14 California gifted children and of the 28 children who became eminent authors provided a basis for choosing from their number those who may be considered child writers of most outstanding superiority. Because samples of the writings of each child at each age were not available, it was not possible to lay down a set criterion by means of which such children could be selected. However, the ratings furnished fairly conclusive evidence that certain children had, in the opinion of the judges, produced very superior juvenilia, and that certain others had not done so. In the more doubtful cases consideration was given to such matters as versatility, persistence of interest in writing, etc. A rank order of literary merit of writings has been attempted for the fourteen California gifted children. This ranking should not be interpreted as a basis for prognosis of future attainments but only as an evaluation of past performance.

Beatrice and *Verda,* rank 1½. Early, prolific, and continuous production of juvenilia of an exceptionaly high order characterizes both of these subjects.

Wanda, rank 3. Continuous and prolific production of prose and verse of exceptional literary merit is noted in Wanda's case. She is a close rival of Beatrice and Verda.

Jeanette, rank 4. Early production of superior prose, followed by more recent writing of very exceptional verse.

Edith and *Ethel,* rank 5½. Superior and continuous writing of poetry. Ethel has written some prose of high quality.

Ruth, rank 7. At age 15 Ruth wrote several poems of exceptional superiority. She would have received a higher ranking but for the fact that her attempts at literary production have been sporadic.

Margaret and *Vivian,* rank 8½. While the writings of Vivian and Margaret are rated as very good, they do not evidence the general superiority which is characteristic of those of the children receiving higher ranks. Between these two and the first seven there seem to be very marked differences in general merit. Vivian and Margaret were consequently not included in the final group.

Ralph, James, Juanita, Pauline, and *Walter* then follow in order, with ranks from 10 to 14. The writings of these children are rated as decidedly superior to those of average children, but they lack the exceptional superiority, age considered, which characterizes the works of Beatrice, Verda, Wanda, Jeanette, Edith, Ethel, and Ruth. In the cases of Juanita, Pauline, and Walter, interest in literary production has been of rather ephemeral nature. Ralph's writings have improved decidedly as he has grown older, and had he shown marked interest and exceptional ability prior to age 15 he would have been included in the final group.

Because of the incompleteness of the data for eminent writers, no attempt has been made to rank them in order of literary ability evidenced as children. Inspection of the ratings of the literary productions indicated clearly that Browning, Bryant, Burns, Byron, Coleridge, Cowper, Emerson, Franklin, Freneau, Hamilton, Hawthorne, Holmes, Johnson, Keats, Longfellow, Lowell, Macaulay, Milton, Poe, Pope, Shelley, Tennyson, Thackeray, Whittier, and Wordsworth wrote very exceptional juvenilia, age considered. The evidence was somewhat uncertain in the cases of Dryden, Jefferson, and Thoreau. In all cases in which only one or two juvenilia were available for an individual who was included in the final group, other data, such as early productions not selected as "best works," undated juvenilia, information concerning amount of early writing, etc., were taken into consideration.

Summary

1. Gifted children, possible candidates for selection as outstanding child writers of exceptional mental superiority, were studied in three groups:

a) 1,672 California gifted children, whose progress was being followed by Dr. Terman and for whom extensive data were available.

b) 271 children who had later become eminent and who were rated in Dr. Cox's study as having had childhood IQ's of 140 or over. For them considerable data, though not so extensive as for the California gifted children, were available.

c) Ten children not included with the 271, and who later achieved eminence in literature and were rated as having had childhood IQ's of 140 or over. The writer has secured rather extensive data for these individuals.

2. From these 1,953 gifted children, 42 were selected as showing unusual merit as child writers. Fourteen of these were members of the California gifted group, and 28 were individuals who had later attained eminence in English or American literature.

3. A number of the best writings of these children were chosen by three judges for final evaluation and study.

4. The writings so selected were presented to five or seven judges for evaluation on a tentative scale of literary merit, the steps of which were evaluated by the judges prior to making the ratings.

5. Best averages were secured for the ratings of this literature. The reliability of these weighted ratings was found to be in the neighborhood of .90.

6. After a consideration of all the data available, seven of the fourteen California gifted children, and twenty-five of the twenty-eight children who later attained eminence in literature, were chosen for further study as showing outstanding superiority as child writers.

CHAPTER XXIV

THE TENTATIVE SCALE AND ITS USE

In this chapter selections will be given representing as many steps on the composite scale of merit as could be illustrated by the literature rated. The selection receiving the lowest rating was considered "almost as good as the average work of tenth-grade pupils"; the one considered the best was rated as "better than the average work of authors considered good, but not as good as the best ten in the English language." While the range of merit of these selections does not extend low enough for all school purposes, it is adequate for rating the writings of children exceptionally gifted in literary expression.

The selections have been chosen so as to represent as little disagreement as possible among the judges as to the quality of the literature at the various levels or steps on the scale. The validity of the scale rests upon the qualifications of the judges assisting in the study. Its usefulness will depend upon the ability of those using it to make judgments on other literature comparable with those made by the judges in this study. Where possible both prose and poetry are given at or near each of the steps on the scale.

It is expected that the scale will prove particularly useful to teachers of English; it should also be helpful to school administrators and psychologists, who frequently have their attention called to children regarded as literary prodigies by parents and friends. The procedure to be followed in arriving at a decision as to the probable literary merit of the writings of such a child may be outlined as follows:

1. Several of the child's productions, prose or poetry, or both, should be collected. Age at the time of writing each selection should be ascertained.

2. If possible, typed copies, from which the name and age of the author have been omitted, should be prepared.

3. Copies of the selections, together with the Tentative Scale, should be submitted to several individuals trained in literature. There should be at least five or six such judges, preferably persons who are not acquainted with the child

or with his writings. Ratings by a single judge are too unreliable to be of much value. The judges should be asked to read and study the Tentative Scale carefully, then to read each production to be judged, and to give it the numerical rating of that selection in the scale which it resembles most in general literary merit. Interpolation between steps should be permitted; e.g., a production might be rated 80 if judged to be between the scale values 88 and 73.

4. The ratings of the judges on each production should be averaged.

5. The ratings of the child's productions at various ages should be compared with the ratings of the juvenilia of eminent writers at comparable ages.

6. Interpretation should be made conservatively and provisionally, for the Tentative Scale is offered as an aid to interpretation rather than as a basis for prediction.

TENTATIVE SCALE FOR EVALUATING LITERARY MERIT

110 Slightly better than the average work of the 30 or 40 authors considered good, but not of the best 10 in the English language[1]

LINES WRITTEN BENEATH AN ELM IN A CHURCHYARD. 54[2]

Written by Byron at age 19

Spot of my youth! whose hoary branches sigh,
Swept by the breeze that fans thy cloudless sky;
Where now alone I muse, who oft have trod
With those I love, thy soft and verdant sod.
With those who, scattered far, perchance deplore,
Like me, the happy scenes they knew before:
Oh, as I trace again thy winding hill,
Mine eyes admire, my heart adores thee still,
Thou drooping Elm! beneath whose boughs I lay,
And frequent mused the twilight hours away;
Where, as they once were wont, my limbs recline,
But ah! without the thoughts that then were mine:
How do thy branches, moaning to the blast,
Invite the bosom to recall the past,
And seem to whisper, as they gently swell,
"Take, while thou canst, a lingering, last farewell!"

When Fate shall chill, at length, this fevered breast,
And calm its cares and passions into rest,

---

[1] No prose selection was available for this step of the scale.
[2] Refers to serial number in Table 94.

Oft, I have thought, 'twould soothe my dying hour—
If aught may soothe, when Life resigns her power—
To know some humble grave, some narrow cell,
Would hide my bosom where it loved to dwell;
With this fond dream, methinks, 'twere sweet to die—
And here it lingered, here my heart might lie;
Here might I sleep where all my hopes arose,
Scene of my youth, and couch of my repose;
Forever stretched beneath this mantling shade,
Pressed by the turf where once my childhood played;
Wrapped by the sod that veils the spot I loved,
Mixed with the earth o'er which my footsteps moved;
Blest by the tongues that charmed my youthful ear,
Mourned by the few my soul acknowledged here;
Deplored by those in early days allied,
And unremembered by the world beside.

102 Slightly better than the average work appearing in modern literary magazines such as *Poetry, Bookman, Atlantic Monthly*, etc.

A FRAGMENT. 91

Written by Byron at age 15

When, to their airy hall, my Fathers' voice
Shall call my spirit, joyful in their choice;
When, pois'd upon the gale, my form shall ride,
Or, dark in mist, descend the mountain side;
Oh, may my shade behold no sculptured urns,
To mark the spot where earth to earth returns!
No lengthened scroll, no praise-encumbered stone;
My epitaph shall be my name alone:
If that with honor fail to crown my clay,
Oh! may no other fame my deeds repay!
That, only that, shall single out the spot;
By that remembered, or with that forgot.

102 Slightly better than the average work appearing in modern literary magazines such as *Poetry, Bookman, Atlantic Monthly*, etc.

A FULL VINDICATION. 13

Opening paragraphs of a pamphlet written by Hamilton at age 17

Friends and Countrymen:

It was hardly to be expected that any man could be so presumptuous as openly to controvert the equity, wisdom, and authority of
the measures adopted by the Congress—an assembly truly respec-
table on every account, whether we consider the characters of the
men who composed it, the number and dignity of their constituents,
or the important ends for which they were appointed. But, however
improbable such a degree of presumption might have seemed, we

find there are some in whom it exists. Attempts are daily making to diminish the influence of their decisions, and prevent the salutary effects intended by them. The impotence of such insidious ones is evident from the general indignation they are treated with; so that no material ill-consequences can be dreaded from them. But lest they should have a tendency to mislead, and prejudice the minds of a few, it cannot be deemed altogether useless to bestow some notice upon them.

And first, let me ask these restless spirits, whence arises that violent antipathy which they seem to entertain, not only to the natural rights of mankind, but to common-sense and common modesty? That they are enemies to the natural rights of mankind is manifest, because they wish to see part of the world enslaved by another. That they have an invincible aversion to common-sense is apparent in many respects: they endeavor to persuade us that the absolute sovereignty of Parliament does not imply our absolute slavery; that it is a Christian duty to submit to be plundered of all we have, merely because some of our fellow-subjects are wicked enough to require it of us; that slavery, so far from being a great evil, is a great blessing; and even that our contest with Britain is founded entirely upon the petty duty of three pence per pound on East India tea, whereas the whole world knows it is built upon this interesting question, whether the inhabitants of Great Britain have a right to dispose of the lives and properties of the inhabitants of America, or not. And, lastly, that these men have discarded all pretension to common modesty, is clear from hence: first, because they, in plainest terms, call an august body of men, famed for their patriotism and abilities, fools or knaves: and of course the people whom they represent cannot be exempted from the same opprobrious appellations; and secondly, because they set themselves up as standards of wisdom and probity, by contradicting and censuring the public voice in favor of those men.

A little consideration will convince us that the Congress, instead of having "grossly misunderstood, carelessly neglected, or basely betrayed the interests of the colonies," have, on the contrary, devised and recommended the only effectual means to secure the freedom, and establish the future prosperity of America on a solid basis. If we are not free and happy hereafter, it must proceed from a want of integrity and resolution in executing what they have concerted, not from the temerity or impolicy of their determinations.

Before I proceed to confirm this assertion by the most obvious arguments, I will premise a few brief remarks. The only distinction between freedom and slavery consists in this: In the former state a man is governed by the laws to which he has given his consent, either in person or by his representatives; in the latter, he is governed by the will of another. In the one case, his life and his property are his own, and in the other, they depend upon the pleasure of his master. . . . .

88 As good as the average work appearing in modern popular magazines such as *Good Housekeeping, American, Saturday Evening Post,* etc.

INDIAN WAR SONG. 77

Written by Bryant at age 16

Ghosts of my wounded brethren, rest,
Shades of the warrior dead!
Nor weave, in shadowy garment drest,
The death-dance round my bed;
For, by the homes in which we dwelt,
And by the altar where we knelt,
And by our dying battle-songs,
And by the trophies of your pride,
And by the wounds of which ye died,
I swear to avenge your wrongs. . . . .

88   As good as the average work appearing in modern popular magazines such as *Good Housekeeping, American, Saturday Evening
Post,* etc.

MALOCCHIO. 37

Written by Wanda at age 14

There were only four of them in the Club smoking room. Carter,
book-collector and confirmed bachelor, was enthroned in his favorite
arm-chair, smoking his usual vile pipe, and reading the latest number
of the "Bibliomaniacs' Magazine." Brand, wealthy and a jewel-expert
by avocation, was listening with a resigned expression to Wickson,
the club bore. Finally, gentle old Doctor Pierce was playing his
eternal game of solitaire, using a magazine on his lap for a table.

The door opened, and a mån entered breezily. He greeted them
with the assurance of one whose popularity is established.

"Hello, Carter, Brand, Wickson. Good afternoon, Doctor. I say
Carter, what's this I hear about your moving heaven and earth to
get a little piece of coral? I thought your specialty was books."

Carter, looking up, grunted. The newcomer understood the tone,
and pressed the point. "Story in it, eh? Tell us."

He drew a chair up to the fire and sat down. The others, except
the Doctor, edged a little nearer.

"You're right in thinking there's a story in it," Carter began.
"It's the most uncanny experience I've ever had. The beginning dates
back nearly a year.

"I was walking along a corridor in the Mercantile Building one
morning, on my way to my office, when a little man came up and
spoke to me. He was very short, scarcely five feet, and with long
curly iron-grey hair. He wore big tortoise-shell spectacles that seemed
to hide half his face. 'There, sir,' said he, pulling a book out of his
pocket. He had an odd accent, like an Italian or Spaniard who
had been taught English by a cockney Londoner. 'Mr. Carter, would
you look at this book? I'll sell it to you for five dollars.'

"Brand, you're a jewel expert. Did anyone ever offer you a magnificent diamond of the first water, flawless, and which you were
able to tell was genuine, for less than the cost of the setting?"

The question was rhetorical, but Brand answered it. "Never! I wish they had."

"If someone had, what would you have done?"

Brand laughed shortly. "Snapped it up, I guess. Perhaps it wouldn't be moral, but I guess I'm a Philistine."

"Wickson?"

"Oh, of course I should refuse it, and tell the man it was very valuable," said the little man self-importantly.

"Doctor?"

The old man considered, putting a card down. "I think," said he gently, "that in those circumstances I should follow the example of neither Mr. Brand or Mr. Wickson. Rather, I should say, 'My dear friend, this gem is worth a great deal more than the sum you have named. I cannot afford to buy it at a just valuation, but I will give you so much,' and name the amount I could afford."

"Well, I was put in that position. The book he offered me was a very rare copy of the first edition of Stevenson's *The Wrecker,* autographed and in excellent condition. Naturally I hesitated, wondering if there might be something wrong.

" 'No?' said the little man. 'I give it to you for four dollars—three—two! I give it to you for nothing!' He pushed it into my hands and fled away.

"He had vanished around a corner before I found my voice, so I walked on slowly, examining the book slowly as I went. I kept it at the office for some days, in case it should be claimed, but nothing turned up about it. So, after a couple of weeks, I took it home and put it in my sets of Stevensons. My collection of his works, you know, is pretty complete, but this was one of the best things I had ever secured. Then I forgot about it for some time.

"About six weeks later I had a small group of friends at my home—chiefly collectors like myself. The conversation naturally turned to old books, and I told them the story of this one which I had so strangely acquired.

"I leaned back in my chair and reached up to pull the book out of the bookcase behind me. It fell open in my hand. Glancing down, I saw that it was open at one of the illustrations—the one showing the auction of the wreck. One of the figures in the foreground caught my eye. It's impossible to define evil exactly, but I swear that there was the very essence of concentrated evil in that pictured face! The eyes—it was a three-quarter view—seemed to be glaring into mine in a way that frightened me.

"I shut the book quickly and handed it to the man next to me. It passed the rounds, and then I put it back.

"The uncanny thing was that two of the men who had handled it longest were seriously hurt in an automobile accident on the way home that evening.

"Of course, that was only a coincidence. But a few days later I took the book down again, to paste in my bookplate. The next night I was awakened by smoke in my room, and when I jumped up I discovered that the house was on fire. A good deal of damage was done, too, but none of my books were hurt.

"And so it went. Every time I touched the book, something

happened—never anything directly attributable to its influence, of course, but it got to be more than a coincidence. It was no longer any wonder to me that its former owner had wished to get rid of it!

"I mentioned the matter to one of my closest friends, an Italian. He made me tell him everything. When I had done, he said gravely, 'Only once have I heard of a case like that. My friend, the face you mentioned, in that illustration, has the Evil Eye—*e malocchio*.'

"I laughed, but I was close to belief. You may talk of your 'enlightened ages,' but if you had been haunted as I had, you would have been ready to believe any explanation. I asked him if there was anything that could be done about it.

"'Myself, I do not know,' he said, 'but I have a friend who is very wise in such matters.' So he introduced me to the Contessa, whose last name I have forgotten. She listened to my tale and gave me written directions for removing the curse. So far as I can remember them they were like this:

"'Secure one of the *corni* (the little hands of coral or gold, with fingers crooked to form a pair of horns, and which many Italians wear to avert the Evil Eye). Wrap it in a thrice-folded leaf of parchment made from the skin of a young lamb, on which has been inscribed the Lord's Prayer and the words, "Get thee behind me, Satan." Make a fire of charcoal and burn the packet in it. Sprinkle the book, inside and out, with the resulting ashes, and lay it away for a week. It is wise to have it blessed by a priest.'

"Well, I did it. It wasn't hard to get the coral, though it was expensive. Don't grin that way, Harris; I'm not superstitious, but what would you?"

He paused.

"Well?" asked Brand.

"Did it work?" demanded Harris.

Carter pulled a book out of his pocket. "There it is," he said. "Look at it."

It fell open of itself at one of the illustrations, which was, as Carter had said, a representation of the auction of the wreck. In the foreground was one figure—that of a man leaning forward a little, as if to see someone at the right of the picture. The face was seen in three-quarters. Brand examined, gasped, and passed it on to Harris, who gave it to the Doctor.

The half-seen eyes—were closed! Where the outline of iris and pupil should have been was only a delicate, pale tracing of a pair of lids. There was a long pause as they looked it over and over.

"What are you going to do with it?" asked the Doctor.

"Heaven knows!" said Carter simply. Astonishing, isn't it? Do you think that was really caused by the coral and the holy water and all? I don't know, I'm sure. At any rate, nothing's happened to me since, and I've carried the book around with me every day."

"I'd like to buy it," said Harris abruptly.

"Only over my dead bank account," struck in Brand. "Carter, if it's on sale, I'll give ten times what it's cost you."

"No," said Carter, "But if you like I'll put it up at auction. The affair has rather shattered my nerves, and I shan't mind getting rid of it."

So it was done. The book was knocked down to Brand for one hundred and forty-five dollars. Three days after the sale, he received a letter.

"Dear Brand: (it read)

Heaven knows, I'm sorry that the price should have gone so high, although I know that you can well afford it. My beautiful story—a romance purely, invented on the spur of the moment. I have such a reputation as a yarner that I hated to disappoint Harris when he asked if there was a story in the coral—actually intended for a wedding present, by the way. As for the foundation of the tale, I enclose the letters which go with it, and which are self-explanatory. If, after reading them, you feel that you have been cheated, I shall be glad to buy the book back.

JOHN CARTER"

One of the two enclosures was dated in 1904, and had the letter-head of "Robert Moss, Agent." Its faded typewriting suggested one of the earliest machines. It read:

"Dear Sir Arthur:

As to the matter of the book about which you enquired: I have been able to locate only one copy of any of Mr. Stevenson's works, at least of the description you required. Its name is *The Wrecker*. It is offered at a price which I fear would make it prohibitive, owing to a peculiarity which might interest you. In one of the illustrations, the most notable figure is portrayed with closed eyes; an oddity which I am assured is not the case with other examples of the same work. However, I shall be very glad to hear from you.

Respectfully,

ROBERT MOSS"

The second was of recent date, and in a girlish, modern hand:

"Dear Jack:

I have just come across the oddest superstition! We dined with the Contessa Montevarchi our last night in Rome. During the conversation she happened to mention the corni, or horns of good luck. Having never heard of them, I asked what they were. She explained that they were little hands of gold or coral, with fingers in an odd position, worn by many people to avert the Evil Eye. I scoffed at the idea of there being such a thing, but she was quite serious about it, and even named a person who has the Evil Eye. Several people nodded in recognition of the name, and my partner said, 'That is quite true.' I won't repeat the name, first because I can't spell it, and second because it might be libel or something. However, the Contessa went on to say that not only living people but pictures can have it. She herself had known a picture in one of the galleries which had it, and which finally had to be covered up because of its influence, which kept people away. The spell, or whatever you call it, was later removed by some mysterious recipe.

Incidentally, I might hint that I should love one of those corals (the gold ones aren't so nice) for a wedding present.
We send love.

Your devoted sister,
MARGARET CARTER"

But Brand kept the book. He said he might as well.

73 As good as the average work of college seniors

IDLE THOUGHT. 132

Written by Ethel at age 11

Light and rosy (so it seems),
Is the path that leads to dreams;
Glad, the time that we spend there,
    Ah, reality so bare.

Swaying with the summer breeze,
Revelling beneath green trees;
Far and wide our fancies soar,
    And return to earth is sore.

In the land of Fancy fair—
Nothing, nothing matters there,
But—as Father Time goes on—
    Idle dreams die, with the dawn.

72 Almost as good as the average work of college seniors

REFLECTIONS OF A STUDENT. 30

Written by Walter at age 16

The clock on the wall has a queer habit. It's one of these governed by electricity from the main office. It jerks as each minute passes. In the quiet of the room, broken only by the droning of reciting students, the jerks resound. Oh, but the intervals between— ages, aeons. All eternity passes between those jerks as we sit here droning forth the dead languages of the almost forgotten inhabitants of Rome.

That queer bulldog-like face that peers over the desk at us and barks forth obscure sarcasms appears a vague white blur. The bass voice booms, the clock jerks, cries and shouts are heard in the distance. A group of boys are matching pennies sheltered from view by books carefully piled. The faint click breaks the whispering silence. The class breaks into argument. The teacher, now no longer a blur, raps for silence. The strokes bark out like rifle shots on a hot day.

In front of me there are three flies. Are they males and females or females and males? How distant from us seems sex. How unnatural emotions. The girls are not mates, merely like myself, chained captives. In this air of pedantry it seems impossible to think of love, of mating. We are mere clay to be modelled in the hands of the blur at the front of the room.

64   As good as the average work of college sophomores

LIGHTS. 133

Written by Margaret at age 12

Each shining like a fallen star that in the heavens high
Once lost its tiny footing and came trembling from the sky;
I see them from the window of the house upon the hill,
And there I like to sit and dream, when all the world is still.

The lights are all a-twinkle like the real stars up so far,
And like the ones up in the sky, I wonder what they are.
There are some so large and silent, all standing in a row
Like silent, watchful sentinels—they're public ones, I know.

Electric signs are flashing in a maze of green and red—
They rival constellations in the heavens overhead.
But oh, the ones I like the best are those that here and there
Send out a cheery, homelike light, to brighten up the drear.

I kneel there by the window, and I breathe the cool night air,
And think how very bright the lights are shining everywhere.

64   As good as the average work of college sophomores

IN THE GARDEN OF ALLAH. 29

Written by Vivian at age 12

Once in the vast, sandy stretches of the Sahara, there was a small, green oasis that looked like an emerald as it glistened and shone in the center of an ocean of golden sand. This beautiful emerald hue was due to the tall, slender green palms that surrounded a small lake of cool, sweet water, as clear as crystal.

In this oasis lived an Arab sheik, El Harlan by name, and with him lived his beautiful daughter, Myrzia.

One afternoon, as sheik El Harlan sat in his tent smoking, he espied Myrzia walking on the outskirts of the oasis. El Harlan had always loved his daughter very dearly. As he sat there watching her and thinking how beautiful she was, he suddenly caught sight of two horsemen riding swiftly over the sand. The sheik called to his daughter, but she did not hear him, neither did she see the horsemen.

Sheik El Harlan called his men together and they watched the outlaws. When they reached the oasis they rode around the outskirts of it until they reached Myrzia. One of them grabbed her up on his horse and then like arrows they sped away, as softly and silently as they had come.

The sheik and his men swiftly mounted their Arabian steeds, but by the time they were out on the desert the kidnappers were gone, and with them Myrzia.

El Harlan set out for a nearby oasis where the young sheik, Le Annanna lived. He was an admirer of Myrzia. By the time the sheik and his men reached that oasis it was dark. "I am sure," said Le Annanna, "that the bandits will stay to-night at the oasis of the cave. Let us go there tonight." So that night the two men set out over the sand, by the light of the moon, who sent her bright cold rays down upon them.

By midnight they reached the oasis where the two bandits were sitting by a fire. Poor Myrzia was tied to a horse.

As soon as the bandits saw the two men they mounted their horses and were off across the sand again, with the two sheiks in close pursuit. "The man with the white robe has Myrzia on his horse. Don't shoot, or you will kill her," said El Harlan.

A hot pursuit now followed. But the bandits' horses were tired while the others were fresh, so the two sheiks gained on the bandits. Finally Sheik El Annanna drew near to the bandit in white and sent a bullet through him, while El Harlan peppered the other. Then Le Annanna loosened Myrzia's bonds and they started back to the oasis.

At about four o'clock they reached the oasis. As El Harlan reached his tent, he noticed Myrzia and Le Annanna were not there. Then he turned around in the saddle and on the outskirts of the oasis he saw two forms—one of a man on horseback, and the other of a girl resting in his arms.

Sheik El Harlan smiled and rode on to his tent. All was as still as death in the majestic Gardens of Allah.

---

54   As good as the average work of twelfth-grade pupils

CHRISTMAS. 59

Written by James at age 7

Hurrah for Christmas
And all its joys,
That come that day
To girls and boys!

---

53   Almost as good as the average work of twelfth-grade pupils

THE COUNTESS OF MORCAS' PEARL. 39

Written by Beatrice at age 8

I had started for my customary evening walk down the street. When I had gone a few steps I observed a great crowd around a stately mansion. Out of its midst my esteemed friend, William Powers, disengaged himself and hurried toward me. "The Countess of Morcas' priceless pearl is stolen," he explained in rather a low and hurried tone. "Would you have the goodness to come with me while I try to discover a clue, Mr. Jones?"

"With great pleasure," I replied. We at once presented ourselves at the door. Mr. Powers rang the bell in a business-like manner. A maid looked out. Her face portrayed great anxiety. "Tell the Countess that Mr. Smith and Mr. MacDonald would like to see her," he announced and nudged me. In a minute we gained admittance.

As soon as we entered, Mr. Powers whispered in her Ladyship's ear that her servants must leave the room. As soon as they had left he said in a rather friendly tone, "I must confess, Countess, that the incognito worked admirably; your servants did not even suspect. You must know," he added to me, "that in a large household it is necessary for a detective to have a false name." "And now," he continued, "we will proceed to business. Would you give me your leave, your Ladyship, to examine the room in which the theft took place."

"Most gladly," the Countess replied, and led the way to a small chamber draped in white.

Silently he proceeded to examine the room. At last he uttered a cry of triumph, dived into a recess, and brought forth a bit of tobacco. "What did I tell you? Glory!" he cried jubilantly, "I know something at any rate, Countess," examining it carefully—"This isn't your fine gentleman's tobacco. It's the coarsest sort. I suspect you will find the thief among your menials."

"Do you think so?" exclaimed the Countess in great surprise. "Then I must be careful."

While he was talking he was continuing his search and finally as he disappeared behind a curtain he uttered a second exclamation. The Countess and I were in a great state of anxiety and perturbation. At length he issued from behind the curtain bearing a bit of carpet. On it was the print of a man's foot.

"What do you gather from that, Mr. Powers?" I asked.

"Why," he responded, "it is obvious: we have here one more link. I will now, with your permission, withdraw to study these two things"—waving the bit of tobacco and the footprint.

"Wait a second," cried the Countess, "I am going to present you with a bouquet of flowers, Mr. Powers, and your friend also. You must wait for a second." She then led us down into the garden. "Now, Mr. Jones, wouldn't you relish a bunch of roses and lilacs?" and forthwith a mammoth bunch was presented to me. "Nothing can be more suitable for Mr. Powers," continued our hostess laughing, "than a bunch of snapdragons—he's such a crack detective! And now," she finished, "I think I have loaded you with the choicest products of our garden."

"Yes, indeed," I responded, bowing, and my companion added gallantly, "The flowers are fair but they bear no comparison to the Countess of Morcas."

"I fear you are flattering me," said the Countess, blushing deeply. But suddenly recollecting herself, "If you must go now, Mr. Powers, do work your hardest to discover my pearl."

"I can answer for my friend," I assured her. "I am sure that he will try to do his best."

Just then a servant came running down the path and gasped,

"Your Ladyship, your Ladyship, you should not be out. The chill winds are blowing and you know that your constitution is delicate."

"Well, I suppose if I must, I must," she said with a sigh. "I beg your pardon, gentlemen, for leaving you so precipitously, but I am the 'servant of my servants'," she added as she went off with a swift gait towards the house.

We proceeded toward the carriage. "Quite a remarkable woman, that," I remarked to my companion.

"Quite," he responded. Just then a passing gust of wind blew my wig off my head. I stopped in some confusion and put it on again.

"Accidents will happen," I remarked to my friend as we got into the coach.

"They certainly will," he replied. "By the way," he continued after we were seated, "isn't the Countess charming? Seems to me she would be more suitable as a princess, Mr. Jones."

"Much more suitable," I agreed.

"But now," he held up the bouquet, the carpet and the tobacco dreamily, and played with them. "Do you know that these things are most often the basis upon which a detective forms his theory?"

"No?"

"It is so." We had by this time reached my house.

"Sorry to leave you," said I, alighting, "but Mary (my wife) only allowed me to go on condition that I return home early." At once I disappeared into the house.

.   .   .   .

Mary and I were having a comfortable little chat before the fire when there came a tug at the doorbell and an apparent workman of about seventy years was admitted. "Sorra to disturb," he murmured, "but oi've wan wee thing that oi'd like to show ye. I thought perhaps ye might know wat it is."

"What did you say?" I said absent-mindedly.

"I was going to say that I've something that I'd like you to look at," he responded, smiling at my evident astonishment, as I watched the drooping figure of the old Irishman grow up into the stately form of my true friend, Mr. Powers.

"Magic!" I exclaimed.

"Gracious!" cried Mary. "But," she added, recovering from her astonishment, "come, take a chair, Mr. Powers. Ye must be sair weary," she added mischievously, with a capital imitation of the old Irishman.

William and I laughed heartily while she disappeared from the room, to return shortly with some glasses of wine. We drank the health of Mrs. Mary Jones.

"What was it you wanted to say to me?" I asked after we had finished.

"Why nothing," he responded, "except this. Look!" and held up a pearl as round as a marble and about as large, and of a magnificent pink luster.

"The Countess of Morcas' pearl!" I exclaimed, astonished.

"The very same," he responded jubilantly.

"Why, you remember my bunch of snapdragons was rather damp, for Rogers, the gardener, had just been watering. Therefore as

soon as I got home I shook them over a sink to get off a little of the
water. Just then the largest one opened and out it tumbled."

"What luck!" Mary exclaimed, astonished, "indeed!"

"Now," I questioned, "have you any evidence of the thief?"

"Not yet," he responded, "but I have a plan. We know it is a
servant. As it promises rain tomorrow, and the clay in the garden
preserves imprints easily, as soon as the servants have gone in we'll
examine the footprints. The one that tallies with the one in the house
will, it stands to reason, be that of the thief. It's clear as water."

. . . .

The next day was cloudy. It had rained over night. The servants
had been called in; everything had apparently gone well. We lost no
time in measuring the footprints. One was like that on the carpet.
"Quite lucky," I remarked.

"Not so very, though," he replied, and then suddenly, "Hello,
what's this?" There was a face looking down from the upper window with an expression of dread and doubt. Then the owner of it
seemed to ascertain who we were for it disappeared with almost as
great rapidity as it had come. "That's the thief!" exclaimed Mr.
Powers, and at once we rushed toward the house. "Lead us at once
to your mistress," excitedly commanded Mr. Powers.

"Yes sir," answered the maid, astonished.

It seemed an age to us while she was gone. At length she returned and said for us to "step this way, please, sirs." We at once
complied and found ourselves in a room with the servants. We
looked about but no face tallied exactly with that seen at the window.

"Did anyone go away?" Mr. Powers demanded of the Countess.

"Why, yes," she said. "There was old Rogers, the gardener. He
said that he had an appointment with a friend at the present hour."

"Well, he hasn't," Mr. Powers informed her. *"That man is the
thief!"*

"You don't say so?" exclaimed the Countess, starting up.

"I certainly do! But let us waste no time in talking; we must at
once search for the thief." At once we proceeded to search all over
the house, but not a trace of the man. At last we looked from a window over the back and saw a trail of footprints corresponding with
the others.

The man was gone!

Discouraged, we retraced our steps. "At any rate," Mr. Powers
comforted me, "as the walls are of marble (the Countess was worth
millions) and the gates are locked, the thief must be somewhere in
the garden." The garden was a spacious one.

"By good luck," observed my companion, "I have all the materials necessary—handcuffs, pistols, etc. I have two along, so take
this one," and he handed me a Colt revolver. We at once dispersed
to different parts of the garden and proceeded to search. We at
length came upon the same footprints and by following them up (I
called the other assistants) came upon the man behind a monstrous
arbor of roses.

We at once rushed upon him; there was a brief struggle and we
had him. Mr. Powers pulled the handcuffs out and in a trice had

them on him. We stood regaining our breath for a few minutes, while I remarked, "At last! Thank goodness we have him!"

"Quite so," answered my friend. "But the thing I now suggest is turning him over to the police. He'll be much more comfortable at headquarters."

The excitement of that hour I shall never forget! We hailed a cab and drove to the police station. At last we got there. The man had been very sullen from the time when we captured him and had not uttered one word. "Well," I remarked to our captive, "You've had a rather hard time of it, eh?"

He shook his head. "No," he nodded sullenly.

"I have a suspicion," I continued, "that name, Rogers, is not your true one." He looked away.

At length the turnkey came and conducted him to his cell. We went out to the coach and drove home. Still not a word from my friend.

.   .   .   .

At about five in the morning I received a message. It ran thus:

"Dear Mr. Jones:

We have had a coincidence that I think you would like to hear. We tried the prisoner at midnight as we did not want to lose any time. It has been proven that he is a noted criminal and that his real name is Pryor. When I come to see you, I shall explain the case more fully.

Yours truly,

WILLIAM POWERS"

I was delighted and at once started for headquarters. When I arrived I was met by my friend. "Hello, old boy!" he said. "I was just hoping you would come now; in fact, I was going out to wait for you."

"Where is the prisoner?" I asked.

"Where do you suppose? In cell number nine. By the way, I've great news for you. I've been courting the Countess and she accepted me today. The marriage is going to be tomorrow at 10:30 and . . . ."

Well, there is no more to relate. It is sufficient to say, as most stories do, "They lived happily ever after."

47   Slightly better than the average work of tenth-grade pupils

LETTER TO HIS UNCLE. 38

Written by Hawthorne at age 9

December, 18—

Dear Uncle:

I hope you are well, and I hope Richard is, too. My foot is no better. Louisa has got so well she has begun to go to school, but she did not go this forenoon because it snowed. Mamma is going to send for Doctor Kitridge today, when William Cross comes home at 12 o'clock, and maybe he will do some good, for Doctor Bradshaw has not, and I don't know as Doctor Kitridge will. It is about 4 weeks yesterday since I have been to school, and I don't know but it will be four weeks longer before I go again. I have been out of the office two or three times and have set down in the step of the door, and once I hopped out into the street. Yesterday I went out in the office and had 4 cakes. Hannah carried me out once, but not then. Elizabeth and Louise send their love to you. I hope you will write me soon, but I have nothing more to write; so good-bye, dear Uncle.

Your affectionate nephew,
N. H.

45 As good as the average work of tenth-grade pupils

THE BREAK OF DAWN. 78

Written by James at age 12

The sun went down in a darkened sky,
From a world of desolation;
Women and children and men also
In the pangs of dire starvation.

The sun went down in a darkened sky
From the battlefield of war,
Away from the terrible sickening sights
Of men covered with bloody gore.

The sun went down in a darkened sky,
Away from the scene of a little town
Shelled and shattered and torn to pieces,
And her defenders being shot down.

The sun went down on scenes of horror,
Horrors of a bloody war.
When the sun in the East came up,
Peace was standing at the door.

And so at the end of another day,
Instead of war's great girth,
Th' world was enveloped with brotherly love,
And liberty and justice encircled the earth.

CHAPTER XXV

RESULTS OF RATINGS, WITH ILLUSTRATIONS

In Table 95 the selections rated, classified by age of author, are listed by title together with name of author (fictitious in the case of the California gifted children), and "best average" of the ratings assigned. The number following each title is the serial number of the selection used for purposes of identification. By use of the serial number it is possible to find in Table 90 what judges rated any particular selection and what the individual ratings were. In this table, the selections marked by an asterisk are included in the Tentative Scale and are reproduced in the preceding chapter. Those marked by a dagger are reproduced in this chapter.

TABLE 95
AVERAGE RATINGS OF INDIVIDUAL JUVENILIA
ARRANGED BY AGE OF AUTHOR

Age	Author	Rating	Title	No.
5	Verda	69	†The Place I'd Like to Be	151
7	Beatrice	56	Why the Bunny Has a Cotton Tail	28
	Beatrice	85	†My Prayer	80
	Beatrice	71	A Picture, a Riddle	98
	James	54	*Christmas	59
	Verda	65	There's a Drop upon the Pavement	147
8	Beatrice	68	The Magic Pencil	26
	Beatrice	53	*The Countess of Morcas' Pearl	39
	Macaulay	85	†Olans the Great	121
9	Beatrice	48	The Dandelion	116
	Hawthorne	47	*Letter to His Uncle	38
10	Beatrice	76	The Church in the Woods	62
	Beatrice	79	A Fog Picture	82
	Beatrice	61	My Castle	100
	Beatrice	69	An April Shower	117
	Bryant	86	†After a Total Eclipse of the Sun	110
	Edith	72	The Mill	134
	Jeanette	63	The Faucet That Was Always Leaking	33
	Verda	65	How Santa Claus Came to Give Presents	111
	Verda	90	†The Mountains	129
	Walter	42	A Story	16
11	Beatrice	82	†Music under Pines	120
	Beatrice	75	Fire Fairies	135
	Edith	71	The Prairie	42
	Ethel	74	The Plant of Herkii	17
	Ethel	63	Winter	96
	Ethel	73	*Idle Thought	132
	Scott	89	†In Awful Ruins Aetna Thunders Nigh	101
12	Beatrice	83	†The Fable of the Missionary and the Untutored Child of Nature	1

Age	Author	Rating	Title	No.
	Franklin	86	†One of the "Dogood Papers"	21
	Freneau	84	The Village Merchant	55
	Hawthorne	70	Days of My Youth, Ye Fleet Away	125
	Johnson	82	†To a Young Lady on Her Birthday	142
	Johnson	90	Translation of *Horace*, Book II, Ode ix	124
	Ralph	63	Out of India	6
	Walter	72	*Reflections of a Student	30
	Wordsworth	77	On Anticipation of Leaving School	81
17	Bryant	84	Introduction to "Thanatopsis"	113
	Burns	93	†Handsome Nell	148
	Byron	84	To Caroline	73
	Coleridge	80	To the Muse	70
	Cowper	87	On Finding the Heel of a Shoe	94
	Freneau	81	The Pyramids of Egypt	149
	Hamilton	102	*A Full Vindication	13
	Jefferson	73	Letter to His Guardian	11
	Juanita	79	The Scimitar of the Sun-God	10
	Juanita	66	The Bonehead	22
	Juanita	66	Witch Molly	35
	Juanita	86	Farewell	144
	Longfellow	105	Italian Scenery	58
	Milton	93	On the Death of a Fair Infant	46
	Pope	104	Autumn: The Third Pastoral	83
	Ralph	81	When the Kid Drove	5
	Ralph	78	Twenty Feet Down	31
	Thoreau	72	Excerpt from His Journal	23
	Wordsworth	91	†An Evening Walk	99
18	Bryant	104	A Love Song	95
	Byron	92	The Prayer of Nature	130
	Coleridge	89	Music	51
	Jefferson	83	Letter to a Friend	34
	Longfellow	80	Hymn of the Moravian Nuns of Bethlehem	122
	Lowell	87	Follow This Narrow Path to Where the Grass	143
	Poe	91	†The Happiest Day, the Happiest Hour	52
	Poe	90	Dreams	71
	Ralph	72	Phillippe Mendet	18
	Ralph	81	A Philosophy	150
	Shelley	99	†Queen Mab	57
	Thackeray	56	Mrs. Ramsbottom at Cambridge	27
	Thoreau	78	Our Punishments	9
	Whittier	99	†The Deity	49
	Whittier	93	The Vale of the Merrimac	68
19	Browning	99	Pauline	112
	Byron	110	*Lines Written beneath an Elm in a Churchyard	54
	Dryden	86	To His Friend John Hoddeson	106
	Emerson	98	Good-bye	74
	Freneau	82	The Rising Glory of America	131
	Keats	96	To Hope	48
	Keats	86	Sonnet to Solitude	67
	Longfellow	92	Burial of the Minnisink	104
	Lowell	87	Invocation and Epilogue to Class Poem	140
	Milton	79	At a Vacation Exercise in the College	139
	Shelley	75	Omens	119
	Tennyson	94	Timbuctoo	136
	Thoreau	78	On Story-Telling	36
	Wordsworth	86	Lines Written While Sailing a Boat at Evening	118

Space is not available for the reproduction of all the juvenilia listed in Table 95. Those which follow have been selected partly on the basis of their intrinsic interest, partly for their brevity, and partly to secure a wide sampling of authors. They are arranged by age.

THE PLACE I'D LIKE TO BE 151

Verda, age 5

Average Rating, 69

The place I'd like to be
Is where the spreading tree
    Spreads its shade
    And is made
By the gentle hand of God
In the rich, black mud.
And the brooklet ripples down
To the other end of town,
And the roses are in bloom,
And the violets give perfume,
And the blue grass waves like bushes,
And in the brook here wave rushes,
—But instead—a dingy town!

MY PRAYER 98

Beatrice, age 7

Average Rating, 85

Comment: "More literary merit than 81, but springs from the psychology and vocabulary of a twelfth-grade pupil."—JUDGE E.

Oh, Master of fire! Oh, Lord of air,
Oh, God of waters, hear my prayer!
Oh, Lord of ground and of stirring trees,
Oh, God of man and of pleasant breeze,
Dear Father, let me happy be—
As happy as a growing tree!

OLANS THE GREAT 121

Macaulay, age 8

Average Rating, 85

Comment: "Imitative quality makes it difficult to place."—JUDGE E.

Day set on Cambria's hills supreme,
And, Menai, on thy silver stream.
The star of day had reached the West.
Now in the main it sunk to rest.
Shone great Eleindyn's castle tall:
Shone every battery, every hall:
Shone all fair Mona's verdant plain;
But chiefly shone the foaming main. . . . .

THE MOUNTAINS 129

Verda, age 10

Average Rating, 90

The sighing pines, the hemlocks tall and grand,
The massive oaks, that seem to stir with life
And inter-life, with nesting birds. The rocks,
That hold us still in wonder and in awe,
Grim patriarchs of battles fought by none
That breathe the breath of life, unhuman warriors:
The storm—the hurricane—the aging years.
Here we see trees struck down by one of these—
Uprooted—blackened—robbed of all their life;
And yet the quiet rocks live calmly on.

The river flows majestically along,
Feeding and watering a thousand trees—
Ten thousand flowers—a million blades of grass.
The trees decay, and, falling, meet their doom;
The grass turns brown and dies within a year;
The flowers wither in one happy day;
And still the river staidly flows along,
Calm and unchanging through the span of time.

The birds! Ah, harbingers of happy days!
Who flutter in the air, and chirp, and trill,
Who swoop to catch a glistening drop of foam
From off the river's dancing surface bright.
Ye come to make your home within the woods,
As do the squirrels, who leap and frisk and play
And chatter in the treetops, till the wood
Seems like a Babel tower once again.

The mountains! Ah, eternity is theirs!
Unchanging, yet so different each day.
Each day some flower or tree or bird is dead;
Each day some new thing blossoms into life.

AFTER A TOTAL ECLIPSE OF THE SUN 110

Bryant, age 10

Average Rating, 86

How awfully sublime and grand to see
The lamp of day wrapped in obscurity.
To see the sun remove behind the moon,
And nightly darkness shroud the day at noon;
The birds no longer feel his genial ray,
But cease to sing and sit upon the spray.
A solemn gloom and stillness spreads around,

Reigns in the air and broods o'er all the ground.
Once-smiling Nature wears another face,
The blooming meadow loses half its grace.
All things are silent save the chilling breeze,
That in low whispers rustles through the trees.
The stars break forth and stud the azure sky,
And larger planets meet the wondering eye.

Now busy man leaves off his toil to gaze,
And some are struck with horror and amaze,
Others of noble feelings more refined
Serenely view it with a tranquil mind.
See God's bright image strikingly portrayed
In each appearance which his power had made.
(Fixed in their hearts cool Meditation sate,
With upraised eye and thoughtful look sedate.)

Now bursts the Sun from silence and from night,
Though few his beams, they shed a welcome light;
And Nature's choir, enlivened by his rays,
Harmonious warble their Creator's praise.
The shades of darkness feel his potent ray,
Mine eye pursues them as they flee away;
So from the greyhound flies the tim'rous hare,
Swift as the dart divides the yielding air.

"IN AWFUL RUINS AETNA THUNDERS NIGH" 101

Scott, age 11

Average Rating, 89

In awful ruins Aetna thunders nigh,
And sends in pitchy whirlwinds to the sky
Black clouds of smoke, which, still as they aspire,
From their dark sides there bursts the glowing fire;
At other times huge balls of fire are toss'd,
That lick the stars, and in the smoke are lost:
Sometimes the mount, with vast convulsions torn,
Emits huge rocks, which instantly are borne
With loud explosions to the starry skies,
The stones made liquid as the huge mass flies,
Then back again with greater weight recoils,
While Aetna thundering from the bottom boils. . . . .

MUSIC UNDER PINES 120

Beatrice, age 11

Average Rating, 82

Dreamily parting the silence,
Reaching up far to the sky,

Under the slow-swaying pine tops,
Floats the melodious sigh.

All through the balm-laden fragrance,
Harmony soaring on wings
Bearing a strange incantation,
Softly and sweetly it sings.

ODE TO SOLITUDE   137

Pope, age 12

Average Rating, 86

Comments: "Alexander Pope."—JUDGE A.
"Delicate, uneven cadence is good, reticence of quietly regretful last
stanza effective; but the piece is somewhat typical of many in the seventeenth century and early eighteenth century, when poets frequently yearned
(usually without sincerity) for solitude and peace. This by Pope."—JUDGE B.

Happy the man whose wish and care
  A few paternal acres bound,
Content to breathe his native air
  In his own ground.

Whose herds with milk, whose fields with bread,
  Whose flocks supply him with attire,
Whose trees in summer yield him shade,
  In winter fire.

Blest, who can unconcern'dly find
  Hours, days, and years slide soft away,
In health of body, peace of mind,
  Quiet by day.

Sound sleep by night; study and ease,
  Together mixt; sweet recreation:
And innocence, which most does please
  With meditation.

Thus let me live, unseen, unknown,
  Thus unlamented let me die,
Steal from the world, and not a stone
  Tell where I lie.

THE FABLE OF THE MISSIONARY AND THE UNTUTORED CHILD OF NATURE   1

Beatrice, age 12

Average Rating, 83

Now, behold, there was once an Untutored Child of Nature whose
abode was in the wildest wilds of Africa, whose name was Itchy-
galoop. And he lived in primitive bliss and ate mangosteens and

fried pig, and his drink was the limpid waters of the brook. And he wore a neat but not gaudy garment of leaves, and used no hair tonic.

And it came to pass that a Missionary came unto those wilds and when he beheld Itchy-galoop with his incumbrous garments he was aghast and said unto him:

"Untutored Child of Nature, the way thou goest thou wilt inevitably end up in perdition, so come to my tent and be baptized tomorrow at nine A.M."

And Itchy-galoop was awed by the majestic and noble aspect of the Missionary's nose, and consented.

And the Missionary was glad, and said unto him: "I will now proceed to civilize thee." So he got out his second-best pair of pants and a violet shirt and arrayed Itchy-galoop therein.

And it came to pass that when Itchy-galoop had learned to read, the Missionary presented him with a book of the science of medicine and hygiene. And Itchy-galoop looked therein and was dismayed. He saw plainly that it was a miracle he had survived so long, and began industriously to study.

And he boiled the limpid water of the brook before he quaffed thereof, and partook no more of fried pig which is hard to digest, and washed his mangosteens before he ate of them. And he thumped his chest doubtfully, and felt of his pulse, and foresaw that he was dying of tuberculosis and heart disease. And he said, "Yea, it is a certainty that I have every disease in this book from appendicitis on." So he took unto a folding couch that the Missionary had brought and groaned when he thought he ought to.

And when he had survived for a week in this precarious state he awoke one morning with a feeling of unaccountable happiness. And he said unto himself, "This is verily the light-heartedness before the end," and felt his pulse. And suddenly it came to him that the sky was blue and that he was feeling better than ever in his life before. A great conviction dawned on him and he arose and went in search of the Missionary and said to him with menacing aspect, "Get out of here on the double-quick, and if you come into my vision perambulating around this vicinity again I will immediately examine into the contents of your cranium with my primeval stone hatchet."

And Itchy-galoop stood on a high hill and when the speck of Missionary had faded into the distance he took the book and wrapped his trousers around it and threw it far out into the sea. And he sighed with happiness and went and ate some mangosteens without washing them.

MODERATE VIEWS   107

Hawthorne, age 12

Average Rating, 81

Comment: "Pure imitation of moral cant spooned out to the eighteenth- and nineteenth-century child by such poets as Watt and Southey."— JUDGE B.

With passions unruffled, untainted by pride,
By reason my life let me square;

The wants of my nature are cheaply supplied,
  And the rest are but folly and care.

How vainly through infinite trouble and strife,
  The many their labors employ,
Since all that is truly delightful in life,
  Is what all if they please may enjoy.

LINES TO THE MEMORY OF SIR WILLIAM PITT 85

Macaulay, age 13

Average Rating, 96

Comments: "The utter smoothness of the rhythm almost precludes any necessity of idea—but the jerk of repetition in the last line catches attention."—JUDGE B.
"Moore?"—JUDGE E.
"Perhaps Tennyson."—JUDGE F.

Oh, Britain! dear Isle, when the annals of story
  Shall tell of the deeds that thy children have done,
When the strains of each poet shall sing of their glory,
  And the triumphs their skill and their valour have won.

When the olive and palm in thy chaplet are blended,
When thy arts, and thy fame, and thy commerce increase,
When thy arms through the uttermost coasts are extended,
And thy war is triumphant, and happy thy peace;

When the ocean, whose waves like a rampart flow round thee,
  Conveying thy mandates to every shore,
And the empire of Nature no longer can bound thee,
  And the world be the scene of thy conquests no more:

Remember the man who in sorrow and danger,
  When thy glory was set, and thy spirit was low,
When thy hopes were o'erturned by the arms of the stranger,
  And thy banner displayed in the halls of the foe,

Stood forth in the tempest of doubt and disaster,
Unaided and single, the danger to brave,
Asserted thy claims, and the rights of his master,
Preserved thee to conquer, and saved thee to save.

CHRISTMAS 123

Wanda, age 13

Average Rating, 95

Today is Christmas.

Somewhere this morning dawned
One of a thousand like it;

A golden sun in a metallic sky,
Shining, here, upon fair green hills;
Yonder, on stifling jungle; or again
On the salt-crispened tops of cold, blue tossing waves,
Or on far-stretching leagues of burning sand.

And somewhere, great, soft flakes are falling slowly,
Drifting against some quiet bank and lying still,
Hiding some muddy patch of ugliness.
(Once, last night, the wind blew back
The curtains of the heavy-lying clouds.
Then, for an instant,
Poised in blue darkness shone one golden star,
And faintly came the echo of a carol).

But here, the day is misty.
Gray fog
Eddies about me, blown by a wet wind.
It brushes with soft benison the grass,
Wreathes in strange patterns, lifts and dips again;
Through it one little candle casts its light,
Throwing a welcome from my friend's high window.
A church-bell chimes in gravely measured cadence.

For sunshine is the Greater Glory,
And snow is bright, pure adoration,
But mist is Peace.

A GLOVE   84

Beatrice, age 13

Average Rating, 93

She left her glove, and cold and void it seemed
To fill the place where her warm hand had lain,
As empty as the heart of one who dreamed
And lost his dream, and found it not again.
The fingers, curved and grasping on the air
Made the same gesture that had bid farewell—
O poor illusion! There was nothing there!
Perhaps some vagrant breezes—who can tell?

This glove has compassed many times, I know
A dearer hand than many angels own:
I cannot kiss the kindly hand, and so
I kiss this quickly, now I am alone.
There! Lie there, little glove! But do not tell
Our secret to the one I love so well!

THE BATTLE OF LOVELL'S POND   86

Longfellow, age 13

Average Rating, 81

Cold, cold is the north wind and rude is the blast
That sweeps like a hurricane loudly and fast,
As it moans through the tall waving pines lone and drear,
Sighs a requiem sad o'er the warrior's bier.

The war-whoop is still, and the savage's yell
Has sunk into silence along the wild dell;
The din of the battle, the tumult, is o'er,
And the war-clarion's voice is now heard no more.

The warriors that fought for their country, and bled,
Have sunk to their rest; the damp earth is their bed;
No stone tells the place where their ashes repose,
Nor points out the spot from the graves of their foes.

They died in their glory, surrounded by fame,
And Victory's loud trumpet their death did proclaim;
They are dead; but they live in each Patriot's breast,
And their names are engraven on honor's bright crest.

ON THE DEATH OF A YOUNG LADY   127

Byron, age 14

Average Rating, 89

Hush'd are the winds, and still the evening gloom,
    Not e'en a zephyr wanders through the grove,
Whilst I return to view my Margaret's tomb,
    And scatter flowers on the dust I love.

Within this cell reclines her clay,
    That clay, where once such animation beam'd;
The King of Terrors seiz'd her as his prey;
    Nor worth, nor beauty, have her life redeem'd.

Oh! could that King of Terrors pity feel,
    Or Heaven reverse the dread decree of fate,
Not here the mourner would his grief reveal,
    Not here the Muse her virtues would relate.

But wherefore weep? Her matchless spirit soars
    Beyond where splendid shines the orb of day;
And weeping angels lead her to those bowers,
    Where endless pleasures virtuous deeds repay.

And shall presumptuous mortals Heaven arraign!
And, madly, Godlike Providence accuse!
Ah, no, far fly from me attempts so vain;—
I'll ne'er submission to my God refuse.

Yet is remembrance of those virtues dear,
Yet fresh the memory of that beauteous face;
Still they call forth my warm affection's tear,
Still in my heart retain their wonted place.

A LETTER 146

Bryant, age 14

Average Rating, 88

Once more the Bard, with eager eye, reviews
The flowery paths of fancy, and the Muse
Once more essays to trill forgotten strains,
The loved amusement of his native plains.
Late you beheld me treading labor's round,
To guide slow oxen o'er the furrowed ground;
The sturdy hoe or slender rake to ply,
'Midst dust and sweat, beneath a summer sky.

But now I pore o'er Vergil's glowing lines,
Where, famed in war, the great Aeneas shines;
Where novel scenes around me seem to stand,
Lo! grim Alecto whirls the flaming brand.
Dire jarring tumult, death and battle rage,
Fierce armies close, and daring chiefs engage;
Mars thunders furious from his flying car,
And hoarse-toned clarions stir the raging war.
Nor with less splendor does his master hand
Paint the blue skies, the ocean and the land;
Majestic mountains rear their awful head,
Fair plains extend, and bloomy vales are spread.
The rugged cliff in threatening grandeur towers,
And joy sports smiling in Arcadian bowers;
In silent calm the expanded ocean sleeps,
Or boisterous whirlwinds toss the rising deeps;
Triumphant vessels o'er his rolling tide,
With painted prows and gaudy streamers glide. . . . .

AN ODE 88

Cowper, age 14

Average Rating, 88

To rescue from the tyrant's sword
Th' oppress'd—unseen and unimplor'd,
To cheer the face of woe;

From lawless insult to defend
An orphan's right—a fallen friend,
And a forgiven foe;

These, these, distinguish from the crowd,
And these alone, the great and good,
The guardians of mankind;
Whose bosoms with these virtues heave,
O, with what matchless speed, they leave
The multitude behind!

PATTERN 75

Jeanette, age 15

Average Rating, 94

A green rimmed sky,
A purple tree,
A pale blue wind a-blowing—
And a great round moon
From the far off sea
Like a copper platter glowing!

And moon, and tree,
And blue high lands
Send scornful shadows flying
Across the gold
Of desert sands
To where the day is dying.

THE RAINBOW 97

Ruth, age 15

Average Rating, 90

Comment: "Vague, and not too rhythmical; showing great sensitiveness to delicate impressions."—JUDGE B.

Born on the sunset
Spanning the sky and forming
A gigantic arc in the heavens
Iridescent and glowing
Pale shades softly blending;
Formed by the shimmering
Veils of the Deities,
Or lingering mists of the air.
Brightly circling the heavens
Then fading into
Dim fantasies
Leaving lasting impressions
Of Nature's rare and beautiful
Innermost secrets.

FIRST ADVENT OF LOVE   145

Coleridge, age 15

Average Rating, 89

O fair is Love's first hope to gentle mind!
As Eve's first star through fleecy cloudlet peeping;

And sweeter than the gentle south-west wind
O'er willowy meads, and shadowed waters creeping,

And Ceres' golden fields;—the sultry hind
Meets it with brow uplift, and stays his reaping.

NIGHT   79

Edith, age 15

Average Rating, 84

Miles o'er the emerald seas, and across the golden sand,
Beyond where the plumed palm trees give shade to a burning land,
Is a deep-mouthed, rocky cave, lost in the purple hills,
Still as a lonely grave, with a silence that awes and thrills,
In its depths, forlorn and weird, asleep on a massive throne,
Where a torch, as if it leered, makes a smoky, flickering zone
Of devil-dancing light upon the shadowy walls,
Sits the sable-winged Night, queen of those Stygian halls.

Her skin is white as death, and her black cascade of hair,
Stirred by her gentle breath, gleams in the dull red glare.
Her arms are bound with chains which clank if she slightly stir,
For she, while Phoebus reigns, is the sun-god's prisoner.

The Moon sleeps by her side, with her silver wings outspread,
White as a lace-clad bride, who lily-like lies dead.

Hark! Down the silent halls where strange phantom shadows quake,
The sound of light foot-falls and a thousand echoes wake.
'Tis Hesperus! In his hand he bears a golden key;
Obeying the Day's command, he sets the prisoner free.
She moves her lovely head, she raises a queenly arm,
Like waking from the dead, she breaks Apollo's charm.
She opens her deep green eyes and in a gentle tone
She bids the Moon arise, and leaves her lofty throne.
Her silken hair shakes down around her pallid face,
Her shimmering sable gown discloses her every grace.
As she moves down the blackened hills, rocky and jagged and steep,
She stoops to the earth and fills her arms with poppies of sleep;
Then, like a graceful bird, with the white moon by her side,
With never a wing-beat heard, she rises and seems to glide
Over the darkened earth, far in the heavens deep,

Silencing sounds of mirth, scattering poppies of sleep.
Still as a dream she flies, never a wing-beat heard,
She moves through the quiet skies like the shade of some great bird;
Still as the dreams of love that through the shadows creep;
Still as a dream of love—scattering poppies of sleep.

IRISH MELODY 63

Thackeray, age 15

Average Rating, 84

Comments: "A clever parody on Moore's 'The minstrel boy to the war has gone.' Note the knowledge of contemporary politics and the shrewdness of the last point."—JUDGE B.
"Probably by Thackeray."—JUDGE F.

Mister Sheil into Kent has gone
On Penenden Heath you'll find him;
Nor think you that he came alone,
There's Doctor Doyle behind him.

"Men of Kent," said the little man,
"If you hate Emancipation,
You're a set of fools." He then began
A cut and dry oration.

He strove to speak, but the Men of Kent
Began a grievous shouting,
When out of the wagon the little man went,
And put a stop to his spouting.

"What though these heretics heard me not!"
Quoth he to his friend canonical,
"My speech is safe in the *Times,* I wot,
And eke in the *Morning Chronicle.*"

PARAPHRASE OF PSALM CXIV 65

Milton, age 15

Average Rating, 80

Comment: "Milton."—JUDGE F.

When the blest seed of Terah's faithful son
After long toil their liberty had won,
And passed from Pharian fields to Canaan land,
Led by the strength of the Almighty's hand,
Jehovah's wonders were in Israel shown,
His praise and glory were in Israel known.
That saw the troubled sea, and shivering, fled,
And sought to hide his froth-becurled head

Low in the earth; Jordan's clear streams recoil,
As a faint host that hath received the foil.
The high huge-bellied mountains skip like rams
Amongst their ewes, the little hills like lambs.
Why fled the ocean? and why skipped the mountains?
Why turned Jordan toward his crystal fountains?
Shake, Earth, and at the presence be aghast
Of Him that ever was and aye shall last,
That glassy floods from rugged rocks can crush,
And make soft rills from fiery flint-stones gush.

DEATH   61

Edith, age 16

Average Rating, 95

Comment: "Excellent but for the last line."—Judge F.

And this is death? This carven marble face,
The effigy of one we loved so well,
Lies on its pillow, white as are the blooms
That early spring has heaped upon his bier.
His last sharp agony has wiped away
The furrows left by years of wearing pain,
And now he seems to sleep a dreamless sleep.

Joy is not there, nor woe, nor any look
Known to the world of which he was a part.
All mortal struggle he has left behind
Like broken shackles lying on the ground.

He is so still, so silently at rest
That, having come into his heritage
Of lasting peace, he seems to ask no more.
His eyes are closed. If he could open them
Perhaps they would reveal celestial joy
That is not meant for human sight to see,
Such happiness as can be only earned
By years of useful life and noble thoughts.

Dear face! You have fulfilled the task assigned.
The last page in your book of life is filled;
The writing there is done in your own hand.
May rest, such rest as souls like you deserve,
Be yours until eternity is done.

Farewell, until my heart has ceased to beat,
Until I, too, lie peacefully asleep,
Until my timid spirit ventures forth
Into the great unknown where you have gone.
That time seems years ahead, unthinkable,
For I have just begun the road of life.

But if I die before experience
Has taught me death is not a thing to fear,
If, still remembering my happy life,
I stagger out into the Ages dark
With frightened feet, and hands that wildly grope,
With streaming eyes, and lips that cry for help,
A lost child looking for a friendly face,
O Grandfather, be there to guide my way.
Let not the hollow darkness swallow me.
Be there to take me into your strong arms,
And comfort me with reassuring words,
Telling me not to fear eternity
Nor grieve for those that I have left behind.
I should not fear the darkness with you near,
But realize that Eternity means Peace.

TO THE AUTHOR OF THE ——— JOURNAL   21

ONE OF THE "DOGOOD PAPERS"

Frankiin, age 16

Average Rating, 86

Comment: "Clever imitation of *Spectator* and *Tatler* papers."—JUDGE B.

Discoursing the other Day at Dinner with my Reverend Boarder, formerly mentioned, (whom for Distinctions' Sake we will call by the Name of Clericus), concerning the Education of Children, I asked his Advice about my Son William, whether or no I had best bestow upon him academical Learning, or (as our Phrase is) bring him up at our College: He persuaded me to do it by all Means, using many weighty Arguments with me, and answering all the Objections that I could form against it; telling me withal, that he did not doubt but that the Lad would take his Learning very well, and not idle away his Time as too many there nowadays do. These words of Clericus gave me a Curiosity to inquire a little more strictly into the present Circumstances of that famous Seminary of Learning; but the Information which he gave me, was neither pleasant nor such as I had expected.

As soon as Dinner was over, I took a solitary Walk into my Orchard, still ruminating on Clericus' Discourse with much Consideration, until I came to my usual Place of Retirement under the great Apple Tree; where having seated myself, and carefully laid my Head on a verdant Bank, I fell by Degrees into a soft and undisturbed Slumber. My waking Thoughts remained with me in this Sleep, and before I awaked again, I dreamt the following Dream.

I fancied I was travelling over pleasant and delightful Fields and Meadows, and through many small country Towns and Villages; and as I passed along, all Places resounded with the Fame of the Temple of Learning. Every Peasant, who had wherewithal, was preparing to send one of his Children at least to this Place; and in this Case most of them consulted their own Purses instead of their

Children's Capacities: So that I observed a great many, yea, the most Part of those who were travelling thither, were little better than Dunces and Blockheads. Alas! Alas!

At length I entered upon a spacious Plain, in the Midst of which was erected a large and stately Edifice: It was to this that a great Company of Youths from all Parts of the Country were going; so stepping in among the Crowd, I passed on with them, and presently arrived at the Gate.

The Passage was kept by two sturdy Porters named Riches and Poverty, and the Latter obstinately refused to give Entrance to any who had not first gained the Favour of the Former; so that I observed many who came even to the very Gate, were obliged to travel back again as ignorant as they came, for Want of this necessary Qualification. However, as a Spectator I gained Admission, and with the Rest entered directly into the Temple.

In the Middle of the great Hall stood a stately and magnificent Throne, which was ascended by two high and difficult Steps. On the Top of it sat Learning in awful State; she was apparelled wholly in black, and surrounded almost on every Side with innumerable Volumes in all Languages. She seemed very busily employed in writing Something on half a Sheet of Paper, and upon Enquiry, I understood she was preparing a Paper, called the ———— Journal. On her right Hand sat English, with a pleasant, smiling Countenance, and handsomely attired; and on her left were seated several antique Figures with their Faces veiled. I was considerably puzzled to guess who they were, until one informed me (who stood beside me) that those Figures on her left Hand were Latin, Greek, Hebrew, etc., and that they were very much reserved, and seldom or never unveiled their Faces here, and then to few or none, though most of those who have in this Place acquired so much Learning as to distinguish them from English, pretend to an intimate Acquaintance with them. I then inquired of him, what could be the Reason why they continued veiled, in this Place especially. He pointed to the Foot of the Throne, where I saw Idleness, attended with Ignorance, and these (he informed me) were they who first veiled them, and still kept them so.

Now I observed that the whole Tribe who entered into the Temple with me, began to climb the Throne: but the Work proving troublesome and difficult to most of them, they withdrew their Hands from the Plow, and contented themselves to sit at the Foot, with Madam Idleness and her Maid Ignorance, until those who were afflicted by Diligence and a docile Temper had well nigh got up the first Step. But the Time drawing nigh in which they could in no Way avoid ascending, they were fain to crave the Assistance of those who had got up before them, and who for the Reward perhaps of a Pint of Milk, or a Piece of Plum Cake, lent the Lubbers a helping Hand and sat them, in the Eye of the World, on a Level with themselves.

The other Step being in the same Manner ascended, and the usual Ceremonies at an End, every Beetle-Skull seemed well satisfied with his own Portion of Learning, though perhaps he was just as ignorant as ever. And now the Time of their Departure being come, they marched out of the Doors to make Room for another Company, who waited for Entrance. And I, having seen all that was to be seen, quitted the Hall likewise, and went to make Observations on those who had just gone out before me.

Some I perceived took to Merchandizing, others to Travelling, some to one Thing, some to another, and some to Nothing; and many of them from thenceforth, for Want of Patrimony, lived as poor as Church Mice, being unable to dig, and ashamed to beg, and to live by their Wits was impossible. But the most Part of the Crowd went along a large beaten Path, which led to a Temple at the further End of the Plain, called the Temple of Theology. The Business of those who were in this Temple being laborious and painful, I wondered exceedingly to see so many going towards it; but while I was pondering this Matter in my Mind, I spied Pecunia behind a Curtain beckoning to them with her Hand, which Sight immediately satisfied me for whose Sake it was that a great Part of them (I do not say all) travelled that Road. In this Temple I saw nothing worth mentioning, except the ambitious and fraudulent Contrivances of Plagius, who (notwithstanding he had been severely reprehended for such Practices before) was diligently transcribing some eloquent Paragraphs out of Tillotson's Works, etc., to embellish his own.

Now I bethought myself in my Sleep, that it was Time to be at Home, and as I fancied I was travelling back thither, I reflected in my Mind on the extreme Folly of those Parents who, blind to their Children's Dullness, and insensible of the Solidity of their Skulls, because they think their Purses can afford it, will needs send them to the Temple of Learning, where, for Want of a suitable Genius, they learn little more than how to carry themselves handsomely, and enter a Room genteelly (which might as well be acquired at a Dancing-School) and from whence they return, after Abundance of Trouble and Charge, as great Blockheads as ever, only more proud and self-conceited.

While I was in the Midst of these unpleasant Reflections, Clericus (who with a Book in his Hand was walking under the Trees) accidentally awakened me; to him I related my Dream with all its particulars, and he, without much Study, presently interpreted it, assuring me that it was a lively Representation of HARVARD COLLEGE.

I remain, Sir,

Your humble Servant,

SILENCE

TO A YOUNG LADY ON HER BIRTHDAY 142

Johnson, age 16

Average Rating, 82

Comments: "I suspect it is Pope."—JUDGE C.
"Isn't it Pope?"—JUDGE D.
"Samuel Johnson."—JUDGE F.

This tributary verse receive, my fair,
Warm with an ardent lover's fondest prayer.
May this returning day forever find

Thy form more lovely, more adorn'd thy mind;
All pains, all cares, may favouring Heaven remove,
All but the sweet solicitudes of love!
May powerful nature join with grateful art,
To point each glance, and force it to the heart!
Oh then, when conquer'd crowds confess thy sway,
When ev'n proud wealth and prouder wit obey
My fair, be mindful of the mighty trust:
Alas! 'tis hard for beauty to be just . . . .
Those sovereign charms with strictest care employ;
Nor give the generous pain, the worthless joy:
With his own form acquaint the forward fool,
Shown in the faithless glass of ridicule;
Teach mimic censure her own faults to find,
Nor let coquettes to themselves be blind,
So shall Belinda's charms improve mankind.

HANDSOME NELL   148

Burns, age 17

Average Rating, 93

Comments: "Burns? The adored 'sweet simplicity' of the late eighteenth and early nineteenth century. Note the moral implication and the tone of teaching in the last two stanzas."—JUDGE B.
    "Burns."—JUDGE F.

> Oh, once I loved a bonnie lass,
> Ay, and I love her still;
> And whilst that honour warms my breast,
> I'll love my handsome Nell.
>
> As bonnie lassies I hae seen,
> And mony full as braw;
> But for a modest, gracefu' mien,
> The like I never saw.
>
> A bonnie lass, I will confess,
> Is pleasant to the ee,
> But without some better qualities,
> She's no the lass for me.
>
> But Nelly's looks are blithe and sweet,
> And, what is best of a',
> Her reputation is complete,
> And fair without a flaw.
>
> She dresses aye sae clean and neat,
> Both decent and genteel:
> And then there's something in her gait
> Makes ony dress look weel.

A gaudy dress and gentle air
May slightly touch the heart;
But it's innocence and modesty
That polishes the dart.

'Tis this in Nelly pleases me,
'Tis this enchants my soul;
For absolutely in my breast
She reigns without control.

AN EVENING WALK   99

Wordsworth, age 17

Average Rating, 91

. . . .

How pleasant, as the sun declines, to view
The spacious landscape change in form and hue!
Here, vanish, as in mist, before a flood
Of bright obscurity, hill, lawn, and wood;
There, objects, by the searching beams betrayed,
Come forth, and here retire in purple shade;
Even the white stems of birch, the cottage white,
Soften their glare before the mellow light;
The skiffs, at anchor where with umbrage wide
Yon chestnuts half the latticed boat-house hide,
Shed from their sides, that face the sun's slant beam,
Strong flakes of radiance on the tremulous stream;
Raised by yon travelling flock, a dusty cloud
Mounts from the road, and spreads its moving shroud;
The shepherd, all involved in wreaths of fire,
Now shows a shadowy speck, and now is lost entire.

Into a gradual calm the breezes sink,
A blue rim borders all the lake's still brink;
There doth the twinkling aspen's foliage sleep,
And insects clothe, like dust, the glassy deep:
And now, on every side, the surface breaks
Into blue spots, and slowly lengthening streaks;
Here, spots of sparkling water tremble bright
With thousand thousand twinkling points of light;
There, waves that, hardly weltering, die away,
Tip their smooth ridges with a softer ray;
And now the whole wide lake in deep repose
Is hushed, and like a burnished mirror glows,
Save where, along the shady western marge,
Coasts, with industrious oar, the charcoal barge. . . . . .

QUEEN MAB 57

Shelley, age 18

Average Rating, 99

Comments: "Extraordinary richness of verse form and occasional image causes me to rank rather high this morbid and sentimental subject. Shelley."—JUDGE B.

"This sounds like Shelley."—JUDGE D.

How wonderful is Death,
Death and his brother Sleep!
One, pale as yonder waning moon
With lips of lurid blue;
The other, rosy as the morn
When throned on ocean's wave
It blushes o'er the world:
Yet both so passing wonderful!

Hath then the gloomy power
Whose reign is in the tainted sepulchres
Seized on her sinless soul?
Must then that peerless form
Which love and admiration cannot view
Without a beating heart, those azure veins
Which steal like streams along a field of snow,
That lovely outline, which is fair
As breathing marble, perish?
Must putrefaction's breath
Leave nothing of this heavenly sight
But loathesomeness and ruin?
Spare nothing but a gloomy theme,
On which the lightest heart might moralize?
Or is it only a sweet slumber
Stealing o'er sensation,
Which the breath of roseate morning
Chaseth into darkness?
Will Ianthe wake again,
And give that faithful bosom joy
Whose sleepless spirit waits to catch
Light, life, and rapture from her smile?

Yes! she will wake again,
Although her glowing limbs are motionless,
And silent those sweet lips,
Once breathing eloquence,
That might have soothed a tiger's rage,
Or thawed the cold heart of a conqueror.
Her dewy eyes are closed,
And on their lids, whose texture fine
Scarce hides the dark blue orbs beneath,

The baby Sleep is pillowed:
Her golden tresses' shade
Her bosom's stainless pride,
Curling like tendrils of the parasite
Around a marble column. . . . .

THE DEITY 49

Whittier, age 18

Average Rating, 99

Comment: "Conventional rehearsal of scriptural material, here rendered effective by the poetic verbal effects."—JUDGE B.

The Prophet stood
On the high mount, and saw the tempest cloud
Pour the fierce whirlwind from its reservoir
Of congregated gloom. The mountain oak,
Torn from the earth, heaved high its roots where once
Its branches waved. The fir-tree's shapely form,
Smote by the tempest, lashed the mountain's side.
Yet, calm in conscious purity, the Seer
Beheld the awful desolation, for
The Eternal Spirit moved not in the storm.

The tempest ceased. The caverned earthquake burst
Forth from its prison, and the mountain rocked
Even to its base. The topmost crags were thrown,
With fearful crashes, down its shuddering sides.
Unawed, the Prophet saw and heard; he felt
Not in the earthquake moved the God of Heaven.

The murmur died away; and from the height,
Torn by the storm and shattered by the shock,
Rose far and clear a pyramid of flame,
Mighty and vast; the startled mountain deer
Shrank from its glare, and cowered within the shade;
The wild fowl shrieked—but even then the Seer
Untrembling stood and marked the fearful glow,
For Israel's God came not within the flame!

The fiery beacon sank. A still, small voice,
Unlike to human sound, at once conveyed
Deep awe and reverence to his pious heart.
Then bowed the holy man; his face he veiled
Within his mantle—and in meekness owned
The presence of his God, discerned not in
The storm, the earthquake, or the mighty flame.

THE HAPPIEST DAY, THE HAPPIEST HOUR 52

Poe, age 18

Average Rating, 91

Comment: "Early nineteenth century. Conventional romantic self-pity and misty vagueness. Includes a bad rhyme or two, and is only fairly powerful as verse. Probably by Poe."—JUDGE B.

The happiest day, the happiest hour
My seared and blighted heart hath known,
The highest hope of pride and power,
I feel hath flown.

Of power! said I? Yes! such I ween;
But they have vanished long, alas!
The visions of my youth have been—
But let them pass.

And pride, what have I now with thee?
Another brow may ev'n inherit
The venom thou hast poured on me—
Be still, my spirit!

The happiest day, the happiest hour
Mine eyes shall see, have ever seen,
The brightest glance of pride and power,
I feel—have been:

But were that hope of pride and power
Now offered, with the pain
Ev'n then I felt—that brightest hour
I would not live again:

For on its wing was dark alloy,
And as it fluttered, fell
An essence, powerful to destroy
A soul that knew it well.

CHAPTER XXVI

CASE NOTES ON GIFTED JUVENILE WRITERS

In Volume II of this series Dr. Cox has given case summaries of the early mental development of eighteen of the twenty-eight eminent authors represented in the juvenile productions rated in this study. The eighteen include Burns, Byron, Coleridge, Cowper, Dryden, Emerson, Franklin, Hamilton, Hawthorne, Jefferson, Johnson, Longfellow, Macaulay, Milton, Pope, Tennyson, Thackeray, and Wordsworth. The present writer has perpared similar case summaries of the remaining ten eminent authors (Browning, Bryant, Freneau, Holmes, Keats, Lowell, Poe, Shelley, Thoreau, and Whittier) and for the seven best writers of the California gifted group (Beatrice, Edith, Ethel, Jeanette, Ruth, Verda, and Wanda). In the preparation of these case summaries the same rubrics were followed as were used by Dr. Cox, except for the addition of headings relating to test data.

BEATRICE (b. 1912)

I. *Family standing.*

Beatrice's father is a surgeon, six of whose paternal ancestors in direct line were physicians. Other relatives in this line, of French and English extraction, include a Lord Mayor of London, an artist who was knighted, and several American statesmen and diplomats. Less is known concerning Beatrice's maternal ancestry, which is Swedish-German. Her maternal grandfather was an artist. Her maternal grandmother was of a family in which considerable musical talent has appeared. The mother was a teacher of music before her marriage. Beatrice is an only child and was born twelve years after her parents' marriage; her development and training have absorbed the major portion of their attention and interest.

II. *Development to age 17.*

1. Interests. An early, continuous, and intense interest, first in hearing or reading, then in producing, stories and verses, is especially noteworthy. Music (including improvising on the piano), drawing and painting, clay modeling, dancing, swimming, tennis, and natural science have been absorbing interests.

2. Education. Until the age of 11 Beatrice read and studied at home under her mother's direction. Formal instruction to this age

included as a rule from ten to twenty minutes of arithmetic instruction daily. At 11 years Beatrice entered the ninth grade of a private day school for girls, which she attended for two and a half years. Her last year of high-school work was done in a private boarding-school for girls. She entered university at 14-8 and graduated at 17.

3. School standing and progress. In Beatrice's first two and a half years of high school she earned thirteen units of high-school credit, and in the last year seven additional units, all of A grade. In her college work she has received A and B grades in English and language courses, and mostly C's in science. (The science courses were taken in pursuance of a long-standing intention of becoming a physician, but this has recently been abandoned in favor of an exclusively literary career.) She fell just short of Phi Beta Kappa honors.

4. Friends and associates. Beatrice's early contacts with other children were very much restricted. She had few playmates among neighborhood children before entering school, and few intimate friends in high school or college.

5. Reading. Beatrice was able to read books of the difficulty of *Heidi* before she was 5 years old, although she had had no formal instruction in reading. Reading has been a major interest from that time on, five or six hours per day often being devoted to it. At 5 years she read such books as *Silas Marner* and Charles and Mary Lamb's stories. At 8 years she had a wide acquaintance with the classics of English and American literature, as well as with the works of such modern writers as Maeterlinck, Barrie, Stevenson, Mark Twain, Tarkington, etc. At 8 years she had read approximately 750 books; at 10 years approximately 1,500. At 15 years she was reading French and German with facility and had read many of the classics of French and German literature. She had also done some reading in Spanish. Her speed of reading and memory for what she has read have always been considered remarkable by her associates and teachers.

6. Production and achievement. Beatrice began making up and telling stories at 2½ years, and rhymes at 3 years. Few of her compositions were preserved before she was 6, at which age she was given a typewriter and began recording them herself. From the age of 6 until she was 11 or 12 she often illustrated her stories and poems by crayon or water-color drawings, some of which have been reproduced in the report by Terman and Fenton.[1] Her writing has been continuous and prolific and has included many types of prose and verse not sampled by the selections reproduced in chapter xxiv; e.g., a long poem in Spenserian stanza, one in Scotch dialect, one in Chaucerian English, etc. Her first novel, about 120 pages in length, was completed just before her eighteenth birthday. The products of her clay modeling and painting in oils and water-color have been very favorably commented upon by a teacher in a well-known school of art.

---

[1] Terman, Lewis M., and Fenton, Jessie C.: "Preliminary Report on a Gifted Juvenile Author," *Journal of Applied Psychology*, Vol. 5, 1921, pp. 163–178.

7. Evidences of precocity. (See also II, 1, 2, 3, 5, 6.) The mother's "baby-book" records the following: at 16 months Beatrice had learned the letters I, A, O, and T by asking what the letters on her blocks were. At 19 months she was talking in sentences, said everything clearly, and knew the entire alphabet. At 20 months she supplied the words in eleven English and six German folk songs, and built balanced towers of blocks without assistance. At 22 months she began repeating nursery rhymes she had heard, although no effort had been made to teach them to her. At this age she counted objects to twelve, put together block picture puzzles, knew her own full name and that of her father, and began making up little stories concerning pictures she saw. At 2 years she recited the story of "The Three Bears," changing the pitch of her voice for each of them. At 25 months she picked the front door key out of a string of eighteen keys, although she had never had any distinguishing mark called to her attention. She knew the primary colors at this age. At 26 months she sang "Swanee River" with correct intervals. At 27 months she surprised her parents by reciting three poems, one of eight lines, and two of sixteen lines each. The poems had been read, but not taught to her.

Further evidence of precocity of development could be given at length, if space permitted.

8. Test data. Scores on a large number of intelligence and achievement tests are available for Beatrice. Several of those here given are quoted from the report by Terman and Fenton. It will be seen that her scores on these tests are very high. The literature tests given her at age 15-3 were not adequate measures of her ability along this line, as her scores were practically perfect. The test data on character and personality are too scanty to justify conclusions.

a) Intelligence and achievement tests. "Six weeks before Beatrice's eighth birthday she tested 14-10 by the Stanford Revision; IQ 188. . . . . Her score on the Army Beta test was 71, which is about the norm for 14 years. Thus her IQ measured by a non-verbal scale was 175. By the National Intelligence Tests she graded above 15 years (score, Form A, 152.8; Form B, 123), and by the Terman Group Test considerably higher (score 151, median for grade 12). On the Trabue Completion Tests, B and C, her score (17.5) equaled the mean for third or fourth year high school pupils. She took the memory span test for digits (oral presentation) with a class of twenty-one graduate students, beating ten and tying four. Her extreme memory span is nine digits, direct order, and seven digits, reverse order. On the Kelley Construction Test, which was given her by Dr. Kelley, her performance resembled that of a normal child of 9 or 10 years. . . . . She is at her best in vocabulary, information, language completion, and memory, and at her worst in tests involving arithmetical processes.

"On the Woody tests for addition, subtraction, multiplication, and division, her scores correspond to the medians for grade six. On the Kansas Silent Reading Test she scores at median for the eleventh grade, on the Thorndike Handwriting Scale at median for the eighth grade, on the Starch Grammatical Scale (A) at median for the eighth grade, on the Starch Punctuation Scale (A) at median for the sixth grade, on the Teachers College Spelling Scale (List 16) at median for eighth grade, and on the Grier test of information in zoölogy and physiology considerably better than standards given by Grier for second term high-school pupils. . . . ."

At age 11-6 Beatrice's score on the General Information test used in the California gifted children survey was above high school senior norms. At age 14-2 her score on the Thorndike Examination for High School Graduates was 85, or considerably above the average of Stanford freshmen.

b) Literature tests. At age 7-10½ Beatrice's score of 7 on the Abbott-Trabue Exercises in Poetic Appreciation was at the median for second-year college students. At age 15-3 she made a perfect score on the test, a performance which is equaled by few graduate students in English. At 15 her score on the Burch Tests of Comprehension in Literature was 119 out of a possible 128, and at this age she defined correctly 136 of the 150 words of the Inglis Vocabulary Test. The latter score is above the norm for college graduates.

c) Tests of character and personality. The only test of this series given to Beatrice was that dealing with plays, games, and amusements, which indicated that her play knowledge was much greater than that of average children of her age. (She was then just 10.) Her play interests resembled those of much older children, and were noticeably masculine, possibly because of a preponderance of boy playmates. The plays and games for which she expressed preference were ordinarily social and active. At age 11, her occupational preference was for a career which combined literary production with the practice of medicine, and her school-subject preferences were, in order, for literature, composition, and drawing.

EDITH (b. 1909)

I. *Family standing.*

Most of Edith's ancestors have been of the professional class, chiefly engineers, ministers, and teachers. Her father is a mining engineer of some note. Her paternal grandfather was a minister, her maternal grandfather, a mining engineer. The mother was a school teacher before her marriage. Edith has two brothers, one five and one seven years younger than herself.

Some of Edith's relatives (notably her father and her maternal grandfather) have shown interest in literary composition, but none has achieved note in letters.

II. *Development to age 17.*

1. Interests. From about the age of 3 Edith was much interested in the sands, rocks, plants, and insects of the Arizona and Nevada deserts, where her father's work kept the family in mining camps until after Edith was 11. Other major interests were in reading, dramatic games, presenting original plays with the aid of playmates, writing verses and stories, drawing, and painting.

2. Education. Edith entered school in the third grade at age 7-8, and attended a public school in Arizona for 4 years. When the family moved to California, in 1920, Edith entered junior high

school. She transferred to a private school for girls when in the tenth grade and was graduated from high school at age 17-5.

3. School standing and progress. Edith's school marks have been almost without exception A's and B's. During her senior year of high school she made an honor record in both examinations and class work, with grades of A or A+ throughout.

4. Friends and associates. Until Edith was past 11, her friendships with individuals outside the family were very much restricted because of her environment. Since the age of 11 she has had many friends, usually among those near her own age. Most of her intimates have been girls with literary tastes.

5. Reading. Edith learned to read at about the age of 6 by asking her mother what various words were. A little later the mother gave her some instruction by the phonetic method. Edith has rather consistently read more than the average child of her age, and has preferred reading matter of a superior quality. At 6 to 8 years she read fairy tales, Fabre's animal and nature stories, *St. Nicholas,* the *Jungle Books,* etc.; from 11 to 12 she especially liked such works as *Ivanhoe, Treasure Island,* and *Oliver Twist;* at 13 she enjoyed *Jane Eyre, The Little Minister, The Little Shepherd of Kingdom Come,* and *Deerslayer.*

6. Production and achievement. Edith's first poem was written just before her sixth birthday. She composed very little before the age of 8 or 9, but since then has usually spent from two to ten hours per week in writing, according to her own estimate. She has written stories, lyric poems, dramatic monologues, plays in verse (rhymed and unrhymed), and epic poems. Some of these have been published in school papers and annuals.

Edith seems to be more interested in literary than in artistic production. That her ability in the latter field has been recognized by her teachers and classmates is attested by the fact that she was chosen art editor of the high-school annual during her senior year.

7. Evidences of precocity. (No specific record, beyond II, 1, 2, 3, 5, 6.)

8. Test data. The data available for Edith include intelligence and achievement tests, and tests of character and personality, given at the time of the California gifted children survey, plus some literature tests given her in connection with the present study. The tests of character and personality indicate normal and healthy attitudes. Conclusions as to the other tests must be rather tentative, because these tests are known not to be adequate measures for bright children of her age. Her scores were all high, and indicate very superior mental ability and achievement.

a) Intelligence and achievement tests. At 13-0 Edith's Stanford-Binet mental age was 18-0, her uncorrected IQ 138, and her corrected IQ 148. When she was in the low ninth grade, at age 13-5, her Stanford Achievement score equivalents were: arithmetic age, 18-2; reading age, 17-11; spelling age, 17-3; general information and language usage, above high school norms.

b) Literature tests. These were given at age 18-4. Edith's score on the Burch Comprehension Tests (119 out of a possible 128) far exceeds high school norms. She correctly defined 133 of the 150 words of the Inglis Vocabulary Test, exceeding the norm for college graduates. Her score of 11 on the Abbott-Trabue Exercises in Poetic Appreciation exceeded the norm for graduate students in English.

c) Character and personality tests. Edith took these tests at age 14-0. Her responses to the Plays, Games, and Amusements Blank indicated that her play interests resembled those of children of her own age, that she preferred non-social, rather quiet, and sedentary games, that her knowledge of plays and games was greater than that of average children of her age, and that her play preferences were noticeably masculine. (Gifted girls at ages above 10 generally make more masculine scores on this blank than do unselected girls.) Her scores on the Raubenheimer-Cady character tests indicated very desirable social attitudes, trustworthiness, emotional balance, and a tendency to understate rather than overstate. Her scores on the Wyman Interest Test indicated that she was somewhat more intellectual and social than average children, but rather below them in activity interests. On the Interest Blank her interests and abilities were noted as being markedly even. Her school subject preferences were for drawing and composition, and her occupational preference was for literary work.

III. *Development after 17.*

As has been mentioned, Edith graduated from high school at age 17-5. Since then she has attended university, making chiefly A and B grades. She joined a sorority during her freshman year and has lived at the sorority house most of the time. Her social adaptation in college has been exceptionally good. While she has not participated extensively in the university literary activities, several of her poems have appeared in the college literary magazines under pseudonyms.

ETHEL (b. 1913)

I. *Family standing.*

Little is known concerning Ethel's remote paternal ancestry. Her father was of Swiss extraction and was a hardware merchant until his death in 1921 at the age of 44 (the cause of his death is reported as nervous breakdown following an automobile accident). The father's father was a farmer. Ethel's mother has been a teacher of piano since the father's death. Ethel's maternal grandfather, several of whose ancestors and relatives are listed in Burke's *Landed Gentry,* was a physician. These maternal relatives were Irish; many of the men of the family were physicians. Ethel has no siblings.

II. *Development to age 17.*

1. Interests. A very marked dramatic tendency was observed in Ethel when she was quite small. Her play usually consisted in making up games and acting out stories. As a child she had a very pleasing soprano voice, and sang at entertainments, on radio programs, etc. Although she plays the piano well, she is not especially interested in instrumental music. Since the age of 11 or 12 she has

shown marked interest and ability in drawing and painting. She
has told stories and composed verses since before the age of 5.

2. Education. Ethel attended kindergarten for five months when
she was 3½ years old, but did not enter first grade until age 6½.
Her first three and a half years of school work were done in the
public schools of the Arizona city in which the family lived before
the father's death; her subsequent schooling has been in California.

3. School standing and progress. Ethel has skipped four half-
grades, and is now (1928–29) a senior in high school. While her
school grades have not all been A's and B's, they have always been
satisfactory, and the general quality of her school work has assisted
her in obtaining an unusual number of double promotions.

4. Friends and associates. As Ethel is an only child, most of her
associates have been schoolmates. As a child she never played well
in large groups, because other children thought her too "bossy," but
usually played with one or two friends near her own age. During
her high-school years she has shown a tendency to adolescent
"crushes."

5. Reading. Ethel learned to read at 5 years of age, with very
little instruction. She asked what the letters were, then what different words were, and was soon reading simple stories. She has
always read a great deal more than the average of children of her
age and has preferred reading matter of a superior quality. At 7 and
8 she read O. Henry's and Kipling's works, at 9 and 10 such books
as *Aesop's Fables*, *Gulliver's Travels*, *Pilgrim's Progress*, *Wizard of
Oz*, and Seton's *Woodland Tales*. Her subsequent reading has acquainted her with a large number of English and American classics.

6. Production and achievement. (See also II, 1.) Ethel's early
productions were not recorded. Most of those written since the age
of 9 or 10 have been lyric poems, though she has written a few
stories. Because she is interested in music and drawing as well as
in literary production, her creative efforts are divided between them.

7. Evidences of precocity. (See II, 1, 3, 5, 6. There is no other
specific record.)

8. Test data. Ethel's Binet IQ is equaled by not more than two
or three children in 10,000. Her achievement test scores are high and
fairly uniform. Her scores on literature tests indicate marked superiority of knowledge in this field. The social attitudes revealed by
the various tests of character and personality are quite normal.
These scores, in the words of the field worker who tested Ethel, "do
not in the least do justice to her feeling for 'the right word in the
right place'."

a) Intelligence and achievement tests. At age 8-10 Ethel's National Intelligence Test score was 107 (mental age equivalent 12-2),
placing her well within the best 1 per cent of her age group. Her
Stanford-Binet mental age was 15-1, making her IQ 171. Her subject
ages on the Stanford achievement battery at age 9-1 were: arithmetic
age, 11-8; reading age, 15-11; language usage, 16-4; spelling, 12-6;
general information, 13-10.

b) Literature tests. At age 14-2, soon after Ethel's completion of
the tenth grade, her score on the Burch Tests of Comprehension in
Literature was above high-school norms. At that time she defined

correctly 117 of the 150 words in the Inglis Vocabulary Test, which equals the mean of college juniors. Her score of 8 on the Abbott-Trabue Exercises in Poetic Appreciation equals the mean of college juniors and seniors.

c) Character and personality tests. At one month past her ninth birthday, Ethel's scores on the Plays, Games, and Amusements Blank indicated a play knowledge equal to that of average children of her age, play interests resembling those of somewhat older children, play knowledge and interests that were neither noticeably masculine nor feminine, and preference for noticeably non-social and quiet or sedentary games. The Raubenheimer-Cady battery of character tests taken at age 10 showed desirable social attitudes, a tendency to underestimate her knowledge, average trustworthiness of performance in the face of temptation not to follow the rules laid down, and average emotional stability. On the Wyman Interest Tests her interests were rated as decidedly intellectual, somewhat more social than average, and decidedly below average in activity lines. Her school subject preference at that time was for reading, and her occupational preference for acting and singing.

JEANETTE (b. 1911)

I. *Family standing.*

Most of Jeanette's male paternal relatives have been business and professional men. Her father, of French and English extraction, is manager of the state agency of a large insurance company. His father was an English squire who became a business man in Canada and later in the United States. Jeanette's mother holds two college degrees and was a teacher before her marriage. The maternal grandparents are of German ancestry. The mother's father is a noted Chicago pediatrist; the mother herself was a teacher of music before marriage. The mother's only brother is a noted obstetrician and gynecologist, and is on the teaching staff of one of the leading medical colleges of America.

Jeanette has two siblings, both brothers and younger than herself. The younger of the brothers is a member of the California group; the other tested at 125 IQ.

II. *Development to age 17.*

1. Interests. The development of any marked hobby or interest except those of reading and original literary composition has been practically precluded in Jeanette's case, as arthritis deformans since the age of 2½ years has permitted little physical activity. She made a medium-sized collection of dolls and a fairly large one of books before the age of 10. She was also interested in making up plays and directing her playmates in performing them.

2. Education. Because of Jeanette's physical disability she was taught at home until the age of 10, when she entered the fifth grade of a public school.

3. School standing and progress. Jeanette's school work has been of very superior quality, in spite of somewhat irregular attendance. She was a member of the high-school honor society, and a par-

ticipant in the literary activities of the school. Her grades have been practically all A's. She graduated from high school at age 17-0.

4. Friends and associates. While Jeanette has never been able to participate physically in group games and activities, she has always been a leader, and her remarkably sunny disposition has won her many friends. In high school her intimates were young people with literary interests.

5. Reading. A maid in the home taught Jeanette to read at the age of 5 years. Reading has since then been one of her chief pleasures. At 5 to 6 years she especially enjoyed the Perkins "Twin" series; from 7 to 8, St. Nicholas magazine and John Martin's books; at 9 to 10, Pyle's Robin Hood and King Arthur; at 11 to 12, the works of Scott and Dickens; from 15 to 16, the works of Whitman, O. Henry, Daudet, Kipling, Walpole, and Thackeray.

6. Production and achievement. Jeanette's first poem, written at 7½ years, was for a magazine contest and was published. Most of her early works were stories and plays. She wrote little from 11 to 13, but since then has written a great deal of lyric verse. Some of her works have been published in connection with magazine contests and in school papers and annuals.

7. Evidences of precocity. (See also II, 1, 3, 5, 6.) As a very small child Jeanette remembered rhymes easily and always filled in the rhyme with another appropriate word if she had forgotten the original. Her general mental superiority was early recognized by her parents and by others who came in contact with her.

8. Test data. The writer is convinced that Jeanette's test scores are not adequate measures of her ability, as in giving them no allowance was made for her physical weakness and tendency to fatigue. Her comparatively low scores on drill subjects are not surprising when it is realized that her previous home instruction had included very little drill in arithmetic and spelling. The literature tests given her several years later are seen to be inadequate as measures of a child of her age and ability. Jeanette's personality traits are characterized as normal by the ratings and by somewhat limited test data secured.

a) Intelligence and achievement tests. Jeanette's Stanford-Binet mental age at age 10-4 was 15-3; IQ 153. Her subject ages on the Stanford Achievement Test at age 11-0 were: arithmetic, 13-9; reading, 17-3; language usage, 17-11; and spelling, 14-4. She had attended school for only a few weeks when these tests were given her. The age equivalent of her General Information Test score was 16-3.

b) Literature tests. When Jeanette was just 16 years of age, her score on the Burch test was above high-school norms. At the same age she defined correctly a higher percentage of words on the Inglis Vocabulary Test than the average of college graduates (134 of 150 words). She made a perfect score (13) on the Abbott-Trabue Exercises in Poetic Appreciation, exceeding the norm for graduate students in English.

c) Character and personality tests. As indicated by the Plays, Games, and Amusements Blank at age 10-6, Jeanette's play knowledge was much greater than that of average children of the same age, her play interests resembled those of much older children, her knowledge of games and her play preferences were neither noticeably masculine nor feminine, and the plays and games for which she expressed preference were socially normal and rather sedentary. She was not able to be present when the Raubenheimer-Cady tests and the Wyman Interest Test were given. Her school subject preferences were for English and history, and her occupational preference was for writing.

RUTH (b. 1909)

I. *Family standing.*

Ruth's father, who was a merchant from age 18 to 70 (now retired), was born in France and is probably of Jewish ancestry. Little is known concerning his relatives, except that his father was a farmer near Paris. Ruth's mother is a very successful teacher of vocal music. She sang in concerts from the age of 12, in grand opera from age 17 to 27, and has taught vocal music since the age of 17. The maternal ancestry is German and probably Jewish. The mother's father was a merchant. Ruth has one sibling, a brother four years older than herself, who is a clothing salesman.

II. *Development to age 17.*

1. Interests. Ruth's most persistent interests have been in reading, music, active games, and athletics. She plays the piano well, and has given piano instruction. Science and mathematics appealed to her in high school. The desire to write appeared rather suddenly at about age 15, but waned within a year or two.

2. Education. Ruth entered the first grade of a California public school at age 6. She was graduated from high school at 17-4.

3. School standing and progress. School work has always been easy for Ruth. Her grades have been mostly A's and B's with an occasional C. She received two double promotions in elementary school. She held several elective school offices, most of them when in high school.

4. Friends and associates. Members of the family, and neighbor children and schoolmates of both sexes, usually a little older than Ruth, have been her chief associates. She has been an enthusiastic Girl Scout since the age of 12 and has many friends in that organization.

5. Reading. Although Ruth learned to read at 5 years by asking her mother the words in her picture books, she read very little before entering school. When she was in the elementary grades her reading, though voluminous, was rather indiscriminate, perhaps due to lack of literary standards in the home. Ruth's high-school courses in English seem to have raised the quality of her reading choices and to have given her a taste for literary classics and the better modern literature.

6. Production and achievement. (See also II, 1.) A collection of her lyrics, written at 15, was published privately and received some favorable reviews. "The Rainbow" (p. 411) is taken from this collection. Some book reviews have been published in the

National Girl Scout magazine. Ruth has also written one or two plays and has participated in high-school journalistic activities.

Ruth's athletic prowess is attested by the fact that she won a tennis championship in San Francisco at the age of 12.

7. Evidences of precocity. (No specific record beyond that given in II, 1, 3, 6.)

8. Test data. As in the case of Edith, most of the test scores for Ruth may be considered as minimal measures, since the tests used are known to be inadequate as measures of gifted children of her age. In the case of the literature tests she admitted not having taken sufficient time to be accurate; the tests were given just prior to her departure for a summer vacation in Hawaii and she hurried through them in order to meet other appointments. This procedure seems to have been responsible for errors which resulted in scores too low to represent her actual knowledge. Normality and balance are indicated by her scores on the battery of personality tests.

a) Intelligence and achievement tests. Ruth's Terman Group Test score at age 12-2 was 167 (mental age equivalent 17-6). At 13-0 her score on the National Intelligence Test was 157, and at 13-2 her Binet mental age was 18-6, giving her an uncorrected IQ of 141, and a corrected IQ of 152. She took the Thorndike Test at 17-2, making a score of 83, which is a little above the mean of Stanford entering freshmen. When she was in the high eighth grade (at age 13-4), her Stanford Achievement Test subject ages were: arithmetic, 18-6; reading, 17-1; language usage, 18-6; and spelling, 15-10. The age equivalent of her General Information score was above high-school norms.

b) Literature tests. All these tests were taken at age 18-3. Ruth's score (109) on the Burch Tests of Comprehension in Literature was above the high-school norms. She defined correctly 119 of the 150 words in the Inglis Vocabulary Test, equaling the mean of college juniors. Her score of 7 on the Abbott-Trabue Exercises in Poetic Appreciation equaled the mean of college sophomores.

c) Tests of character and personality. Ruth's age was 13-3 when she took these tests. Her play knowledge was much greater than that of average children of her age, her knowledge of games, and play preferences were noticeably masculine, and the plays and games for which she expressed preference were more active than average. Her social attitudes, as measured by the Raubenheimer-Cady character tests, were average for her age and sex. The same tests gave her an average score with respect to overstatement, trustworthiness, and emotional balance. Her Interest Test Scores indicated that she was decidedly intellectual, more social than average, and equal to average in activity interest. On the Interest Blank her interests and abilities were noted as markedly even, her interest in school subjects was general rather than specific, and her occupational preference was for music.

III. *Development after 17.*

After high-school graduation, Ruth entered university (age 17-6). She is doing her major work in bacteriology and is making a very satisfactory record. She might have carried on some further work in journalism had she received some encouragement, but as she was assigned routine work with which she was already familiar she soon discontinued it.

VERDA (b. 1911)

I. *Family standing.*

Business and professional men have been numerous in Verda's paternal ancestry. Her father, who is of Scotch-Irish extraction, has been a life insurance salesman since the age of 19 and has succeeded well in this field. He has considerable mechanical, musical, and literary ability, as well as unusual qualities of social leadership. Verda's mother is of English and French ancestry. She is descended in direct line from Governor Bradford of "Mayflower" fame, and is related through both English and French lines to many noted individuals. She is a prominent member of the College Women's Club of her city. Verda has no brothers or sisters.

II. *Development to age 17.*

1. Interests. Puppet theaters, a spool village, dramatizing games, more active types of play, decorative work, puzzles, and collections were more or less passing interests in Verda's childhood. She began making up rhymes and tunes before the age of 3, and soon thereafter began drawing pictures. These interests have been very persistent. Reading has also been a persistent interest.

2. Education. After some home instruction, Verda entered school in the high fourth grade at age 8-7, attending only the last two months of the school year. Her elementary schooling was obtained in a private school and her high-school work in a public high school.

3. School standing and progress. Throughout her school career almost all of Verda's marks have been A's. School work has been very easy for her. She has had no extra promotions since entering school, because her parents preferred not to jeopardize her social development. She was granted a scholarship at the private elementary school because of her superior ability and in high school was a member of the school honor society. (A more extended account of Verda's school record is given in chapter xiv, pp. 254 ff.)

4. Friends and associates. Most of Verda's early playmates were neighbor children. Since she entered school most of her friends outside the family have been schoolmates, though she has many friends among her parents' social group. Her intimate friends are a few classmates of superior ability.

5. Reading. Soon after she was 4 years old, Verda brought a story-book to her parents and showed them she could read. She had had no formal instruction in reading, but had been read to. From that time on she read a great deal, though much play with other children was also insisted upon by the parents. The exceptional quality of her reading at various ages is illustrated by the following examples: before 5 years, nursery rhymes, small story-books, *Something-to-do, Little Folks;* 5 to 6 years, *St. Nicholas, John Martin's Book, Boys' and Girls' Bookshelf;* 7 to 8 years, good poetry, Alcott's books, *Huckleberry Finn, Real America in Romance;* 9 to

10 years, *David Copperfield, Pickwick Papers, Hans Brinker, Laddie, As You Like It;* 11 years, *Journeys through Bookland, Biography of a Grizzly, Don Quixote, Gulliver's Travels, Little Citizens, Boys' Life of Mark Twain,* Franklin's *Autobiography, Idylls of the King;* 12 years, *Old Curiosity Shop,* Roosevelt's *Letters to His Children, Biography of Johnny Appleseed,* etc.

6. Production and achievement. Before the age of 2, Verda began making up and telling stories to her parents. Some of them were rather elaborate tales. The mother recorded a few of them. Her first poem was composed at 2 years, 9 months, when she was recovering from a double mastoid operation:

> "Mamma dear,
> Here's a spear.
> Don't you 'tick it
> In my ear!"

Other verses and many stories followed. Comparatively few of these early efforts have been preserved. She learned to print by 5 years, however, and "The Place I'd Like to Be" (p. 402) was printed without spaces between the words. By the age of 16 she had written many lyric poems, one or two novels, several skits, some plays, several short stories, and newspaper articles. At age 15 she collaborated with her father in writing an operetta of some length which was produced by a social club to which the parents belong. The father wrote part of the verses, while Verda wrote the lyrics and composed the music for the songs and choruses. She improvises on the piano a great deal and occasionally records her musical compositions. In 1926 she won a gold medal in a piano contest.

7. Evidences of precocity. (See also II, 1, 3, 5, 6.) Her parents noticed her phenomenally rapid mental development when she was a mere infant. Her first words were spoken at 7 months, and she was talking in sentences at 15 months. She hummed a tune at 17 months. At 22 months she could name all the primary colors. She counted to thirteen at 25 months, and to thirty at 44 months. At the latter age she could name all and print most of the letters of the alphabet, and had memorized a poem of some length. Additional data of this kind could be cited at length.

8. Test data. The phenomenal mental ability shown by Verda is equaled by only five or ten children in 100,000. Since she was a member of the Outside-Binet group, our test information concerning her school achievement is scanty. Other records indicate all-round achievement as superior as her intelligence. Her scores on the literature tests given her in 1927 are almost perfect. Ratings and other data supplement the test findings as to Verda's character and personality, and indicate that her social balance and attitudes in general are very desirable.

a) Intelligence and achievement tests. Our first test of Verda was at age 11-1, in a demonstration before a group of teachers. At that time her mental age was 18-1, her uncorrected IQ 163, and her corrected IQ 175. On this examination Verda passed all the tests given her except one (enclosed boxes, 16-year level). On this occasion the examiner omitted a few of the most time-consuming tests in order to finish within fifty minutes. At age 11-7, when given the complete examination, she passed every test, earning a mental age of 19-6, an IQ of 170, and a corrected IQ of 186. At age 16-4 her score on the Thorndike Test was 109, one of the highest scores on this test ever made by a woman. Unfortunately, no tests of school achievement were given her when she was tested at age 11-7.

b) Literature tests. These were given at age 15-8, when Verda had just finished the eleventh grade. Her score on the Burch Tests of Comprehension in Literature was 120 out of a possible 128. She defined correctly 142 of the 150 words in the Inglis Vocabulary Test, far exceeding the norm for college graduates. On the Abbott-Trabue Exercises in Poetic Appreciation her score was 12 out of a possible 13, which exceeds the norm for graduate students in English.

c) Tests of character and personality. At age 11-7 Verda's scores on the Plays, Games, and Amusements Blank indicated that her play knowledge was very much greater than that of average children of her age. Her knowledge of games and her expressed play preferences resembled those of average children of the same age, and were neither noticeably masculine nor feminine, and the plays and games for which she expressed preference were noticeably non-social, rather inactive, and intellectual. On the Interest Blank she indicated that her school subject preference was for dramatics, and her occupational preference for a career which would combine wifehood and motherhood with writing. Verda was not given the other tests of the character-personality battery.

III. *Development after 17.*

At age 17-0 Verda entered college. She is participating in student activities, athletics, and dramatics, besides writing a column and news articles for the daily newspaper.

WANDA (b. 1912)

I. *Family standing.*

Wanda's father is a business man and manufacturer. Many of his relatives have been merchants, teachers, and community leaders. Wanda's paternal ancestry is English-Scotch, her maternal ancestry Scotch-Irish. In the maternal line there have been many Southern plantation owners, statesmen, legislators, judges, orators, and political writers. The mother is a prominent club woman. Wanda has a maternal half-sister and a full brother, older than herself, and a sister younger, all of whom are members of the California gifted group.

II. *Development to age 17.*

1. Interests. Wanda's interests in reading and writing seem to have overshadowed her other hobbies. She early showed interest, and some ability, in music, and had piano lessons until her fourteenth year, when her mother found her reading a book while she practiced. She is said to play the piano well. Cooking has been a hobby with her for some years.

2. Education. During Wanda's third and fourth years she visited, rather than attended, the kindergarten of the private school near her

home. At age 5-2 she entered the first grade of the school. Except for four months in the public schools of a midwestern state, where the father was temporarily managing a large factory, all her elementary schooling was carried on in the private school mentioned. At age 12 she entered a public high school which emphasizes the domestic arts. This school was chosen by the parents to counterbalance her somewhat bookish tastes.

3. School standing and progress. In the elementary school Wanda was advanced as rapidly as her ability and social contacts seemed to warrant. She was ready for high-school entrance at 12 years, and for college at 16. She decided to wait a year before entering college, and is now (1928–29) doing secretarial work in connection with a women's club.

4. Friends and associates. Most of these have been school friends and members of the family. Her intimate friendships have been with a few girls somewhat older who are interested in writing.

5. Reading. Wanda seems to have learned to read at the age of three, without instruction, while visiting the private school. Her reading has always been of superior quality and voluminous in quantity. At all ages she has preferred books usually read by much older children, as is seen by the following examples: 3 to 6 years, "Peter Rabbit" series, "Mother Goose," school readers to the third; 7 to 8 years, *Little Women,* Altscheler's historical tales; 9 to 10 years, works of Ibsen, Dickens, Mary Roberts Rinehart, Oscar Wilde, Cooper, Scott, Shakespeare, the Bible; 11 to 12 years, Wiggin, Bacheller, Ian Hay, Kipling, Stevenson, Twain, Daskam, Barrie, O. Henry, etc. Beginning with the age of 13 or 14 she has read many French classics (in French). Her favorite serious reading has for years been history, especially the history of France.

6. Production and achievement. According to the report of her mother, the family noticed Wanda's literary tendencies before she was three years old. By the time she was 6 an excellent choice of words was observable in school compositions and in little stories written for her own amusement. None of her productions written before the age of 12 was preserved. Since then, to quote from one of her mother's letters, "She is a very happy child so long as her typewriter works and white paper does not fail."

Wanda has been especially interested in short-story writing, but has also written lyric verse, essays, plays, and reviews. Many of her stories fill over twenty typed pages each. A few selections have been published in school annuals.

7. Evidences of precocity. (See also II, 1, 3, 5, 6.) The parents noticed her unusual fund of knowledge and desire to learn when she was quite small.

8. Test data. These data indicate marked mental superiority, with a special bent toward literature. Wanda's traits of character and personality are rated as normal by the tests used.

a) Intelligence and achievement tests. On the National Intelligence Test at age 9-4 Wanda's score was 134, corresponding to an IQ of 166. Her Binet mental age at age 9-10 was 15-6, IQ 172. Another Binet at age 11-10 gave her a mental age of 18-6, uncorrected IQ 156, corrected IQ 171. When she was in the high seventh grade, at 10 years, 11 months, her reading age (Stanford Achievement Test) was 18-3; her arithmetic age, 17-6; nature study and science age, 17-1; history and literature age, 17-7; language usage age, 17-6; spelling age, 18-0.

b) Literature tests. Wanda scored 119 of a possible 128 points on the Burch Tests of Literary Comprehension at age 14-11. This score is far above high-school norms. At the same age she defined correctly 145 of the 150 words on the Inglis Vocabulary Test, a truly phenomenal performance. She scored 11 on the Abbott-Trabue Exercises in Poetic Appreciation, thus exceeding the norm for graduate students in English. These tests were inadequate to measure a child of Wanda's ability.

c) Tests of character and personality. All these tests were given a month before Wanda was 11 years of age. Her scores on the Plays, Games, and Amusements Blank rated her play knowledge as greater than that of average children of her age. Her play interests resembled those of children somewhat older; her knowledge of games and her play preferences were neither noticeably masculine nor feminine, and the games she preferred were socially normal and ordinarily active. Her social attitudes, as reflected in the Rauben-heimer-Cady battery of character tests, were average for her age and sex; she estimated her knowledge more accurately than the average child; she made a high score in trustworthiness; and in emotional balance she rated at the average of unselected children of her age and sex. On the Wyman Interest Test her interests were rated as somewhat more intellectual than average, and equal to the average in sociability and activity. Her school subject preference was for English, and her occupational preference for literary work.

The reader may find it interesting to compare in detail the above case summaries with the following summaries for ten eminent writers. As has been stated, summaries for the remaining eighteen eminent writers will be found in Volume II of this series.

ROBERT BROWNING (1812–89)

(Estimated IQ 165. Reliability coefficient of data, .60.)[1]

I. *Family standing.*

Both of Browning's parents were Dissenters. His father, who as a young man had wished to be an artist, was a clerk in the Bank of England. He is said to have "known Greek, Latin, French, Spanish, Italian, and Hebrew," and to have had a well-rounded education. He was a lover and collector of books, and encouraged his son's literary efforts. Browning's paternal grandfather rose from a clerkship in the Bank of England to be head of a department. The Brownings were of the English middle class. Browning's mother was born

[1] This reliability coefficient represents the statistical adequacy or inadequacy of the factual information on which the IQ estimate was based. Its derivation is explained in Volume II, pp. 73 ff.

in England of German parentage. One of her uncles by marriage is said to have been wealthy. Little else is known about her or her family.

II. *Development to age 17.*

1. Interests. Browning showed diverse interests from an early age. He was very imaginative and much interested in nature, music, art, and the drama. Drawing and painting (a drawing of his at 2 years and 3 months has been preserved), writing and producing plays (he directed a troupe of playmates), improvising on the organ, piano, and spinet, were all strong interests in childhood and adolescence. The revolutionary ideas of Shelley and Keats appealed to him when he was about 16. Although quite a student, he was fond of athletics and enjoyed fencing, boxing, riding, and dancing.

2. Education. After receiving some home teaching in reading, Browning was sent to a dame school before the age of 5, but was soon withdrawn. He attended preparatory school from the age of 8 or 9 to 15. The next year was spent in study with a French tutor. Because Browning was a Dissenter, Oxford and Cambridge were not open to him, and at 16 he therefore entered the newly established non-sectarian University of London. The new and unfinished nature of the institution appealed to him so little that he left it after about a year and pursued his studies alone from that time on.

3. School standing and progress. Browning is said to have made an excellent school record.

4. Friends and associates. Browning seems to have made few school friends, at least partly because of his self-confidence and his intolerance of school ways. His most intimate childhood friendships were with his sisters, both of whom had literary tastes. Some boy cousins who were interested in music were also close friends. As Browning grew older many of his friendships were with individuals interested in literature.

5. Reading. Browning read widely from his father's well-chosen library, which seems to have been more extensive than any school library to which he had access.

6. Production and achievement. (See also II, 1.) While Browning's earliest production seems to have been in the field of drawing, he is said to have composed verses before he could read and to have imitated Ossian's verses when he was only 5. At 12 he began a volume of poems which he later destroyed because he was not satisfied with his early work.

7. Evidences of precocity. (See also II, 1, 6.) It is related that Browning was taken out of dame school because he wrote and spelled so well as to excite the jealousy of the parents of his classmates. He read and wrote before he was 5.

III. *Development from 17 to 26.*

Most of this period Browning spent in travel on the continent, and in getting acquainted with other literati. "Pauline," written at 19, and "Paracelsus," written at 21, received some uncomplimentary reviews. "Sordello," begun when Browning was 25 or 26, was not published until later.

REFERENCE

Griffin, W. Hall, and Minchin, H. C., *The Life of Robert Browning*, Methuen, London, 1910.

WILLIAM CULLEN BRYANT (1794–1878)

(Estimated IQ 170. Reliability coefficient of data, .75)

I. *Family standing.*

Bryant numbered among his ancestors John Alden, Priscilla, and other New England pioneers. Of his father, who was a physician, it is said that he was well-read and fond of books, that he knew several languages, played the violin, and "delighted in poetry and music." The paternal grandfather was also a physician. Bryant's mother, who was brought up on the frontier and had little schooling, is said to have been "a woman of good sense, who promptly condemned deceit or injustice," and a splendid wife and mother.

II. *Development to age 17.*

1. Interests. Nature, reading, and poetry appealed to Bryant from early childhood. As a youth he became interested in science, and acquired a smattering of chemistry and botany from his father's books. Though he had some reputation as a scholar, he was fond of outdoor sports, and it is said that "he was one of the fastest runners in school, and was fairly good at ball games."

2. Education. Bryant was sent to school before he was 5, but did not attend regularly for the first year or two. At 12 he was sent to study Latin with an uncle who was a minister, and within eight months was able to meet sophomore requirements in that subject at Williams College. Two months were then spent in studying Greek with another minister, after which Bryant studied alone to meet other college entrance requirements. At 16 he matriculated at Williams College as a sophomore. After one year there he wished to attend Yale, but as the family could not afford to finance his studies any longer he returned home.

3. School standing and progress. (See also II, 2.) Bryant excelled in most of his studies, especially in spelling and geography, but did not care for such tasks as learning the catechism.

4. Friends and associates. Bryant's father was always his especial counselor. The boy's intimate friendships seem to have been with his parents and brothers and sisters rather than with school and other acquaintances.

5. Reading. From childhood Bryant read "greedily." When he found he could not go to Yale, he is said to have read all the books in his father's library which he had not already perused (including the medical works).

6. Production and achievement. Bryant early expressed a desire to be a poet and wrote verses about everyday happenings, letters in verse, etc. At 10 he had produced a rhymed version of the Book of Job which his relatives thought remarkable. Some lines about his school were published in a local newspaper when he was 10 or 11. His father was so well pleased by "The Embargo" (written at 13 years) that he had it printed, and sold several hundred copies of it.

A number of Bryant's lyrics written at 15 or 16 were published in the local newspaper. Even his early poems showed excellent versification and rhyme.

7. Evidences of precocity. (See also II, 1, 2, 5, 6.) According to his mother's report, Bryant walked alone at 12 months, and knew all the alphabet before he was 17 months old.

III. *Development from 17 to 26.*

During Bryant's period of indecision as to his vocation, following the year at Williams, he almost decided to enter the army. He became interested in law, however, and began reading it in the office of a lawyer in a town near by. He assisted the lawyer very creditably with his practice and his political activities, and had no difficulty in securing admission to the bar at 21. He started the practice of law in a small community, but soon accepted a partnership in a larger town. He purchased the entire business within a year or two, and was well established as a lawyer by the time he was 25 or 26. He married at 26 years.

The study and practice of law did not interfere with Bryant's literary tendencies. When he was 19 or 20, his father found by chance and submitted to the *North American Review* the first draft of "Thanatopsis" (written at 17) and some other poems. These created quite a sensation with the editors and the reading public. "To a Waterfowl" (written at 20 and published a little later) was very well received. Bryant was now assured of a public for his poems and for the critical prose which he began to write. His position in contemporary literature was fairly well established by his twenty-sixth year.

REFERENCE

Bigelow, John, *William Cullen Bryant*, Houghton Mifflin, Boston, 1890.

PHILIP M. FRENEAU (1752–1832)

(Estimated IQ 160. Reliability coefficient of data, .53.)

I. *Family standing.*

Freneau's family is related to many individuals who have been prominent in American history. His father, paternal uncles, and paternal grandfather traded with the West Indies and were rather wealthy. The paternal grandfather was a French Huguenot who came to the American colonies in the seventeenth century; the paternal grandmother was of Dutch and French ancestry. Little is known of Freneau's mother except that her name was Agnes Watson and that she was twenty years younger than her husband. She is said to have been well-educated and "a woman of rare good judgment."

II. *Development to age 17.*

1. Interests. It is reported that Freneau was very patriotic from early childhood. No interests are mentioned besides an interest in nature, zeal for his country, and a desire to write verse. He is said to have read French and Latin satirists in order that he might develop a satiristic style.

2. Education. Freneau's mother superintended his studies until he was 9 years old. He then began the study of Latin and Greek under a minister. From 14 to 16 he attended a Latin grammar school, and at 16 he entered Princeton, graduating in 1771.

3. School standing and progress. Freneau is said to have been a very superior scholar. During his first year at college his excellent work attracted the attention of the president of Princeton.

4. Friends and associates. No specific record was found, beyond members of the family, more distant relatives, and school friends. He seems to have had no friends of marked literary tastes.

5. Reading. No specific record, beyond mention of his great interest in reading from the time he learned to read.

6. Production and achievement. Although Freneau seems to have been interested in writing from an early age, no verses written before he was 16 have been preserved.

7. Evidences of precocity. (See II, 1, 2, 3. No further record.)

III. *Development from 17 to 26.*

At 17 Freneau wrote "The Pyramids of Egypt" and at 19 "The Rising Glory of America," dramatic dialogues in blank verse. These were published privately several years later. He started the study of divinity immediately after his graduation from Princeton at 20, because his father had wished him to become a minister, but soon found himself unfitted for that occupation or for teaching. He then considered the study of law, but found he did not care for it. During this period of indecision as to his vocation he went to Jamaica on a visit, and while there wrote some poems descriptive of nature and some love poems. As soon as he heard that the American Revolution had begun, he returned to the United States and engaged in the war as owner and captain of a privateer.

REFERENCE

Austin, Mary S., *Philip Freneau, the Poet of the Revolution,* A. Wessels Co., New York, 1908.

OLIVER WENDELL HOLMES (1809–94)

(Estimated IQ 155. Reliability coefficient of data, .53)

I. *Family standing.*

The Holmes family, several of whom held positions of trust and responsibility in their communities, first settled in New England early in the seventeenth century. Oliver Wendell Holmes' father was a minister. His mother, who was descended from the early Dutch colonists of New York, is said to have been cheerful, social, and sympathetic. Holmes is said to have resembled his mother more than his father, especially in temperament and disposition.

II. *Development to age 17.*

1. Interests. Reading, religion, and writing verses are the only special interests mentioned. In religion Holmes tended more toward his mother's Unitarianism than toward his father's Calvinism.

2. Education. Holmes was sent to dame school at an early age. From 10 to 15 years he attended a school in a neighboring town. At 15 he went to Andover to prepare for college.

3. School standing and progress. Holmes was a good scholar, but seldom led his classes.

4. Friends and associates. No intimate friends outside the family are mentioned prior to his attendance at Andover. His most lasting friendships began there and at Harvard, during college days.

5. Reading. Holmes read widely from his father's large library and from school libraries.

6. Production and achievement. During his school days Holmes wrote some stories and poems which were published in school papers and annuals. As an adult he was very critical of these early efforts, and would not allow them to be reprinted.

7. Evidences of precocity. No specific record. (See II, 2, 3, 5.)

III. *Development from 17 to 26.*

Holmes was graduated from Andover at 17 and entered Harvard the same year. After receiving his A.B. from Harvard in 1829, he took one year of legal work there. As he was not satisfied with law, he began the study of medicine. Following his work in it at Harvard, he studied medicine with famous surgeons in Paris during two post-graduate years. He was a conscientious college and medical student, always being in the upper one-fourth of his classes. During this period he wrote a great deal for school papers and some poems for more general publication. "Old Ironsides" is perhaps the best-known of his early works. Through his attendance at Harvard he became acquainted with many eminent individuals and many who were soon to become eminent, not a few of whom were members of his own class. He was acquainted, though not intimately, with Lowell. His medical study in France was followed by a summer trip to Italy, then he returned to the United States to practice medicine.

REFERENCE

Morse, John Torrey, *Life and Letters of Oliver Wendell Holmes,* Sampson, Law, Morton and Co., London, 1896.

JOHN KEATS (1795–1821)

(Estimated IQ 165. Reliability coefficient of data, .60.)

I. *Family standing.*

Little information is available concerning Keats's ancestry. His father was a hostler who married his employer's daughter and later managed the business. He left a fairly large estate when he died. Keats was then 8½ years of age. Keats's mother is said to have been pleasure-loving. She died in her late thirties from tuberculosis.

II. *Development to age 17.*

1. Interests. The only mention is of his interest in nature and literature (especially poetry).

2. Education. Keats attended the Clarke preparatory school at Enfield, near London. After his mother died, when he was 15, his guardian apprenticed him to a surgeon.

3. School standing and progress. Keats is said to have preferred battles with his schoolfellows to books during his early years in school. During adolescence he became much interested in acquiring knowledge, and studied and read incessantly. He received many prizes and medals, both for regular school work and for literary productions.

4. Friends and associates. Keats was a leader in school and had many friends. He and his brothers were very fond of each other. His friendship with Cowden Clarke, son of his schoolmaster, who first discovered and encouraged his writing, began when he was in school at Enfield.

5. Reading. Keats read widely and voluminously while in school and during his apprenticeship to the surgeon (he still had access to the Clarke school library). He read Latin with considerable facility.

6. Production and achievement. (See also II, 3.) Keats wrote verse in childhood, but kept most of it hidden until his friendship with Cowden Clarke. He did some verse writing during his apprenticeship.

7. Evidences of precocity. (See also II, 3 and 5.) It is said that Keats used rhyme a great deal as a small child. His translation of the *Aeneid* into prose during his fifteenth and sixteenth years is cited as an example of his energy and ambition.

III. *Development from 17 to 26.*

Keats was interested in surgery, completed his training, passed his medical examination, and received an appointment at Guy's Hospital, London. He soon found, however, that he was more interested in writing than in medicine, so left the hospital. He said that he received his greatest impulse toward a literary career from the reading of Chapman's *Homer,* which Cowden Clarke brought to him when he was still a medical student. The sonnet, "On First Looking into Chapman's *Homer,*" was written the next day. He became acquainted with Leigh Hunt, at whose home he lived part of the time, and with other literati in and near London, and spent a great deal of time at writing. His first published volume (1817) was coldly received and harshly reviewed, especially by the *Edinburgh Review.* Keats nevertheless continued his work on "Endymion," which was already under way. He also wrote some dramatic reviews, which are almost his only prose works. He nursed his brother, Thomas, who was ill with tuberculosis, until the latter's death. Keats finally contracted the disease himself, and died in Italy (whither he had gone for his health) at the age of almost 26.

REFERENCES

Colvin, Sidney, *John Keats,* Scribners, New York, 1917. Hancock, Albert E., *John Keats,* Houghton Mifflin, Boston, 1908. Lowell, Amy, *John Keats,* Houghton Mifflin, Boston, 1925.

JAMES RUSSELL LOWELL (1819–91)
(Estimated IQ 165. Reliability coefficient of data, .60)

I. *Family standing.*

The Lowells were early New England settlers of considerable standing. James Russell Lowell's father was a college graduate, a minister, and something of a physician (he had studied medicine abroad when a young man). Lowell's mother was of Scotch ancestry, and is said to have possessed rare beauty of person and of temperament. Her son's love for the romantic, and his imaginative nature, are said to have been inherited from her more than from the father. Both parents were lovers of literature. The home library and collections of rare books were large for the time, and even for the community in which they lived (Cambridge).

II. *Development to age 17.*

1. Interests. Lowell was always very sensitive to nature. He was fond of books and of reading, and had a taste for rare books and beautifully printed volumes. He started collecting rare books at 15 years.

2. Education. As a young child Lowell attended dame school. Later, when preparing for college entrance, he attended a boarding school as a day pupil. He entered Harvard at 15 years.

3. School standing and progress. Languages were especially easy for Lowell, and he received good marks in all his subjects.

4. Friends and associates. While Lowell had many school friends, he had few intimates until college days, when he became acquainted with other young people of intellectual tastes.

5. Reading. Reading was one of his chief pleasures from early boyhood. Spenser and other English poets he particularly appreciated.

6. Production and achievement. Although making up rhymes was one of Lowell's favorite childhood occupations, few of his early productions have been preserved. When in college he used verse frequently in his letters and wrote for college papers and annuals. He wished to follow literature as a vocation, but his family wanted him to be a lawyer since he did not care for the ministry.

7. Evidences of precocity. (See also II, 1, 2, 3, 5, 6.) Lowell is said to have been an excellent student of Latin before the age of 10.

III. *Development from 17 to 26.*

Lowell was chosen to write the class poem for his college class. He became more interested in this task than in such formalities as attending chapel, and had to spend the last few weeks of his senior year with a tutor instead of at Harvard. After considerable vacillation he studied law and was admitted to the bar, but did not practice long, as he found himself more and more interested in writing. He was a member of a circle of young people interested in writing, among whom was Maria White, who became Mrs. Lowell in 1844. A few months before the latter event Lowell and a friend started a literary magazine which published only a few issues. The failure was at least partly due to Lowell's trouble with his eyes, which necessitated his absence from Boston when the magazine was just getting well started.

REFERENCE

Scudder, Horace E., *James Russell Lowell*, Houghton Mifflin, Boston, 1901.

EDGAR ALLAN POE (1809–49)

(Estimated IQ 165. Reliability coefficient of data, .60)

I. *Family standing.*

Poe's father was a lawyer who left the profession to become a none too successful actor. The paternal grandfather, General Poe, was a Revolutionary patriot. Poe's mother was descended from a line of actors. She and her mother were successful singers and actresses who, nevertheless, because of the extreme poverty of the era, were able to earn very little. Poe's father died when the boy was two years old, and his mother a few months later. Poe was reared by the Allans, a childless couple, who wished to give the boy every advantage but who seem to have lacked understanding of his temperament.

II. *Development to age 17.*

1. Interests. Writing plays and producing them with the help of playmates was a strong boyhood interest. Poe was an officer in a boys' military troupe and enjoyed its activities. He was something of an athlete and is said to have been an accomplished swimmer. Early in his 'teens he became fond of gambling and strong drink.

2. Education. Poe first attended a private school at Richmond, Virginia, where his foster-father was in business. When the latter took his family to England for a few years, Poe attended school there. He spent a year after the return from England in preparing for admission to the University of Virginia, which he entered at the age of 17.

3. School standing and progress. "All Poe's schoolmasters acknowledge him very clever." He was usually first or second in his class. While attending preparatory school he was selected as class poet.

4. Friends and associates. The fact that Poe's ancestors had been actors seems to have been something of a social handicap to him, for he had to seek playmates among younger boys and apparently had no intimate friends.

5. Reading. No evidence beyond a statement that Poe always loved reading and read widely.

6. Production and achievement. (See also II, 3.) Poe wrote some verses before the age of 12. These unfortunately were not preserved.

7. Evidences of precocity. (See also II, 1, 3, 6.) "At 6 years Poe could read, draw, and dance, and declaimed well." Later, he quoted Latin verse with ease.

III. *Development from 17 to 26.*

Poe attended the University of Virginia for only one year, as he did not enjoy some of the features of the school. He then ran away and enlisted in the army under an assumed name, but was located by Mr. Allan and discharged by substitute when he was 20. He received an appointment to West Point when he was past 21, but was very shy and reserved there, did not study a great deal, and was finally dismissed for neglect of duties. Mr. Allan supported Poe for some time, though they were not on good terms, but did not mention him in his will. (He died when Poe was 24.) From that time on Poe made his living by writing both prose and verse, which he had been publishing since the age of 18 ("Tamerlane," and other poems, published at 18; second book of verse, published at 20; third book, published at 21 or 22). By the time he was 26 he was writing the prose tales which are now considered to be among his best works, had written some critical reviews, and had had some editorial experience.

REFERENCE

Woodberry, George E., *Life of Edgar Allan Poe,* Houghton Mifflin, Boston, 1909.

PERCY BYSSHE SHELLEY (1792–1822)

(Estimated IQ 165. Reliability coefficent of data, .75)

I. *Family standing.*

The Shelley's were an ancient family in Sussex. One of them came over with William the Conqueror, several were crusaders of note, and many had held positions of trust and honor under the British kings. Shelley's paternal grandfather is said to have been wealthy and avaricious. His son, Shelley's father, was an Oxford man who had had the advantage of considerable European travel. He has been characterized as "a somewhat self-important English country gentleman . . . . who was never able to understand his son." Shelley's mother, who was the daughter of a squire, was noted for her beauty. She seems to have had considerable "good sense," though she was somewhat narrowminded and had a violent temper. Though she was not especially literary in her tastes, she is said to have been an excellent letter-writer. Shelley had four sisters, beauties like their mother, and one brother, all of whom were younger than he.

II. *Development to age 17.*

1. Interests. Science, especially as connected with magic and mystery, was one of Shelley's chief boyhood interests. He bought a solar microscope for his own use, and demonstrated it, as well as his knowledge of chemistry and electricity, to his brother and sisters whenever he was home for a holiday. Reading and dramatics were also major interests. At school he made up plays and acted them with the help of a few friends before his younger schoolfellows.

2. Education. At 6 years Shelley was sent daily to a clergyman's house to learn Latin. He was later sent to Sion House, a school kept by Dr. Greenlaw at Brentford, near London. At 14 or 15 he was sent to Eton.

3. School standing and progress. Shelley seemed to learn almost without study. His marks were good, for the most part, though he did poorly in mathematics, which he did not like, and in dancing, in which his poor motor co-ordination was a handicap. It is said that his teacher at Sion House was prejudiced against him because he refused to laugh at the teacher's jests. Shelley was twice expelled from Eton, for minor offenses, and promptly reinstated at the insistence of his father.

4. Friends and associates. Shelley was badly hazed, both at Sion House and at Eton. He usually submitted to it, but occasionally turned on his tormentors with fury, thus earning the nickname "mad Shelley." Most of his friends at Sion House were younger boys. At Eton he became acquainted with Hogg, a lifelong friend. Some of his Eton friends had literary leanings.

5. Reading. Shelley read voluminously from early childhood. He delighted in tales of magic and mystery and in Richardson's novels, which he obtained through a circulating library. When at Eton he became interested in reading philosophy and similar serious subjects.

6. Production and achievement. Shelley wrote verses, plays, and stories as a child, for the amusement of his brother and sisters, his school friends, and himself, but did not preserve them. One play, written in collaboration with his sister Helen, was sent to an actor, whose comment that he did not think it suitable for acting seems to have discouraged the young playwrights. Shelley made Latin verse with ease as a schoolboy. He wanted to write from an early age, though his surroundings and the family traditions were not at all literary.

7. Evidences of precocity. (See also II, 1, 3, 5, 6.) Shelley had a very retentive memory. It is said that as a little child he repeated word for word, after hearing them once, Gray's lines on "A Cat and a Goldfish." Even as a child he repeated long Latin quotations with ease, and committed to memory Greek and Latin passages almost without effort. Before he could write he told long stories to his brother and sisters.

III. *Development from 17 to 26.*

At 18 Shelley moved from Eton to Oxford, where his school surroundings were much more pleasant, and where he had an opportunity to read much more widely. Plato, Plutarch, and Septuagint, Euripides, and other "solid" works were read in the original during this year. Shelley read French, Italian, Spanish, Latin, and Greek with almost as much facility as English, and often spent sixteen hours a day in reading. With his characteristic energy he also wrote a great deal. The first four cantos of "The Wandering Jew" were refused by a publisher, but "Zastrossi," a mystery tale without much plot, and a volume of verse, were published during his eighteenth year. The poems received such unfavorable reviews that Shelley suppressed their distribution by buying up practically all the copies, none of which are now available. Toward the end of his first year at Oxford he had trouble with his publishers, and with his father (over financial matters). At this time, too, he definitely broke with a cousin, Harriet Grove, with whom he had been in love for years and whom he had hoped to marry. However, he continued writing a great deal, publishing sometimes under a pseudonym, sometimes as a collaborator. "St. Irvyne," a melodramatic romance, some poems, which included "Queen Mab," perhaps the best of his early works, and some pamphlets were published during his nineteenth year. Reviewers criticized his work severely and called him a corrupter of youth. One of the pamphlets, *On the Necessity of Atheism,* which was published anonymously as an appeal for tolerance, aroused the ire of the college authorities, and Shelley was peremptorily dismissed from college. His friend Hogg suffered the same fate when Hogg tried to defend him. It seems probable that the series of shocks he had suffered led to his close friendship with Harriet Westbrook and his elopement with her in 1812. They were happy for a time, but separated in 1814. In 1815 Shelley eloped to France with Mary Godwin, daughter of his publisher. His first long poem, "Alastor," seems to have been inspired by his happiness with her. They travelled through France to Italy, where Shelley became acquainted with Byron and Keats. He wrote a great deal during this period, in spite of the grief occasioned by the suicide of Harriet Westbrook and the death of the three children that had been born to him and Mary Godwin. His works were well received on the Continent, where there was less prejudice against his atheism than in England.

REFERENCES

Brock, A. Clutton, *Shelley, the Man and the Poet,* London, 1909. Dowden, Edward, *Life of Shelley,* London, 1886. Hogg, Thomas Jefferson, *Life of Shelley,* London, 1858.

HENRY DAVID THOREAU (1817–64)

(Estimated IQ 155. Reliability coefficient of data, .53)

I. *Family standing.*

Thoreau's paternal ancestors, who were of French extraction, came to America in the eighteenth century from the island of Jersey. Many of the ancestors in this country were farmers and ministers. Thoreau's father was a pencil manufacturer. Information concerning his mother is confined to statements that she was a brilliant woman and very talkative. Her father was a minister and later a lawyer. Thoreau had two sisters and one brother, all of whom were school teachers.

II. *Development to age 17.*

1. Interests. Only nature and reading are mentioned. Thoreau had considerable mechanical ingenuity and assisted his father in manufacturing pencils.

2. Education. Thoreau studied at the village school, then at the academy at Concord. He entered Harvard at 16 years.

3. School standing and progress. He was an apt scholar and always stood high in his classes.

4. Friends and associates. His sisters and brother, especially the latter, were his closest friends. He had many college friends, but few intimates.

5. Reading. Thoreau read widely, both at school and at home. (The home library was rather large.)

6. Production and achievement. We have no records to indicate that Thoreau was especially interested in writing during his boyhood, although a few notes and essays which have been preserved show some promise of the style and ability which appeared in his later work.

7. Evidences of precocity. (See II, 2, 3, 5.) Several incidents reported by friends of the family indicate that his courage and his ability to conceal his feelings developed early.

III. *Development from 17 to 26.*

Following his graduation from Harvard at 20, Thoreau taught school successfully for one or two terms, but found he did not enjoy teaching. He became interested in the Transcendental movement, and contributed both prose and verse to its organ, *The Dial.* He drew much of the material for the essays he wrote during this period from the journal he began to keep at 18 years.

REFERENCE

Sanborn, Franklin D., *Henry D. Thoreau,* Houghton Mifflin, Boston, 1888.

JOHN GREENLEAF WHITTIER (1807–92)

(Estimated IQ 155. Reliability coefficient of data, .43)

I. *Family standing.*

Whittier's paternal ancestry was perhaps French Huguenot. His immediate paternal ancestors were farmers. The more remote ones had come to America with the early colonists. His maternal ancestors were Quakers. His mother was 21 years younger than his father, and seems to have understood the boy better. The family is well described in "Snow Bound."

II. *Development to age 17.*

1. Interests. Reading, nature, and farming are mentioned. He seems to have enjoyed farming, even though many of its tasks were very difficult for his never robust health.

2. Education. Whittier learned to read at home, then attended school somewhat irregularly for several years.

3. School standing and progress. No record.

4. Friends and associates. No specific record beyond members of the family, neighbors, and schoolmates.

5. Reading. Whittier gained an extraordinary familiarity with the few books (mostly classics) in the home library by reading and re-reading them. Reading and hearing the poems of Burns when he was 14 is said to have kindled his interest in verse writing.

6. Production and achievement. Whittier's earliest poems have not been preserved. The influence of Burns is said to have been noticeable in some of them. Whittier wrote secretly until he was 19; none of his verses had been discovered or published until then.

7. Evidences of precocity. (See also II, 5, 6.) His fund of information was considered remarkable in view of his limited schooling and opportunities.

III. *Development from 17 to 26.*

Some of Whittier's verses published when he was 19 were so well received that he was encouraged to obtain further training and to continue writing. He saved his money for a year, attended the neighboring academy the next year, taught for a term, then returned for another year at the academy. By the time he was 23 or 24 about a hundred of his poems which had been published in local newspapers had gained for him considerable reputation throughout New England. He acted as editor for two or three newspapers and a magazine or two for a few months each during the two or three years which followed. His first book, *Legends of New England,* was published when he was 24. He began writing essays in literary criticism during his twenty-fifth year. He had become something of a politician and was interested in temperance and abolition, but had not yet allied himself with the latter cause. He found it impossible to live in the city for a long period of time, as his health was much poorer there than when he was on the farm.

REFERENCE

Carpenter, George Rice, *John Greenleaf Whittier,* Houghton Mifflin, Boston, 1903.

CHAPTER XXVII

THE PREDICTION OF LITERARY ACHIEVEMENT

VALUE OF A RATING SCALE FOR LITERARY MERIT

One would hardly be justified in attempting to devise methods for the prediction of adult literary accomplishment. Too many factors other than natural ability go to determine the amount and merit of achievement. Interest, zeal, health, opportunity, encouragement, chance of reward, and the presence or absence of competing abilities and interests are only a few of these. To ask or expect accurate prediction would obviously be absurd.

If equal influences were brought to bear upon all children to get them to write to the very limit of their ability, and if we could be sure that ability in childhood and in adult life were perfectly correlated, then prediction would be possible. Neither of these presuppositions can be realized. We cannot in any present-day society fully equalize opportunity and encouragement for all, and we have yet no positive proof that a child's literary ability retains the same relative degree of superiority or inferiority from childhood to full maturity. It is true that all we know about mental growth changes favors the hypothesis that in the vast majority of cases mental abilities are not subject to rapid deterioration or saltatory improvement. So far as general intelligence is concerned, "once gifted, always gifted" is the rule, though a rule that doubtless has exceptions.

It is reasonable to believe that this rule holds for special abilities as well as for general intelligence. At any rate the presumption lies sufficiently in this direction to warrant us in paying serious attention to the merit of a child's literary productions. The child who has written supremely well in comparison with average children will probably have the ability to write supremely well as an adult, whether he actually does so or not. For educational purposes it therefore becomes very important to be able to rate the merit of superior juvenilia.

The tentative scale here offered for this purpose has numerous shortcomings. It would be possible to make a better collection of samples for use in standardization. The collection used was especially weak in the number and variety of prose writings. The steps of merit as defined in the instructions are more or less vague. The tentative scale would have been both more accurate and more valid if the judges had been more numerous and if they had been more expert critics of literature than they were. The two latter conditions, unfortunately, are not easy to fulfill. Notwithstanding its recognized faults, it is believed that the scale will be in some degree useful. How useful will depend largely on the manner in which it is applied, and in this connection it must be particularly emphasized that a sample whose merit is to be estimated should be rated by at least three or four judges.

No number of judges, however, can rid us of the essentially conventional nature of art standards. What true excellence is we do not know. The criterion of excellence fluctuates from period to period with the change of ideals, social forms, and cultural background. This must be freely admitted. At the same time an unbiased examination of the literary juvenilia of a Milton or a Pope or a Goethe will convince anyone that great superiority of performance in one age or country can be detected by standards which are usable also in an age or country far removed. The fluctuation of standards makes our comparisons less accurate, but it does not make them valueless.

What the Use of the Tentative Scale Has Shown

The use of the tentative scale with the gifted subjects has yielded results of considerable interest. We have found, for example, that the juvenilia of eminent authors are usually very superior to the productions of average children, but that the degree of superiority for a given author varies greatly from one sample of his work to another. There is some evidence that the most eminent writers produced on the whole better juvenilia than the less eminent, though satisfactory proof of this is lacking. The most interesting disclosure is that some of the gifted California subjects have, in the opinion of the judges who made the ratings, shown about as much literary promise as any of the twenty-eight eminent authors had shown at corresponding age. This is brought out with rather startling effect in Figure 9.

It is possible, of course, that another set of judges selected on a different basis would have given different results; for example, judges of more extreme literary sophistication. That the relative merits would be entirely overturned by another set of judges is hard to believe. There can be no reasonable doubt of the rare merit, age of writer considered, of such juvenilia as Jeanette's "Pattern," Ruth's "The Rainbow," or Macaulay's "To the Memory of William Pitt." Verda's "The Mountains," written at age 10, may not be exactly as meritorious as Wordsworth's "An Evening Walk," written at 17; Wanda's "Christmas" and Beatrice's "A Glove," both written at 13, may or may not be better than Byron's "Death of a Young Lady," written at 14, or Pope's "Ode to Solitude," written at 12 and included in his collected works. That these productions are of a grade of excellence extraordinarily rare in children of their age is, however, indisputable. Not one child in ten thousand or perhaps a hundred thousand has ever equaled at age five the achievement of Verda in her poem "The Place I'd Like to Be."

Even so, prophecy regarding future accomplishment would be unsafe. Any one of a hundred things might conceivably prevent the fruition of literary ability in any one of these subjects. Nothing has been demonstrated beyond the superiority of achievement to date.

In examining Figure 9 one is struck by the lack of smoothly progressive improvement from age to age. This is partly a matter of chance, for chance has entered both in the preservation of juvenilia and in the present sampling of those preserved. It remains true, however, that a child writer may attain a grade of excellence at 10 or 12 years which is not reached again until several years later. Beatrice at every age up to 15 has written poems (not here reproduced) far inferior to her "My Prayer," composed at age 7. Similar if less extreme observations could be made of a majority of the writers studied.

A Search for Possible Differentiating Factors

It was hoped that an examination of all available facts regarding the environment, early interests, and mental development of the total group of child writers, thirty-five in all, would disclose environmental circumstances or youthful traits common to all or nearly all of the group and distinguishing them from children of equally high IQ who have given less evidence of possessing unusual literary ability. This hope, unfortunately, was not realized. Whether we compare eminent authors with other eminent individuals, or gifted child writers with others of the Stanford gifted group, no clearly differentiating characters are found in the data at hand.

The average IQ of the seven California juvenile writers is 165, or higher than that of the gifted group as a whole, but in all probability no higher than would be found for the half-dozen or so who are most gifted in science or mathematics. The average estimated childhood IQ of the eminent authors is about the same as for our California subjects, but in Dr. Cox's group of three hundred subjects, philosophers averaged 170, revolutionary statesmen 160, and scientists 155. It is clear, therefore, that gifted child writers can not be distinguished from other gifted children on the basis of either estimated or tested IQ.

Such factors as family standing, income, and environment serve to differentiate in some degree child writers from children of the general school population, but only as gifted children in general are differentiated from unselected children. In the majority of cases the families have been in only fairly comfortable circumstances, although a few have had independent incomes of some size (e.g., Byron and Pope), and a few others have had the handicap of at least mild poverty (e.g., Burns and Whittier). The neighborhoods in which these children were brought up may likewise be characterized as superior, as were those of the entire group of gifted children studied by Dr. Terman. The same was true, in general, with those of the eminent men and women studied by Dr. Cox for whom the pertinent information could be secured. The intelligence of the parents, as judged by the fathers' occupation and other data available, resembles that of parents of other highly gifted children, but does not offer a means of distinguishing child writers.

School progress furnishes no better criterion of outstanding literary ability than the other items that have been mentioned. Several of the children have been very much accelerated in school, but this does not distinguish them from other highly gifted individuals. Their greater interest in literature and original composition was often evidenced by the winning of medals, prizes, and other distinctions of the sort, but gifted children of far less literary accomplishment often win similar distinctions.

Dr. Terman's data indicate that a strong liking for reading is rather characteristic of gifted children as a group. Dr. Cox's study corroborates this finding. This trait is especially noticeable in the children here studied, but not to any diagnostic extent, for while they surpass the general run of gifted children in this respect, we have no evidence that they greatly surpass other children as highly selected for general mental ability.

A marked tendency to dramatic play at an early age characterizes many of these children. The California gifted girls who were chosen as exceptional child writers cared little for play with dolls, except that they used dolls as puppets in plays which they composed. However, our cases are two few to be conclusive.

Gifted children in general have been found to have more hobbies than unselected children, but in this child writers are hardly different from other gifted children. There are indications, however, that their hobbies are apt to be related to their interests and abilities along literary lines. Macaulay began to acquire a library of his own at six years; Scott in childhood made a collection of ballads; Lowell started collecting rare books at 15; Jeanette made a fairly large collection of books before the age of 10; Beatrice's library consisted of about three thousand volumes when she was 15 years of age; at 16 Franklin saved money by boarding himself in order that he might buy books. Other examples could be given.

Special talents along other than literary lines do not serve to separate the children here studied from other gifted children. Browning played the organ, piano, and spinet, and improvised on them; Verda shows marked ability in original musical composition; Browning and Thackeray were caricaturists from an early age; Beatrice has since childhood shown talent in drawing. Others in the group have shown no unusual ability along any of these lines.

Though none of the immediate relatives of the child writers has achieved eminence in letters, we can draw no conclusion from our data as to whether there is or is not a hereditary factor involved. How many are the children who wrote exceptionally well as juveniles but whose writings were lost or whose interests waned, we cannot say. The clues to this which we are able to find in the study of Dr. Cox (as in the case of Robert Boyle, Humphry Davy, Hugh Miller, and others) indicate that early interest in letters is by no means certain to be followed by eminent achievement in that field. The relationship between literary ability in childhood and later distinction in literature is not shown by our data, though one may well believe that some relationship exists. We have at present no certain criteria by which to select child writers who will achieve eminence in literature, nor can we on the basis of later achievement select with certainty individuals whose juvenilia will show exceptional merit.

In the course of the present study, extensive information was secured from each of the seven California subjects regarding method of writing, early play, associates, reading preferences, literary comprehension, and poetic appreciation. These data were supplementary to the hundred or more pages of material on heredity, development, school progress, etc., already available for each child as a member of the gifted group. The biographical material for the eminent authors was also searched for information on these points. This type of data proved to be of so little value as an indication of literary ability or as a means of identifying gifted child writers that a summary of the material does not seem worth while.

An attempt was made by non-experimental methods to secure information regarding imagery types and imaginative trends, but was abandoned because of lack of opportunity to carry out the work under laboratory conditions. Investigation along this line might prove very fruitful, especially if a comparative study could be made of two fairly large groups of children of equal IQ but differing notably in ability to write. A detailed comparison of the profiles of two such groups in many kinds of standardized tests would also be extremely interesting. One would especially like to know what the relative standing of two such groups would be in general vocabulary, certain specialized vocabularies, diction and language usage, sense of rhythm, verbal memory, reading ability, spelling ability, arithmetical ability, appreciation of humor, linguistic invention, various fields of information, mental masculinity or femininity, introversion-extraversion, and trends of interests, preferences, and aversions. Dr. Strong has secured data by the use of his Occupational Interest Test which point clearly to the desirability of further trial of this type of test in the differentiation of potentially gifted writers.

At present our only criterion of exceptional literary ability in childhood is the production of superior juvenilia. Other elements, such as early tendency to dramatic play, marked interest in reading, etc., may have some bearing on the problem, but the data we have been able to secure on these points offer no basis for differentiation or prediction. We must turn to actual accomplishment in writing. It should again be emphasized, however, that demonstrably superior literary accomplishment in childhood does not in itself offer a satisfactory basis for predicting adult literary achievement. Of this no better proof could be offered than the fact that whereas the twenty-eight eminent writers whose superior juvenilia were studied were all men, there is not a single boy among the seven California children who have shown most literary promise. Three boys were included in the fourteen cases tentatively selected for study, but their best productions were unquestionably inferior in merit to those of all the girls. We have no certain explanation of this rather astonishing finding. It hardly seems reasonable to suppose that the subjective criteria of merit which our judges had in mind tended to favor the writings of girls over those of boys, although it is conceivable that such may have been the case. It is more likely that girls of today who have superior literary ability are much more likely to give evidence of it through preoccupation with writing than are boys, who have so many other interesting things to do. Until recently the reverse was almost certainly the case. For all we know there may be several boys in the California gifted group who have as much natural literary ability as the best endowed of the seven girls. The fact that a child has not produced superior juvenilia is by no means proof that he could not have done so or that he will not later write brilliantly. On the other hand, the production of superior juvenilia, although not a guaranty of adult literary achievement, is at least suggestive of promise. The next approach to the problem should be by methods of more analytical and experimental nature than the circumstances of the present study permitted.

REFERENCES

1. Abbott, Allan, and Trabue, M. R., "A Measure of Ability to Judge Poetry," *Teachers College Record,* March, 1921, pp. 101–126.
This is the first published description of the Abbott-Trabue *Exercises in Poetic Appreciation.* The reliabilities of the tests when used with groups of different maturity and training are given in some detail.
2. Binet, Alfred, "M. François de Curel," *L'Année Psychologique,* Vol. 1, 1894, pp. 119–173.
The most comprehensive of Binet's early studies of the creative imagination of dramatic authors.
3. Binet, Alfred, "La Création Littéraire—Portrait Psychologique de M. Paul Hervieu," *L'Année Psychologique,* Vol. 10, 1904, pp. 1–62.
Probably the most objective of Binet's studies of creative ability in literature.
4. Binet, Alfred, and Passy, Jacques, "Études de Psychologie sur les Auteurs Dramatiques," *L'Année Psychologique,* Vol. 1, 1894, pp. 60–118.
The authors here discussed are Sardou, Dumas fils, Daudet, Pailleron, Meilhac, MM. de Goncourt, and Coppée, who were interviewed in their homes or offices by Binet and Passy, as to their heredity, life history, habits of work, and especially as to their opinions concerning the imagination.
5. Burch, Mary C., "Determination of a Content of the Course in Literature of a Suitable Difficulty for Junior and Senior High School Students," Ph.D. Thesis, Stanford University, 1926. 156 pp. (Unpublished.)
By sampling and testing the author determined the difficulty of a large number of selections commonly taught in high-school literature classes. The reliability of her test battery is given as .95. Her findings indicate that in the present teaching of literature in the junior and senior high school the material presented is beyond the comprehension of about 75 per cent of the class. The *Tests of Comprehension in Literature* (now published by Stanford University Press) developed by Dr. Burch in connection with this study were given to the California gifted children who evidenced exceptional ability as child writers.
6. "Certain Literary Debutantes," *Scribners,* February, 1921, pp. 249–50.
This article maintains that many children have as much literary ability as Daisy Ashford and Opal Whitley, and that more culture in the home would make for better literary work in high school and college among children in general.
7. Cox, Catharine M., *The Early Mental Development of Three Hundred Geniuses, Genetic Studies of Genius,* Volume II, Stanford University Press, 1926. 842 pages.
A valuable historiometric study of the early mental development of 300 European and American men of eminence who were born between 1450 and 1850. IQ estimates were made on the basis of the material available in each case. The study indicates that these men of eminence were all above the average in ability as children.
8. Currie, Mary M., "Enfants Trouvés of Literature," *Nineteenth Century,* July, 1904, pp. 126–141.
The writer discusses her collection of the juvenile works of would-be writers, some of whom later attained fame and wished to suppress their early publications. Examples of the verse quoted show some good lines, with many mediocre and poor ones. The juvenilia of better known writers are not quoted.
9. Mearns, Hughes, *Creative Youth,* Century Co., 1925. 234 pages.
10. Nixon, H. K., *Psychology for the Writer,* Harper and Brothers, New York, 1928. 322 pages.
The bibliography is extensive and well-chosen.

11. "Poems of Children," *Poetry*, July, 1916, pp. 191–194; July, 1917, pp. 197–202; July, 1918, pp. 202–207.

The poems of Hilda Conkling figure prominently in these short collections. Some of her poems are rather juvenile in tone; some of them contain pleasing word pictures.

12. Robinson, A. M., "Horace A. Wade, America's Youngest Author and the World's Only Boy Novelist," *Overland*, n.s., Dec., 1921, pp. 29–32.

A popular account of the habits of work of Horace Wade. He is said to have written as many as 5,000 words at one sitting during his twelfth year. "He was always very much absorbed in his writing, and felt it was inspired. He made no corrections after the first writing of his articles and novels."

13. Swisher, W. S., "A Psychoanalysis of Browning's 'Pauline,'" *Psychoanalytic Review*, Vol. 7, 1920, pp. 115 ff.

14. Terman, Lewis M., et al., *Mental and Physical Traits of a Thousand Gifted Children, Genetic Studies of Genius*, Vol. I, Stanford University Press, 1925, 648 pages.

15. Terman, Lewis M., and Fenton, Jessie C., "Preliminary Report on a Gifted Juvenile Author," *Journal of Applied Psychology*, June, 1921, pp. 163–178.

16. Toulouse, Édouard, *Enquête Médico-Psychologique sur les Rapports de la Superiorité Intellectuelle avec la Névropathie: Émile Zola*, Société d'Éditions Scientifiques, Paris, 1896, 282 pages.

17. Wells, Frederick L., "A Statistical Study of Literary Merit," *Archives of Psychology*, Vol. 1, 1906. 30 pages.

PART IV. SUMMARY

CHAPTER XXVIII

RETROSPECT, PROSPECT, AND SUMMARY

More than fifteen years have passed since the researches set forth in these volumes of *Genetic Studies of Genius* were first definitely planned; it is twelve since the senior author began devoting each year a portion of his salary to the collection of data on bright children in the hope that once a beginning had been made funds would somehow be found for a realization of the larger plan. Although the undertaking entered upon so long ago is still far from completed, the first stage has been compassed, and it may not be unprofitable to cast a backward glance of appraisal over the problem that has been set, the labors that have been expended, and the factual information that has been garnered. There is further reason for such a review in the fact that the additional volumes which are in prospect can probably not appear until several more years have elapsed.

CIRCUMSTANCES FAVORING THE INVESTIGATION

Although every large-scope research has its inevitable disappointments—and the present one is no exception—the work since its beginning has been attended far oftener by good than by ill fortune. If the value of the results thus far obtained is less than it should have been, the blame therefor cannot be charged to unlucky circumstance.

In the first place, more liberal financial support was secured than had been hoped for, amounting in all to more than $60,000 for the three volumes that have been completed. It would be in ill grace to dwell upon the fact that more could have been accomplished if larger funds had been available. That could always be alleged. There is reason enough to feel profoundly grateful that an investigation looking so far into the future for its practical results could be financed at all. There was no promise to do anything during the course of the investigation to benefit any individual gifted child. There was no suggestion of devising improved methods for the educational treatment of these

463

gifted children. It was avowedly and solely a fact-finding project, one that could appeal only to donors wise enough to understand that knowledge must precede reform and with faith to believe that once the pertinent knowledge has been obtained reform is ultimately sure to follow.

In the second place, the senior author has reason to be thankful for his extraordinary good fortune in the collaborators and assistants whom the undertaking has attracted. In ability, in devotion, and in enthusiasm they measured up to the task without exception. Their labors were, almost literally, Herculean. When one considers the havoc to the investigation that even moderately incompetent assistants could have wrought, and the number of assistants the task required, it is remarkable that there is nothing whatever to regret from this source. It was as though only the best had presented themselves and as though these had been inspired throughout to their utmost limit of efficiency and devotion.

In short, the investigation has been favored by attending circumstances of every kind. Teachers and school officers have willingly co-operated in all possible ways, often at the cost of much labor and inconvenience. It was feared that many parents would resent the intrusion into their domestic affairs, but not more than one in a hundred has shown an unfriendly attitude toward the investigation and all but a small minority have rendered willing assistance. Newspaper publicity was recognized from the beginning as a possible danger, but almost without exception the California newspapers have respected the desire of the University that the study should be allowed to proceed in silence. The published results as later set forth in the earlier volumes of the series have been accorded favorable consideration by school people and by psychologists. These facts taken together indicate the seriousness with which the problem of the gifted child is everywhere regarded and give reason to hope that researches in this field will continue.

Program for Future Research

It is believed that the dual approach to the problem adopted at the inauguration of this research has fully justified itself. On the one hand, children of superior intellect must be identified, studied, and followed through life; and, on the other hand, superior adults, whether living men and

women or historic geniuses, must be followed backward to
the period of childhood. The researches of Volumes I and
III have employed the former of these methods, those of
Volume II the latter. It is obvious that additional researches
in both directions will be necessary to complete the program
that has been initiated. Of the living group of subjects at
least two more follow-up studies should be made, one of
them not later than 1940 and the last not earlier than 1950
or 1960. It is probable, therefore, that the task will have to
be completed by other hands than those which began it. But
that will not matter. Regardless of the life or death of any
one person, it is hardly conceivable that after another quar-
ter-century or more a final appraisal should not be made of
the lives and achievements of the gifted subjects concerning
whose childhood and early abilities so much objective information has been collected. It may well be that this final appraisal will be only the better if it is carried out by someone
who in his psychological training and outlook represents a
later generation than that which now holds the stage.

Later researches by the second method—the study of the
early mental development of genius—should be in two directions. (1) They should include studies of the childhood
of a large number of living individuals who have risen to
eminence by reason of their achievements. It would be difficult to overestimate the value of a study of this kind that
would include five hundred or a thousand of the country's
most eminent men and women who have reached the stage
of later maturity, for by this method it would be possible to
unearth facts of great importance that usually are not accessible to the biographers of historic geniuses. (2) Researches
of the kind set forth in Volume II should be continued, particularly in the form of more minute and intensive studies
of the early lives of individual geniuses. Herein lies the
great opportunity of the psychological biography, and, one
may add, of the psychological autobiography. It is to be
hoped that the time will come when all who have achieved
eminence will hold it an obligation to posterity that they
should attempt an analysis of their childhood traits and of
the environmental influences that played upon them in the
formative period. One could not expect that all such attempts would be entirely successful, judged from the psychological point of view; the outcome in most cases would

probably be far from satisfactory. There would be notable exceptions, however, and, if the practice became general, techniques of reporting would no doubt be developed to improve the range and accuracy of autobiographical data for the period of childhood.

It would be an interesting psychological problem to devise a technique for the purpose just indicated. A method of getting at the problem empirically would be for someone, twenty or thirty years hence, to secure from the California gifted subjects detailed reports and self-analyses which could be checked against the test scores and other objective or partially objective records obtained for these subjects during their early years and preserved in the files at Stanford University. Such reports should include estimates by each subject of his natural abilities in various directions, self-ratings on interests in several typical fields, analyses of personality traits, and detailed testimony on such matters as early reading, health, school progress, school marks, hobbies, play life, and environmental circumstances. By comparing the ratings and reports thus obtained with the earlier records it would be possible to find out what kinds of childhood data are most accurately and what kinds are least accurately reported in middle and later life. Moreover, by varying the method of obtaining the report it might be found possible to increase the amount and to improve the validity of almost every kind of biographical information. It is to be hoped that someone will take advantage of the opportunity offered by our records to carry through an investigation of this type.

The most important thing accomplished by Dr. Catharine Cox in the researches described in Volume II was to show that in the vast majority of cases the great geniuses of history gave unmistakable evidence of intellectual superiority in early life. While there are some who will hold that this fact hardly needed to be proved, it must be remembered that for nearly a hundred years the opposite belief had been widely held not only by common opinion but by scientists of repute. The work of Dr. Cox established beyond question the existence of important correlations between the mental abilities of childhood and those of mature life. Mental maturation proceeds by developmental processes, not by successive transformations. Not only later abilities, but later interests as well, are foreshadowed in the preoccupations and behavior of childhood. How close the correlations are and just what developmental changes are most likely to occur are matters for further researches to determine. The rôle of environmental influences and also the rôle of character and personality traits in the achievements of geniuses are other problems of crucial importance which could be touched upon only more or less incidentally in the investigation reported in Volume II. Along these and many other lines this work should be continued until the early life of every outstanding genius has been laid open in so far as extant records make this possible.

Once the social significance of intellectual genius has been fully grasped, one may confidently expect that the preservation of dependable data concerning the childhood period will be given special attention in the case of living geniuses, and that the task of the future psychologist-biographer will thus be immeasurably simplified. It may not be absurd to suggest that the time may come when every intellectual giant will have officially assigned to him a psychologist whose duty it will be to record the facts of his development, to secure objective measures of his abilities and of his personality traits, and to evaluate the influences of nature and nurture that have entered to make him what he has become—a kind of psychological Boswell. Scientists think nothing of going to such pains to solve the mysteries connected with a meteor that strikes the earth or a comet that approaches our planetary system, yet a phenomenon of this kind offers less of marvel and infinitely less that has immediate importance for mankind than the advent and the career of a genius like Aristotle, da Vinci, Shakespeare, Newton, Goethe, Beethoven, or Einstein. It would be well for us to find out, if possible, how such golden eggs are laid and nurtured.

Is the Rôle of Genius Diminishing?

The idea has been advanced that the rôle of genius will be less important in the future than in the past; that such factors as the education of the masses, the preservation and widespread publication of every new idea or invention, and the ever increasing specialization of achievement are bringing us to the point where the genius will no longer be neces-

sary to cultural progress. According to this view, every
advance that accumulated knowledge makes possible will
be accomplished anyway by the specialized toil of hordes of
suitably trained but intellectually mediocre workers.

That important scientific discoveries are sometimes
made by fairly commonplace intellects may be freely admitted, also that this is probably more likely to occur today
than at any previous time in the world's history. It does not
follow from this that the rôle of genius has grown less important. To believe so is to hold a poor opinion of the possibilities of science, of art, and of life itself. It is more reasonable to believe that the mounting quantity and growing complexity of knowledge call more insistently for the masterful
genius today than ever before. Disrupted social and economic orders, from England to Japan and from Canada to
the Argentine, are calling almost in vain for statesmen of
genius and vision. The air, the sea, and the bowels of the
earth offer more powerful incentives to the engineer and
the inventor than ever have been offered. Millions still lan-
guish and die of diseases which the brain of man now, for
the first time, has some chance to conquer. The breaking up
of long-established religious sanctions calls for moral leaders, and the call is answered by Comstockery and moronic
prohibitions. Lawmaking in most countries, and perhaps
nowhere more than in the United States, is chiefly the product of fourth-rate minds.

Precisely because of the increasing complexity of civilization and of science the call for genius now comes from
hundreds of places from which it did not come in the days
of Aristotle or even of Benjamin Franklin. The former was
able to systematize existing knowledge so well that his formulation satisfied the best minds for a thousand years, while
a formulation of 1930 is more than likely to be demolished
by a new fact before the end of 1931. Electricity was only
one of several things about which Franklin learned nearly
all that anyone of his day could possibly learn; but in the
field of electrical science alone there is now room for hundreds of scientific intellects as gifted as that of Franklin. The
sheer momentum of cultural forces may insure that some
progress can be made by the moderately gifted, and that
previous advances can be held even by mediocre minds;
even so, the demand for intellect of truly giant proportions

is incomparably greater in the twentieth than in any previous century. Where the call once broke the silence only at
long intervals, it beats now an incessant tattoo. We seek
advances in so many more directions than formerly because
the perceptual possibilities of advance are ever becoming
clearer and more numerous.

The truth appears to be, not that superior ability is likely
to go begging, but that it will become more and more at a
premium. This probably holds not only for ability of genius
order but for the less exceptional grades of superiority as
well. There will always be problems aplenty which do not
call for genius but which the average mind cannot grapple
with successfully. No really difficult problem was ever
solved by a strictly average mind or by a mind that was
near-average; the problems that can thus be solved are *ipso
facto* not difficult and would never be so regarded.

It is quite possible that no intellect of heroic stature will
emerge from the thousand gifted subjects of the present investigation. By the laws of chance one could hardly be expected, for after all the selection was made from only about
a quarter-million children of the California school population. The Oxford Rhodes scholars are far more highly selected than our gifted group, yet from the hundreds who
have gone from the United States during the last twenty-five
years none has thus far risen to over-towering eminence.
The appearance or non-appearance of supremely eminent
individuals is not, however, in point here. The point is that
there is abundant work in this day and age for IQ's of 140
or 150, and that it is probably at this level that rightly directed educational endeavor can be most effective. Great
geniuses, those of truly heroic stature, are at best so rare
that they can never be a matter of very general educational
concern; the school's practical problem in this direction is
with the best ten or twenty out of a thousand.

Specific Aims of the Present Researches

It is with the brightest four or five out of a thousand that
Volumes I and III of this series are concerned. It is their
characteristics—physical, intellectual, social, and moral—
which we have attempted to delineate, their development
which we have attempted to trace. The investigations which

have been carried out for this purpose, although purely scientific in their immediate aim, have in their ultimate end been motivated by considerations of practical import, as is doubtless true of the majority of scientific investigations in every field. In this case the purpose has been to build up a foundation of pertinent and verifiable factual material upon which improved educational methods can at some time be securely based.

What, can it be reasonably claimed, has been accomplished toward this end? At best, certainly, not more than a modest fraction of the total that is needed. Perhaps the author and his co-workers should be content if it can be said that an honest beginning has been made and that the foundation stones they have set will not have to be torn away and replaced. That much, they would fain believe, has been accomplished.

DEFINITION OF THE GROUP FOR WHICH THE CONCLUSIONS ARE VALID

In advance of a final discussion of results it may be well to remind the reader once more that the generalizations to be offered can be held to apply only to a group selected as this group was selected, namely, on the basis of a Stanford-Binet IQ of 140 or higher; also that possibly 10 or 15 per cent of the total number who could have qualified according to this criterion were missed by the methods of sifting employed. (See Volume I, chapter ii.) Although it is impossible to say how those who were missed would have differed from those who were identified, the number of these was fortunately not large enough to distort conclusions seriously. It is more important to bear in mind the arbitrariness of the line set for inclusion of subjects and the probable error of the intelligence score through which the line was drawn. Many children whose found IQ's were appreciably below 140 may have had higher IQ's than some whose test scores satisfied the criterion. There is roughly one chance in seven that a child whose measured (found) Stanford Binet IQ is 135 has a true Stanford-Binet IQ of 140. There is roughly one chance in sixteen that a measured IQ of 130 should really have been as high as 140. There are corresponding chances that measured IQ's of 145 or 150 should not have been above 140. These estimates are based upon a probable error of 4 IQ points for Stanford-Binet test scores. The probable error is somewhat less than this in the mental age range of five to ten years, but at the levels above twelve or fourteen is probably greater. In any case it cannot be claimed that the group studied is composed of all the children above a certain (true) level of intelligence and of none but those. Because the selective method is fallible, the result is only an approximation to this. The criterion set is one which is satisfied by about 4 children in 1,000 of the urban pre–high-school population of California. This is at the rate of 1,000 in 250,000.

SEX RATIO IN THE GIFTED GROUP

As the sex ratio in the pre–high-school groups of subjects is about 116 boys to 100 girls, a gifted group of 1,000, selected as ours was selected, contains about 538 boys and only 462 girls. At the high-school level a method of selection somewhat similar to that used in the elementary grades but employing the Terman Group Test instead of the Stanford-Binet as the final criterion gives a sex ratio of 212 boys to 100 girls, or 680 boys to only 320 girls in a group of 1,000. (Volume I, chapter iii.)

These facts are very challenging, especially when considered in connection with the fact that among historic geniuses, eminent living scientists, and other outstanding groups the large majority (usually above 90 per cent in any group) are males. In Volume I four hypotheses were examined in the search for possible explanations: biased selection; sex ratio in families of the gifted children; differential death rate of embryos; and sex difference in variability. Analysis of the data seemed to rule out the first two explanations and to suggest the possibility that either or both of the last two may have been to some extent accountable. The vastly greater excess of boys at the upper age levels than at the lower was at the time explained as possibly due to the difference in method of selection of subjects in the upper and lower age ranges.

The follow-up study sheds no further light on the sex ratio in the younger group, but suggests another explanation of the greater excess of boys at the upper age levels; namely, that gifted girls do not maintain their intellectual superiority in adolescence as well as boys do. Whether this is to be thought of in terms of decreasing variability of the girls with increasing age, or as an earlier cessation of intellectual growth on the part of the girls, the result is the same. It is probable that all the facts regarding sex ratios are accounted for as follows: (*a*) a slightly greater male variability, explaining the relatively small difference in the number of boys and girls found in the pre–high-school grades; and (*b*) an earlier cessation of mental growth on the part of the girls, resulting in the large sex difference in numbers of gifted children at the high-school level.

Composite Portrait of the Gifted Child

A large part of both Volume I and Volume III has been devoted to a delineation of the characteristic traits of gifted children considered as a group. This seemed necessary because of the large amount of erroneous opinion that has been disseminated in connection with this aspect of the problem. Further justification for making this one of the major objectives of the research is found in the fact that the educational issue as to what the school should or should not do with gifted children hinges largely on their group characteristics. We believe that the data secured have enabled us to delineate these characteristics faithfully, at least so far as the main outlines are concerned. There is probably no part of the study which has yielded conclusions less likely to be materially modified by further investigation. It seems to have been satisfactorily demonstrated that:

1. Gifted children come predominantly from family stocks of decidedly superior intellectual endowment and of slightly superior physical endowment;

2. These family stocks have greatly decreased in fecundity during the last two generations and have already reached the point where they are not maintaining themselves;

3. The mean IQ of siblings of children who are in the IQ range above 140 is about 123, or almost exactly what would be expected if the correlation between siblings in the general population were in the neighborhood of .45 or .50;

4. Intellectually gifted children, either because of better endowment or better physical care, or both, are as a group slightly superior to the generality of children in health and physique and tend to remain so;

5. Children above 140 IQ are not as a group characterized by intellectual one-sidedness, emotional instability, lack
of sociality or of social adaptability, or other types of maladjusted personality;

6. Indeed in practically every personality and character
trait such children average much better than the general
school population;

7. In social-intelligence ratings, social interests, and play
activities, gifted children as a group are either normal or
superior;

8. In mental masculinity and femininity gifted boys rate
on a par with unselected school boys of corresponding age,
while gifted girls deviate significantly from the norm of
their sex in the direction of greater masculinity;

9. In the character traits measured by the Raubenheimer-Cady tests the typical gifted child of nine years is on a
par with unselected children of thirteen or fourteen years;

10. In trait ratings by teachers gifted children show their
superiority to the average most of all in intellectual and volitional qualities and least in physical and social traits;

11. In school progress the typical gifted child is accelerated by 14 per cent of his age, but in actual mastery of the
school subjects (as shown by achievement tests) he is accelerated by more than 40 per cent of his age;

12. At the age of ten years there is no correlation between achievement test scores and the number of years
gifted children have attended school;

13. As a rule gifted boys maintain or almost maintain
their relative superiority to the common run in intelligence,
at least through the period of adolescence;

14. Girls somewhat more often than boys show a drop
in the IQ as adolescence is approached, or soon thereafter;

15. School achievement as a rule continues through high
school and college to be in line with the IQ originally found
in 1921–22;

16. Subject failures in high school are practically never
incurred by children of this grade of intelligence;

17. Nearly three-quarters of the total marks earned in
high school by gifted girls, and nearly half of those earned
by gifted boys, are of A grade;

18. Gifted children of the senior high-school year test
on the average above the 90th percentile of the general run

of high-school seniors on the Iowa High-School Content Examination, or from 1.5 to 2.0 S.D.'s above the mean of high-school seniors in general;

19. More than 90 per cent of gifted boys and more than 80 per cent of gifted girls (in this group) go to college, most of them remaining to graduate;

20. Those who graduate from high-grade universities win Phi Beta Kappa or other graduation honors about three times as frequently as do the general run of graduates from such institutions.

The twenty generalizations in this list could have been multiplied several times, but they are among the more significant features of the portrait. A few of them are more or less specific to this group of subjects, but the large majority will in all probability be found to hold for any gifted group selected from the school population of any city or country by means of any of the better forms of intelligence tests when the criterion for admission to the group is set in the neighborhood of 140 IQ. There is every reason to believe that they will be found valid, though in somewhat less degree, for representative groups of children in the IQ range of 120 to 140.

It is to be hoped that the superstitions so commonly accepted relative to intellectually superior children have been permanently swept away by the factual data these studies have presented. It is simply not true that such children are especially prone to be puny, over-specialized in their abilities and interests, emotionally unstable, socially unadaptable, psychotic, and morally undependable; nor is it true that they usually deteriorate to the level of mediocrity as adult life is approached. Educational reforms in the direction of special classes, special curricula, and special classroom procedures can now be confidently formulated upon this foundation of established truth. If special classes and special procedures are to be opposed, it must henceforth be upon other grounds than those which have been most commonly alleged. One would like to believe that the stage is set for one of the most important educational reforms of the century; a reform that would have for its end the discovery, conservation, and intensive cultivation of every form of exceptional talent.

Relative Permanency of the Characteristic Traits of Gifted Children

The most important single outcome of the follow-up investigation is the abundant and conclusive evidence that for the group as a whole the picture did not greatly change in the period that elapsed between the studies summarized in Volume I and Volume III. With minor exceptions, what was true of these children in 1921–22 was true of them in 1927–28. During this period, however, there were changes in the background of the picture which are likely at times to deceive the reader. What is here referred to is the fact that the school population with which it is necessary to make our comparisons was a much more highly selected population at the time of the follow-up study than in 1921–22. This has been alluded to many times in the exposition of the findings, but it cannot be too often emphasized. There are few who appreciate how much the composition of a class of high-school seniors has been affected by the retardation and elimination of their less-gifted fellows. This holds true, though to a less marked degree, of high-school freshmen, and of course to a far greater degree of students enrolled in superior universities.

Moreover, it is constantly necessary to make allowance for the fact that the gifted group usually averages some two years younger than the school population with which it is compared. In 1921–22 the comparisons in school achievement were in most cases age comparisons; in 1927–28 they were of necessity grade comparisons, because of the absence of age norms for achievement tests at higher levels. In 1921–22 less than one child in a hundred of the general school population rated as high in achievement as the typical gifted child of the same age. In 1927–28 about one high-school senior in ten rated as high in achievement as the typical gifted child of the same grade but two years younger. The latter showing is approximately as favorable as the former, although it might not appear so to one not fully cognizant of all the factors entering into the comparison.

Individual Changes in Rate of Intellectual Growth

The composite portrait method is useful, just as concepts and generalizations are useful in the shorthand of thinking.

Nevertheless, the composite portrait, like any other kind of average, has its limitations. In telling what is true of a group, it fails to convey any sense of the uniqueness that is to be found in each of those who compose the group. In the present instance too exclusive concentration of attention upon what is true in general hinders us from recognizing the variety of trait combinations that the fact of personality necessarily implies, and obscures all those characteristics which are exceptions to the rule. It is in giving a more vivid impression than did Volume I of the "exceptions to the rule" that the present volume makes one of its most important contributions.

For example, it is true that the gifted subjects as a group have held their own intellectually, but it is no less true that some of them have changed significantly in their intelligence ratings. In interpreting the findings on this point the reader will need to bear in mind the factors mentioned in chapter iii which complicate the issue: the probable error of a Stanford-Binet score, the fact that the Stanford-Binet as at present standardized yields scores with older subjects which are too low, and the fact that the tests in the scale which measured the younger subjects in the original survey do not test exactly the same functions as those in the upper ranges which measured the same subjects at the time of the follow-up study. The same factors are involved in greater or less degree in the case of retests by other intelligence scales. The Herring-Binet not only lacks "top," but because of faults of standardization it yields IQ's much below those of the Stanford-Binet. The Terman Group Test measures in part other functions than those measured by either the Stanford-Binet or the Herring-Binet, and like both of these it is inadequate to measure the brighter half of our adolescent subjects.

For the reasons just given, and others, it is impossible to make a quantitative statement of the exact degree to which IQ's tend to maintain themselves. Considering the evidence from all sources, including intelligence tests, achievement tests, school marks, etc., it appears that the IQ's of boys tend to remain constant and those of girls to decrease. One finding out of harmony with this conclusion is that at all ages girls retain a certain superiority over boys in school marks, but it has long been known that for one reason or another, or for several reasons, girls make a far better showing per unit of intelligence than boys do in the matter of class marks.

Making due allowances for complicating factors in measuring IQ constancy, one can hardly avoid the conclusion that there are individual children in our gifted group who have shown very marked changes in IQ. Some of these changes have been in the direction of IQ increase, others of them in the direction of decrease. The important fact which seems to have been definitely established is that there sometimes occur genuine changes in the rate of intellectual growth which cannot be accounted for on the basis of general health, educational opportunity, or other environmental influences. The opinion has often been advanced that something like this is true, but convincing evidence has hitherto been lacking, previous data having been limited entirely to retests by a single fallible intelligence without supporting evidence.

OTHER DEVIATIONS FROM CENTRAL TENDENCIES OF THE GROUP

The group studied shows far more variability in other traits than in constancy of IQ. One finds among the subjects extreme deviation from the group average in every physical, mental, and personality trait: size, strength, athletic ability, health, scientific ability, artistic ability, literary ability, mental masculinity and femininity, fair-mindedness, social and activity interests, vocational interest, social intelligence, leadership, interest in school work, ambition, and moral dependability. One member of the group became definitely psychopathic and committed suicide; one is serving time in a state reform school after an extended career as a delinquent. The group in fact contains disharmonic personalities of almost every type. Several cases of these have been described in Part II, particularly in chapter xix. Other behavior and adjustment problems include cases showing inferiority complexes, inordinate conceit, "wildness," disobedience, untruthfulness, social deficiency, dishonesty, and extreme laziness. There are several cases of marked inversion with respect to mental masculinity and femininity, though it must be said that the significance of such inversion is not yet fully understood. (For examples, see case descriptions beginning on pp. 326, 328, and 330.) A considerable number of the subjects are so lacking in ambition, or in ability to work consistently toward even a moderately distant goal, that after leaving school they either remain content with inconsequential positions or drift aimlessly from job to job.

The other side of the story would take longer to tell, because there are so many more instances of extreme deviation in the direction of personality balance, stability of character, and successful accomplishment. Examples of heroic self-sacrifice and of courageous struggle against such handicaps as ill health, poverty, parental ignorance, race prejudice, and other unfavorable circumstances of environment have been described in chapter xvii, and the list of such case studies could have been greatly extended. The group contains several musicians of genuine promise, one of whom has already taken rank as one of the outstanding musical composers and musical theorists of America (chapter xx). Among the subjects are at least a half-dozen who have produced literary juvenilia comparable to the best produced by eminent authors at corresponding age. Three or four have shown unusual promise in art. The number who have evidenced exceptional ability in science is so large that it will be surprising if thirty or forty years hence the group is not well represented in starred lists of the type illustrated by Cattell's 1,000 American men of science.

The Case Studies

The reader will doubtless agree that the case studies of Part II and of chapters x and xxvi are among the most valuable features of this report. Their value is enhanced by the fact that they are all more or less of the longitudinal type. Cross-section case studies of children are always unsatisfying; one is so curious to know how the scene is likely to shift with the passing of years. The same is true to some extent of those herein presented, but for these we have at least two points of reference, separated by an interval of six or more years. Even two points locate a curve of development much better than one! It would be fortunate if in future follow-up researches with our gifted group every member of it could be represented by a biographical case study. It is conceivable that this could be satisfactorily carried out with an average space allotment of five or ten pages each, though the range might well be from one to fifty pages or more. There is one of the subjects (Henry Cowell) who already merits a full-sized biography.

Among the brief case studies we have been able to assemble for this volume, there are several of special interest. Examples are: Millie (pp. 248 ff.), who holds the world's record for early reading; Beatrice (p. 423), gifted poet, novelist, and artist; Verda (pp. 254 ff. and 434 ff.), gifted poet and brilliant student; Roger (pp. 262 ff.), injured by injudicious acceleration in school; David (pp. 266 ff.), a Bachelor of Arts at the age of sixteen and under psychological observation since the age of seven; Bertha and Jerome (pp. 272 ff.), two extreme instances of decrease in IQ; Marshall (pp. 283 ff.), handicapped by frailty, lameness, poverty, bad heredity, and sordid environment; Harriet (pp. 286 ff.), a gifted negro girl; four children of a Japanese-American marriage (pp. 289 ff.); Barbara and Marguerite (pp. 298 ff.), a pair of identical twins; Ronald (pp. 306 ff.), a problem boy; Emmett and Alfred (pp. 310 ff.), illustrating the combined effect of unfortunate heredity and extremely unfavorable home environment; Blake (pp. 319 ff.), who committed suicide; Renwick (pp. 328 ff.), a gifted musician showing inversion in the mental masculinity - femininity trait; Roberta (pp. 330 ff.), our most masculine girl; and Francis (pp. 338 ff.), a gifted young scientist.

An especially interesting sketch, psychologically, is that of P. J. B., described in chapter xxii. This case is unique, for the subject, so far as we know, is the only person whose development in infancy has been minutely recorded and who has been subjected to psychometric study as late as the high-school period. Biographical material of this kind possesses such extraordinary interest and value that it should be collected in great quantities, as in time it doubtless will be. There are few things in this entire report as interesting as P. J. B.'s babyhood drawings (pp. 346–47) viewed in the light of her later development.

MISCELLANEA

Numerous partial summaries which have preceded render it unnecessary to make this concluding chapter a complete summary of the follow-up results. We have merely called attention to some of the findings which seem to us of particular interest or significance, hoping that the reader will turn for more detailed information to the main body of the report where the data are presented in full. It remains only to mention certain results of secondary or minor importance which happen to be of more than passing interest.

The Strong Test of Occupational Interests has shown that although our gifted subjects who are in college are able to judge their occupational interests fully as accurately as do college students in general, there are a good many of them who are looking forward to occupations which the test scores indicate to be out of line with their interests. The Strong test lays no claim to infallibility, but it has demonstrated its usefulness to a degree that in our opinion warrants its wholesale application with college students. Clinical use has been made of the test with many members of our group who sought our advice because of uncertainty with regard to choice of a vocation, and in every case it has helped to throw light on the problems involved.

The high ratings earned by some of the literary productions of several members of the group provoke a number of questions. One would especially like to know why the seven most talented in writing are all girls, and whether these children are really as well endowed in literary ability as the eminent authors whose juvenilia were of the same merit as theirs. It is impossible, of course, to answer either of these questions. As for the first one, the most reasonable guess is that the sex difference is one of interest and preoccupation rather than of ability. Boys have so many more interesting things to turn to than girls have; moreover, the writing of poetry has less prestige value among boys than it has among girls. The group probably contains children of both sexes whose natural literary gifts compare favorably with those of authors who have attained a secure place in literature, but whether these children are destined to make the most of their native abilities in this field only time can tell.

The instance just cited is only one of many which suggest the existence of hidden potentialities in a group of the type with which we are here concerned. From the Zyve Test of Scientific Aptitude it appears that there are gifted potential scientists in the group who will never study science. It is probable that the group contains hidden talents of correspondingly superior grade in music, art, mathematics, language, engineering, social leadership, and other fields of human endeavor. There are so many things that go to determine whether prodigious talent in a given line will result in prodigious achievement. A child may have many talents, but the complexity of present-day civilization is so great that in most cases only one or two of them can be fully realized even under the most favorable circumstances. And circumstances are not always favorable. Ill health, poverty, unwise educational guidance, accidental personal contacts, unhappy home life, unfortunate love affairs, parent fixations, lack of ambition, sheer indolence, and personality defects are factors which, operating in combination or even singly, may prevent the fruition of the most exceptional talent. The world's supply of genius is probably many times as great as it would be judged to be from the amount which comes to light. The supply itself is the product of heredity—a gift of Nature which no amount of nurture can substitute for; but whether the raw material furnished by heredity ever realizes its potentialities depends upon nurture factors over which, theoretically at least, man has control. The discovery and cultivation of hidden talents and genius thus becomes one of the most important functions of organized society.

The greater the intellectual gifts of a given child the more difficult is the problem of making the most of these gifts. In some respects it is to be regretted that exceptionally superior intellectual endowment shows itself so early, that is, is accompanied by so much precocity in mental development. The difficulty in the situation arises from the fact that extreme precocity unavoidably complicates the problem of social adjustment. The child of eight years with a mentality of twelve is inevitably to a greater or less extent a social misfit. Neither holding such a child to lock-step progress nor promoting him to the level of his ability offers a satisfactory solution. Special classes for the gifted do not altogether eliminate the problem, but they are the nearest thing we have to a solution.

It is noteworthy that the Special Ability group, composed of children who in 1921–22 had shown outstanding talent in drawing, painting, or music, but whose IQ's did not enable them to qualify for admission to the gifted group on the basis of general intelligence, have in a majority of cases turned out most disappointingly. At the present time nearly all the subjects we have who show any real promise in these special fields of accomplishment are those who qualified for the group on the basis of general intelligence instead of on the basis of special talent. This, we believe, is significant in the highest degree, for it suggests the important rôle played by general intelligence in making possible superior accomplishment in a special field. This finding cannot be explained on the theory that our Special Ability group was more or less a chance selection and so does not truly represent the type of child it is supposed to represent. On the contrary, extraordinary pains were taken to locate the most promising subjects of this type in a school population of more than a quarter-million children. The only conditions were that the child must have given some evidence of specialized talent and must have an IQ of less than 140. Untold labors were expended in hunting down all children who had given evidence of unusual special talent, and all of the outstanding cases located were tested. Those who obtained an IQ of 140 or above were admitted to the Regular group; those of lower IQ were classed in the Special Ability group. It is the latter group that has made such a poor showing in the follow-up research.

Finally, attention may be called to one of the eugenic aspects of our problem. Data collected regarding the spouses of the gifted subjects who have married show that, notwithstanding a marked tendency toward marital selection in the usual direction, the spouses appear to be in a majority of cases less well endowed than the gifted subjects who have married them. A certain regression of spouses toward the mean of the general population is to be expected, is indeed perhaps inevitable, but it is on the whole regrettable and something that should be counteracted in so far as possible by eugenic education. The argument sometimes brought forward that the most highly gifted ought to select mates somewhat less gifted than themselves in order to insure a better all-round balance of traits in their offspring can hardly be regarded as valid in the light of the personality scores and ratings which these researches have yielded.

APPENDIX

APPENDIX

In the following pages the protocols which were used in securing information from parents, teachers, and the subjects themselves are reproduced in full, though in reduced type. The content of certain of them was in part determined by the desire to make the information which they yielded as comparable as possible with that secured in 1921–22. Notwithstanding the limitations of the questionnaire as a tool of research, its use in a study of the present type could hardly be avoided. As a matter of fact, the information secured by the following blanks supplemented in a very helpful way the data secured by tests and measurements.

GIFTED CHILDREN FOLLOW-UP

HOME INFORMATION BLANK

(For parents of children up to and including nineteen years old.)

Mail to *Professor Lewis M. Terman, Stanford University, California*

Full name.. Present age................................

School or college now attended................................Grade (high or low) or college year

If in school, name of class teacher.......................... Name of principal...............................

Present occupation, if not in school...

Address (if away from home)...

Parent or guardian...

Address of parent or guardian... Telephone...............................

This report made out by... Date...............................

Note: I appreciate very greatly the splendid co-operation that the parents of our group of a thousand superior children have given during the past five years. This year a grant of $10,000 enables us to make a more complete study of the educational and intellectual status of the boys and girls of the group than has been possible since 1922. We are now counting on the same interest and enthusiastic support that has been offered in the past.

As previously, the information gathered in this investigation will be held strictly confidential; it will be kept in locked files at Stanford University, and will be used for statistical purposes only, without the use of names. Please omit nothing, however confidential the information requested may be, or however unimportant it may seem to you. The fullest scientific and practical contribution of our study to an understanding of the nature and special needs of the gifted child will only be possible if we can secure a continuous record for every boy and girl of the group over a period of many years.

In order to avoid the danger of causing undue self-consciousness, parents are urged not to say anything about the special information which is sought in this blank, or to tell their child the exact result of the mental tests. *Publicity of every kind should be avoided.* Do nothing which could possibly stimulate vanity or self-consciousness.

[*Page 1*

485

I. PHYSICAL DATA

1. General health since 1922 has been good, fair, poor. (Underline)
2. Illnesses since 1922...
   After effects, if any...
3. Accidents since 1922...
   After effects, if any...
4. Surgical operations since 1922...
   Was recovery normal?...
5. Has colds very frequently, frequently, occasionally, only rarely. (Underline)
6. Wears glasses?............... When first worn?............... Serious eye trouble?...............
7. Has suffered from headaches?........... At what age?........... How often?.....................
8. Is hearing excellent, good, fair, poor? (Underline)
9. Has had serious digestive trouble recently?..................... At what age?.....................
   How serious? ....
10. Signs of special nervousness?............... How shown?...
11. Has shown a marked tendency to worry?........... Over what?.............................
12. Usual hour of going to sleep?........... Of waking?........... Is sleep sound?...............
13. (If girl) Has menstruation begun?..................... At what age?.............................
    (If boy) Has voice changed?............... At what age?.............................
14. Organic diseases (as of heart, kidneys, lungs, etc.)...

II. EDUCATIONAL AND SOCIAL HISTORY

1. Month and year that eighth grade was completed...
   Month and year that high school was completed...
   Month and year that college was completed...
2. If no longer in school, give date of leaving school.....................Last grade or
   college year of attendance........................... Reason for leaving.......................
3. Diplomas received........................... What school or college?...........................
4. Any long absences from school since 1922?............... How long?...............................
   Reasons for irregularity...
5. Liking for school very strong, fairly strong, slight liking, positive dislike. (Underline)
6. Desires to go to college?..................... Are plans being made to attend?...................
   What college? ....
7. Private tutoring since 1922 (out of school)

Subject	From what age to what age	Hours a week (including practice)	Ability shown—very superior, superior, average, inferior, very inferior
Music			
Drawing			
Painting			
Dancing			
Language			
Other subjects			

8. Ability recently noted in special fields (as music, mathematics, science, nature study, mechanical ingenuity, art, dramatics, handiwork, etc.). Give brief description of the development of specialized ability, if any..

....

....

....

9. How has leisure time been spent during the last two or three years? (Examples: games, hiking, reading, writing, study, experiments, hobbies, music, making collections, working with machinery or tools, sewing, household work, etc.) ....

....

....

Describe briefly any special projects or hobbies that have been carried on recently ....

....

....

10. In general ability is gaining, holding his own, or losing ground? (Underline)

11. Is very tractable, fairly tractable, rather headstrong, very headstrong regarding disciplinary matters? (Underline)

12. Are there any tendencies at present toward selfishness, lack of studious interests, intolerance of social customs, lack of ambition, or lack of moral integrity?............................ Describe..

....

....

13. Is teased by others very frequently, frequently, occasionally, rarely, never? (Underline)

14. Is considered by others of the same age as "queer" or different?............................

....

....

15. In regard to opposite sex, shows a great interest, moderate interest, indifference, aversion? (Underline)

16. Especially significant events of last few years such as long trips, emotional experiences, marriage, etc..

....

....

488

THE PROMISE OF YOUTH

III. FAMILY AND HOME

1. Present occupation of father (if living)...

2. Present occupation of mother (if living)...

3. Special accomplishments, activities or honors of father during last five or six
years ....
....
....

4. Special accomplishments, activities or honors of mother during last five or six
years ....
....
....

5. Special accomplishments, activities or honors of other relatives during last
five or six years..
....
....

6. Brothers or sisters born during last five or six years: (Mark with cross [X]
any half-brothers or sisters).

First name	Boy or girl	Date of birth	In school?

7. Members of the family, or other relatives as close as grandparents or uncles
and aunts who have died during the last five or six years: (Mark with cross
[X] any half-brothers or sisters).

Relationship (to your child)	Age at death	Year of death	Cause

8. Have parents separated or been divorced during the last five or six years?..........
.... If so, when?...
Has either parent married during the last five or six years?...................................

9. Other information that would help us understand this boy or girl............................
....
....

INTEREST BLANK, 1927–1928

(For children under twenty years old.)

NOTE: I am asking your help in a study of the way young people develop from youth to maturity. A few years ago you took some tests which showed what your interests and capacities were at that time. Your co-operation this year will be even more useful and valuable, because you have now had several additional years of active experience.

Please answer all the questions frankly, and do not omit any. The information will be held strictly confidential; it will be kept in locked files at Stanford University, and will be used for statistical purposes only, without the use of names. When this blank is filled out, mail it to:

Professor Lewis M. Terman, Stanford University, California

Name .... Age............ Grade or college year....................
Address (if *not* at home).. Telephone.....................
Name of school or college.. City.......................
Date of filling out this blank...

1. What studies have you liked most during the last two or three years?...............
....

2. What studies have you liked least?...
.... Reason?.......................

3. If you are at college, what is your major subject?...................

4. About how many hours a week (outside of school hours) do you spend on school (or college) studies?.................

5. About how many hours a week do you spend on *general reading* (not school studies)? ....

   What kind of reading do you enjoy most: e.g. travel, history, essays, plays, adventure stories, science, poetry, short stories, novels, detective stories, etc.? ....Name a few books and magazines you have enjoyed recently ....
....

6. Below are several different kinds of things to do. On the line before each thing, put a figure (1, 2, 3, 4, or 5) to show how well you like to do that kind of thing. Put a 1 if you like it very much; put a 2 if you like it fairly well; put a 3 if you neither like it nor dislike it; put a 4 if you rather dislike it; put a 5 if you dislike it very much.

........Studying.

........General reading (books, magazines, newspapers).

........Practicing music, drawing, dancing, etc.

........Games that require little physical exercise.

........Games that require lots of exercise.

........Spending time with several other persons.

........Spending time with one other person.

........Spending time alone.

........Going to parties, picnics, dances, club meetings, etc.

........Using tools or working with apparatus and machinery.

........Sewing, cooking, knitting, housework, etc.

........Being leader in a team or club and managing other persons.

7. When you have an hour or two that you can spend just as you please, what do you like to do best?..................

8. At what age did you first begin to enjoy doing this?.....................How did you first happen to become interested in doing this?.................

9. Name all the collections you have been making during the last four or five years, and tell how large the collections are.
....
....

[*Page 1*

10. What have you made or constructed yourself during the last four or five years? (Examples: built a canoe, made dresses, wrote poetry, composed some music, etc.)

Thing done	Your age at the time	Was it very good, fairly good, or poor?
1.		
2.		
3.		
4.		
5.		
6.		

11. Name all the offices or honors you have held during the last five years. (Examples: class officer, scout officer, club officer, actor in plays, scholarship prize or honor, member of band, orchestra, debating team, athletic team, school committee, school paper, etc.)

Position or honor	Your age at that time
1.	
2.	
3.	
4.	
5.	
6.	

12. Do you prefer to be with people who are older, younger, or the same age as yourself? ....
Briefly describe your best chum...
....Age of chum?................

13. Name all the paid jobs you have had during the last five years.

Job	How long did you work at this job?	Hours per week	Your age at the time	Compensation per week
1.				
2.				
3.				
4.				
5.				
6.				

Present job? ....

14. Have you decided yet what life vocation you wish to follow?................ If so, what occupation? ....
Under what circumstances did you make this choice? (E.g., what influences determined the decision—such as school or college courses, advice of relatives, teachers, or friends, reading, close-hand observation, etc.?)................................

15. Have any disappointments, perplexities, failures, or bereavements ever exerted a prolonged influence upon you?................ If so, briefly describe, stating your age at the time...

16. Do you consider that any single person, book, philosophy, or religion has had a profound influence on your life?...
If so, what was it?...
Age at which such influence, if any, began...

[*Page* 2

INFORMATION BLANK

(For children of twenty years or over; combines Home information Blank and Interest Blank.)

Name .... Age.................................
Address .... Telephone.....................
Name of school or college, if in school.................................... Grade or college year........
Date of filling out this blank..

1. Month and year that eighth grade was completed...
   Month and year that high school was completed...
   Month and year that college was completed...

2. If no longer in school, give date of leaving school.................Last grade or college
   year of attendance........................ Reason for leaving.................................

3. Diplomas received................................ What school or college?.....................

4. Any long absences from school since 1922?............... How long?.............................
   Reasons for irregularity ....

5. If not in college, do you desire to go?........Are you making plans to attend?........
   What college? ....

6. What studies have you liked most during the last two or three years?...............
   What studies have you liked least?.................................... Reason?................

7. If you are at college, what is your major subject?...

8. Have you belonged to a social fraternity, sorority, or house club?.......................
   Which one? ....
   If a member, are you glad you joined?...

9. Especially significant events of last few years such as long trips, emotional
   experience, engagements, etc...
   ....

10. Are you married?.................. If so, give date...
    Names and ages of children, if any...
    ....

11. General health since 1922 has been good, fair, poor. (Underline)

12. Illnesses, accidents, or surgical operations since 1922...................................
    .... After effects?...............................

13. Any tendencies toward nervousness, or worry?.................. Over what.................
    ....

14. Present occupation of father, if living.................. Of mother.........................

15. Members of the family or other relatives as close as grandparents or uncles
    and aunts who have died during last five or six years. (Give relationship, age
    at death, year of death, and cause.)...
    ....

16. Any other significant information regarding recent family history?.....................
    ....

[*Page 1*]

17. What have you made or constructed yourself during the last four or five years? (Examples: built a canoe, made dresses, wrote poetry, composed some music, etc.)

Thing done	Your age at the time	Was it very good, fairly good, or poor?
1.		
2.		
3.		
4.		
5.		
6.		

18. Name all the offices or honors you have held during the last five years. (Examples: class officer, scout officer, club officer, actor in plays, scholarship prize or honor, member of band, orchestra, debating team, athletic team, school committee, school paper, etc.)

Position or honor	Your age at that time
1.	
2.	
3.	
4.	
5.	
6.	

19. Name all the paid jobs you have had during the last five years.

Job	How long did you work at this job?	Hours per week	Your age at the time	Compensation per week
1.				
2.				
3.				
4.				
5.				
6.				
Present job?				

20. Have you decided yet what life vocation you wish to follow?................. If so, what occupation? ....
Under what circumstances did you make this choice? (E.g., what influences determined the decision—such as school or college courses, advice of relatives, teachers, or friends, reading, close-hand observation, etc.?).........................

21. Have any disappointments, perplexities, failures, or bereavements ever exerted a prolonged influence upon you?...
If so, briefly describe, stating your age at the time.................................

22. Do you consider that any single person, book, philosophy, or religion has had a profound influence on your life?...
If so, what was it?...
Age at which such influence, if any, began...

23. Additional information ....

GIFTED CHILDREN FOLLOW-UP

(For parents of Regular and Outside-Binet and Special Ability cases under twenty.)
(For teachers of children not yet in college.)

Name..........................

Date..........................

TRAIT RATING BLANK

Rated by..........................

Mail to *Professor Lewis M. Terman, Stanford University, California*

Parent—Teacher——
(Underline)

DIRECTIONS: In each trait or characteristic, compare this boy or girl with the *average* for his *age*. Then make a small cross somewhere on the line to show how much of the trait he possesses. The ratings will be held absolutely confidential.

Locate your cross *any place on the line* where you think it belongs. It is not necessary to locate it at any of the little vertical marks.

EXAMPLES: In *Example 1*, the cross shows how one boy was rated for health. In *Example 2*, the cross shows how the same boy was rated for prudence and forethought.

EXAMPLE 1. HEALTH.

Extraordinarily good health. Almost never sick. Vigorous.	Decidedly superior health	Rather superior health	Average for age	Rather weakly or sickly	Decidedly weakly or sickly	Extremely weakly and sickly. Extreme lack of vigor.
		X				

Was your judgment on the above trait very certain, fairly certain, rather uncertain, very uncertain?

EXAMPLE 2. PRUDENCE AND FORETHOUGHT.

Extraordinary prudence. Always looks ahead. Never sacrifices future good for present pleasure.	Decidedly more prudent than average	Rather more prudent than average	Average for age	Rather happy-go-lucky	Decidedly happy-go-lucky	Extreme lack of prudence. Never looks ahead. Lives wholly in the present.
			X			

Was your judgment on the above trait very certain, fairly certain, rather uncertain, very uncertain?

TRAIT 1. PERSEVERANCE.

Extraordinarily persistent in overcoming difficulties. Extremely steadfast.

| Decidedly persevering | Rather persevering | Average for age | Gives up rather easily | Decided lack of perseverance | Easily discouraged and gives up at slightest difficulty. |

Was your judgment on the above trait very certain, fairly certain, rather uncertain, very uncertain? (Underline)

TRAIT 2. FONDNESS FOR LARGE GROUPS.

Extraordinary fondness for large groups. Unhappy when alone. Devoted to parties, picnics, etc.

| Decidedly social | Rather social | Average for age | Rather solitary | Decidedly solitary | Invariably avoids groups. Always prefers to be either alone or with one or two close chums. |

Was your judgment on the above trait very certain, fairly certain, rather uncertain, very uncertain? (Underline)

TRAIT 3. LEADERSHIP.

Extraordinary qualities of leadership. Gets others to do his will. Not easily influenced.

| Decidedly a leader | Rather tends to be a leader | Average for age | Rather tends to follow | Decidedly a follower | Always a follower. Never takes initiative. Suggestible and easily influenced. |

Was your judgment on the above trait very certain, fairly certain, rather uncertain, very uncertain? (Underline)

TRAIT 4. POPULARITY WITH OTHER CHILDREN.

Extraordinarily popular. Universal favorite. Is sought after and has many friends.

| Decidedly more popular than average | Rather more popular than average | Average for age | Rather less popular than average | Decidedly less popular than average | Extremely unpopular. Disliked and shunned. A social outcast. |

Was your judgment on the above trait very certain, fairly certain, rather uncertain, very uncertain? (Underline)

TRAIT 5. DESIRE TO EXCEL.

Extraordinary pride in accomplishment and desire to excel. Does his utmost to stand first.	Decidedly anxious to excel	Rather anxious to excel	Average for age	Rather little ambition	Decidedly weak ambition	No pride in accomplishment. No ambition to excel. Almost never does his best.

Was your judgment on the above trait very certain, fairly certain, rather uncertain, very uncertain? (Underline)

TRAIT 6. FREEDOM FROM VANITY AND EGOTISM.

Extraordinarily free from egotism or vanity. Shrinks from praise or admiration.	Decidedly modest	Rather modest	Average for age	Rather vain	Decidedly vain	Extremely egotistical and vain. "Fishes" for praise. Always showing off.

Was your judgment on the above trait very certain, fairly certain, rather uncertain, very uncertain? (Underline)

TRAIT 7. SYMPATHY AND TENDERNESS.

Extraordinarily tender and sympathetic. Kind on principle. Abhors cruelty.	Decidedly more than average sympathy	Rather more than average sympathy	Average for age	Rather less than average sympathy	Decidedly less than average sympathy	Extreme lack of tenderness or sympathy. Rarely does a kind act. Tendency to cruelty.

Was your judgment on the above trait very certain, fairly certain, rather uncertain, very uncertain? (Underline)

TRAIT 8. CONSCIENTIOUSNESS.

Extraordinarily conscientious. Keen sense of duty. Does right for right's sake. Always dependable.	Decidedly more conscientious than average	Rather more conscientious than average	Average for age	Rather less conscientious than average	Decidedly less conscientious than average	Extreme lack of conscientiousness. No sense of duty. Does wrong for any advantage. Not dependable.

Was your judgment on the above trait very certain, fairly certain, rather uncertain, very uncertain? (Underline)

TRAIT 9. DESIRE TO KNOW.

Extraordinarily strong intellectual curiosity, and broad interests. Insistent on knowing. — Decidedly above average curiosity — Above average curiosity — Average for age — Rather weak curiosity — Decidedly weak curiosity — Extreme lack of intellectual curiosity. Mentally inert. Few interests. Rarely asks questions.

Was your judgment on the above trait very certain, fairly certain, rather uncertain, very uncertain? (Underline)

TRAIT 10. ORIGINALITY.

Extraordinary ability to think things out for self. Original, resourceful, and inventive. Excels in reasoning. — Decidedly above average — Rather above average — Average for age — Rather below average — Decidedly below average — Extreme lack of originality and resourcefulness. Always depends on teacher or book.

Was your judgment on the above trait very certain, fairly certain, rather uncertain, very uncertain? (Underline)

TRAIT 11. COMMON SENSE.

Possesses common sense and judgment in extraordinary degree. His advice always highly valued. — Decidedly above average — Above average — Average for age — Below average — Decidedly below average — Extreme lack of common sense and judgment. Opinions not taken seriously by anyone.

Was your judgment on the above trait very certain, fairly certain, rather uncertain, very uncertain? (Underline)

TRAIT 12. GENERAL INTELLIGENCE.

Extraordinary all-round intelligence. — Decidedly above average — Rather above average — Average for age — Rather below average — Decidedly below average — General intelligence extremely inferior. Almost feeble-minded.

Was your judgment on the above trait very certain, fairly certain, rather uncertain, very uncertain? (Underline)

GIFTED CHILDREN FOLLOW-UP

SCHOOL INFORMATION BLANK

(For teachers of children not yet in college.)

Mail to Professor Lewis M. Terman, Stanford University, California

Note: The information requested in this blank is being collected for about 1,000 children and young people of very superior intelligence or special talent. The majority of this group were first tested by members of the research staff from Stanford University in 1922. The school record and general development of each member of the group will be followed for as many years as possible. We confidently hope that through this careful study of the individual development of a large number of gifted boys and girls we may eventually throw light on the factors causing mental superiority, the means by which superior mental ability may be recognized, and the methods which are suited to the education of gifted children.

The present follow-up has been made possible by a special grant of $10,000. We hope to have the same splendid interest and co-operation from the teachers and professors in whose hands the education of this group now lies that we received from the teachers who were educating these boys and girls in 1922. In order that the results of the investigation may have the greatest possible practical and scientific value, will you please answer *all the questions indicated upon this blank (upon which you have information), however confidential the information requested may be or however unimportant it may seem to you.* The information will be held *strictly confidential;* it will be kept in locked files at Stanford University, and will be used for statistical purposes only, without the use of names.

In order to avoid the danger of causing undue self-consciousness, teachers are urged not to call the student's attention to the fact that he (or she) is being studied. Please do not say anything about the special information which is being sought in this blank. *Publicity of every kind should be avoided.* Do nothing which could possibly stimulate vanity or self-consciousness.

When this blank is filled out, will you kindly mail it to me at Stanford University. I wish to express the deepest appreciation for the time and thought which this assistance represents. It is upon such co-operation that the ultimate success and value of the entire investigation depends.

LEWIS M. TERMAN

Name..Age (years and mos.)...

Name of school or college...City..

Grade (H or L) or college year ....How long have you known this boy or girl?..

This report made out by..Your position............................

Your address..Date ....

I. PHYSICAL DATA.

    1. General health is good, fair, poor. (Underline.)

    2. Symptoms of general weakness, if any..

    3. Is vision (without glasses) normal, somewhat defective, very poor? (Underline.)

        Nature or defect, if any..Wears glasses?...................

    4. Is hearing normal, somewhat defective, very poor? (Underline.)

    5. Signs of special nervousness?................................How shown?...........................

    6. Organic diseases (as of heart, kidneys, lungs, etc.)................................

    7. Other facts of interest regarding physical status................................

    8. Is above information based mainly on examination by a doctor?...............

    Nurse's examination...........................Your own observations?...........................

II. RECORD OF STUDIES.

  1. Compared with the average student of the same school grade or college year, the quality of this student's general academic work is very superior, superior, high average, average, low average, inferior, very inferior. (Underline.)

  2. Does the student show very extraordinary ability in any special subject or subjects? ....
What subjects? ....
How shown? ....

      ....
      ....
      ....

  3. Is the student especially weak in any subjects?...
What subjects? ....
What are the reasons, if known to you?...

      ....
      ....
      ....

III. GENERAL INFORMATION.

  1. Has attendance been very regular, fairly regular, rather irregular, very irregular? (Underline.)

  2. Describe the student's attitude toward school or college.................................

      ....
      ....
      ....

  3. Is the student's companionship especially sought, rather avoided, neither? (Underline.)

  4. Does the student respond well to discipline?.............If not, explain.............

      ....
      ....
      ....

  5. Has the student shown any unusual or abnormal sex interests or sex behavior?.....................If so, what?...

      ....
      ....
      ....

  6. Describe any social or moral peculiarities not listed above.................................

      ....
      ....
      ....

  7. In the remaining space add any other facts which will help characterize this student, or add to our understanding of his abilities, disabilities, or peculiarities ....

GIFTED CHILDREN FOLLOW-UP
REPORT ON HOME VISIT

(For Regular, Outside-Binet, and Special Ability cases within field workers' range)

Name of subject..

Name of field assistant..Date..

1. How is child developing (including check-up on guide sheet observations, etc.)?
2. Where is child in school? Name of school, grade, liking for school?
3. Plans for later education. Means of financing.
4. Vocational ambitions.
5. Special abilities.
6. Social traits—how does he get on with others, how many chums, plays at home or elsewhere, leadership, association with opposite sex.
7. Inter-family relationships. (a) Parents. (b) Sibs. (c) Attitude of parents or subject on subject's inclusion in group, newspaper publicity.
8. Sacrifices for or by child, including changes in family circumstances.
9. Can child take responsibility? Is he encouraged? Is he willing?
10. Conduct problems, character traits in general.
11. Sibs: names, schools, and grades; or occupations.
12. Type of home and neighborhood, cultural evidence, advantages and disadvantages.
13. Comment. (a) General impression. (b) Suggestions.

(42 blanks follow here)

Note which pairs of siblings resemble each other in physical appearance:
a. Enough to be taken as identical twins..
b. Almost enough to be taken as identical twins.........................
c. Decided family resemblance...
d. Slight family resemblance...
e. No noticeable resemblance...
f. Marked difference in type...
g. Extreme difference in type...

GIFTED CHILDREN FOLLOW-UP
REPORT ON CONFERENCE WITH TEACHER

(For school visits of Regular, Outside-Binet, and Special Ability cases in field workers' range, and not yet in college.)

Name of subject..

Name of field assistant..Date..

Name of teacher..Grade............School..........................

1. How is subject getting on—how satisfactory a student?
2. In what studies especially good, and in what especially poor?
3. Social traits, how many chums, leadership, association with opposite sex, etc.
4. Conduct problem, character traits in general.
5. Family influence, co-operation, etc.
6. Comment by field assistant. Impressions and suggestions.

GIFTED CHILDREN FOLLOW-UP
REPORT ON CONFERENCE WITH CHILD

(For child visits of Regular, Outside-Binet, and Special Ability cases in field workers' range.)

Name of subject...

Name of field assistant.. Date.................................

1. Physical appearance (size, carriage, deformities, facial expression, etc.).
2. Manner (forwardness, shyness, poise, conceit, speech defects, sense of humor, etc.).
3. Interests (hobbies, studies liked, sports, ambitions).
4. Attitude toward school.
5. Comment.

SUPPLEMENTARY BLANK
(Sent to subjects who were married)

Note: I have been interested this year to find that, in the group of young people whose progress we are following, 25 per cent of those who have reached the age of 23 or more are now married. Accordingly we are anxious to make a little statistical study of the husbands and wives of the members of our group who are married. We would appreciate it greatly if you would fill in and return the questionnaire below. In summarizing this information, like other information that you have furnished us, of course no use will be made of names.

LEWIS M. TERMAN

Your name ....

Name of your husband or wife ....

Exact nature of his or her present work...

What vocation does he or she expect to follow as a life career...........................

Highest grade or college year of academic schooling...

Diplomas received................................What school or college..............................

Present occupation of his or her father...

Present occupation of his or her mother...

Other information that you think would be of interest...

INDEX

INDEX

Abbott, A. A., 368, 459

Abbott-Trabue Exercises in Poetic Appreciation, 367

Accidents, in relation to IQ changes, 52

Achievement, illustrative case studies, 196 ff.; ratings by field visitors, 192 ff.; in relation to IQ changes, 47 ff.

Achievement quotients, 86 f.

Achievement tests, 86 ff.; in relation to IQ changes, 47 ff.; tests used, list of, 8

Activities preferred, 120 ff.

Activity interest, 130 f.

Age-grade status, 64 ff.; of High School group, 227 f.

Almack, John C., 367

Artistic ability, 240 f.

Attendance, 71 f.

Austin, Mary S., 442

Avery, G. T., 31

Bailey, Margery, 368

Baldwin, B. T., 30, 58

Barr Scale ratings of occupational status, 135 ff., 137; of fathers of gifted children, 219; in relation to IQ changes, 55 f.

Behavior problems, 178 ff., 306 ff.

Bigelow, John, 441

Binet, Alfred, 459

Biography, psychological interpretation of, v, 248, 465 ff.

Blake, William, 361

Boyle, Robert, 457

Brock, A. Clutton, 449

Browning, Robert, 366, 381, 401, 423, 438 ff., 456

Bryant, William C., 366, 381, 387, 399, 400, 401, 403, 410, 423, 440 f.

Burch, Mary C., 87 f., 368, 459

Burch Test, *see* Stanford Test in Comprehension of Literature

Burks, Barbara S., vi, 11, 59, 350, 364

Burns, Robert, 366, 381, 401, 418, 423, 455

Byron, Lord, 366, 381, 384, 385, 400, 401, 409, 423, 454, 455

Cady tests, 148, 149 f., 181

Cady, Vernon S., 181

Carlyle, Thomas, 161

Carpenter, George R., 451

Carroll, Herbert A., 45

Cases of gifted children:

—A. family, 289 ff.

—Albert, 305

—Alfred, 179, 310 ff., 479

—Barbara, 298 ff., 479

—Beatrice, 361, 364, 367, 380, 393, 399, 400, 402, 404, 405, 408, 423 ff., 454, 456, 479

—Bertha, 271 ff., 479

—Blake, 319 ff., 479

—Carlotta, 179

—Charles, 305

—Charlotte, 296 f.

—Clara, 275 ff.

—Cowell, Henry, 248, 322 ff., 479

—Dalton, 204

—Daniel, 296

—David, 266 ff., 479

—Delbert, 206

—Dickson, 203

—Dollie, 206

—Donald, 257 ff.

—Donaldine, 324 ff.

—Dora, 252 ff.

—Doris, 295 f.

—Edith, 365, 367, 381, 399, 400, 412, 414, 423, 426 ff.

—Edwin, 279 ff.

—Eleanor, 198

—Emmett, 179, 310 ff., 479

—Ernest, 201

—Ethel, 365, 367, 381, 391, 399, 400, 423, 428 ff.

—Eva, 179

—Fitzhugh, 204

—Floyd, 304

—Francis, 338 f., 479

503

Emerson, Ralph W., 366, 381, 401, 423
Emotional stability, in relation to IQ changes, 53; test of 9, 148, 149 ff.
Employment of gifted children, 137 ff., 232
Environmental influences recognized by gifted subjects, 127 ff.
Environment of gifted children, 478; handicaps of, 283 ff.; illustrative case studies, 198, 203 ff.; ratings by field visitors, 192 ff.; in relation to IQ changes, 55 ff.
Eye disorders, 215; *see* Vision, defective

Fair-mindedness, test of, 9, 149, 151 ff., 289
Farnsworth, Paul R., 351
Fenton, Jessie C., 361, 424, 460
Follow-up procedures, field work, 13, 18 ff.; schedule, 8
Franklin, Benjamin, 366, 381, 401, 415, 423, 456
Fraternity membership, of High School group, 234
Freneau, Philip M., 366, 381, 401, 423, 441 f.
Fuller, Florence, 19
Future research, plans for, 464 ff.

Galton, Francis, 3, 4
Garrison, C., 30
General weakness, 211
Genetic Studies of Genius:
—Vol. I, 4, 6, 7, 67, 72, 73, 74, 76, 79, 81, 86, 116, 120, 124, 130, 136, 148, 149, 153 ff., 164, 165, 169, 177, 184 ff., 209, 211, 213, 214, 215, 216, 219, 222, 227, 239, 240, 288, 469, 471, 475
—Vol. II, v, 3, 23, 118, 178, 241, 423, 438, 455, 456, 457, 465, 466
Genius, modern rôle of, 467 ff.
George Washington University Social Intelligence Test, 9, 162 ff.
Glover, James W., 235
Goethe, Johann W., 248, 453

Goodenough, Florence L., 11, 18, 271, 345
Grades, skipping, 67
Graduation from school, age of, 68
Graduation honors, 107
Griffin, W. Hall, 440

Hamilton, Alexander, 366, 381, 385, 401, 423
Hancock, Albert E., 444
Handicaps of gifted children, 283 ff.
Hawthorne, Nathaniel, 366, 381, 397, 399, 400, 401, 406, 423
Headaches, 212
Health, 209 ff.; in relation to IQ changes, 51 ff.
Hearing, 215
Heredity, as shown by sibling tests, 223 ff.
Herring-Binet test, 41, 43 ff.
Herring, J. P., 43
Herrington, L. P., 162
Highest levels of ability and social adjustment, 172 ff., 264 ff.
High School group, 16, 136, 217; age-grade status of, 227; compared with Regular group, 37, 229; co-operation of, 229; educational plans of, 228 f.; offspring of, 236; social traits of, 234; spouses of, 237 f., 482; vocational plans of, 230 ff.
Hocking, Adeline, 216
Hollingworth, Leta S., 45, 173, 267
Holmes, Oliver W., 366, 381, 400, 423, 442 f.
Holzinger, K., 31
Home environment, illustrative case studies, 198, 203 ff.; ratings by field visitors, 192 ff.; in relation to IQ changes, 55 ff.
Honors, 107, 125 ff.
Hotz Algebra Tests, 8, 91 ff.
Hotz, Henry G., 91

Infancy, in relation to later development, 248 ff., 340 ff.
Intellectual interest, 130 f.